# Sitting in Darkness

# Sitting in Darkness

NEW SOUTH FICTION, EDUCATION,

AND THE RISE OF JIM CROW COLONIALISM,

1865–1920

Peter Schmidt

UNIVERSITY PRESS OF MISSISSIPPI

Jackson

www.upress.state.ms.us

The University Press of Mississippi is a member of the Association of American University Presses.

Copyright © 2008 by University Press of Mississippi
All rights reserved
Manufactured in the United States of America

First printing 2008

∞

Library of Congress Cataloging-in-Publication Data

Schmidt, Peter, 1951 Dec. 23–

Sitting in darkness: New South fiction, education, and the rise of Jim Crow colonialism, 1865–1920 / Peter Schmidt.

p. cm.

Includes bibliographical references and index.

ISBN-13: 978-1-934110-39-3 (alk. paper)

ISBN-10: 1-934110-39-6 (alk. paper)

1. American fiction—Southern States—History and criticism. 2. Southern States—In literature. 3. African Americans in literature. 4. Education in literature. 5. Race relations in literature. 6. Imperialism in literature. 7. Citizenship in literature. 8. Reconstruction (U.S. history, 1865–1877) in literature. 9. Literature and history—United States—History—19th century. 10. Literature and history—United States—History—20th century. I. Title.

PS261.S34 2008

813'.409896073075—dc22                                      2007028023

British Library Cataloging-in-Publication Data available

To all those scholar-teachers who applied for research
funding and were turned down—persist anyway.

Fiction's not novel
Critique doesn't rate
Why work with modes so
Out of date?

Future then present
Drifting past, I'm
Likely to turn up
Out of time.

# Contents

# Contents

# Acknowledgments

Working in this brier patch of a book for a decade, I've been helped to find my way by a good number of friends and colleagues. Some assisted very graciously after they were imposed upon, while others helped unconsciously—their insights on other matters wound up being useful. When you're working on a book, especially in its later stages, everything seems connected, but having talkative and intelligent friends from whom you can steal, I mean borrow, sure helps too. The people named below are responsible for an uncounted number of whatever good ideas may be in the book—but none of its errors.

At Swarthmore College I benefit from few social boundaries separating the disciplines: we can easily get to know colleagues in many different fields who will be reading different authors and asking different questions. To my colleagues who gave their time to listen to me and respond, accept my thanks: you were a generous well from which I could drink. Your teaching and published work inspires me. Particular thanks to Phil Weinstein, Chuck James, Patty White, Nat Anderson, Kendall Johnson, Bakirathi Mani, and Anthony Foy—our "Americanist krewe" in the English Department here; plus Kathryn Morgan, the late Jerry Wood, Allen Kuharski, Miguel Díaz-Barriga, Braulio Muñoz, Allison Dorsey, Bruce Dorsey, Sarah Willie, Farha Ghannam, Tim Burke, Keith Reeves, Rick Valelly, Carol Singley, and colleagues and friends in the TriCo American Studies reading group. I'd also like to single out Christopher Densmore of the Swarthmore Friends Historical Library at Swarthmore College for the special assistance he gave. I must invoke the name of Paul Gaston as well—an example of someone who, though connected to this northern college with Quaker roots, was able to make a distinctive contribution to the critical study of the New South.

Colleagues elsewhere have been friends and inspiration too and caused trouble for my ideas when I most needed it. Thanks to Amrit Singh and Shelley Fisher Fishkin, José Limón and Sarita See, Jack Matthews and Scott Romine, Herman Beavers and Jennifer Rae Greeson, Leigh Anne Duck and Ifeoma Nwankwo, Jon Smith and Deborah Cohn, John Lowe and Katherine Henninger, George Handley and Karla Holloway, Natalie Ring and Tara McPherson, Patsy Yaeger and Susan Donaldson, Mab Segrest and Rebecca Mark, plus Katherine McKee, Annette Trefzer, and Charles Reagan Wilson at Ole Miss and Michael Kreyling at Vanderbilt. *Muchísimas gracias también* to all the folks in the Society for the Study of Southern Literature who participated in two conferences on global perspectives on the U.S. South in México and Mississippi, which includes most of those named above and many others: I've learned to ask new questions because of you. I would like in particular to single out Barbara Ladd, Riché Richardson, Hosam Aboul-Ela, and Jay Watson for your wit and insights on our SSSL "Global South" panel on teaching strategies and the current state of graduate and undergraduate education, plus the insights you've given me in many other ways. I won't name everyone who participated in all the panels and discussions that made these "Global South" conferences so rich (and such a good time), but you know who you are. A pat on the back, too, to the sensible soul who, after a long day of conference papers and arguments, suggested we move to the pool for a good game of water volleyball.

Andrew Doolen wrestled with several earlier versions of this manuscript and certainly helped it to become a better book; I thank him for his patience as well as for his astute advice. At the University Press of Mississippi, Anne Stascavage, Shane Gong, and Todd Lape ably assisted with technical matters, while Seetha Srinivasan, Hunter Cole, and Walter Biggins provided support and patience and skepticism—in approximately that order—when they were most needed, during the impossibly long process of this book's gestation in the dark.

# Sitting in Darkness

# Introduction

Never in the history of this country has there been a generation of writers who came into such an inheritance of material as has fallen to these younger writers of the South. Behind them, fading away in the distance, but still clear to the eye and most intelligible through its ruined picturesque landmarks, [lies] the vast landscape of the old regime. On its hither border, war; and on the hither side of war, peace again. In the first what gorgeous colorings; what groupings of figures and races; what scenes of caste, wealth, indolence, and pride; what phases of morals, manners, conduct, and faith; what pleasures and crimes and virtues and pursuits; what a whole world apart—the social world of the old South—unlike all that ever went before or can ever come again! In the second, what ruination and downfall; what struggles and passions, heroism and cowardice, love, parting, and death; poverty, sickness, and famine; hatred, humiliation, insult, and prostration! In the third, what wrongs and sufferings; what broken hearts and broken strength and broken fortunes; what forgiveness, reconciliation, growth, wealth, newmindedness, expanding sympathies, larger happiness, sweeter bread, clearer skies! Is there in all this material any element wanting that could enter into the groundwork of a new literature of the imagination, deep, serious, passionate and powerful?

—WALTER HINES PAGE, "Literature in the South"

The contradiction between these noble ideals and the actualities of our conduct generated a guilt, and unease of spirit, from the very beginning, [and] ... the American novel at its best has always been concerned with this basic moral predicament.... [B]y the twentieth century and after the discouraging and traumatic effect of the Civil War and the Reconstruction it had gone underground, had become *understated*. Nevertheless, it did not disappear completely.

—RALPH ELLISON, "Hidden Name and Complex Fate"

Two photographs document two schools a world apart, one in Tuskegee, Alabama, and one in Hawaii: Booker T. Washington's famed Tuskegee Institute and Uldrick Thompson's Kamehameha School for Girls and Boys. In the Tuskegee photograph, a class of about thirty boys and girls endure what appears to be a history lesson while sitting in rows on unpadded wooden benches. The girls wear beautiful dresses and blouses, each unique, with their hands in their laps and their hair often pinned up in a bun. The boys wear suit jackets and ties and have taken off their military-style caps with stiff, short brims and crests in

3

Fig. I.1. Francis Benjamin Johnston, ["History class, Tuskegee Institute"], 1902. Library of Congress, Prints and Photographs Division, LC-USZ62-64712

the front and placed them on the benches. All are facing to their right, where a wall-length blackboard holds the day's lesson. A second blackboard is behind them, filled with a map of the early United States east of the Mississippi. Above the blackboards are pictures of Lincoln, Washington, and McKinley, each decorated with a pair of flags. This photograph from 1902—once part of the many materials put forth by Tuskegee to document its success for students, parents, supporters, and the nation—now has migrated to Web sites covering Tuskegee and Alabama history.

Historians at the Kamehameha School in Hawaii have also put documents from their archives onto a Web site, including photos of the boys' and girls' graduating classes around the turn of the twentieth century and information about where they were working several years later. One photograph commemorates a class of twenty-three young men who graduated in 1900. Some sit on the floor, others on chairs, others standing tall, all arranged around the white-bearded central figure of the school president. They wear dark suits, high starched collars, black bow ties, and polished boots. Their names include Solomon Leleo, Joseph Poo, Charles Paehaole Davis, Louis Thompson (son of the president?), Henry Ontai, Charles Molokai "aka Charles Frederick Kauhane," Archibald Hapai, and Joseph Aea. Jobs held in 1902 included clerk, engineer or brakeman with a local railroad, student at Oahu College, timekeeper for the Waianae Sugar Company,

Fig. I.2. Photo used with permission from Kamehameha Schools

schoolteacher, "cattle raiser," guard at a reform school, machinist, and mounted policeman, among other professions.

The Kamehameha girls' class of 1900 was nineteen strong, but only eight are in the photograph. The young women are all seated in high-necked white lace dresses and one, in the center, perches on an ornately carved, high-back wooden chair that is almost a throne. All have wrist corsages of Hawaiian flowers. Their names, like the men's, often mark their mixed American and Hawaiian identities as well as the importation of labor to Hawaii from Japan and the Philippines, among other areas: Margaret Anahu, Nancy Aki, Esther Akuna, Emma Kaipu, Hannah Kaipu, Malia Sakuma, Elizabeth Robinson, Maria Piihoi, Rose Aloiau, Mrs. Louisa Kakaha Harbottle, Mary Yoshioka Yanagihara. Two years after their graduation, they have gone to many different islands in Hawaii with jobs such as "matron's assistant" at a girls' school, teacher of sewing and dressmaking, student at the Normal school for teachers in Honolulu, office assistant, and inter-Hawaiian island telegraph operator.

How can we understand the schools' seemingly unlimited aspirations expressed for their students in the face of the realities of racial discrimination in Alabama and Hawaii in the 1900s? After all, the U.S. South had entered one of the darkest periods of its history, where blacks had lost the right to vote and strict new laws validating segregation and economic stratification were reinforced by lynching. McKinley's photograph in the classroom at Tuskegee is telling, not just because he was president but also because the U.S. government programs that

5

McKinley and his successor Theodore Roosevelt enthusiastically supported in the new post-1898 colonies used the Tuskegee Institute as a model for constructing a successful educational system for people of color in the colonies, even as they instituted policies of segregation abroad as well as at home, causing many blacks to flee the South.

Meanwhile, in Hawaii, the Kamehameha School graduated its pupils into a world where most could find respectable employment, but the islands on which they lived had recently had their economic and political status utterly changed by a political coup by white elites backed by U.S. troops. A democratically elected Hawaiian government including many native-born Hawaiians was overthrown in 1893 by a group of businessmen, many of them wealthy sugar plantation owners, determined to control the islands, expand their wealth and markets, and make Hawaii an official territory of the United States. By 1900 the success of their project had been assured beyond their wildest dreams, while Hawaii had turned out to be the first piece of the United States' new overseas empire in the Caribbean and the Pacific. The Kamehameha School surely was helping grow Hawaii's middle class for people of color, including many mixed-race students, but the school's role in challenging the new structures of power being put in place in Hawaii and the South Pacific could only be small.

Two pictures, two footnotes to history.[1] But the intense gazes of the students in these photographs and their unknown fates should inspire us to ask larger questions about the roles that schools for people of color played at the turn of the twentieth century, and what connections, if any, we might find between developments in the New South and those in the new U.S. colonies, particularly on the matter of education and citizenship. Debates over U.S. expansionism were haunted by the specter of Reconstruction, particularly the suggestion that people of color would prove impossible to "civilize" in colonial schools, just as they supposedly had in the U.S. South after the Civil War. Consider two cartoons that appeared in 1899. The first, from a Detroit newspaper, depicts U.S. soldiers in the Philippines, one dead on the ground while another hauls a native up a hill toward a newly built schoolhouse flying an American flag.

Racial "uplift"! The native faces backward, a spear in one hand and a look of terror or incomprehension on the face while being hauled uphill to school by a figure who looks rather like the "Rough Rider" Teddy Roosevelt. Also worthy of notice is the hallucinatory mix of racial signifiers here: Spear, grass (?) skirt, earring and bracelet, and dark skin denote a tropical "native," but except for the U.S. presence these could be all signs of Africa, not the Asian Pacific or the Caribbean. And the wild-eyed, uncomprehending stare and wide lips are stereotypes straight out of blackface minstrelsy. One set of plantation histories merges with another, U.S. South into South Pacific, as any variety of "colored" difference in the white U.S. imaginary tends to revert back to the black Other. The cartoon's mixture of

**THE WHITE MAN'S BURDEN.**—*The Journal, Detroit.*

Fig. I.3. *Literary Digest XVIII.* 7 (18 February 1899): 180

bravado and despair (or disgust) aptly captured the bluster and anxieties swirling around debates both pro and con regarding the wisdom of ambitious U.S. plans to transform its new colonies.[2]

My second introductory example of the nexus between Reconstruction and post-1898 U.S. colonial discourse comes from Louis Dalrymple, the house cartoonist-illustrator for *Puck*, the satiric New York weekly that was decidedly pro-McKinley and used "imperial" as a term of praise. In the double-page cartoon at the center of the 25 January 1899 issue, Uncle Sam is teaching the principles of civilization wielding a very long stick over some recalcitrant new students. The caption reads: "SCHOOL BEGINS. Uncle Sam (*to his new class in civilization*). 'Now, children, you've got to learn these lessons whether you want to or not! But just take a look at the class ahead of you, and remember that, in a little while, you will feel as glad to be here as they are!'" The four slouching troublemakers Uncle Sam addresses are students of color labeled Philippines, Hawaii, Porto Rico, and Cuba.

Behind them, studying in very orderly fashion, are older male and female students representing territories on the way to becoming states: Arizona and New Mexico and Alaska, with Texas (1845) and California (1850) up front as successful role models. Interestingly, "Alaska" differs from the others in being dark-skinned, but she too is a model of perfect schoolroom decorum.

Fig. I.4. "School Begins"

What is the intended message of this 1899 cartoon? That even these new dark-skinned delinquents would eventually learn their lessons and become states (or at least prosperous territories)? Or that, as betrayed by their scowls, their character and intelligence are too low for them to learn? At the door to the schoolhouse stands what appears to be a Chinese child carrying a book and casting a wary eye at a blanketed and befeathered Indian on a stool reading the ABC's upside-down. And off to the other side, in the back, a black man with bulbous red lips, wide eyes, and a bucket stands on a ladder cleaning the school's windows—perhaps he was not a graduate of this particular school of "civilization," but rather the beneficiary of one of the new "industrial" southern schools training Negroes to enter the workforce.

Dalrymple's cartoon's text conveys messages just as important as its visual codes. The schoolbook cover on the teacher's desk reads, "U.S. First Lessons in Self Government," with paper underneath naming the new pupils. The blackboard texts in the back allude to contemporary debates on the Senate floor about the proper interpretation of the Declaration of Independence's phrase "the consent of the governed":

THE CONSENT OF THE GOVERNED IS A GOOD THING IN THEORY, BUT VERY RARE IN FACT. ENGLAND HAS GOVERNED HER COLONIES WHETHER THEY CONSENTED OR NOT. BY NOT WAITING FOR THEIR CONSENT SHE HAS GREATLY ADVANCED THE WORLD'S CIVILIZATION. THE U.S. MUST GOVERN ITS NEW TERRITORIES WITH OR WITHOUT THEIR CONSENT UNTIL THEY CAN GOVERN THEMSELVES.

Fig. I.5. Four Bad Students

Over the door is a sign even more pointed about the lesson that *Puck*'s readers as well as obstreperous new colonies should learn: "THE CONFEDERATE STATES REFUSED THEIR CONSENT TO BE GOVERNED. BUT THE UNION WAS PRESERVED WITHOUT THEIR CONSENT." Evidently, the southern states finally learned their lesson. Would the new colonies learn theirs?

Pro-imperialist senators in 1898 confidently explained how a theory of limited consent—the "consent of *some* of the governed"—underwrote the tutelary policies of U.S. colonialism. Soon after, their reasoning was picked up in national journals such as the *Literary Digest* and *Puck* and linked to the supposed lessons of Reconstruction. These claims would quickly be adopted and elaborated by public intellectuals such as Franklin Giddings and Woodrow Wilson, who, like Louis Dalrymple, would sharply distinguish between the civics lessons good white pupils representing the New South could learn versus the slower progress southern blacks or other people of color were destined to make. Furthermore, Dalrymple's caricatures of the new colonies basically recycle iconography from anti-Reconstruction cartoons savaging the idea of civics education for blacks— such as this illustration that appeared in an 1874 *Harper's* article on black schools in the South (fig. I.6). As these schoolchildren move away from the schoolhouse steps on the far left, they gradually degenerate from students to unruly pickaninnies to running pigs. This graphic, by an unnamed artist, aptly matched the anonymous *Harper's* essay that accompanied this illustration, "On Negro Schools," which marked rising doubts in the North in 1874 about Reconstruction. The narrator tempered his praise of southern schools for blacks by insinuating that too much education would either be wasted on blacks or would take too well and spoil them for the menial labors for which they were best suited.[3]

9

SCHOOL'S OUT—HURRAH!

Fig. I.6. "School's Out"

How can we explain the fact that so soon after the vast majority of whites rejected Reconstruction as a fool's errand so many embraced even more ambitious programs—including schoolhouses and carefully designed curriculums—for social and political reconstruction in the new colonies? Might we discover any links between the arguments justifying the rise of Jim Crow white rule in the South and the post-1898 discourses of U.S. colonialism?

## 1

Let us first approach such large questions by pondering recent developments both within and outside of the academy concerning how to treat late nineteenth- and early twentieth-century U.S. history.

The National Constitution Center, which opened in Philadelphia in 2003, deploys state-of-the-art multimedia to package U.S. constitutional history as the story of "Freedom Rising." As if to silence any unspoken fear that power may no longer reside with the "people" but with corporations and other institutions, every display at the center implies that power does indeed remain in "our" hands. Our government never functions for long without the majority's consent, so the story goes, for power always remains checked and balanced and democracy remains freely flowing. At one display, visitors may stand at a lectern, follow a prompter, and recite the presidential oath of office as if they themselves were being sworn in. Looming above on a large screen is a video image of the reciter merged with an unchanging background image of a "live" swearing-in ceremony, complete with a generic white-haired male Supreme Court justice administering the oath. The spectacle proves an irresistible photo-op. Another popular moment comes when visitors conclude their trip in the Signers' Hall. They may pose next to life-sized and individualized bronze statues of the signatories of the Constitution, all clustered in the room as if in casual conversation. Here we may discover Alexander Hamilton's hauteur, James Madison's feistiness, Gouverneur

Morris's peg leg, or that many signers were now unknown young plantation owners from the Carolinas. Mr. Benjamin Franklin presides over the whole scene, glancing skeptically over his spectacles, one of the only signers seated (he had gout).[4]

Despite the Constitution Center's exploitation of the pleasures of spectacle and walking in the footsteps of the powerful, many of the displays do confront tough issues and crises in U.S. constitutional history, focusing on debate and difficulty, not illusory consensus and participation. The designer of the American Experience exhibits inside the center, Ralph Appelbaum, has said that "if people get the idea that the Constitution is a living process of dialogue and compromise, that alone is an important lesson" (quoted in Vienne 99). In several displays devoted to the 1890–1910 period, for example, we can hear and read denunciations of corporate power by the People's Party, arguments pro and con about the Pullman Railroad strike and the government's violent response, the details of a Supreme Court decision that overturned a law limiting bakery workers to no more than sixty hours per week, and other items. What is missing, though, is any focus on issues of power—the voices quoted are presented as if they were all equally "heard" and influential in the "compromises" that supposedly were the pragmatic outcomes of all U.S. constitutional conflicts.

Also conspicuously absent in the Constitution Center's presentation of 1890–1910 history is sustained coverage of the United States' war with Spain in 1898 and the vociferous debates that ensued regarding whether the United States should or should not acquire "dependencies" such as Cuba, Puerto Rico, and the Philippines, and, if so, what their status should be. This is an odd omission, since the events in Hawaii in 1893 and the victory over Spain in 1898 inspired a lengthy national argument over the constitutional issues raised by these new "territories." Many felt the islands should be given their independence, others that they should become colonies governed for the benefit of the inhabitants and the United States. In 1898 and 1899 alone, articles and editorials were published in newspapers and influential journals such as *Literary Digest* and the *Forum* with titles such as "Citizenship in the United States," "Isolation or Imperialism?" "The Moral of the Cuban War," "Annexation and Universal Suffrage," "The School System of Porto Rico," "Is Our Army Degenerate?" "A Lost Eden—Cuba," "The Conditions of Good Colonial Government," and "The Struggle for Commercial Empire." Many of these pieces focused on complex constitutional and philosophical questions. Was a colonial empire compatible with democracy? Could inhabitants of the new colonies become U.S. citizens? Would the Declaration of Independence's credo of no government instituted without the "consent of the governed" apply to the colonies? What about the Constitution, especially the Bill of Rights and the Fourteenth Amendment, guaranteeing all citizens their due "privileges and immunities"? What kinds of governments, if any, should the United States install, and should it create a public school system? What should be our economic ties? One wonders why such a lively and complex moment in U.S. constitutional history would be completely passed over by the National Constitution Center.

Speaking of lesions in our historical memory, anyone who researches the United States' new colonial ambitions after 1898 may discover other odd omissions from the public record. For instance, how can we explain that just at the moment in the late 1890s when democratic rights for blacks and other people of color residing in the United States were being eviscerated, there were lively debates in newspapers, public policy journals, and Congress over how to *bestow* limited voting rights to those living in the new colonies?

Another spectral absence in our public memory of the 1880–1920 period is surely that of Reconstruction itself. Other reform movements in U.S. history may have produced more durable results than Reconstruction, but they were neither more ambitious nor more broadly based, and they did not alter the U.S. Constitution as profoundly as the Reconstruction era's Thirteenth, Fourteenth, and Fifteenth Amendments. (The Fourteenth, promising equal protection of the laws to all citizens, is the most important and contested amendment passed since the Bill of Rights.) Reconstruction's very name suggests a vision of total, not piecemeal, reform. Reconstruction had fervent adherents (as well as opponents) in all branches of the U.S. government, including the U.S. military, as well as in nongovernmental organizations, especially religious and reform groups. Reconstruction's idealistic dreams and ignominious fate inspires and shadows all later reform movements. U.S. history may be full of cycles of reform and reaction, but Reconstruction has a special place in our history as an experiment in creating multiracial democracy that was rapidly repudiated by a majority only a few years after its adoption. The building of new schools was one of the Reconstruction reforms that some found long overdue, but it gave others apoplexy. What was it about Reconstruction that provoked both open defiance and quiet renunciation by whites—not just those in the New South but a majority in the rest of the country—even among those who just a few years before had seemed so enthusiastic about Reconstruction reforms?

At the same time that the United States displayed ambitious plans for regime change and social transformation in its new Caribbean and Pacific colonies after 1898, there was much talk of regime change at "home" as well, particularly in those southern states in which legacies of Reconstruction reforms and governments still held on. Many white supremacist "Redeemer" governments had already come to power across the South by 1898, of course, but their efforts to eradicate all vestiges of Reconstruction's influence accelerated after that date. For example, possibly inspired by U.S. Army and Navy victories over Spain earlier in 1898—and by events in Hawaii, where white business and military leaders united to overthrow an elected government—in November 1898 a group of armed white citizens attacked the multiracial government in Wilmington, North Carolina, executing many blacks and burning and looting the city's black business district, beginning with its newspaper office. Accounts that soon appeared in newspapers and magazines with mostly white readership expressed outrage at a black man denying the rape charges against him and depicted the escalating events as if whites were being besieged by angry barbarians: "White Men Forced to Take Up Arms for the Preservation of Law and Order" was how a headline in the Wilmington *Morning Star* put it. Most events of the 1890s elsewhere in the South were less dramatic, for they involved laws rather than looting and lynching, but the effects of all these counter-measures on middle-class and well as working-class blacks were devastating. The strange career of Jim Crow has been well documented, but much less investigated has been the question of whether news from the new U.S. colonies influenced developments at home, especially regarding the consolidation of white power and segregation in the South.[5]

Even though Reconstruction was denounced, lynched, and buried in what was intended to be an unmarked grave, Reconstruction also had what is surely one of the strangest afterlives of any major U.S. reform movement: it became *the* prime model for U.S. colonial policies abroad. How and why such a posthumous career occurred is a largely untold story. U.S. history is haunted by the ghosts of Reconstruction—not just ideals and promises betrayed at home, but also the ways in which Reconstruction's disciplinary discourses were appropriated for the purposes of projecting U.S. state power at home and abroad. Such unquiet ghosts seethe softly beneath the surface of our national memory.

Progressivism—the key reform movement in the United States in the late nineteenth and early twentieth centuries—has largely been understood as a reaction to and accommodation of the growing power of corporate capitalism and labor agitation in the industrial North and the West. But when developments in the New South and overseas are made part of the story, another defining ingredient of Progressivism comes sharply into focus. Progressivism involved a *federal* attempt to reconstruct the meaning of Reconstruction, correcting its "mistakes" while appropriating, containing, and redefining its key ideals and methods, especially regarding the making of new citizens via educational and other reforms.

In *Sitting in Darkness* I trace how Reconstruction narratives of "uplift" were revised both to justify Jim Crow at home and to persuade many skeptical Americans that the U.S. imperial destiny abroad meant the reconstruction of its newly acquired colonies, with special emphasis on limited suffrage rights and new education systems. When the contradictions of Progressivist racial policies are studied, too often this is still done by separating domestic and international developments rather than looking at them together. This book's primary title is taken from a scathing essay by Mark Twain, "To the Person Sitting in Darkness," excoriating U.S. colonial policies in the Philippines—practices exemplifying a late nineteenth- and early twentieth-century version of "globalization" discourse that held the "white man's burden" was to bring civilization to those mired in darkness. I propose a new analytical frame—Jim Crow colonialism—for understanding the paradoxical mix of citizen-building and subjection at the heart of Progressivist discourse at home and abroad. Yet Progressivism's alchemical combination of uplift and containment did not come out of nowhere. We can see its sources in the ways in which much Reconstruction discourse—especially by whites—defined the proper limits of educating ex-slaves to be citizens.

Since *Sitting in Darkness* is primarily a work of literary criticism, however, my approach here is not to offer yet another general history of Reconstruction, Progressivism, or U.S. colonial policies. Rather, I seek to bring to the foreground a host of under-studied fictional texts that *enact* narratives of education and citizen-building in the postwar U.S. South. These fictions allow us to gain unprecedented critical perspective on the contradictions in Reconstruction that helped doom it to failure. They also illuminate why Jim Crow colonialism, in contrast, became such a powerful and long-lasting force in U.S. history, even though it, too, had manifold contradictions and many opponents.

Being fiction, the individual works studied in *Sitting in Darkness* do not present uniform views either for or against Jim Crow colonialism. Fictional texts are multivocal and cannot have their "positions" on historical issues simply defined via plot paraphrase or claims about a single ideological stance that they do or do not take, or that their authors held. The shaping of space and time in fiction is inevitably multilayered, convoluted, and in motion, even as fictional narratives also attempt to bring order and flatness and direction to such flux, mapping coordinates and urging definitive conclusions. The works considered here subjected all the rationales for and against black citizenship and multiracial democracy in the United States to a volatile process of testing and debate and complication—one that was often far less predetermined than what passed for debate in other discursive arenas in the public sphere. I read these fictions for their ideological agendas, certainly, but I pay equal attention to their textual complexities, to the ways in which narrative as it unfolds in time irrevocably complicates the absolute truths and binary oppositions that ideology strives to maintain as inevitable and permanent and right.

## 2

No epoch of U.S. literary history is arguably less investigated, more fragmented, and more poorly understood than that of Reconstruction and the New South, from the end of the Civil War to the great cultural flowerings of the 1920s that have been variously named Modernism, the Harlem Renaissance, and the Southern

Renaissance. In contrast to social-historical studies of the U.S. New South period from 1865 into the 1920s, literary history for this era currently has no powerful paradigm-shapers who have decisively reorganized the field.[6] Literary historians are doing valuable and honorable work on the post-1865 South, but like other allegedly regional literary histories, it tends to be condescended to when not ignored entirely. The real "action" in cultural studies using original sources and paradigm-generating theories of interpretation, it is often assumed, occurs elsewhere.

Recent conferences, anthologies, and books, however, suggest that a change may be occurring in scholarship on the U.S. South—particularly in literature and cultural studies—that may be as momentous as those paradigm-breaking shifts in southern studies that emerged after World War II in conjunction with a renewed civil rights movement and the rise of Faulkner's reputation. Some of the most decisive and invigorating influences in recent years on American studies as a field have come from so-called postcolonial studies' critiques of nation-centered history writing. More than any other intellectual movement, postcolonial studies has enabled many historians to critique rather than validate "American exceptionalism," the United States' appropriation of itself as an exceptional and exemplary American or New World culture while casting other countries in the Americas and the Caribbean as failed or less successful variants. The United States' many attempts to define itself as different from the model of modernity for other New World countries is increasingly studied within a new historical framework that stresses how the legacies of colonialism and imperialism affect all the cultures of the Americas. Because the U.S. South's deep involvement in plantation slave and post-slavery economies also affected many other areas of the Americas and the Caribbean, rethinking the history of the U.S. South in hemispheric terms is increasingly understood to be central, not secondary, to any effort to make U.S. studies be more genuinely comparative, inter-American, and critical of imperial narratives asserting U.S. cultural difference and superiority.

Such a trend is part of what many scholars and journals are now calling the transnational or postnationalist turn in scholarship on the United States, including southern studies.[7] Earlier models that emphasized the "southern" difference within a national context were fruitful for scholarship and actually helped *produce*, not refute, nationalist discourse in U.S. studies. But it is now common to speak of the "U.S. South," not merely "the South," as one way of signifying a paradigm shift to a more hemispheric and global, not exceptionalist, understanding of slavery and post-slavery cultural histories, including those of former Confederate states. Of course, any thorough analysis of the post-slavery world that focuses on the cultural legacies of colonial plantation systems should not do so to the exclusion of the many other "Souths" that existed alongside rice, cotton, and tobacco fields filled with sharecrop labor. These different Souths must include non-plantation rural areas, the new urban centers which grew more rapidly after the war than they ever had before, population flows crossing regional and national borders, and cultural events such as the fact that after the collapse of Reconstruction in 1877 short stories and novels by authors both black and white depicting changes in the postwar South proved immensely popular with a nation-wide U.S. readership.

"No more monoliths, please!" C. Hugh Holman requested in his famous 1983 valedictory essay to scholars of the U.S. South, urging them to emphasize variety and complexity in the region and its connections to the larger world, rather than constantly reiterating narratives about a true and timeless South and its supposedly exceptionalist values. Holman's essay brimmed with a sense of excitement about new changes and opportunities in the field, confident they would give us a richer sense of past traditions, not cut us off from them. Prophetic of many contemporary developments in cultural studies as Holman's essay is, it serves as an example that contemporary cultural historians would do well to heed. For Holman's essay was remarkably modest, disguising large ambition with self-deprecating charm and a witty way with anecdotes—a mix that is, of course, very recognizably southern.

The very next essay in that 1983 issue of *Southern Literature in Transition* took a very different tack toward its subject. Another emeritus scholar, Cleanth Brooks, sought to swim against the current of change he sensed was occurring in southern studies by stubbornly reiterating familiar arguments that "the differences that mark off the South are of long standing and are in fact rooted in the distant past" (4). Against a culture of homogenizing sameness and a love of abstraction, the U.S. South for Brooks continued to stand as an exceptional subculture within the great American consensus, with a special history, identity, sense of tragedy, and a deeper appreciation of timeless values and the transcendental.[8]

More recently, in *Inventing Southern Literature* (1998), Michael Kreyling has given us an invigorating critique of such a belief in a shared vision supposedly unique to the U.S. South of "the past, history, and the timeless" (to use Cleanth Brooks's phrase). Borrowing from Benedict Anderson, Karl Mannheim, and others, Kreyling understands such a "South" not as a "real" and constant identity that directly expresses itself in culture, but as an ideological construction or imagined community involving selective remembering and forgetting, historical origins, and moments of crisis: "From the polemical writings of the Agrarians to recent works of criticism, biography, literary history, and even film reviews, the established formula is repeated, the narrative of forgetting and making continued" (ix). Kreyling's analysis of how academic anthologies and scholars helped "invent" dominant notions of the South has some limitations, including its almost exclusive focus on the role played by academics at elite institutions in shaping powerful cultural narratives. But his book and other recent ones—like Patricia Yaeger's *Dirt and Desire* (2000), Houston Baker's *Turning South Again: Rethinking Modernism/ Re-Reading Booker T.* (2001), and John Lowe's *Bridging Southern Cultures* (2005)— set high standards for self-analysis and self-criticism in southern U.S. studies and are part of the paradigm shift now occurring in this field, influenced by all the changes Hugh Holman welcomed so generously, plus postcolonialism, new historicism, and other new cultural studies theory and practice.

Kreyling's analysis of southern literature anthologies and the invented South basically begins in the 1920s, with the Agrarians and those who argued with them and followed them. But what role might *earlier* New South elites have played in crafting the fiction that the U.S. southern cultural tradition was singular and known to all? Could the post-1877 New South have had a vision of a shared tradition—or even a Southern Renaissance—that was promoted before the 1920s? And what role, if any, could the New South have played in the invention of "American literature" itself, especially as it was then being constituted in the universities?

During the period of the rise of the New South, circa 1877 to the 1920s, English literature professors first made themselves central to any proper liberal arts program offered by universities in the United States to train the next generation of citizens and gentlemen. At this same time, many institutions of higher learning in both the South and elsewhere began offering courses in American (i.e., U.S.) as well as British literature and history. What role did the U.S. South play in these national developments? How might we best understand why these changes in literary study and canon formation in the United States at the university level occurred just when the nation itself was transforming and expanding its imperial identity on a global stage, while also (controversially) absorbing more immigrants from other nations than ever before?

After the U.S. Civil War, the building and organization of universities in the country entered its most important period of development. Creating professorships and eventually departments teaching not just English but also U.S. national and regional literary traditions was understood to be a crucial agent for reasserting shared ethnic (read Anglo-Saxon) cultural unity for a new generation of young men who would lead a nation inundated with immigration, racial and class strife, and industrialization while still recovering from a ruinous Civil War.

Between the 1890s and the 1920s, just when New South racial policies were having their maximum influence on the nation's so-called Progressivist thinking about race, history, civil rights, national destiny, and colonialism, a good number of anthologies and histories of U.S. southern literature were published, along with explanations for why such a canon of writing needed to be defined and implemented in high school and university humanities courses. A sampling includes these:

William Malone Baskerville. *Southern Writers: Biographical and Critical Studies.* Two volumes. Nashville and Dallas: Publishing House of the M.E. Church South, 1903.
Carl Holliday. *A History of Southern Literature.* New York: Neale, 1906.

Edwin Anderson Alderman, Joel Chandler Harris, and Charles William Kent, eds. *Library of Southern Literature. Compiled Under the Direct Supervision of Southern Men of Letters.* Seventeen volumes plus a one-volume supplement. New Orleans and Atlanta: Martin and Hoyt, 1907–1923. This anthology included selections from and biographical essays on over three hundred authors.

Caroline Mays Brevard. *Literature of the South.* New York: Broadway P, 1908.

The Southern Historical Publication Society. *The South in the Building of the Nation: A History of the Southern States Designed to Record the South's Past in the Making of the American Nation; To Portray the Character and Genius, to Chronicle the Achievements and Progress and to Illustrate the Life and Traditions of the Southern People.* Twelve volumes. Richmond: Southern Historical Publication Society, 1909. Includes volume 7, *The Literary and Intellectual Life*; and volume 8, *Fiction*. Postwar writers treated as canonical include Joel Chandler Harris, George Washington Cable, Mary Murfree, Thomas Nelson Page, James Lane Allen, Ellen Glasgow, Mary Johnston, and Grace King.

Edwin Mims and Bruce Payne, eds. *Southern Prose and Poetry for Schools.* New York: Scribners, 1910.

Simultaneously during the late nineteenth and early twentieth century, many other studies and anthologies sought to define a canon of American literature for inclusion in the new English literature courses that were being instituted for the first time in many U.S. universities. Consider the following list:

Charles F. Richardson. *A Primer of American Literature.* Boston: Houghton, Osgood, 1878.

Brander Matthews. *An Introduction to the Study of American Literature.* New York: American Book Co., 1896.

William Cranston Lawton. *Introduction to the Study of American Literature.* New York: Globe School Book Company, 1902.

Lorenzo Sears. *American Literature in the Colonial and National Periods.* Boston: Little, Brown, 1902.

Fred Lewis Pattee. *American Literature since 1870.* New York: Century Company, 1915.

Bliss Perry. *The American Spirit in Literature: A Chronicle of the Great Interpreters.* Volume 34 in the *Chronicles of America*, edited by Allen Johnson. New Haven: Yale University Press, 1921.

Vernon Louis Parrington. *Main Currents in American Thought.* Volume 3: *The Beginnings of Critical Realism in America, 1860–1920.* New York: Harcourt, Brace, 1930.

These texts and others deserve an extended comparative analysis that cannot be undertaken here. But what patterns might we find if we briefly examine their statements about history, memory, and the function of regional and national traditions?

To begin with, the above anthologies of southern literature place their projects firmly within narratives celebrating new U.S. nationalism and colonialism. Cataloguing regional traditions and differences is seen not as antithetical to nationalism, but as a *foundational* stage for nationalism's growth. In his article "The National Element in Southern Literature" in *The Library of Southern Literature*, John Bell Henneman argued that the Civil War was "a true line of demarcation between the old and the new. Its close introduced a period of great expansion and development and change everywhere" (14: 6276). In one of several introductory statements for the same anthology, editor Charles Kent wrote:

> In presenting to the public this first effort to represent comprehensively and in adequate amount the literary life of the Southern people of the United States, the editors deem it wise to make clear, if may be, the purpose and plan of this pioneer work. This they do without any apology for the task they voluntarily assumed and with no plea save that the book be received, not as a manifestation of any vainglorious or sinister sectionalism, but as a direct and serviceable contribution to the history of our national literature. (1: xv)

Sectionalism is "serviceable," serving national unity, not separatist; its expression of regional cultural traditions models national power on a smaller scale.

Thus we should not be surprised to find tropes of imperial power applied by scholars to their concepts of both sectional and national maturity, in cultural development as well as politics. Kent calls the *Library* anthology's subject an "imperial" though sectional territory (1: xv), a paradox explained by his co-editor Edwin Alderman's essay on "Sectionalism and Nationalism" in another volume, *Southern Prose and Poetry for Schools*: "The story of America, in a large way, is the story of imperial sections, reaching up after self-consciousness, and social and industrial unity, and then reacting upon each other, sometimes blindly, sometimes helpfully, to achieve a national unity and a national spirit" (388). Slavery warped and deflected the South's proper contribution to the nation's unity, but since the rise of the New South all has changed: each section of the country may now develop as a little nation-state, and as they approach cultural maturity all contribute without conflict their individual strengths to a diverse yet unified national whole. At least that is the claim. Most remarkable here is how, in the post-1898 United States, expansive imperial power functions not just abroad but internally, as an expression of the proper development of state power. Furthermore, when Alderman and others use the imperial trope, they apply it to broad aspects of *cultural* development: this, too, is understood to mature toward absolute unity and integration. In short, Progressivist imperialism models a narrative of development on the micro-level of local and state power, as well as on the macro-level of the expansive nation-state, and it envisions military, political, economic, and cultural developments all converging into unity.

Edwin Alderman's contributions to *The Library of Southern Literature* also provide pre-1920 examples of the claim for a tragic southern exceptionalism to U.S. optimism. Such statements would later in the century become very familiar, in the writings of the Nashville Agrarians in the 1930s and (to rather different ends) in C. Vann Woodward's *The Burden of Southern History* (1961), to choose just two examples. These later arguments for recurrent southern difference are worth pondering in the context of *The Library of Southern Literature*. Alderman wrote:

> It is difficult to imagine how the Nation could have been fostered into maturity without the influences that came from the South. Under the play of great historic forces this region developed so strong a sense of unity within itself as to issue in a claim of separate nationality, which it was willing to defend in a great war. No other section of our country has ever known in its fullest sense so complete a discipline of war and defeat; nor has any group of men or states ever mastered new conditions and reconquered peace and prosperity with more dignity and self-reliance. Here then would seem to be all the elements for the making of a great literature—experiences of triumph and suffering, achievement and defeat. (1: xx)

If the Civil War was caused by a perverted sense of nationalism, "a claim of separate nationality," the New South, Alderman claimed, corrected that error with heroic re-conquering—its destruction of the perverted influences of federal Reconstruction. The pain of southern whites during the Civil War and Reconstruction is here reinscribed as a transition from the trauma of being colonized to the mastery of a successful post-slavery regional identity that, for the first time in southern history, was inspirational for rather than threatening to U.S. national identity.

Alderman's colonial tropes are integral to his claims. The reintegration of the South figures as a necessary stage in the development of the South's and the United States' discipline, self-reliance, and imperial destiny. Such signs of maturity and modernity are rooted in the disciplinary experience of tragedy and loss unique (so it is claimed) to the experience of all white southerners. In tracing the history of claims that the special "burden" of southern history is an understanding of loss, we must acknowledge their roots in the white New South, including the Lost Cause movement commemorating the Civil War. As David Blight, Nina Silber, Charles Reagan Wilson, Nell Irvin Painter, Edward Ayers, and others have shown, Lost Cause and Decoration Day romanticism must be understood paradoxically: it simultaneously asserted southern difference yet reaffirmed national affiliation. After the rise of the New South this form of southern exceptionalism was generally seen as an exceptional contribution *to* national unity, not a negation of it. Further, it was the white southerner's experience with being colonized, so the argument went, that would make U.S. imperialism abroad exceptional, not repeating the errors of Reconstruction or of other, European empires. Yet (as I will argue in more detail in upcoming chapters) there were remarkable but usually repressed *parallels* between the disciplinary regime of Reconstruction, especially in education and politics, and federal modernization projects after 1898 in the new colonies.

The men constructing the canon of southern literature also asserted that "local color" short stories in the national magazines (many of them contributed by southerners) brought to maturity a new literary form, the short story, that would be one of the United States' signal contributions to world literature. "The short story has indeed become the national mode of utterance in the things of the imagination," the "most distinct contribution America has made to literary forms," according to Edwin Mims of Vanderbilt University (8: lvii). Professors stressed that teaching stories such as Thomas Nelson Page's "Marse Chan" as part of the study of American literature in the nation's classrooms would be indispensable for bestowing a new generation of citizens with a proper understanding of the meaning of the Civil War and the right relation between blacks and whites. If "industrial education" was the correct format for socializing a duly regulated and productive working class, especially among people of color, a curriculum balancing the arts and sciences with practical training was the educational format most attuned to creating shared values and a sense of national unity in those whites who would have full citizenship rights and responsibilities. A national literature, properly taught, would play an indispensable role in educating a new generation of governing elites. A key paper on the subject was Woodrow Wilson's "University Training and Citizenship" (1894).[9]

In the bold new Progressivist alliance between a reinvigorated U.S. nationalism and the new humanities curriculums in the universities, southern schools of advanced learning played a most important role. J. B. Henneman lauded the 1876 opening of Johns Hopkins University in Baltimore, "halfway between North and South," as "the first instance of German university methods fully applied to American conditions, destined to revolutionize the attitude of education in America and particularly to exert a deep influence upon the training of young Southern scholars." Henneman noted that Vanderbilt University in Nashville was also founded in the 1870s and celebrated the birth of these institutions—along with newly ambitious expansion at the University of the South at Sewanee, Tulane University in New Orleans, Washington and Lee University, and the University of Virginia—as indispensable southern contributions to the institutionalization of American intellectual independence (*Southern Literature* 14: 6280). Further, "chairs of English Literature and of History are receiving the greatest emphasis in nearly every Southern college and university, and their work is usually conceived beyond the sectional on behalf of the national ideal and the widest appeal" (14: 6288–6289). In other words, the public intellectuals creating a New South canon also positioned the South as a key player in the construction of a liberal arts curriculum (including English and American literature) that would help constitute a new generation of white Progressivist leaders.[10]

Not coincidentally, this new southern canon, properly constituted and taught, would demonstrate the proper relations between the races, both at home and abroad. It was a canon for the validation of Jim Crow colonialism. *The Library of Southern Literature* played a particularly ambitious role in accomplishing this goal. Its work included defining not just what authors and texts should be studied, but how syllabi might be organized and taught. (The *Library*'s intended audience was not just professors and students at the universities, but also private citizens who wanted to extend their education.) The anthology divided southern writing into three major phases, the First National Period, the Period of Division (the Civil War and Reconstruction), and the Second National Period. Volume 16, edited by Lucian Lamar Knight, included fifty "Reading Courses" on novelists who were "Historical," "Romantic," "Society," "Problem," or "Psychological" (the last category included Kate Chopin and Ellen Glasgow); plus many other courses on "Local Color" and other short story writers, "Poetry," "Drama," "Dialect Writers," "Essays," "Oratory," "Letters," "Great Public Issues" (including "The Tragedy of Reconstruction" and "The Race Problem"), and other categories. Knight even designed one set of study courses—divided into the categories of "Stories of Cracker Life," "Stories of Creole Life," "Negro Dialect Stories," "Mountaineer Stories," "Miscellaneous"—entitled "The Southern Literary Renaissance" (16: Reading Courses 8–17).[11]

In Edwin Mims and Bruce Payne's *Southern Prose and Poetry for Schools* (1910), the contributor Edwin Alderman elaborated the nationalist/imperial agenda behind such invocations to a Southern Renaissance beginning in the 1880s. He spoke openly of the New South's coming "Golden Age," which he envisioned as succeeding New England's centrality to the growing nation. If New England was dominant throughout the early stages of U.S. national development, particularly in the period from 1800 to 1860, Alderman believed that the Progressivist future belonged to the South. Note the highly Matthew Arnold–like language used: "Between 1870 and 1906 these same forces have worked on the side of the South. Her Golden Age is yet to be. Excess of success, and replacement of its labor population, have tended to change the ideals of New England democracy, to destroy its homogeneity, to deaden and pervert somewhat its idealism." Note also Alderman's euphemism: "Replacement of the labor population" means the influx of non-Anglo-Saxon immigration, particularly from Ireland and Italy and Eastern Europe and China in the nineteenth century, destroying New England's alleged ethnic "homogeneity." After a long period of war and struggle, Alderman's reunited South is now poised to take New England's place of leadership: "reinfused into its old idealism for steadfastness and pride of locality," now tempered with "a splendid quality of nationalism." "Is it strange that all this should turn to it [the South] the eyes of a country that feels it to be the last repository of ancient freedom and ancient faiths?" ("Sectionalism" 397). If immigration in urban areas in the North, Midwest, and West threatened the nation's Anglo-Saxon gene pool, in other words, it was the South's destiny to be the repository of the nation's "original" ethnic and cultural memory, the region that more than any other would produce a literature teaching those core character values—idealism, self-discipline, heroic love of freedom, and fit leadership—that would help the United States compete against other empires on the world stage. Left unspoken in such a catalogue, but very much present, was the implication that none of this could happen without the New South instructing the nation why and how to allow full power to white supremacy. The nation could still be multiethnic and multiracial, just as the canon of southern literature could make room for stories of "Cracker" or "Creole" life and Negro dialect tales. But when it came to defining what was universal, one shared Anglo-Saxon cultural tradition of "ancient freedom and ancient faiths" was destined to dominate.

## 3

Since the re-emergence of W. E. B. Du Bois's *Black Reconstruction* (1935) in historians' understanding of their own profession's history, it is now common to speak of how whites' post-1880s reinterpretation of Reconstruction and the New South's rise—exemplified by the "Dunning school" of historians, named after William A. Dunning of Columbia University and his cohorts at many other top universities—exercised unfortunate hegemony over more than a generation of historians. But equal critical attention should be paid to the ways in which the New South's canonization of southern literature—and its description of why a southern canon reinforced a national one—provided crucial terms, categories, narratives of development, and other components of literary history that helped shape how American literature itself was first understood and consumed. Such an assertion does not claim the South was the only source of inspiration for how the idea of a mature nationalist American literary tradition was formulated in the late nineteenth and early twentieth century. But the New South's role in this process has been much too neglected.

At first, in glancing over representative narratives from the 1880s to the 1920s defining U.S. literary tradition, it may seem that the South is repeatedly cast as the antithesis to American realism, optimism, and modernity. True, but something more complex is also at work. Consider some of the key organizing binary oppositions for conceptualizing American literary themes urged by influential historians such as Fred Pattee, Vernon Louis Parrington, and others. Early twentieth-century tomes defining the new field of American literature frequently treated the South as either pariah or paragon, America's Other or an enduring source of its most foundational values. William Lawton's brief chapter on the literature of the South in his *Introduction to the Study of American Literature* (1902), for example, defined the South almost entirely via negatives: "no Kipling, only a hostile Nemesis in the person of Mrs. Stowe, arose to give them adequate artistic expression." Yet although the Civil War supposedly vanquished southern literary traditions as thoroughly as its armies were beaten by the Union, "that vanished phase of our civilization was the most picturesque, indeed the most retarded and medieval, form of Anglo-Saxon life then existing" (301). For readers assuming civilization was essentially the creation of Anglo-Saxons, such a description of the South surely seemed rather two-edged: retrograde, perhaps, but was it therefore not also essential? Lorenzo Sears, publishing in the same year, made similar claims. He conceded the South made valuable cultural contributions to American literature in marginal areas, such as "local color" stories and historical fiction, but he gave an Orientalist turn to Lawton's suggestion that in an age of new empires the South still lived in another time: "The drowsy land in which they dwell is a land of cypress shadows, of blazing sunlight, of crimson and purple, of broad bayou and majestic river; and there are oriental aspects in the life which is lived amid all this splendor of color and luxuriance of climate. It is a remnant of Romance civilization from the old world brought into the new, that the inheritance of this country from all the empires may be complete" (411–412).

In 1915 Fred Lewis Pattee brought out his acclaimed *American Literature since 1870*, whose thesis was that the Civil War "shook America awake, it destroyed sectionalism, and revealed the nation to itself" (15). It was a process that (following the trope at the heart of the World's Columbian Exposition in 1893 in Chicago) Pattee called "the Second Discovery of America." In this narrative, Pattee gave the South a more complex role to play than that of America's Other. In Pattee's account, the U.S. South oscillates between retarding what is most "American" and embodying its very best qualities. Pattee traces through the heart of American culture a perpetual conflict between dreamy decadence and retreat versus practical "realism"; sectionalism as opposed to nationalism; perpetual adolescence versus cultural maturity and manhood. In many of Pattee's binary oppositions, the South always falls on the wrong side. Yet for Pattee the breakthrough that led to U.S. cultural maturity after the 1870s was the democratization of culture once controlled by elites—and it was a writer born in the South, Mark

Twain, who best embodied the new spirit of realism, critique, innovation, and cultural mixture that Pattee argued proclaimed America's literary coming-of-age. Pattee's binary opposition between decadent sectionalism and mature nationalism also governs the primary binary of colonial discourse, that between primitivism and civilization. In essence, Pattee claimed that after the 1870s the white South transformed itself from dependent colonial subject to fit colonial master— and that after doing so it could finally join the national consensus. (In making such a move, incidentally, Pattee had to downplay Twain's anti-imperialist writings—the beginning of a trend in Twain studies that continued until the 1960s.) Other forces were important, too, in displacing New England elites from their control over U.S. national culture. But for Pattee the New South, embodied by Mark Twain, was an indispensable agent in this transformation.[12]

Bliss Perry, the powerful long-time editor of the *Atlantic Monthly*, published his *The American Spirit in Literature: A Chronicle of the Great Interpreters* in 1921, as volume 34 in Yale University's *Chronicles of America* series. In some ways, Perry saw the South as still grieving over old losses or perpetually trying to play catch-up to other more rapidly advancing regions of the country. But following white New South historians and novelists, Perry argued that the emergence of a mature U.S. nationalism could not have occurred without the stimulating example of the New South: "within a dozen years after the close of the War and culminating in the 1890s, there came a rich and varied harvest of Southern writing, notably in the field of fiction. The public for these stories, it is true, was still largely in the North and West, and it was the magazines and publishing houses of New York and Boston that gave the Southern authors their chief stimulus and support. It was one of the happy proofs of the solidarity of the new nation" (246). That new sense of America's cultural coming-of-age was defined by Perry and the *Chronicle of America* series in quintessentially Progressivist and imperialist terms. Seeking to imitate the history of the country itself, the Yale series culminated in volumes 43 through 48, a set called *The Era of World Power*, including volume 46, *The Path of Empire*. Almost as an afterthought, the series was supplemented by two volumes of other American chronicles—*Canada* and *Hispanic Nations*. This was Woodrow Wilsonian literary history at its most striking.

The most influential history of U.S. literature in the first half of the twentieth century was probably Vernon Louis Parrington's *Main Currents of American Thought*, including volume 3: *The Beginnings of Critical Realism, 1860–1920*, published in 1930. When examined in light of his predecessors, Parrington's famous thesis about U.S. culture has a distinctly familiar rather than innovative ring to it: the story of America is the struggle between Enlightenment Man and Economic Man, the romance of egalitarian democracy versus the quest to define progress primarily in material and market-centered terms. For Parrington, who completed volume 3 during the Great Depression, literature's revolt against the desecrations caused by ungoverned capitalist development and collapse could take several forms, from romantic escapism to Pattee-like critical engagement. Although Parrington's primary modern literary hero of critical realism, Theodore Dreiser, was an urban northerner, southern writers from Jefferson to Twain to Glasgow played a crucial role for Parrington in defining a healthy American "Enlightenment" tradition to counter the country's obsessive focus on the pursuit of wealth.

The South, it is true, also exemplified for Parrington U.S. cultural failure confronting the challenges of industrial capitalism. Henry Grady and other New South leaders "surrendered" to the fragmenting energies of industrial development. Other New South figures clung to an over-simplified, compensatory vision of a pastoral past in local color and plantation fiction (Parrington xix–xxi). Parrington's negative assessment of the bulk of New South fiction and nonfiction was indebted to one of his southern heroes, Ellen Glasgow, and proved highly persuasive to a new generation of literary historians, who concluded that the vast majority of New South writers formed a stagnant eddy rather than one of the "main currents" in U.S. literary history. Thus 1930 signaled the beginning of the end of the pre-1920 New South's literary prestige—with Mark Twain the great exception, of course. This winnowing of older New South writers worth reading was greatly accelerated by the rise of Faulkner's reputation after World War II as *the* modern southern writer.

For those of us who stubbornly believe that the best literature intervenes in its era rather than merely reproducing that era's ideologies, we remain empowered by Parrington's vision of literature's *critical* function, in both senses of the word. Too bad Parrington's mainstream left submerged so many southern artists from 1865 to the 1920s who actually provided fine examples of just the critical, interventionist fiction-writing he claimed he most valued. Pattee's and Parrington's arguments for critical realism, carefully modified, are still relevant today. They can allow us to distinguish between New South traditions that validated dominant narratives of U.S. imperial unity under white supremacism versus those that heroically attempted a critique and an alternative.[13]

In sum, New South anthology makers between 1865 and the 1930s bequeathed to us several different narratives of literature's relation to its era and to the nation-state. Some argued that art should serve a Progressivist narrative of utopian state formation and imperial reach. Theirs was a highly coded narrative of Anglo-Saxon racial superiority, but more often than not it was cast as a tradition that was not racially based, but rather created universals and offered them for all the world to share. In their vision, the New South modeled for the nation successful race-relations management—in other words, new colonial forms compatible with the new, corporate forms of capitalism. Others (most notably the Agrarians, but they had many New South precedents) offered the counterargument that aesthetic form contested the fallen world of history and validated instead the supposedly universal ideals of a past cultural whole that had been abandoned by the corrupt modern age. They wanted to be fugitives from Progressivism and asserted the South's eternal difference from the nation. Often presenting themselves as pastoral and anti-industrial, proponents of eternal values rather than modern ones, the Agrarians, in fact, invented unities defining the South that served a quite contemporary strategic function, that of shoring up what they took to be proper, stable hierarchies between classes and races, not to mention gender roles.

What both these narratives of southern reunion or difference share is the assumption that any regional or national tradition had to be shaped and defined by cultural elites. As Edwin Alderman warned in the passage quoted earlier, "Excess of success, and replacement of its labor population, have tended to change the ideals of New England democracy, to destroy its homogeneity, to deaden and pervert somewhat its idealism." From Alderman's august perspective, slavery had once marred the nation's allegedly homogeneous composition and universal ideals, but just as that blot had been removed the South and the nation became stained in a new way, due to the polyglot racial and cultural mixtures caused by immigration, migration, and the general disrespect of proper boundaries of all kinds. In the face of such unruly population and cultural flows, it was the frightening responsibility of regional and national elites to reassert homogeneity and coherence in the places where it most mattered—at the loci of economic and political power and, just as importantly, at the sites where regional and national memory were shaped and stored via narratives defining what "American" ideals were and who could embody them.

Whenever we seek *alternative* theories of regional or national U.S. culture to counter either of the above narratives—in other words, when we adapt Pattee's and Parrington's ideal of critical realism for the twenty-first century and focus on all the ways in which narratives are complicit with, yet struggle against, the fallen secular world of which they are a part—we might turn for some of our models to the contrarian writers discussed in *Sitting in Darkness*—particularly Lydia Maria Child, Ellwood Griest, Albion Tourgée, Mark Twain, Marietta Holley, Aurelio Tolentino, Frances E. W. Harper, Sutton Griggs, George Marion McClellan, Walter Hines Page, W. E. B. Du Bois, and George Washington Cable. These authors heroically tried with various degrees of success to embody in their texts what a relatively egalitarian and multiracial—not racially stratified—democracy would look and sound like, how it would act, and how it would remember its own history. It was a vision of the nation's destiny that had never yet been realized, much less fully expressed.

Two questions guide *Sitting in Darkness*: What was education's role in constructing the limits of citizenship for blacks and, later, new colonials abroad? And what role did fiction play in shaping and/or questioning these discourses of education? Throughout this study, key concepts involving nation, racial formation, narration, memory, and other topics have influenced my readings, but theoretical arguments for the most part are made to play a secondary, not primary, role. The majority of the book's chapters mix history, biography, and attentiveness to the texture of a work's sentences and larger structures as they unfold themselves in time when read. My intent is to synthesize the best of the new methods in cultural studies with older forms of literary appreciation that were more thoroughly author- and text-centered, yet also broad and ambitious in their historical range—works such as Sterling Brown's *The Negro in American Fiction*, Jay Hubbell's *The South in American Literature*, or Edmund Wilson's *Patriotic Gore*.

Recent historians of Reconstruction and its aftermath, such as Eric Foner and Saidiya Hartman, have added remarkable achievements to the great legacies of John Hope Franklin and C. Vann Woodward. In different ways, Foner and Hartman emphasize that postbellum civil rights discourse linking education and citizen-making was full of contradictions, burdens, and instabilities. Seemingly liberal Reconstruction discourses affirming freedom, banning discrimination, and sanctioning "uplift" also naturalized the subordination of blacks to whites. Instead of finding a simple opposition between liberty and bondage in postwar history—between, say, the repressive Black Codes passed by southern legislatures and Reconstruction's reforms—Hartman demonstrates how both were profoundly implicated in the modern forms of state-sanctioned racism that replaced slavery. She traces how discourses of education and development for blacks were so intent on "fashioning obligation" and codifying and containing blackness that they created a double-bind of equality and exclusion, endlessly entangling the two. Hegemony may enforce unequal power relations through the choices it presents, not just through repression.

What is most needed in New South cultural history now is a way of uniting analysis of domestic scenes of subjection and self-making with a focus on the U.S. government's evolving foreign policies during the late nineteenth and early twentieth centuries, particularly where the education of the newly colonized was concerned. Historians of the postwar period have focused primarily on the actions of both governments and private citizens (often those running charitable foundations), using legal texts, newspapers and journals, and textbooks and handbooks, particularly those associated with Reconstruction, plus the occasional fictional text. What happens if an extensive array of short stories, novels, and other texts of imaginative literature by blacks and whites is added to the mix, while local histories are conjoined with global ones?

Creating such a synthesis is the goal of *Sitting in Darkness*. The majority of the following chapters survey a range of post–Civil War imaginative texts, mostly novels, that directly deal with the issue of black education and citizen-making in the U.S. South. Their focus is not just on schools and schoolteachers, but on the many other scenes of instruction and community-making that were essential to black communities' survival after the war. These chapters do not just read these texts' arguments pro and con regarding the education of southern blacks, but also chart a distinct shift from the private to the public sphere as the focus of attention. Further, I demonstrate that these authors understood that the construction of *white* identity and community was precariously involved in the fate of black self-development. Ironically, an unease about such racial interdependency proves to be as motivating for authors like Thomas Dixon, who was rabidly racist, as it was for Walter Hines Page and George Washington Cable, notorious liberals on matters of black education and civil rights. And after the immigration boom in the 1890s and early 1900s and the annexation of colonies in the Caribbean and the Pacific, such a sense of the compound fate of the races only increased. In imaginative works published in the 1890s and after, we can see authors struggling mightily to figure out what the United States' new colonial empire abroad meant for domestic racial relations.

The first two sections of this study mark opposing premises in the debates over education and citizenship in the postwar era. As the overlapping chronologies of parts 1 and 2 imply, these arguments should be understood to unfold in continuous dialectical opposition, not in successive stages. Part 1 gathers authors who for the most part believed that the United States was destined to become a multiracial democracy and that such an evolution was a good thing, a beacon for the world. In particular, these authors not only describe why only a liberal arts education can foster the critical thinking skills necessary for an informed citizenry on which democracy depends, but also *embody* those educational ideals in the ways their texts are designed, in the experiences they give their readers. With varying degrees of success, however, these writers also struggle against a discourse for re-creating black dependency that was also their inheritance from Reconstruction.

Part 2's chapters focus on just how powerful that rhetoric of dependency was, and why. Dependency models for black education perhaps functioned most powerfully when they presented themselves as narratives of uplift and development, not suppression. To tell this story adequately, we must attend to the ways in which in the 1890s and after the meaning of Reconstruction was rewritten by New South and national Progressivist intellectuals and leaders to endorse Jim Crow segregation at home and U.S. colonial expansion abroad. Imaginative literature played a key role in creating this revisionist history. Simultaneously, such models for uplift and containment were also vigorously critiqued by writers such as Mark Twain and Aurelio Tolentino, who castigated "white man's burden" rhetoric as profoundly hypocritical, and by openly racist authors like Thomas Dixon and Owen Wister, who worried that whites would be unable to seize their racial destiny without heroic models of white supremacism in action. As the reader of *Sitting in Darkness* moves through parts 1 and 2, he or she will notice a necessary broadening of the education theme from a focus on black schools and their curricula to questions of educational models for citizenship that applied to whites as well. An emerging irony should also become clear: whites were profoundly split regarding how best to educate whites to be superior, with some favoring the liberal arts and others a kind of indoctrination by hypnosis and the purification rituals of lynching.

Part 3 analyzes four texts that despite their flaws should be much better known. The section functions in *Sitting in Darkness* not so much as a synthesis to the dialectic set in motion in parts 1 and 2, but rather as a climactic dramatization of all that dialectic's tensions and torsional complexities. In this section too, this book's education theme is far broader than the topic of black schools, though black schools play key roles in all the texts considered. These authors eloquently show why the goal of a liberal arts education should be to create independent and critical citizens of all races, not dependent subjects divided by the color line. In so doing, they carry to a new level of complexity the educational project undertaken by the authors featured in part 1. If we seek to imagine a reworked canon of New South authors and texts that would serve neither southern nostalgia nor imperial narratives of nationhood, the fascinating early twentieth-century responses to Jim Crow colonialism considered in part 3 should have an honored place in any such alternative New South archive.

I offer *Sitting in Darkness* to teachers who would like to teach in new ways and to students eager to learn new things. I also offer it in the name of the many writers and texts herein included that have been unfairly neglected in U.S. cultural history, forced to sit in its shadows or brier patches, even in an era of active canon reformation and anthology creation. Let us remember the gazes of the students in the photographs at the start of this chapter, and let us try to recapture the sense of excitement and possibility of New South literary history suggested by the Walter Hines Page and Ralph Ellison quotations chosen as this introduction's epigraphs. It is time to make the relevance of U.S. Reconstruction to the literary history of post-slavery societies mis-stated or *understated* no more—time to make the old New South pure-D *new* again. In the end, *Sitting in Darkness* is not a pessimistic title, though it expresses a good deal of pain. The same is true for this book's hidden narrative, its dark archive.

# PART I

# Black Education in Fiction from Reconstruction to Jim Crow

## DISCOVERING A LIBERAL ARTS MODEL FOR CITIZEN-BUILDING IN A MULTIRACIAL DEMOCRACY

Chapter 1 opens *Sitting in Darkness* by surveying debates involving black education during the Reconstruction period and after, mixed with an analysis of fictional texts published in the late 1860s and the 1870s that capture both the hopes and anxieties of the early Reconstruction era, especially in regard to the Freedmen's Bureau's and various Christian missionary societies' ambitious plans to build and staff a network of schools across the U.S. South for black children and teenagers. Published fiction allows us to chart several competing models for black educational instruction as well as a distinct shift in national attitudes toward black schools between 1865 and the end of Reconstruction.

In pro-Reconstruction authors, private scenes of instruction (Lydia Maria Child and Ellwood Griest) evolve into an understanding that schools must be profoundly public and institutional endeavors with a liberal arts curriculum (represented here first by Albion Tourgée, followed by Frances E. W. Harper, Sutton Griggs, and George Marion McClellan). The authors in this section all depict scenes of instruction in their fiction, many of them involving schoolteachers and children, but others broadening the definition of when and where acts of education may take place to include other forms of interaction that were central to community-building—including informal conversation, reading group discussions, and speeches. There is considerable less unanimity when it comes to defining the goals and methods of education, however. Most of the texts focused on in chapter 1, plus Tourgée's novel *A Fool's Errand*, employ an imitative model of learning, wherein blacks are shown to progress by rote learning; the importance of good models of hygiene and behavior is stressed as much as the three R's. So too is black subservience to proper forms of authority, so that black behavior in freedom does not become anarchic. As well as stressing the importance of imitation in learning, this educational model also teaches proper power relations: it describes itself as teaching self-reliance, but what it actually models is dependency and subordination.

Beginning with Tourgée's second novel, *Bricks without Straw*, a different educational model comes to the foreground in part 1's analysis, one far more in tune with what was desired by the majority of newly freed blacks in the South. Historians of Reconstruction have extensively documented that the ex-slaves had the highest possible expectations for education: the majority wanted a well-funded public school system for their children with the most modern and ambitious curriculum possible. This other model of education is best described as a liberal arts curriculum; it mixes the teaching of "practical" arts that would be immediately applicable to gainful employment along with solid instruction in math, reading, and, more broadly, the humanities (including history and literature) and the natural sciences. This curriculum employed some learning by rote imitation, but active critical thinking and independent investigation were crucial components. As such, the liberal arts model represents a profoundly different vision not just of how human beings learn, but of the purpose of freedom itself. Liberty is understood to bring with it the responsibility to be actively engaged in community-building, not merely the pursuit of individual wealth. It also requires a robust critical intelligence—that is, independent thinking and the active creation of new knowledge, not the copying of what is already known. At base, the liberal educational model sees schools as agents of justice, slowly reforming social inequities and imperfections. Without schools teaching such principles, it was believed, blacks could never be citizens and U.S. democracy would never be able to cure its flaws and realize its promise.

A dependency model and a liberal arts model: these competing versions of education will be familiar to readers who are acquainted with the notorious rivalry that occurred in the late nineteenth and early twentieth century between Booker T. Washington and W. E. B. Du Bois, as summarized by the scathing assessment of Washington's "industrial education" methods that was a key component of Du Bois's *The Souls of Black Folk* (1903). Both saw schools as the best way for black communities to progress. But beyond that they found little common ground. Washington's and Du Bois's famous confrontation, however, represents a culmination of a long history that commenced well before either of them began their careers as public intellectuals and activists. In many ways, their two positions represent eloquent syntheses of earlier debates; neither position was strikingly original.

Chapter 1 explains why in many ways Washington's vision of education was a creation of the Reconstruction era, when federal and private philanthropical energies converged to create classroom disciplinary models for "uplift" via imitation and the acknowledgment of distinct limits for black progress. After briefly tracing the origins of this model in Reconstruction discourse, especially the work of Lydia Maria Child, chapter 1 then demonstrates how the imitative model expressed hidden (or sometimes not so hidden) assumptions about black inferiority and the need to contain black aspirations within acceptable limits, and why this model, even though it was associated with Reconstruction, proved so attractive to some after the rise of white supremacist rule in the New South after 1877. My test cases are two stories by Constance Fenimore Woolson that reached a national audience in 1878 and 1879 and signaled a distinct shift in the majority's attitude toward black schools. Later, in part 2 of *Sitting in Darkness*, I return to an analysis of the dependency model and its strange career: the black schools that implemented it, including Booker T. Washington's Tuskegee Institute, became exemplars after the 1890s for the design of colonial education systems in the new U.S. colonies abroad. One of this book's central terms, "Jim Crow colonialism," describes how so-called Progressivist reforms in the New South and the federal government created a new system of racial stratification and labor control at home and abroad that was even more profoundly a global capitalist system than the plantation slave economies that it replaced. And unlike in the old slave system, where education was seen as a threat, in the new colonial system the control of a carefully *delimited* educational model for people of color was encouraged—and the New South provided the model.

The dependency model of education had important critics well before Du Bois. Chapters 2 through 5 in part I chronicle several: Tourgée, Harper, Griggs, and McClellan. All of these authors had extensive involvement in educational theory and practice, either directly or indirectly. They used their fiction to define the methods, goals, and dangers facing black educators who sought to implement an alternative model, a liberal arts curriculum, into black schools, as well as exploring how liberal arts values should also govern other important sites where information was exchanged in black communities. In varied ways, these authors stress three elements of a liberal arts model for education: teaching agency (self-reliance and community empowerment); teaching a complex sense of black and U.S. history; and instituting a critique of nationalism—what Griggs calls *imperium*—in all its forms, including both black nationalism and U.S. imperialism. These writers recognize that the goals of instruction should be far more ambitious than merely learning a skill-set. Education should create active citizens and thinkers who have internalized democratic values of inquiry, not the passive imitation of external authorities. Far from ceding "practical" results to other educational models, the defenders of the liberal arts model stressed how such a vision of education was crucial for black survival under Jim Crow. Independent-minded citizens may discover hidden truths about the past and envision possibilities for the future that were unimaginable for previous generations—including the ability to foretell the day when the United States would become the first genuinely multiracial democracy in the world.

Although black grade schools and institutions of advanced learning are portrayed with great affection by all the authors chronicled in chapters 2 through 5, none finds that these schools (and other arenas where education takes place) achieve the goals they demand for black education. Tourgée's best novel, *Bricks without Straw*, ends mostly in despair. But in reconceiving how to portray blacks in fiction and in providing a detailed brief for why black public schools in the New South needed federal protection, Tourgée's novel is hardly nihilistic, despite its pessimism. More optimistic, Harper's idealized portrait of her schoolteacher heroine is also riddled with contradictions the author cannot resolve—color and class divisions that bedeviled black communities as they sought a unified response to Jim Crow. Griggs's novel *Imperium in Imperio* (1899) provides us with the most detailed portrait of what an ideal liberal arts syllabus for a black school might actually look like, at least in the author's opinion. (It focuses on great speeches by rebels such as Martin Luther, Patrick Henry, and Louis Kossuth.) But the novel's strength comes from its daring analysis of how national forms of hypocrisy over racial identity and the aims of education have been internalized by the psyches of black leaders, vitiating their attempts to respond to Jim Crow by building a self-reliant nation within a nation. Griggs's critique of imperious leadership should be read not only as an anatomy of the dangers of black nationalism popular in his era, but also as a critical response to U.S. colonialist nationalism in the post-1898 world. Finally, George Marion McClellan's moving portrait of an "Industrial and Normal" (teacher-training) school for blacks in Alabama turns on the irony that despite the school's success, its relatively conservative curriculum does not teach its students about the complex and tragic history that occurred on that school's very site during Reconstruction and slavery times. That instructional burden is left to McClellan's narrator, who models for his readers what it means to have a deep understanding of the meaning of black history.

## Chapter One

# Changing Views of Post–Civil War
# Black Education in the Fiction of
# Lydia Maria Child, Ellwood Griest, and
# Constance Fenimore Woolson (1867–1878)

Don't know much about history . . .

> —"Wonderful World," music and lyrics by Sam Cooke, Lou Adler, and Herb Alpert

Wake up all you teachers, got to teach a new way.

> —"Wake Up Everybody," Harold Melvin and the Blue Notes; music and lyrics by
> V. Carstarphen, J. Whitehead, G. McFadden

The fundamental cause of our failure in human education . . . is due to the fact that . . . the world regards and always has regarded education first as a means of buttressing the established order of things rather than improving it. . . . The object of all education is the child itself and not what it does or makes.

> —W. E. B. DU BOIS, *Darkwater, Du Bois Reader*

Nowhere does the United States' conundrum over Reconstruction reveal itself more starkly than in the discourse surrounding the role of public education in the postwar South, especially black schools. Should the fall of the Confederacy be taken as an opportunity to set up for the first time a public education system for blacks in the South? If so, how should it be structured and financed? What should the curriculum be? Should the schools primarily be a system to reinforce class and racial divisions dangerously undermined by the currents of the war and emancipation? Or should such schools rather be an education in citizenship rather than subordination, in how to claim one's new place in a new nation? Furthermore, what role was played by fictional narratives (as opposed to government reports, journalism, etc.) in shaping the debates surrounding black education? Were there key shifts in the representation of black schools from the heyday of Reconstruction to the late 1890s, when the new imperialism offered the opportunity of translating the southern education experiment abroad?

As education historians Robert Morris and James D. Anderson have eloquently documented, many ex-slaves linked a publicly funded universal educational system with their aspirations for citizenship and progress. Their vision of
black educational goals, moreover, was not dependent upon the definitions promoted by white elites; indeed, they were often at odds with such a limited vision.
Blacks as a whole also had a profound sense of how deeply their vision of a new
life was threatened. As early as a month after the formal end of the Civil War,
protest meetings for blacks were organized in many southern states to denounce
an emerging network of repression linking denial of voting rights, reneging on
wage contracts, terrorist violence, and retrenchment on promises for new public schools. To pick just one example of what John Hope Franklin has called
"Reconstruction, Confederate style," in Louisiana, President Andrew Johnson suspended a universal school tax recommended by a different branch of the federal
government, the Department of the Gulf's Board of Education (R. Morris 216;
Anderson 9–10). It was an early example of many successful attempts throughout
the South to attack the idea that taxes paid by all should support a public educational system of both black and white schools. Instead, black schools increasingly
were forced to rely on the meager financial support that stressed black communities could give after paying school taxes that went to white schools (Ayers,
*Promise* 420).

Regarding the ideal of a good school for every child, consider the language of
the Ordinance for the newly acquired Northwest Territories (in the Midwest and
elsewhere) passed by the Continental Congress in 1785: "The plats of the town-
ships respectively, shall be marked by subdivisions into lots of one mile square,
or 640 acres, in the same direction as the external lines, and numbered from 1 to
36. . . . There shall be reserved the lot No. 16, of every township, for the mainte-
nance of public schools within the said township." One schoolhouse per township—we need only compare such a vision to the limited programs initiated in
the postwar South for both black and white schoolchildren to see with heart-
breaking clarity how piecemeal Reconstruction's educational vision was, even
before it was subverted. Even the most ambitious of Reconstruction educational
policies never mandated such a comprehensive public school system for blacks
and whites in the South. Reconstruction's relative timidity at the federal level
regarding schools becomes even clearer if we compare its mandates to the southern states with the Morrill Act passed by Congress in 1862. That act stated that,
for each member of Congress, a state would receive thirty thousand acres of public land to sell in order to fund new colleges teaching agricultural and mechanical
arts. Over seventy such "land grant schools" were created in the North, Midwest,
and West because of this act—but not in the South. The act's provisions were
extended to the South not after the Civil War but only in 1890, when they were
mainly used to help create schools for whites. As well as passing various civil

rights bills and other legislation, why didn't the allegedly radical Reconstruction Congress use the Morrill Act as a model for funding a network of primary and secondary as well as advanced public schools throughout the South, once the former Confederate states had ratified their new constitutions and rejoined the Union? How would the history of the South from 1865 into the twentieth century have been different, and more just? Historians are not supposed to ask counter-factual questions. But fiction writers, like poets, stubbornly "dwell in possibility," as Emily Dickinson said. As we shall see, that is certainly the case with Tourgée, Harper, Griggs, and McClellan. And so may teachers and literary historians.[1]

John Hope Franklin has well summarized the educational hopes shared by some whites and the vast majority of newly freed blacks:

The Negroes' avid desire for learning combined with other factors after 1867 to produce a system of public education in the Southern states. One was the anxiety of the poorer whites to overcome their own educational disadvantages. The ante-bellum planters had steadfastly refused to support public education in the belief that only those who could afford it should be educated. They sent their sons and daughters to private schools or had them tutored at home. Without help the poorer classes were unable to educate their children. Another factor was the widespread commitment of Northerners in the South to the idea of universal education. Many were themselves the products of Northern public schools, and they hoped to see similar systems established in the South.... There was, furthermore, the old American ideal that the responsibilities of citizenship, of voting and holding office, could be exercised intelligently only by an educated citizenry. (Reconstruction 108–109)

The Freedmen's Bureau, however, was authorized by Congress only in limited ways to create new public schools in the South. It relied heavily on volunteerism to build and support new schools—southern blacks' own efforts, plus that of northern organizations such as the American Missionary Association. After the war, the Bureau had to operate almost alone in much of the South because "no viable Union military presence existed anywhere outside the towns," historian Randall M. Miller has said (xvi); indeed, it is hard to speak of the Freedmen's Bureau as a single historical agent, given its several incarnations and authorizations, its varied partners and antagonists, and its different record in different states and even counties. At most, the Bureau had only nine hundred agents spread across the entire South. When the Bureau was disbanded in 1870, most black children still did not attend grade school—and many who did were in school only for a few months of the year. Even so, in Eric Foner's estimation, education "probably represented the [Freedmen's Bureau's] greatest success in the postwar South" (*Reconstruction* 144). Nearly three thousand schools with 150,000 total students—from grade schools to sixty-one Normal schools to train teachers and eleven colleges and universities for Negroes—were created in former Confederate states during the first few years after the Civil War via the Bureau, charitable organizations, and community efforts.[2]

Blacks in the South played a central role in creating these new schools. They established temporary classes in all kinds of buildings and "raised money among themselves to purchase land, build schoolhouses, and pay teachers' salaries"; by 1870, blacks had expended over one million dollars on education, though impoverished black communities, especially in rural areas, were often almost wholly dependent upon northern benevolent societies and the Freedmen's Bureau for aid (Foner, *Reconstruction* 96–102). "It is difficult to exaggerate the eagerness of Negroes at the close of the war to secure an education," Franklin asserted (108)—an eagerness confirmed by Foner's much lengthier history of Reconstruction, with moving details such as the fact that blacks hiring themselves out as servants to whites in the late 1860s often insisted on their right to attend night schools (366). After 1868, the Reconstruction state conventions, with blacks playing a leading role, "boldly provided for the support of public schools by special taxes" (Franklin 113). As long ago as 1935, in *Black Reconstruction*, W. E. B. Du Bois correctly argued that "the first great mass movement for public education at the expense of the state, in the South, came from Negroes" (638).[3]

Toward all these developments, "white property owners were outraged" (Franklin 113). White mobs attacked black schoolhouses and other targets, and when "Redeemer" Democrats eventually gained power in the various state legislatures in the 1870s and 1880s, they immediately targeted school-funding arrangements allocating state tax funds to black schools as well as white. Taxes for education were often almost entirely diverted to white schools, and black teachers, if they were paid using state funds at all, received less than whites. The gap between expenditures for black and white pupils steadily widened after Reconstruction began to be undone. State support for public education for whites in the New South was often grossly inadequate as well: in Louisiana, for instance, the percentage of illiterate native whites rose between 1880 and 1890 because of inadequate schools (Foner, *Reconstruction* 588–589). But the southern subversion of universal public education had far worse effects on black communities. From the rise of postwar white rule until well into the twentieth century, blacks throughout southern school districts basically paid much more and received much less. For protesting these kinds of inequities in the Memphis public school system run by an all-white board of education, Ida B. Wells in 1891 was fired from her teaching job (Schechter 72–73).

Although postwar education in the U.S. South has been extensively studied, no focused analysis has been done on the changing representation in fiction of black schools and the schoolteachers (white and black) who taught in them. Yet such fiction is plentiful and had varied, complex contributions to make to national debates about black education after the Civil War and beyond. Comparing and contrasting post–Civil War fiction about black education, we need to discuss a wide range of works so that the cultural battle lines will be seen to be in motion, not statically and simplistically drawn. Pro-Reconstruction whites did not merely join blacks in favor of schools and black advancement, while reactionary whites were against this. The conflict, rather, must be understood to be over what education itself should look like, and whether its goal was to re-enforce or challenge the new configurations that power took in postwar southern U.S. society. Two models for instruction competed. One stressed limited advancement through imitation, with particular emphasis on "practical" education in manual skills; it is most familiarly associated with Booker T. Washington (though he had many precursors, black and white) and was well summarized by Du Bois in *Darkwater* as a focus on what a child manually "does or makes." The competing vision for black education included some manual-labor instruction in the curriculum but was essentially a liberal arts model linking reading, writing, and instruction in American history to citizen-building, a life of community activism, and critical thinking. In writing fiction, Tourgée, Harper, Griggs, and McClellan, in particular, affirmed the latter view, as did Du Bois.[4]

## Lydia Maria Child's *A Romance of the Republic* (1867)

Two years after publishing *The Freedmen's Book*, a schoolbook sententiously mixing life sketches of great men, conduct-guide essays such as "Kindness to Animals" and "The Laws of Health," and advice for citizens, Lydia Maria Child brought out her last and most ambitious novel, *Romance of the Republic*. Like Harriet Beecher Stowe, Wendell Phillips, and William Wells Brown, among many, Child believed that the conventions of popular sentimental romance fiction—which encouraged sympathy and admiration for the oppressed and revulsion for their oppressors— could challenge race prejudice in ways that speeches or laws could not. Since the time of the ancient Greeks, romance narratives were associated with identity loss, trials and tragedy, and the fugitive-hero's journey toward memory recovery, when good triumphs over evil and clarity over confusion. In the conventional ending of romances, family lineage is recovered, usurpers deposed, and a new home and security created. Child felt that all these generic features of romance—especially its essential optimism—made it the ideal narrative genre for readers remaking their identities in a republic. Accordingly, she wrote a narrative intended to make her mostly white middle-class audience identify with heroines who discover their mixed-raced identity and are forced to plunge from a life of privilege into the nightmare of enslavement, then fight their way back to sunshine and citizenship. Once readers' sympathies were engaged, so Child's thinking went, then their racial attitudes would change.[5]

Replete with orphaned daughters, benevolent mentors, treacherous suitors, trials and tribulations, miraculous discoveries revealing hidden histories, and settings that vary from the urban North to New Orleans to the rural South, Child's *Romance of the Republic* concludes full of Reconstruction's heady optimism. A future unblemished by racism is imagined for the light-skinned but still mixed-race protagonists, while another, dark-skinned child, Henriet, presents Child's vision of the true inner reconstruction that only proper education creates. After a period of private tutoring, Henriet presents herself for examination showing off a manuscript book of poems by others (not her own), copied "very correctly, in a fine flowing hand," and a map, also "copied very neatly." Even more praiseworthy, in her mentors' and the narrator's eyes, is the girl's demeanor, full of "ease" and "a pleasing degree of gentleness" (433). A benefactor concludes: "'Really, this is encouraging,' said Mr. Blumenthal, as she left the room. 'If half a century of just treatment and free schools can bring them all up to this level, our battles will not be in vain, and we shall deserve to rank among the best benefactors of the country; to say nothing of a corresponding improvement in the white population'" (433–434).

Twenty-first-century readers, of course, may react more skeptically. They should notice how narrow a vision of education and creativity governs this poor earnest girl's instruction, and wonder too at the sharp notes of condescension and self-praise inflecting Mr. Blumenthal's alleged optimism. This climactic scene in *Romance of the Republic* unfortunately reproduces the limitations of the educational models in Child's *Freedmen's Book*, not to mention that of the Freedmen's Bureau and the northern "missionary societies." All these visions of black education were intent on making sure newly freed slaves defined their freedom primarily in terms of regulating their hygiene, self-discipline, and labor. Such "proper" behavior would allegedly prove that slaves deserved their freedom, but it also demanded black subjects who would not threaten whites' sympathetic gaze.[6]

Child meant Henriet's oral exam scene to suggest, first, that blacks, the most "imitative" of races (433), would respond excellently to good role models; and, second, that blacks' success in schools should in no way be threatening to southern whites, who also under Reconstruction would obtain their own "corresponding improvement" through separate schools. (The novel was not afraid to celebrate interracial marriage, but hedged on the matter of interracial schools.) For Lincoln, in the words of the "Gettysburg Address," the tragedy of the war created a "new birth of freedom"—for *all* citizens. For Child, the promise of that birth could be fulfilled only through postwar Reconstruction.

Child's optimism stemmed from her support of the free labor ideology embraced by many radical Republicans. This ideology believed that free labor did not just lay the foundation for financial independence, but also taught proper social roles. As one of Child's characters intones, black citizens with new-born rights must learn to be "industrious, temperate, and economical," but also must become educated "with a view to the station [i.e., respectable working-class status] you will have it in your power to acquire" (436). In Child's view, independence was impossible without proper parental role-models, especially for citizens who had supposedly been trained by slavery to devalue labor. Child also believed that respect for free labor freed one from race prejudice. She concluded her *Romance* with black characters performing a kind of pro-Reconstruction minstrel show in thanks to their white audience, mixing Mendelssohn, "The Star-Spangled Banner," and John Greenleaf Whittier's song of black freedom as entrepreneurship:

"We own de hoe, we own de plough,
    We own de hands dat hold;
We sell de pig, we sell de cow;
    But nebber *chile* be sold. (433)

At the apex of such a performance demonstrating good mentoring and thankfulness stood Reconstruction fiction. Child believed that fiction had the duty to provide a national model for the regeneration of a nation, and in her most ambitious novel she sought to do just that: move blacks toward realizing the ideal of self-ownership, and whites to seeing that black independence would enrich them as well, strengthening the Republic itself. Despite her ambitious goals, however, Child's understanding of educational practice had a contradiction at its heart: it created not black self-ownership but perpetual indebtedness toward whites. Such a contradiction made it easy for others who held a much more skeptical view of black education to appropriate Child's teaching model for very different ends. Like most whites supporting Reconstruction, Child was essentially promoting education as the "fashioning of obligation," in Saidiya Hartman's apt phrase—a process of rote imitation that created subservient subjects, not citizens, permanent pupils caught in a new form of bondage that passed as uplift.

## Ellwood Griest's *John and Mary; or, The Fugitive Slaves, a Tale of South-Eastern Pennsylvania* (1873)

Northerners controlled the representation of Reconstruction in fiction for the first decade or so after the end of the Civil War, as they were central in defining the agenda of Reconstruction itself. Another revealing postwar fictional text was written by a Pennsylvania Quaker, Ellwood Griest, and published in installments in 1873 in a Lancaster County newspaper, the *Inquirer*, and later in book form. It does not feature black schools, but it warrants discussion here because it defines education in the broadest, most ambitious sense: it seeks to change whites' prejudices by re-educating them about the true meaning of American history. *John and Mary* celebrates blacks and whites collaborating first in the Abolitionist movement and then to create the Underground Railroad. Then it directly links those earlier accomplishments of antiracist activism to the reformist ideals of Reconstruction, grounding those ambitions in biblical imperatives. Finally, the novel is also important because it provides a powerful analysis of all the forces in the South that were actively working to destroy Reconstruction, from Ku Klux Klan terrorism to complacent Freedmen's Bureau operatives who were reluctant to protect black rights when they were violated. Published in 1873, Griest's text prophetically suggests Reconstruction may have already received a fatal wound, just as the novel's leading black protagonist does. Left to mourn and ponder the moral future of his nation is the novel's white protagonist, a white Union officer who had his views of blacks radically changed by fighting alongside them in combat.[7]

Griest was born in 1824 into a Quaker family, was apprenticed as a blacksmith, and as a member of the Union Army during the Civil War spent time in a POW camp and later as a commissary officer with General Philip H. Sheridan in Virginia, New Orleans, and Florida. Griest was a radical abolitionist before the war and after it an active supporter of the Republican Party and Reconstruction.

The main action of *John and Mary* occurs in 1830 and 1865, in Cecil County, Maryland, Lancaster County, Pennsylvania, and then Florida after the Civil War. Two of the primary characters, one black and one white, have their lives intersect because of the Underground Railroad and then again, years later, without at first recognizing each other, while they both are collaborating on U.S. Army and Freedmen's Bureau Reconstruction work. The novel's climactic "recognition" scene, therefore, involves far more than the discovery of shared private histories, important as that is. Griest's text sought forever to pair in the public memory the heroic story of black and white collaboration on the Underground Railroad with Reconstruction's promise to reform U.S. race relations. Griest believed that such organized efforts to help others in need both forwarded the Lord's work and gave immeasurable benefits to society; his text cites as a touchstone Christ's assurance in Matthew 25:40 that "inasmuch as ye did [good works] to the least one of my brethren, ye did it unto me" (150). Revealingly, however, Griest's romance remained quite skeptical of the powers of government or other institutions, especially the army and the Freedmen's Bureau, to effect meaningful social change unless individual human hearts were made contrite and generous, one citizen at a time.

For Griest as well as Child, prejudices were learned and therefore could be unlearned, and nothing worked more forcefully to destroy stereotypes than direct interactions with others who did not confirm those stereotypes. Quakers who opposed slavery on theological and moral grounds are shown to have their inner doubts about blacks erased by direct contact with fugitive slaves, black "conductors" on the Underground Railroad, or black soldiers on Civil War battlefields. Griest writes of a white character, Captain Brown, "[He] had become a good deal attached to Sergeant Evans [a black protagonist], such an attachment as a man will form for one, regardless of rank, color, or caste, who shows in his daily acts those true qualities of manliness that are as rare as they are valuable" (187). For Griest, experience was the best classroom, and it was whites (including northern ones who thought they were liberal on race matters) who were most in need of reconstruction and schooling, not blacks. Such a view is in many ways a more self-critical vision of whites' roles in Reconstruction than Child's.

For this Quaker author, the foundation of democratic citizenship was the responsible use of personal freedom, and only free labor at fair wages could teach discipline and ambition. But Griest turns the familiar free labor ideology around and applies it more trenchantly toward whites, not ex-slaves. In his view, slavery made southern whites slothful, licentious, and violent regardless of whether they owned slaves or not. Griest put the most eloquent denunciation of slavery's effects in the mouth of a white southerner, a native Floridian: "the existence of slavery demoralized everybody" (202). Griest's novel strips slavery of any veneer of civilization it might claim. After surrender, the narrator informs us, the legacy of slavery continued: "Bands of guerrillas were less than ever disposed to adopt the pursuits of civilized life. They had never been accustomed to labor; and now, while the necessity for doing so had been multiplied in consequence of their former slaves obtaining their freedom, their recklessness had been much increased by the circumstances surrounding them during the progress of the war" (157). Reversing clichés of blacks' laziness and barbarism, Griest pointedly applied these to rebel whites, stressing the close connection between slavery's bad habits, the anarchy of the war, and the postwar rise of the "Ku-Klux," portrayed in *John and Mary* as no more than terrorists continuing to war against the U.S. government after the conflict's official end (chapter 13).

Into this cauldron in Florida in 1865 came Captain Brown, Sergeant Evans, and the Freedmen's Bureau. Remarkably, for a book written with an explicitly antiracist agenda, *John and Mary* casts a skeptical eye on the early workings of the Bureau. Local residents hired by the Bureau prove thoroughly prejudiced toward the blacks they are supposed to help; they are drawn to the job for its status and government paycheck. Brown, Evans, and the Bureau have just begun work when Evans is fatally wounded by one of those racist vigilantes.

The last chapters of Griest's text are the fullest depictions I have found in fiction before Albion Tourgée of the violent resistance Reconstruction met in the South.

Griest tried to end his novel on a hopeful note. As Sergeant Evans lies dying, he recounts his memories of his parents being helped by Pennsylvania Quakers to escape slavery. Captain Brown in turn suddenly remembers as a young child seeing frightened fugitives with a baby brought to his parents' home in the middle of the night. That baby, it turns out, grew up to be Sergeant Evans. White and black war heroes are thus further united by recovered memories of their parents' heroic interaction. This shared history of civil disobedience was clearly meant by Griest to signify the link U.S. national memory should make between two different generations of heroes and two phases of antiracist activism—the Underground Railroad and abolitionism and then Reconstruction. Evans dies, but his work (and Captain Brown's) goes on. Evans's mother, the Mary of the novel's title, finds employment working (perhaps as a maid) for the proprietor of a young woman's boarding school in Philadelphia, who promises Mary "good wages, and in addition, to learn her the common branches of education. . . . [In Philadelphia] she remained for many years, and not only learned to read and write, but formed quite a taste for literary acquirements. Her constant contact with persons of good education had also a perceptible effect on her mind and conversation, and she fell gradually into the habit of using such language as prevailed in society of that character. During her residence here she accumulated considerable means" (221–222). With the money this former fugitive slave earned, she could save enough to buy her first home.

Griest complicated this relatively happy ending with forebodings that Reconstruction might not entirely live up to its name; the postwar world that newly educated blacks could create for themselves is shown to be profoundly fragile. The novel finishes with the phrase "home at last" applying to heaven, not fallen human society. Although to some degree the energy supporting Reconstruction was still high in 1873—the Fourteenth and Fifteenth Amendments had been ratified in 1868 and 1870, and key civil rights legislation would pass Congress in 1875—Griest noticed signs of the coming national repudiation of Reconstruction in everyday events, including newspaper and magazine commentary. The historical record of black and white activism for multiracial democracy that Griest's *John and Mary* seeks to commemorate is as fragile a "connecting thread between the present and the past" (214) as Captain Brown's childhood memories, which, forgotten once, may be erased again.

Prominent elements in *John and Mary* portend not romance's conventional forms of resolution but a contrasting vision of the United States trapped in a nightmare of eternal repetition and racial conflict. Mary Brown's worse moment as a fugitive comes when she hallucinates her "master" suddenly stepping out of the woods to reclaim her (114ff). Mary's nightmare proves insubstantial, due to the heroic efforts of blacks and whites to rescue her. But the very mechanisms of Reconstruction that were meant to provide the United States with a similar rescue from racism are pointedly shown to be flawed and inadequate. The only achieved sense of justice and resolution in the novel occurs by Evans's death-bed, as two human beings, a black and a white, discover they share even more than they knew. Mary's education in the postwar era may allow her to join Philadelphia's black middle class, but it is the white protagonist Captain Brown's education that is most profoundly reconstructed by his postwar experience. Revising the phrase Griest applies to Mary's education, which stresses the value of imitating white role models, we might say that Brown's "constant contact" with Sergeant Evans radically reformed his understanding of American democracy, both its promise and its imperfect history.

Griest set out to write a narrative based on a "substantial foundation" of factual truth (219), chronicling events that had actually occurred involving people he knew in the Lancaster area. *John and Mary* presents itself as a properly Quaker chronicle, not a "highly wrought romance" (219), and the narrative is indeed earnest and plain in style and conception. Yet Griest could not help but shape factual details into popular narrative patterns, whether it be Gothic devices to heighten suspense when the fugitives are being pursued, or his concluding gestures toward the happy ending endemic to romance narratives. It may be that in 1873 Griest felt he needed so earnestly to offer his "factual" models of heroism and recovered memory because he already sensed the opportunities and optimism of Reconstruction's original goals were slipping away. Griest hoped that he could counteract such trends by using romance plot conventions to inspire sympathetic identification with the oppressed, so that his readers, just like Sergeant Brown, would have their opinions of blacks and their knowledge of American history irrevocably altered. But Griest's plot also shows how fragile Evans's and Brown's accord is in the face of terrorist violence.

Wendell Phillips, one of Child's and Griest's colleagues in the abolitionist movement, may have been right in 1853 when he said that "the fate of the [N]egro is the romance" of U.S. history, and that "in the thrilling incidents of the escape and sufferings of the fugitive, and the perils of his friends, the future Walter Scott of American would find the 'border-land' of his romance . . . and that the literature of America would gather its freshest laurels from that field" (*Speeches* 132). Following Child, Griest extended the relevance of romance to postwar visions of antiracist reform. Unlike Child, who ended her novel with a tableau full of the paternalist optimism of the immediate postwar period, Griest concluded his 1873 romance with a deathbed scene and a graveyard meditation.[8]

## Constance Fenimore Woolson's "Rodman the Keeper" and "King David" (1877–78)

In the September 1874 issue of *Harper's New Monthly Magazine*, two articles appeared that well reveal the changes taking place in the nation's attitude toward Reconstruction and black schools. One was the final installment of Edwin De Leon's "The New South," full of tables and maps illustrating rises in cotton and rice production, imports and exports, coal mining, new railroad lines, and other indices of postwar material progress. De Leon's article showed little interest in documenting what these changes meant for blacks in the South or analyzing how the signs of progress were very unevenly distributed. His article showed why national magazines such as *Harper's* that had once backed Reconstruction were by the mid-1870s beginning to persuade their readers that federal Reconstruction programs had retarded progress in the South, not advanced it. De Leon's goal was to prove the South was at last "striving to work out her own deliverance from the evils, political, social, industrial, and financial, that have so stifled and oppressed her during eight long years," i.e., 1866–1874 (48: 280). In other words, without seeing the need to argue his point directly, De Leon implied that Reconstruction was a kind of pharaoh's bondage from which the South needed "deliverance" if it were to progress.

The lead article in that September 1874 *Harper's* issue was an illustrated essay, "On Negro Schools." It was written anonymously using the first-person plural, as if the voice of the magazine itself were speaking. This piece's discourse and illustrations (the latter by one "Porte Crayon") well reveal how whites' attitudes toward black education, a key element of Reconstruction, were unstable in 1874. Much of "On Negro Schools" is optimistic regarding black education. The genial narrator interviews a young "embryonic statesman and philosopher" at an unnamed Virginia school, giving him two nickels as a reward, and visits Storer College for blacks in Harper's Ferry, dispensing accolades on its instructors, young scholars, and liberal arts curriculum for training black teachers (49: 457–464). Beneath the narrator's preening optimism, however, lurks doubt and derision, as revealed by the accompanying illustration, "The Great Scholar," which mocks what it purports to praise.

In the article's second half, the narrative voice becomes more openly ambivalent about educated Negroes and focuses on the entire country, not just the South. The persona speaking is white, of course, though its race is unmarked, and definitely middle class. The main issue has suddenly become the negative influence too much schooling may have on "our domestic servants." Educated help may be "more scrupulous in regard to the rights of property in small matters than formerly, when they felt and acted like common owners of the household stuff or farm products. . . . Their manners are more respectful and self-respecting, evincing

Fig. 1.1. "The Great Scholar"

greater deference for the educated superiority of their employers than they ever did for the ownership of their former masters. On the other hand, their cookery has degenerated, their skill in the manual arts is generally decreasing." The illustration accompanying a comment about "our" cook—that she "lets her bread sour while she is agonizing over her long-tailed literary p's and q's"—makes the earnest scholar appear demonic, with tongue (?) sticking out and her turban's ties rather like devil's horns (466–467).

The *Harper's* article concludes by strongly endorsing "industrial schools" training blacks for specific manual employment (468). As the fragile system of black public schools and public-school funding set up during Reconstruction was systematically undermined in the 1870s and 1880s, northern whites increasingly changed their opinions about black education—and the beneficiaries of their philanthropic nickels—in ways rehearsed by "On Negro Schools."[9]

With the limited exception of black voting rights, all of Reconstruction's key proposed reforms—from land redistribution and other economic changes to well-supported public schools and freedom from terrorist violence and discrimination—were systematically attacked as soon as they had begun to be implemented. But forms of resistance that had been improvised at the local and state levels in the early postwar years increasingly became validated on the national level in the early 1870s, even as Reconstruction was reaching a high-water mark in terms of legislation passed by the U.S. Congress and constitutional

Fig. 1.2. "P's and Q's"

amendments ratified by the states. In Nell Irvin Painter's adept summary of the Supreme Court's role:

> The United States Supreme Court reflected the weakening commitment to political revolution in the South. Beginning with the Slaughterhouse Cases of 1873, the Court increasingly used the due process clause of the Fourteenth Amendment to protect corporations from state regulation rather than the civil rights of persons. The *Reese* and *Cruikshank* decisions of 1876, related to antiblack political violence in Kentucky and Louisiana respectively, further limited the scope of the Fourteenth and Fifteenth Amendments by removing individual infringements of civil rights from the purview of federal law. Holding that Congress could legislate only on the actions of states, the Court made it virtually impossible for federal authorities to punish political violence.... In 1883 it ruled the Civil Rights Act of 1875 unconstitutional, thereby permitting discrimination in public accommodations. In 1896 it approved racial segregation, according to the fictional "separate but equal" formula, in *Plessy v. Ferguson.* And in 1898, in *Williams v. Mississippi,* ... [the] Court decided that the Mississippi provisions, which through a series of subterfuges made it nearly impossible for black men to vote, did not constitute racial discrimination because they did not mention race by name. (*Standing at Armageddon* 8)

After the Mississippi constitution quashing of black voting rights was upheld by the Supreme Court, many other southern states that had not implemented such restrictions quickly followed suit (Woodward, *Origins* 321).[10]

National magazines arguably played as important a role as the Supreme Court in dismantling support for Reconstruction. As early as 1871, The *Nation*, a magazine formerly in favor of many Reconstruction reforms, had unequivocally branded Reconstruction a "failure" (Stampp and Litwack 15; Cerny 28). Throughout the 1870s, the evaluation of Reconstruction began to change among northern whites due to shifting coverage of its programs by white newspaper and magazine journalists, cartoonists, and public policy "experts." In 1879, almost two decades before the *Williams* decision, the respected journal the *North American Review* held a symposium on the subject, "Ought the Negro to Be Disfranchised?"

Further, northern-published national monthly magazines competing to capture the increasingly prosperous middle-class market—particularly *Scribner's* (renamed the *Century* in 1881), the *Atlantic Monthly, Harper's*, and the *Nation*—began publishing poems, fiction, and other texts in the 1870s and after that encouraged doubts about the effects of social change sponsored by institutional agencies like the Freedmen's Bureau or even the northern missionary societies, particularly regarding their ability to instill the work ethic among ex-slaves supposedly ignorant of it. As Jay Hubbell long ago pointed out (726–733), *Scribner's-Century*, unlike its rivals, was not identified with northern Republicanism, and as doubts about Reconstruction proliferated it competed for a national audience by opening its pages to white poets, fiction writers, memoirists, and journalists, many of them southerners, who gave readers a distinctly different point of view regarding developments in the South. This journal's rapid circulation growth in the late 1870s and early 1880s caused its competitors quickly to follow suit, and "New South" literature intent on re-interpreting Reconstruction and the South's future achieved a nationwide reach. The Second Civil War was a war of words won by ex-Confederates and their sympathizers who learned how to use the new forms of mass-market media to reach and influence a national audience.

By the 1890s, literature as a whole promoted an increasingly negative portrait of black schools and the black and white teachers who worked in them. Instead, the plantation was substituted for Reconstruction as the most successful site for managing black social development and containment. Only there, the implication was, were contacts between the races not bureaucratic or contractual but caring, personal, even pre-modern, thus better suited (so the "logic" went) to the primitivism of Negro people. Paradoxically, the slavery-less plantation was now envisioned by whites as the ideal locale for nurturing black modernity, via wage contracts, new schools, and a stable relationship with their social "betters"—not a site of brutal labor exploitation, but of citizen-nurturing. Plantation social relations were also portrayed as an ideal counter to white mob violence and groups such as the Ku Klux Klan, all stoutly condemned by the national magazines: The suggestion was that good planter role models positively affected shiftless whites as well as blacks. Black education was still generally advocated, but northern philanthropic support shifted in the 1870s from public schools available for all to private institutions available to far fewer black students and increasingly teaching "industrial" or practical skills, not a full liberal arts curriculum. For most blacks eking out a living as sharecroppers, plantation-run schools were understood by whites as being all that was needed; too much education would be inappropriate for them and counterproductive for the new social order. New South fiction in the national magazines—and journalism such as the Harper's article, "On Negro Schools"—validated such changes.

In part 2 of *Sitting in Darkness* I give a fuller discussion of how Reconstruction's model for fashioning dependent black subjects was appropriated by white supremacists with the rise of the New South, first to promote plantation elites as those who should be in charge of black schools, and then to transform the benevolent planter patriarch model into a colonial education system for the United States' new territories acquired after the 1898 victory over Spain. For now, it is necessary to sketch events that happened after 1877 in the realm of literary representation, so that readers may understand the orthodoxies that had to be fought by adamant defenders of radical black education such as Tourgée, Harper, Griggs, and McClellan.

The southern poet Irwin Russell, writing in black dialect in *Scribner's* in January 1877, put the new orthodoxy best: those who worked with blacks should not be northern do-gooders but "some-un ... what kin talk to 'em bes." The proper goal should be to "Recomstruc' de pore critters, an' help ' em to rise"— but only in ways approved by white southern elites. When Freedmen's Bureau Reconstruction began to be rejected, in literary discourse like poetry and fiction that change was represented not as a repudiation of Reconstructions goals, but as a commonsense reform, taking the process of change away from foolish and ignorant northern idealists and dangerous black radicals. Reconstruction was itself reconstructed, its ideals appropriated for a new agenda—one in which to "rise" was rewritten for blacks to mean rising to their proper (limited) place— and no further—under white rule in the "redeemed" New South.[11]

Poets publishing works in black dialect applying minstrel conventions to postwar "darkies" included Thomas Dunn English, Irwin Russell, Sidney Lanier, Thomas Nelson Page, James Whitcomb Riley, and, eventually, the black poet Paul Laurence Dunbar (though evaluating Dunbar's poems and prose is a more complicated matter). Popular new memoirists, travel writers, and essayists who shaped readers' minds about the possibilities of a post-Reconstruction South included Edward King, "The Great South" (*Scribner's*, 1873); Edwin De

Leon, "The New South" (*Harper's*, 1874); E. L. Godkin ("The White Side of the Southern Question," the *Nation*, 1880); and Henry Grady ("In Plain Black and White," the *Century*, 1885). The ideology of such prose had been foreshadowed in the early 1870s by books such as James S. Pike's *The Prostrate State: South Carolina under Negro Government.* Writers of fiction who found that representations of the South helped their stars rapidly ascend in the 1880s included the northerner Constance Fenimore Woolson and the southerners James Lane Allen, Lafcadio Hearn, Thomas Nelson Page, and Joel Chandler Harris, among many. The 1890s brought even more white southerners to national attention, including Richard Malcolm Johnston, Grace King, Kate Chopin, and Ruth McEnery Stuart.

Two early signposts in the national media that Reconstruction revisionism was underway in fiction were the Constance Fenimore Woolson stories "Rodman the Keeper" (*Atlantic Monthly*, 1877) and "King David" (*Scribner's*, 1878). Woolson's John Rodman is a Union veteran who decides his postwar mission is not to go home but to care for a southern graveyard in which lie fourteen thousand Union soldiers. Eventually, two veterans from opposing sides of the battle lines come to a testy truce, sharing conversation and memories. Woolson's tale thus provided a paradigm for how the country's memorial services might shift from separately honoring Union or Rebel dead—a common practice in the late 1860s and early 1870s, when such commemorations tended to be called Memorial Day in the North and Decoration Day in the South—to honoring all (white) fallen soldiers. This was particularly an issue in the South, as Woolson's story vividly illustrates. The South had many graveyards of soldiers from the "other" side, and as the war's loser its emotions toward the conflict and its aftermath were most turbulent. (Commemoration of black Union veterans was largely left to black communities until much later in the century. Black southerners showed no hesitation honoring all Union dead, however. Ironically, it was black ministers who organized what may have been the first "Decoration Day" in the South, in South Carolina in 1865; the name was only later appropriated by whites for their services for white Confederate dead.)

In Woolson's "Rodman," the Union veteran lowers the American flag every evening. Local blacks honor the soldiers in their own way, with "Swing Low Sweet Chariot." The tale contains much of the dialect humor and character idiosyncrasies that mark the local color genre, stories about rural settings and people in New England, the South, or the Midwest that became hugely popular in the second half of the nineteenth century. In many ways, "Rodman the Keeper" is close in spirit to the most famous work of the British poet Thomas Gray—an American "Elegy Written in a Country Churchyard." The hero's epic labors to write down the names of each of the fourteen thousand dead in a record available to the cemetery's visitors captures perhaps better than any other work of postwar fiction the emotions powerfully flowing behind the newly instituted Decoration and Memorial Day traditions.[12]

"Rodman the Keeper" also contains the perfect description of the revised ideal of black education that much white New South literature and public policy would promote in the 1880s. One of Woolson's characters is "an old black freedman allowing himself to be taught the alphabet in order to gain permission to wait on his master,—master no longer in law,—with all the devotion of his loving old heart." Why did receiving such permission to be a servant require literacy? Doesn't this suggest that for Woolson ex-slaves being paid wages poisoned their personal relations with their betters, ones that Woolson thought should be defined by emotional, not monetary, ties? But the freedman's good heart is shown by the fact that he knows what the proper aim of black education should be: it is to create a literate servant. Admittedly, Woolson's hero Rodman in certain ways is an unreconstructed Reconstructionist. He lectures a white woman who plans to teach that "education will be the savior. Had I fifty millions to spend on the South to-morrow, every cent should go to schools, and for schools alone." But the tale's one portrait of an actual black student suggests a much narrower ambition. Woolson's little parable convincingly shows how the dependency model that was very much a part of Reconstruction could be appropriated and rescripted in the 1870s to become part of the anti-Reconstruction movement, supporting the emergent new forms of white supremacy.

"King David" (1878) is also thoroughly revisionist. A northerner filled with the idealism of early Reconstruction, David King heads to the small black southern hamlet of Jubilee Town to open a school. Most such northern teachers were female, not male. Woolson may have made her teacher male because it gave more authority to his optimism about blacks' learning abilities, and it also gave his concluding disillusionment more sting. The story's message is usually paraphrased to mean that, with blacks, "a little learning is a dangerous thing" (Hubbell 737, quoting the poet Alexander Pope). Certainly the schoolteacher's black charges are more influenced by liquor and incendiary carpetbagger pamphlets than they are by any schoolhouse lesson book. King's ignorant pupils comically invert their teacher's name to "Mars [Master] King David," thereby allowing Woolson to suggest that Reconstruction's dream that blacks might be America's Israelites destined for greatness in a new Canaan of freedom was nothing but a dangerous delusion. Much of the prose features racist portraits of black troublemakers (including black Union soldiers inciting local blacks to drink), plus a narrative voice that urges us to condescend toward King's idealism even as King is made somewhat sympathetic. She puts her sharpest criticism of Reconstruction into the mouth of a southern cynic: "You have brought the whole trouble down upon our heads by your confounded insurrectionary school!" Woolson's suggestion that black schools were basically sites of sedition, not proper education, had many precedents in anti-Reconstruction actions dating to the very beginnings of the postwar period. It also grimly foreshadowed even more extremely negative portraits of black schools as threats in the work of later fiction writers as diverse as Thomas Nelson Page, Thomas Dixon, Joel Chandler Harris, and George Washington Cable.

Older black pupils are portrayed in "King David" in sentimental rather than threatening ways, taking their lessons with utmost seriousness. The narrator is also very serious, and at moments seems even to express the high idealism about blacks' potential expressed by the most radical of Republicans: "sometimes a fine old black face was lifted from the slow-moving bulk, and from under wrinkled eyelids keen sharp eyes met the master's, as intelligent as his own." King's lessons, however, precisely capture the ideological vision of black education-as-imitation that drove most white elites and governed the textbooks compiled for use in Freedmen's Bureau–sponsored black schools. "Our first duty is to educate them," King meditates: "So he began at 'a, b, and c;' 'you must not steal;' 'you must not fight;' 'you must wash your faces.'" Commenting on this program, the narrator shifts to the first person for emphasis: King's disciplinary regime "may be called, I think, the first working-out of the emancipation problem." At such moments, Woolson's vision is very close to Child's, and to the many other projects (such as the Freedmen's instruction book) that taught blacks to copy the proper forms of indebtedness to whites. Otherwise, black freedom was a "problem."

By the story's end, not surprisingly, Woolson's story becomes less subtle and ambivalent in its messages; it makes it clear to her faithful readers that Reconstruction Negro schools were disasters. Blacks are likened to children or dogs whose proper sense of obligation can only be fashioned under the firm discipline of a white master they know and respect—a southern aristocrat, not an impoverished northern do-gooder. Eventually despairing of his mission, David King observes that a "planter spoke to the servant in his kindly way as he passed, and the old black face lighted with pleasure ... [;] none of his pupils looked at him with anything like that affection." King never ceases to feel that his teaching skills are the problem, not his students or the social system in which he has to teach. But King's creator emphatically suggests otherwise. The primary cultural work of Woolson's story was to reassure the guilty conscience of her readers that the best of Reconstruction educational ideals have not been renounced, but with the return of white rule in the New South were going to be realized in more valid, practical ways.

Woolson believed she qualified as an expert on blacks and the South because she wintered there for five years with her invalid mother. When she published her first southern story in 1877, the year the federal government renounced Reconstruction, Woolson set out to use a representative figure like "King David" to school the country on why Reconstruction dreams of education had been fated to fail. She also gave the nation a formula for underwriting the changes that were already underway in the South. With its emphasis on the plantation master as the best teacher for blacks, not a northerner like King, Woolson's little parable marks the turn away from Reconstruction methods for instilling p's, q's, and servitude to those primarily defined by blacks' southern masters. Woolson's title, "King David," indicates the black students' reversal of the protagonist's name, a sign of their affection for him but also of their obdurate ignorance. We may also understand Woolson's title in another way, as signifying the reversal and reinscription of the meaning of Reconstruction itself, as if Reconstruction ideals themselves suffered from a kind of moral dyslexia that could be belatedly reversed and corrected only by the rise of white rule in the New South.

Against such revisionism and the physical acts of violence that accompanied it, many intellectuals and activists who believed in black education labored long and hard. Indeed, their fight only intensified in the decades after the official federal renunciation of Reconstruction in 1877. Four fiction writers should be central to any list of figures who fought against the destruction of Reconstruction's best ideals: Albion Tourgée, Frances E. W. Harper, Sutton Griggs, and George Marion McClellan. For all of them, their most urgent task was rethinking the meaning of education itself, so that learning would not create dependency but intellectual freedom and responsibility, new ways of envisioning the nation's future and its past.

# Chapter Two

# A Fool's Education

ALBION TOURGÉE'S *A FOOL'S ERRAND, THE INVISIBLE EMPIRE,* AND *BRICKS WITHOUT STRAW* (1879–1880)

The pro-Reconstruction novelist who made the greatest impact in the postwar United States was undoubtedly Albion Tourgée, but he found loyal readers only after the battle for strong black schools available to all in the South had largely been lost. Tourgée's account of idealistic Reconstruction agents, *A Fool's Errand* (1879), and his exposé of the terrorist campaigns of the Ku Klux Klan, *The Invisible Empire* (1880), were best-sellers throughout the 1880s, even while the country as a whole had renounced Reconstruction and resigned itself to believing that white southerners, many of them ex-Confederates, knew best about what direction the region should take. Perhaps it was Tourgée's recalcitrant righteousness that most appealed to his readers. Although some surely read his books in order to denounce him as a traitor to his race, many others were drawn to Tourgée because they shared his sense of outrage at the ways in which Reconstruction's limited ideals had been abandoned. Tourgée's mix of idealism and despair struck a strong chord with many; the rhetoric in his novels allowed them to hear their hopes for equality, education, and democracy eloquently reaffirmed, even as his plots increasingly demonstrated that fighting for such ideals in the United States of the 1880s was a fool's errand and could only end in failure. That Tourgée's early works could become best-sellers suggests that the nation was guilty and ambivalent about the betrayal of Reconstruction, even as it moved to make that renunciation inevitable.

There is a second intriguing aspect to the sad story of Tourgée, whose now-unread fictions represent one of the sorriest monuments to fruitless labor in all of U.S. literature. Tourgée's early ideals of black education were very much informed by the paternalist prejudices of Reconstruction education models, which primarily sought to instruct blacks how to imitate the skills deemed appropriate for them by their white superiors. But within the space of one year between the publication of *A Fool's Errand* and *Bricks without Straw*, Tourgée rethought both how his fiction represented blacks and how it defined the aims and methods of black education. His portraits of black leaders shift significantly, from stressing dependency to stressing agency, the right of blacks to define their own destiny. True, Tourgée's change in attitude is imperfectly realized. But it is nonetheless remarkable—and it portends important developments to come. The significance of Tourgée's change in how he signified black freedom has largely been ignored by literary historians, but the main goal of this chapter will be to bring that shift into focus and consider what it means.

## 1

An Ohio native who fought and was wounded in several different Civil War campaigns and spent four months in Confederate prison, Tourgée after the war became a judge in the Superior Court of Reconstruction-era North Carolina. From his very first involvement in the war, Tourgée understood the conflict to be about universal civil rights and racial equality. At first, he saw Reconstruction as the fulfillment of the essential aims of the war. After the nation's retreat on Reconstruction in 1877, Tourgée returned to the North and carried on his campaign for black equality using other means, first fiction based on his North Carolina experiences and then more fiction and tract after tract of nonfiction prose increasingly written in anger and despair about the direction his country was taking.

Between 1879 and 1883 Tourgée published a six-novel set of historical fiction covering the South from the 1840s through the 1870s. More ambitious than any sequence of historical novels published since James Fenimore Cooper and William Gilmore Simms, Tourgée's sextet attempted to diagnose both the causes of the war and a cure for the blight slavery's legacy had cast on whites as well as blacks. For a new Republican president who was a personal friend, James Garfield, he published *An Appeal to Caesar* (1884), which built on arguments made in *Fool's Errand* and *Bricks without Straw* to claim that Reconstruction had failed because the federal government had not forced all southern states to maintain the public school systems for whites and blacks originally mandated in many revised state constitutions of the period. In historian David Blight's words, *An Appeal* "laid out an elaborate critique of national forgetting about the war, as well as a vigorous call for the enforcement of black civil and political rights." Just a few years later, in "The South as a Field for Fiction," Tourgée responded to the spate of New South material in national magazines by lamenting that "our literature has become not only Southern in type, but distinctly Confederate in sympathy" (quoted in Blight 219–220). Tourgée continued his fool's errand against post-Reconstruction ideology for the rest of his life. He tried his hand at medieval romance fiction and then published a novel called *Eighty Nine, or The Grand-Master's Story*, juxtaposing the devious workings of monopoly capitalism with those of the Ku Klux Klan

(1888). Tourgée's most notable action in the 1890s has become famous: he was the lawyer who argued the case for Homer Plessy before the U.S. Supreme Court in 1896. Given Tourgée's impeccable earlier record as the supporter of lost causes, we should hardly be surprised that Tourgée's plantiff lost his suit. But some of Tourgée's arguments for Plessy's rights influenced Justice Harlan's famous dissent—and, through that dissent, all of later U.S. civil rights jurisprudence. In one of his last novels, *Pactolus Prime* (1890), Tourgée gave voice to his anger and alienation by inventing a black narrator whose interior monologues satirize the hypocrisy of the ruling elite, while outwardly he performs classic "darky" routines and shines their shoes. Strange to say, Pactolus also has extraordinarily changeable skin color; it varies from light to extra dark as his fortunes and opinions change. Such a motif is perhaps an appropriate invention for his creator, who as a lawyer in *Plessy* argued that restricting his client's ability to pass as white was an infringement of his property rights. But Tourgée's plot device also makes one wonder how Tourgée conceived of his own "racial" identity. Another late novel is wryly entitled *The Man Who Outlived Himself*, implying that Tourgée both understood his best years were past and yet hoped his work might somehow regain public influence.

Tourgée's was an extraordinary life, filled with the "intransigent idealism" (Edmund Wilson's fine phrase) that inspires jeremiads. Increasingly, though, the hope that stoked Tourgée's narratives darkened to despair; he came to believe that neither government action, education reforms, nor even religion could ever end white racism. His idealism proved fragile after all. The author of the fullest critical study, Theodore Gross, has rightly argued that *Fool's Errand* and *Bricks without Straw* are Tourgée's most important novels, though they share many of James Fenimore Cooper's literary faults: "his use of stereotypes rather than genuine characters, his lack of humor, his unreal dialogue" (122). Earlier, in 1892, Anna Julia Cooper, also an admirer, more wittily made a similar point: "all his offspring [characters] are little Tourgees—they preach his sermons and pray his prayers" (189).

Tourgée is most intriguing today for his ideological content, particularly his various disquisitions on how and why the federal government should have been more ambitious and forceful during Reconstruction. Tourgée's best creation in literary terms may be his occasionally satiric narrative voice, a persona that he called "the Fool," a figure attuned to scathing irony stoked by the contrast between intentions and results. In his novels' third-person narratives, though, Tourgée the novelist was never able to reconcile the Fool's voice with that of the prosecutor's or the lecturer's—perhaps he could not hear the difference. (The Fool no longer believes people can change; but Tourgée the lecturer-lawyer stridently does.) While hardly as supple, humorous, or trenchant as Twain, Tourgée's Fool is not unworthy of being associated with him. Tourgée, too, shared with Twain an increasingly caustic opinion of the damned human race, especially its American representatives, and he also had Twain's tendency to alleviate rising despair by turning to sentimental plot twists and characters whose virtues were perpetually imperturbable. Tourgée's Fool should certainly give him permanent entrée to any canon of U.S. satiric writers.

2

Long ago Theodore Gross intimated that in several key ways Tourgée's *Bricks without Straw* represented a clear advance over *Fool's Errand*, in part because in the sequel to his best-seller Tourgée developed black characters' points of view more thoroughly. Literary criticism has not rushed to explore Gross's insight. Virtually nothing of substance has been published on *Bricks without Straw*. In many ways Tourgée's two best novels embody all of the assumptions, the ideals mixed with arrogance, that motivated Reconstruction. They take for granted the virtue and intelligence of the northerners who came to the benighted South to reform it, and they assume that slavery only partially civilized the Negroes, so that emancipation left them helplessly in need of instruction. As Tourgée developed his black characters in these novels, especially *Bricks*, however, distinctly different stories and understandings of the meanings of black schools and black activism in the postwar South began to emerge.[1]

Written in the summer of 1879, Tourgée's *A Fool's Errand* portrays both newly built official schools and the more informal "Sabbath schools" constructed in black communities in North Carolina. He tells his story through the point of view of the northern reformers Metta and Comfort Servosse, the novel's primary protagonists. Servosse openly advocates building a statewide system of public schools (141), and his daughter Metta was one of thousands of northern white women employed by church missionary associations and other groups to teach the new black schoolchildren. Metta describes the South as if it were a non-Western country, Turkey or Lebanon. She relates with great indignation the slights and insults she suffers at the hands of supposedly respectable whites, including public insults printed in the local paper (42). Tourgée very much intended Metta's experiences to be representative, though her circumstances were remarkably better economically than that of the majority of teachers, black or white, who ventured South.[2] When the Servosses attend a prayer service and political meeting at the new school, Metta presents the black leaders' faulty English for her readers' amusement: "Robert . . . seemed very anxious to display the fact that he could read, and, with comical pride, blundered through 'de free hunner'n firty-fird hymn.'" Yet Metta also admits that several of the points in Robert's sermon are "ludicrously apt" and wise (87), and she contrasts her generous reception at this church with her exclusion from the town's white churches.

Later in the novel Comfort Servosse attends a colored Union League meeting in the schoolhouse/church. The narrator's main focus is not on the blacks but

58

on the opinions of two of the whites in the audience, Servosse and a southern Union sympathizer named Walters. In their opinion, such meetings, despite their limitations, teach the former slaves the rudiments of patriotism and democracy. Ironically, however, the narrator's language in the scene functions in a thoroughly undemocratic way. "If Servosse could have seen what an affront such a meeting was to his neighbors," the narrator intervenes omnisciently, he would have been much less optimistic about the repercussions of Union League activities in the community (111). Tourgée thus creates a distinct hierarchy of points of view, with the omniscient narrator's understanding at the top, Servosse's limited understanding in the middle, and the blacks' respectable but thoroughly rudimentary views in the background, or on the bottom. The narrator's phrase "to his neighbors" (referring solely to the town's whites) excludes blacks from participating in the roles of Servosse's fellow citizens and neighbors, even though Servosse's conversation at the meeting suggests he is attempting to recognize them in these ways. Overall, in *A Fool's Errand* blacks lack initiative or any understanding of means and ends. The only way to educate them is by having them imitate their betters. But their copies will always be marred. They remain "Citizens in Embryo" (the title of chapter 19) whose development must perpetually be managed by far-seeing whites.

In the midst of a trenchant analysis of the personality types of the northerners who were agents of Reconstruction—"martyrs," "self-seekers," and "fools who hoped that in some inscrutable way the laws of human nature would be suspended"—the narrator also implies it was foolhardy to give Negroes the vote: "it seems impossible that the wise men of that day should have been so blind as not to have seen that they were doing the utmost possible injury to the colored race, the country, and themselves, by propounding a plan of re-organization [i.e., Reconstruction] which depended for its success upon the . . . administration of state governments by this class, in connection with the few of the dominant race." (118). Contorted with double negatives and obscurantist diction, this typical sentence of Tourgée's nonetheless reveals that, while critical of northern whites, the text also contravenes itself and validates a common anti-Reconstruction argument of the 1870s: allowing blacks to gain unchecked access to political power retarded, not advanced, democracy and postwar recovery. In many ways, then, *A Fool's Errand* shares much the same ambivalence about black education as Constance Fenimore Woolson did, or the anonymous author of the 1874 *Harper's* article, "On Negro Schools," discussed in chapter 1. Indeed, Tourgée's rather scathing title for his first novel could have been used for Woolson's story about an idealistic teacher's futile efforts.

In several crucial ways *Bricks without Straw*, published just a year later, must be read as a critique of *Fool's Errand*; it is a superior and more daring novel. More scenes are presented to us dramatically, through action and dialogue, rather than summarized by the narrator. Plus, the characters themselves—particularly Tourgée's four heroes—Mollie Ainsley, the northern schoolteacher; Hesden Le Moyne, the southern gentleman who comes to love her; and Eliab Hill and Nimbus Ware, leaders of the black community—are better drawn than anyone in *Fool's Errand* except Comfort Servosse. Tourgée's crucial improvement was that he attempted to rethink the role black leaders and their community would play in his narrative. Eliab and Nimbus are primary, not secondary, characters, with much dialogue and key dramatic scenes; they are the most complex and compelling black characters yet created by a white author, with the possible exception of Herman Melville's Babo in "Benito Cereno" (1856) or the long-suffering twin heroines of Lydia Maria Child's *Romance of the Republic*.[3] Although *Bricks without Straw* retains many of the elements that make *A Fool's Errand* problematic, Tourgée's portraits of Eliab the scholar and intellectual and Nimbus the entrepreneur and man of action—each with his own distinctive speech and worldview—opened new possibilities for U.S. fiction. They allow us to imagine Tourgée, though white, as a missing link between mid-century black writers such as William Wells Brown and Martin Delany and later turn-of-the-century novelists of black resistance such as Frances Harper, Sutton Griggs, Charles Chesnutt, and Pauline Hopkins.

Throughout *Bricks without Straw*, the theme of education is central—black education, yes, but also the education of whites that must be done if the nation is to change its attitude about the possibilities of multiracial democracy. When Tourgée's narrative in *Bricks without Straw* represents black community meetings, black voices are prominent and diverse. Updated spirituals chronicling poll taxes and sharecropping as new forms of oppression educate and entertain: "'Den jes fork up de little tax / Dat's laid upon de poll. / It's jes de tax de state exac's / Fer habben ob a soul!'" (207). Nimbus discusses how to respond to tobacco planters' threats to fire workers who attend political meetings, and answers skeptics by saying the community as a whole—including landowners like him—has the obligation to support the farm workers' collective resistance: "'Ef a man turns off ary single one fer comin' ter dis meetin' evr'y han' dat is ter wuk for him oughter leave him to once an' nary colored man ought ter do a stroke ob wuk for him till he takes 'em back" (198). Like his name, Nimbus Ware's actions suggest that the black community's anger is building like a gathering storm cloud.

Eliab Hill's oratory, in contrast, marks him as one of the educated elite; he appropriates biblical tropes, American Revolutionary allusions, and free labor rhetoric to argue for moderation as well as black solidarity: "The colored people must stand or fall together. . . . It will not do to weakly yield or rashly fight. . . . Remember that while others have given us freedom we must work and struggle and wait for liberty—that liberty which gives as well as receives, self-supporting, self-protecting, holding the present and looking to the future with confidence" (202). Tourgée's narrative voice, it is true, still mediates and condescends, suggesting that Hill was not really understood and noting that, "in accordance with a time-honored custom in that region" (203), the meeting ends with boasting fueled by liquor.

Ware's and Hill's meeting organizing black unity in *Bricks* was held on community schoolhouse grounds (188). The novel's principal heroine, the white northerner Mollie Ainsley, is its teacher, her salary paid by the black community "after Northern benevolence began to restrict its gifts" (187). Tourgée well knew from personal experience and from the testimony he gathered from blacks that their schoolhouses were contested ground. Tourgée's descriptions of white mobs burning and looting black communities in *The Invisible Empire* and *Bricks without Straw* are the fullest accounts in U.S. prose before Ida B. Wells and Charles Chesnutt critiquing terrorism in the service of white supremacy. When the blacks' school is torched soon after the political meeting described above, Tourgée sought to burn into his readers' minds the connection between the Ku Klux Klan's symbols (such as the sheeted costumes and fiery crosses) and the group's documented crimes of arson and murder: "One had hardly time to think, before the massive structure of dried pitch-pine which northern charity had erected in the foolish hope of benefiting the freemen, where the young teachers had labored with such devotion, and where so many of the despised race had laid the foundation of a knowledge that they vainly hoped might lift them up into the perfect light of freedom, was a solid spire of sheeted flame" (*Bricks* 279). Tourgée's text marks its indebtedness to the ex-slave narrative by using footnotes in precisely the same way as did Frederick Douglass or William Wells Brown, authenticating the factual nature of events that may seem fantastical to some readers (289n). Tourgée's rendering also allies this attack on a black settlement to conventions of "captivity" and "frontier" narratives that were very popular throughout the nineteenth century. The town's buildings, especially its schoolhouse, come to represent all the virtues of civilization, contrasted with horrific forms of savagery that emerge from the woods. But here the savages opposing civilization are not war-painted Indians but whites wearing hoods.[4]

However effective, Tourgée's fondness for romantic conventions securely contrasting good and evil—which he inherited from earlier abolitionist and pro-Reconstructionist authors—contained serious problems. Early in *Bricks without Straw*, the blacks seek to have their school also be their polling place. But teacher Mollie Ainsley is wary; she feels such an arrangement linking public education and voting rights will be unnecessarily provocative. There follows an extraordinary scene in which Mollie defends her assessment to blacks who want to celebrate their newfound rights regardless of the consequences. Accurate as a picture of the enthusiasm with which voting rights were greeted by black communities throughout the South,[5] and effective in the way it links the blacks' parade to the "drum and fife" marching associated with Revolutionary patriots (150), the scene quickly threatens to escalate into racial warfare. Most unfortunately, Tourgée opts to resolve the tensions of his scene in a very retrogressive way. His white schoolteacher heroine grabs a sword and, bestride a horse, becomes a kind of Joan of Arc for the Freedmen's Bureau, restoring order and acquiescence.

Preposterously, she receives acclaim from all, black huzzas mixing with white rebel yells (160). In the process of elevating his heroine to her finest moment, Tourgée makes the blacks seem quite witless.[6] Such a narrative "resolution" is representative of a troubling pattern throughout the novel, whereby Tourgée solves his narrative's (and his country's) conflicts by restoring well-meaning whites to the center of the action during moments of crisis. Reconstruction revisionism thus was not just the province of whites explicitly in the anti-Reconstruction, pro–New South camp. In *Bricks without Straw*, Tourgée repeatedly demonstrated that black leaders and communities were primary forces for progressive change during Reconstruction, then retreated into a belief that stable progress could only be managed by white elites.

"What Shall the End Be?" asks the title of the penultimate chapter in *Bricks without Straw*, as if acknowledging that the miraculous resolutions of romance will no longer be adequate. Several of the novel's black characters, including Ware, have just given horrific concluding testimony of harassment, terrorist violence, voting fraud, jail, and exile occurring in the 1870s (482ff). Blacks who attempt to sell the products of their own land are blocked from doing so; others are jailed and have the right to their labor bought under the convict lease system. A pitched gunfight by a county courthouse is fought between blacks and whites intent on overthrowing the remnants of Reconstruction government (484). The anarchic white resistance of the early Reconstruction years has by the end of *Bricks* become systematic. These tales of oppression are told to a white audience that responds with indignation and sympathy—a pattern that Tourgée clearly hopes will be a national reaction to the education his novels provide. The last glimpse of blacks we get in *Bricks* is of homeless exiles in Kansas, Tourgée's prophetic vision in 1880 of the coming Great Migration from the Jim Crow South by those blacks whose hopes have "passed an' gone" (486). Nimbus may be "united with his family and settled for a new and more hopeful start in life" in Kansas under the protection of white benefactors (487). But if Tourgée intended this Reconstruction redux to be hopeful, it reads in just the opposite way, as a mournful afterthought.

The white southern nonconformist Le Moyne has been affected by the rise of white "redeemers" too, driven from power and branded an "enemy of the South" (475). He concludes *Bricks without Straw* with a long disquisition on how Reconstruction failed because it believed ending slavery would change the South, whereas what was needed was a complete reconstruction of its entire "social system," from politics and economics to culture and race relations, using the collective power of the federal government. Coming after black testimony of oppression, and corroborated by it, Le Moyne's concluding peroration is Tourgée's refutation of whites' New South bromides of progress, reform, and reunification that had begun appearing in national magazines. Le Moyne stresses recalcitrant southern difference from the North and argues that little has changed between the vices of the

Old South and the practices now promoted as "New." Unlike the North, which at least acknowledges the ideals of equality, opportunity, and local township democracy even if it does not always live up to them, Le Moyne argues that the South, Old or New, is built on inequality and the control by a privileged few of political power and economic and educational opportunities. One-quarter of the white voters in the former slave states are illiterate, making them much more susceptible to fraud and threat and demagoguery (514). And democracy in the New South is a farce. Local officials are mostly appointed by the state Democratic Party, not locally elected, unlike the township democracies in the North, which act as the "shield and nursery of individual freedom of thought and action," and also provide a fount of economic initiative creating prosperity (506–508). The only solution is education and opportunity for all, but, given southern reluctance to fund a comprehensive system of public schools that would separately serve whites and blacks, the only solution to the education problem is to institute a program much more comprehensive than Reconstruction—the "National supervision of State schools" (518). Le Moyne even believes that if the nation will have a rational, informed debate about what is happening in the New South, it will eventually be able to find the right solution. "Don't try to compel the Nation to accept your view or mine; but spur the national thought by every possible means to consider the evil, to demand its cure, and to devise a remedy" (521). Tourgée tried to stage such a debate in *Bricks without Straw*. White voices (especially Le Moyne's) are given the most prominence, but black voices and testimony participate eloquently. But the most influential "discussion" about the South's future was held in the national magazines, not Tourgée's fiction, and when black voices were heard in those forums, they were mostly the voices of minstrelsy, not voices like Tourgée's Nimbus Ware or Eliab Hill.

A graphic of a schoolhouse spelling book with the words *In Hoc Signo Vinces* ("In This Sign You Conquer") appears rather than the words "The End" on the final page of *Bricks without Straw*. But this attempt by Tourgée to imagine a victorious resolution—by reason, now, instead of a sword—is counteracted by the Fool's sardonic, despairing laughter. Tourgée acknowledged that by 1880 white New South writers, not his fictional heroes, controlled the nation's thinking. Tourgée's early novels expressed not just the progress of their main protagonists, but his goals for the education of the nation, via instructors as diverse as Servosse, Ware, and Le Moyne. His books' ambitious plans for the reconstruction of the postwar republic prove a fool's errand, buildings made using bricks without straw. Yet Tourgée ends each text with a stubborn note of hope. His quixotic campaigns make Tourgée a worthy predecessor not only to important black novelists and social reformists who would emerge in the 1890s and after, such as Frances Harper, Sutton Griggs, and W. E. B. Du Bois, but also to the next generation of white novelists who used fiction to confront New South and U.S. self-delusion—including George Washington Cable, Ellen Glasgow, and Walter Hines Page.

# Chapter Three

# Of the People, by the People, and for the People

## FRANCES E. W. HARPER'S CULTURAL WORK IN
## *IOLA LEROY* (1892)

The subject of Frances E. W. Harper's novel, *Iola Leroy, or Shadows Uplifted* (1892), is nothing less than the duty of black leadership and education in the postwar U.S. South to *make* something of the freedom gained with so much pain and struggle. Harper was about as well qualified to discourse on this topic as any writer could be. Thanks to the detective work of Frances Smith Foster, Paula Giddings, Carla L. Peterson, and others, we now know much more about Harper's travels throughout black communities in the South and the rest of the United States after the Civil War, lecturing on education, culture, the family, and other themes of keen interest to black communities struggling to remake themselves in the aftermath of the war and the fall of Reconstruction.[1]

Many of Harper's lectures, poems, and historical studies have been recovered and reprinted, as well as her only novel. Early in this process of recovering Harper's legacy, *Iola Leroy* was usually discussed in terms of its revision of the tragic mulatta motif in William Wells Brown's antebellum novel *Clotel*. In the 1990s, a dominant topic in Harper criticism became a debate about her strategy of countering negative stereotypes of black women with a light-skinned heroine who embodies to perfection proper middle-class ideals of a woman's self-discipline and responsibilities. In the twenty-first century, Harper criticism has shifted ground somewhat, while continuing to be divided in its assessment of the novel's vision of education and citizenship. Russ Castronovo, for instance, has argued that the book's concluding focus on elite characters as role models "legitimizes citizenship as the architect of inequality" and "bars the 'folk' from sharing equal social resources" (243). Elizabeth McHenry's *Forgotten Readers: Recovering the Lost History of African American Literary Societies*, in contrast, defends Harper's methods as part of a long history of the black middle class working not to secure its own status but to uplift all the race, stressing blacks' responsibilities to overcome divisions of class, color, and, especially, education—all in the face of both vigilante violence and economic and political systems that made black advancement during the Jim Crow era as difficult as possible. Elizabeth Ammons, in turn, in *Conflicting Stories* stressed the contrapuntal structure of *Iola Leroy*, the ways in which it continually juxtaposes different black voices in dialogue and scenes involving educated and illiterate or barely literate blacks. The effect, she convincingly claims, does not separate these characters into different communities but rather shows how they must find a way to progress by working together.

I will argue here that both the novel's most famous classroom scene, the *conversazione*, and the heterogeneous shape of the overall narrative itself enact a profoundly expansive and transformative, not merely exclusivist, educational ideal. In short, the novel's educational method has sometimes been mistaken for being the dependency model, but it is really a classic example of the liberal arts model in action. Recent critical debate over Harper's (and her protagonists') alleged elitism denies the author's understanding of the cultural work that fiction should perform for communities under siege. In Harper's view, novels should honestly depict the struggles all are going through, then demonstrate the ideal traits of character around which *diverse* black communities can restructure themselves. While developing an uplift narrative whose telos is middle-class ideals, *Iola Leroy* demonstrates that progress must be understood as inseparable from a long history of struggle by characters who were never privileged. Indeed, the title character's true education begins when she is plunged out of her world of racial and class privilege and must overcome her prejudice against the black masses as she endures a phase of radical homelessness and identity crisis.

## 1

Harper's contrapuntal technique is especially pronounced in the scenes in *Iola Leroy* that take place after the Civil War. Two of the novel's major characters, Iola and her brother Harry, end up teaching in newly created black schools in the South, and throughout the novel there are discussions of the indispensable role a new educational system for blacks must play to prepare blacks to resist the depredations of Jim Crow and build protective communities. Harper took pains to demonstrate the ways in which interest in education both before and after the war was not centered solely in the small elite class but was widespread throughout all classes and education levels in black communities. She stressed that valuing education was rooted in cultural memory—the many ways in which blacks taught themselves to read and write when it was illegal during slavery, including stealing copy books and having secret meetings that often mixed religious services, hymn-singing, community organizing, and educational instruction. Understated though it is compared to Tourgée or Griggs, Harper's key portrait of the early postwar black schools in action is all the more effective for its dignified plainness and its play with the novel's title trope of shadows uplifted: "Iola had found a schoolroom in the basement of a colored church, where the doors were willingly opened to her. Her pupils came from miles around, ready and anxious to get some 'book larnin'. Some of the old folks were eager to learn, and it was touching to see the eyes which had grown dim under the shadows of slavery, donning spectacles and trying to make out the words" (146). Harper mentions white schoolteachers who came south to teach, but she gives pride of place to newly trained black schoolteachers like Iola Leroy. She never suggests, as Tourgée and the northern missionary societies sometimes did, that school building and teaching were primarily initiated by whites. Indeed, *Iola Leroy* contains a deliciously satiric vignette in which a "gentleman" visits Iola's school and asserts his right to address the children. His topic is the necessity for black self-improvement modeled on "the achievements of the white race." The lecturer is "nonplussed," however, when Iola's charges respond to his speech by mentioning the roles played by money, power, and black labor in *whites'* cultural history (146–147). Such are the dangers of a liberal arts curriculum!

In emphasizing black initiative with schools in her novel, Harper does downplay somewhat the need to train more black teachers and the lack of teaching materials in many of the new schools. Both topics are more thoroughly covered in Tourgée's fiction than in Harper's. But such issues were central to Harper's lecture tours and writings—as was the question of how to define the *goals* of black education, not just its materials and methods. As Carla Peterson has shown, the gradual emergence of postwar black leadership was repeatedly linked to the goal of gaining more black teachers.

On the fears and resentments such schools caused among whites, Harper condensed into a few telling sentences pages and pages of Tourgée: "Very soon Iola realized that while she was heartily appreciated by the freedmen, she was an object of suspicion and dislike to their former owners. The North had conquered by the supremacy of the sword, and the South had bowed to the inevitable. But here was a new army that had come with an invasion of ideas, that had come to supplant ignorance with knowledge, and it was natural that its members should be unwelcome to those who had made it a crime to teach their slaves to read the name of the ever blessed Christ. But Iola had found her work, and the freedmen their friend" (146). When Iola's school is burned down just one page after it is described, Harper shows no interest in turning the attack on the school into a melodramatic set-piece filled with action. She summarizes this crime with brutal briefness and focuses instead on how Iola's schoolchildren respond: as their heart-broken teacher gazes at the smoking ruins of the school, the children try to comfort her by singing spirituals (147).

2

Any discussion of the important ways in which Harper gives a new meaning to education, however, must confront the novel's many forays into high Victorian sententiousness, which contrast rather awkwardly with the narration's "plain style" passages, well shown in the representative excerpt above. Ornate expostulations that were taken to be intellectually elevating by nineteenth-century readers are difficult for many of today's readers of *Iola Leroy* to swallow, no matter how earnestly a syllabus places the work in its historical context. Pious optimism expressed in Latinate abstractions; a belief in a firm line between savagery and civilization; fears that blacks will descend to criminality except for the institutions like the church, school, and marriage; a lecture on how "law ... is the pivot on which the whole universe turns; and obedience to law is the gauge by which a nation's strength or weakness is tried" (249–250)—all of this owes something to Ralph Waldo Emerson, Matthew Arnold, and other Victorian experts on cultural uplift, such as church elders.

Harper's difficulty for some contemporary readers may stem from her determination to wed elements of the novel of education, the ex-slave narrative, and Reconstruction conduct guidebooks. That is, she wanted to write neither a comedy nor a tragedy but a "good, strong book" (262) that would provide for her readers models of virtuous behavior and community-building against all odds (262, 282). Harper felt her book's high responsibilities required that virtue be rewarded and sin punished. Successful black education must be the triumphant antidote to the "duncery of slavery" (145); the "auction block and the slave pen" (282) should be replaced by the *writing* pen and economic empowerment. Such an agenda driving the plot means that virtue must eventually triumph, even in the most outlandish of circumstances. After lengthy bouts of self-denial to prove their respectability, for instance, Harper's heroine and hero fall in love because they share high ideals, not to mention lofty rhetoric; they end the novel living in Jim Crow North Carolina as if it were a cottage home in Eden with morning glories 'round the porch (275). A black Union veteran is able to buy a plantation in the same state and divide it into small homesteads for virtuous black farmers (280)—even while millions of black farmers throughout the South were being driven by whites into share-cropping and enslavement to debt. Even the contradictions of U.S. expansion abroad are absolved with a rhetorical sleight of hand. One speech condemns rising imperial "arrogance, aggressiveness" (260) in the land, but the narrator's conclusion envisions that the solution to "our unsolved American problem" (racism) will be found in greater contact with other lands via trade and colonialism ("glowing with the fervor of the tropics and enriched by the luxuriance of the Orient" [282]).

Despite Harper's taste for rosy resolutions, her novel overall reveals her understanding that a true novel of education subverts too-easy solutions. One wonders whether the happy endings Harper conjured for her characters were greeted in some of the literary societies that discussed *Iola Leroy* with the same trenchant skepticism certain speakers in the "Friends in Council" chapter in *Iola Leroy* received when they spoke too broadly and sententiously (see 246–247 in particular). There are many scenes in the book that teach critical thinking, not self-assured idealism. Iola's entire life history, for one, is presented to the reader as a continual and often painful process of re-education about the certitudes she once believed. In her "fall" from a mistaken belief she is white, Iola must pass not just from the white community to the black, but also through a series of her own prejudiced misunderstandings of what it means to be black. She must learn to renounce class and color-complexion prejudice, not just ignorance. Iola's eventual husband, Dr. Latimer, rightly compares her journey to Odysseus', though given the book's pervasive Christian ethos we might also understand Iola's story as a revised *Pilgrim's Progress* set in a race-obsessed land of temptations and trials. But the novel's insistent focus on a journey toward a just community in this world, not the next, reveals its truest emphasis: not on the eternal verity of predetermined truths, but on unpredictable *process*. Education for the novel's readers as well as its protagonists leads forth into unknown territory, where all must adapt to a world that has no precedents.

Hence some of the most powerful scenes of instruction in *Iola Leroy* occur in everyday conversation, not in a middle-class parlor or a highly regulated school classroom. Such scenes include discussions in markets and kitchens, prayer meetings, a soldiers' camp, and many other sites. This is a crucial point, given the number of critics who have accused Harper of classism. For Harper, neither intelligence nor education is necessarily associated with wealth or security, or even with humble schoolhouses and respectable middle-class conduct, important as these may be for black uplift. And unlike Sutton Griggs or Albion Tourgée (or, as we shall see, any of the white writers who so caustically portray speakers using black schoolhouses to incite mobs), Harper does not emphasize the lecture mode when she portrays the work of education. Rather, she embodies something much closer to the Socratic ideal: education in *Iola Leroy* happens in *dialogue*, when multiple points of view can be expressed, tested, revised. Revealingly, such scenes are plentiful and usually are narrated using Harper's plain rather than ornate style: the characters' talk generally is as important and as full of educational intent as the narrator's interpretations.

Consider Harper's witty opening chapter in *Iola Leroy*, for example, set among black servants buying foodstuffs at a town market in North Carolina near the end of the Civil War. It builds on passages in Frederick Douglass, Harriet Jacobs, William Wells Brown, and other predecessors in demonstrating and deciphering for its readers coded black speech, where one thing is said and another understood. The narrator offers an authoritative analysis of "market-speech" about eggs and butter, using language that is as formal as any employed in the new academic discipline of ethnography: "the shrewder slaves, coming in contact with their masters and overhearing their conversations, invented a phraseology to convey in the most unsuspected manner news to each other from the battle-field." The narrator then translates this code: "if they wished to announce a victory of the Union army, they said the butter was fresh" (9). Soon we see such facility for double meanings in action back on the plantation, when the servants' ability to present one "face" and one language to their mistress is contrasted with other identities and other ways of speaking that emerge behind their mistress's back.

Significantly, Harper stressed this facility among blacks as a skill in reading, writing, and interpretation, even though these slaves are mostly illiterate. Harper intended from the very beginning of her novel to inspire her readers to question too-narrow definitions of literacy, imitation, and education, even while her book enthusiastically promoted the necessity of "book larnin'" for freed slaves. Discussing a Confederate loss in battle, one of the slaves comments, "'I can't read de newspapers, but ole Missus' face is newspaper nuff for me.'" She then discusses some of the lies and rumors she has been told with her fellow servants, and together the group tries to separate truth from falsehood (9–10). Another crucial detail: this second scene is set in a plantation kitchen, with the slaves talking in low voices even as they are setting out to do their work of the day. In such scenes, Harper shows that information was being passed and education occurring not solely in secret meetings away from the plantations in the woods, but at the plantation's very heart, in its most daily activities. Such an interpretation has since the 1960s become the accepted scholarly understanding of "the world the slaves made" in the midst of subjugation, but in the 1890s it was, to put it mildly, rather different from the published accounts in either the popular press or academia regarding how blacks functioned on plantations.[2]

Other scenes of instruction in Harper's novel are scenes of "reconstruction" in the deepest sense. I choose not to discuss here the obvious example, the moment when Iola Leroy discovers her "black" family ties and then decides to use her education to help ex-slaves. Just as revealing of the novel's revisionary strategies are scenes in which Harper's heroine is not the primary focus. After Robert Johnson joins the Union Army in chapter 6, for example, he has a conversation with a young white officer from Maine, Captain Sybil, who has been impressed with Johnson's bravery. "Why not quit this company [an all-colored unit, headed by Sybil], and take your place in the army just the same as a white man? I know your chances for promotion would be better." Johnson defends his decision not to pass (like Iola, he is light-skinned) as a matter of loyalty; the men in his unit "are excellent fighters, but they need a leader." The conversation shifts to the subject of the blacks' bravery, and Johnson explains that his men "seem glad to prove they are something and somebody." The senior officer then returns to the question of Johnson's "difference" in appearance: "you do not look like them, you do not talk like them. It is a burning shame to have held such a man as you in slavery" (43–44). Sybil's well-intentioned liberalism contains a questionable assumption, of course: that the racial category of "Negro" is negative and that any man who can escape it should do so, even though he earlier conceded black soldiers have many admirable qualities, including bravery under fire. Johnson's temperate reply explains that slavery is unjust for all whom it imprisons, regardless of their hue. He then tells Sybil a long story right out of the ex-slave narrative tradition to teach him how blackness can be a source of pride: Tom Anderson, "black as black can be," methodically taught himself to read by carrying book pages hidden in his hat, which, Johnson quips, amounts to "carrying his liberary on his head" (44), linking *library* and *liberation* via the pun. In short, as well as stressing black self-education and race pride, Harper's scene underlines the importance of whites being open to re-education. Sybil's willingness to ask questions and listen and learn is treated (in an understated way) as heroic, equal to anything he might achieve with a gun in his hand.

This scene from chapter 6 ends with a discussion of northern racism. The two soldiers contribute equally. Johnson learns of Sybil's Quaker background and how his religious principles have motivated him to fight. Both conclude the conversation expressing how valuable the encounter has been (43–49). Harper's narrative voice, often ever-present and authoritative, here plays a minimal role; she lets the conversation follow its own course and teach its own lesson. The men *enact* the virtues of democracy and union that the war is supposedly being fought to defend. The understated power of this scene increases when we soon discover that neither Captain Sybil nor Tom Anderson survive the war. Sybil's and Johnson's relative openness toward each other enacts for Harper the hopeful optimism about race relations that characterized the period between the recruitment of black Union troops and the early years of Reconstruction.

A later chapter set after the war, ironically entitled "Open Questions," focuses on a black and white encounter of a very different kind, filled with argument, misunderstanding, and recrimination masked by hypocritical politeness. For Harper this confrontation between the races enacted in an intimate scale the national betrayal of Reconstruction's possibilities by ever-resistant racism. "Open Questions" portrays most whites' closed minds. For Harper, it was not the ignorance of newly freed black schoolchildren that was the nation's primary challenge; it was that the country itself refused to be educated about the history and meaning of its own democracy. In *Iola Leroy*, Harper created a novel of ideas in the most ambitious sense, one that would model a *national* conversation that should be taking place but was not. For all the novel's idealism, though, it also confronts the clear inability of either conversation or education by themselves to cleanse the nation of ignorance or racism.[3]

3

The climactic educational conversation in *Iola Leroy*, of course, is the "*conversazione*" (243) near the book's conclusion. It was meant to function as a Socratic symposium on blacks' future in the United States. Like Harper's contemporaries Anna Julia Cooper and Alexander Crummell (and anticipating W. E. B. Du Bois), Harper asserted the crucial role to be played by the black elite, the so-called Talented Tenth, in the advancement of the race. Harper's version of such a convocation of the black elite is much more formal than other scenes I have discussed, as suits the setting, the well-appointed parlor of a middle-class home. The diction of both the narrator and the characters is mostly not plain style. About a dozen named figures from both southern and northern states, including several professors, a doctor, and a clergyman, read and discuss black uplift and world issues. Robert Johnson at one point explicitly links this gathering to the secret meetings held during slavery times, both to stress the connection and point with pride at the progress made (260).

Harper's conversazione scene in chapter 30 tends to make today's commentators exasperated, even those most sympathetic toward Harper's general goals and methods. During the meeting the membership listens with indefatigable enthusiasm to lectures on patriotism, African colonization, the education of mothers, the moral progress of the race, and a poem entitled "A Rallying Cry." Although conversation is vigorous, with much evidence of differing opinions, the characters tend to sound all too alike. They do not discuss so much as exchange lectures, each filled with high-minded apothegms: "When I look . . . at the ages which have been consumed in reaching our present altitude," begins one member, while another responds to that speech with, "Just now . . . we have the fearful grinding and friction which comes in the course of an adjustment of the new machinery of freedom in the old ruts of slavery" (255).[4] Ironically, nothing may be as culturally and historically bound as expressions of unbounded optimism.

I would encourage readers to focus on the conversazione's *form*, not just the admittedly dated contents of the points individual speakers make. Like many of the earlier conversations in the novel, this colloquium attempts to enact a profound experiment in living democracy—even though those who participate are a relatively exclusive group. The scene validates debate and discussion, not resolution. A speaker's authority is measured by the power of his or her arguments, not his or her social status. In response to the first paper read, for instance, *fourteen* opinions are expressed, many of them commenting on the previous points as well as on the paper itself (246–249). Harper's seminar is thus the polar opposite of the debate scenes in Griggs's *Imperium*, in which the stress is on the power of brilliant oratory to dominate all opinion. Though organized in the name of black liberation, the Imperium for blacks produced a siege mentality and mob behavior that Griggs shows inevitably ends in tragedy and in-fighting. Harper's scenes of instruction work differently.

Harper intended *Iola Leroy* to be a kind of spiritual training manual for new black leadership, but her anatomy of citizenship stressed the dangers of demagoguery as well as the need for a leadership that was humble and responsible. One particularly astute comment (by a "Professor Langhorne") suggests that civilizations that cannot tolerate their own diversity are bound to suffer God's judgment, no matter how "advanced" they are. Referring to the apogee of civilization in medieval Muslim Spain, the professor notes that Spain later "inaugurated a crusade of horror against a million of her best laborers and artisans," expelling Muslims as well as Jews and others during the Reconquista and the Inquisition. "Vainly she expected the blessing of God to crown her work of violence," he concludes (248–249). Harper's contemporary readers would have understood the relevance of this point for the United States in the 1890s, immersed in race and class warfare and on the verge of new imperial ventures. And no less so than Plato's symposium, Harper's may be exclusive in its present version but is theoretically open to all inquiring minds, all those aspiring to remake themselves.

The challenge *Iola Leroy* gives to the Talented Tenth in the black community is to widen the conversation, to allow more to join in. At its best, Harper's novel took pains to demonstrate that interest in educational, social, and political reform and a living experiment in democratic values were widespread within black folk of all educational levels, not just the emerging black elite. The protagonist's development proceeds via the interiorization of viewpoints from many different temperaments and social classes, with Iola Leroy's and other protagonists' growth intended to stimulate parallel acts of reconstruction in the reader's consciousness. Like many students of politics, Harper understood that stable democracies require an engaged (rather than self-centered) middle class interested in the reformation of an entire society, not just the securing of its own status. For her, the emerging black elite had special obligations and required good, strong books to set their sights high.

Yet Harper's novel demonstrating the virtues of a liberal arts education was designed for an even more ambitious audience: the reading public of the entire United States. Too bad that, by the standards *Iola Leroy* set, that pupil had to be graded as basically illiterate. In the decade in which Harper's novel was published, the emerging black middle class was repeatedly attacked, both through lynchings (some of which targeted successful individuals) and through large-scale race riots by whites burning and looting black-owned businesses, as in Wilmington, North Carolina, in 1898.

4

I close with a telling quotation from Elizabeth McHenry's *Forgotten Readers*, and some comments regarding what contemporary postcolonial studies has to teach readers of *Iola Leroy* about the dilemmas faced by new elites emerging when societies evolve out of plantation slave economies. First, McHenry writes: "We might do well to appreciate the significant steps that alternative sites of literary interaction and exchange have taken toward democratizing both literacy and literary study. It is especially true that African American literary societies and reading groups have historically created these alternate sites of literacy, often as a challenge to those formal institutions that denied them access" (314). Key texts in post–Civil War U.S. fiction were part of such an alternative network promoting a liberal arts model of education that taught black independence, not dependency. During the nadir of U.S. race relations, this network of authors and activists developed contrary ways of reading Reconstruction and the New South, including the history of black schools. The novels some of them produced are full of fears and contradictions, but all also honorably sought to school readers in new ways of configuring the United States in the world. By the 1880s and after, a chorus of novelists, historians, and education "experts" sought to refute Tourgée, revise the history of Reconstruction, and rewrite the goals and methods for black education. Sutton Griggs and Frances Harper, among many, rose to the challenge and turned to the novel as well as the lecture circuit to link local and national issues involving education. Their novels employed idealized role models but also counteracted such figures by encoding the subversive energy of skepticism into their narratives. Question authority; do not resolve debates by autocratic rule; strive to remake your world: these are instructional ideals uniting *Iola Leroy* and *Imperium in Imperio*, despite their many differences.

Ultimately, when assessing black leadership in the United States at the turn of the century—including how such leadership was represented in fiction—we need to keep in mind what postcolonial studies tells us about the inherent tensions between popular and bourgeois forms of cultural nationalism in newly decolonized nations. For the situation in which southern blacks found themselves in the postwar United States, regardless of whether they were newly free or born free, was indeed analogous to decolonization. At such a historical juncture, a newly emboldened bourgeoisie tends to position itself to "speak for" the masses, even as it discourages them from direct participation in many forms of governance. Both Amilcar Cabral and Frantz Fanon, for instance, analyzed the mix of timidity and righteousness marking emerging elites in newly decolonized nations. Their critiques share many parallels with contemporary literary critics' unease with Frances Harper's belief (held by many) that the black middle class would be the primary force vanquishing the shadows of slavery. (So too do Fanon's and Cabral's caveats parallel recent historians' critiques of the limited reforms offered by figures such as Booker T. Washington, Anna Julia Cooper, W. E. B. Du Bois, and other such figures.)[5] Yet we have to remember that the black elite so lovingly depicted in *Iola Leroy* was literally under siege when her novel was published; by defining the ideals that should govern this class, Harper hoped to aid black communities' powers of self-defense, not merely shore up one group's self-esteem. For this reason, the dangers of middle-class elitism are memorably explored throughout her book; it is a central, not peripheral, motif from the moment the heroine experiences a "fall" in both race and class status. Leaders can only truly lead, Harper shows us, when they have been educated to remember their rise—the full, complicated history that created them.

The Sutton Griggs novel to be examined next concurs; so too does the George Marion McClellan short story that is the focus of this section's final chapter. *Iola Leroy*, *Imperium in Imperio*, and *Old Greenbottom Inn and Other Stories* are exercises in creating a more generous and multilayered local and national memory—for black families, for the black nation within a nation, and for the United States as a whole. Their authors were as alert to the radical possibilities inherent in the use of fiction as they were to its conformist or elitist ones.

# Chapter Four

# Conflicted Race Nationalism

SUTTON GRIGGS'S *IMPERIUM IN IMPERIO* (1899)

No novel in U.S. literature more vividly captured the excitement and promise blacks felt attending postwar schools than Sutton Griggs's *Imperium in Imperio* (1899). The key protagonists are teachers: Belton Piedmont is hired by a school for Negro students in Richmond, Virginia; Bernard Belgrave teaches for a time in Louisiana. Griggs's text also shows a wide range of education scenes, from small buildings in rural Virginia to informal reading and discussion circles set up by blacks for adults (97) and to respected universities such as Harvard and "Stowe" (Fisk University in Nashville). Griggs depicts students excited not just to be in class but to have black as well as white teachers. (And even a little knowledge proves a dangerous thing: the black students soon demand their teachers not segregate themselves at meals.) Griggs also goes into detail about the students' readings: the novel was apparently intended to influence school curricula, particularly in the subjects of rhetoric and history. Griggs provides a list of authors to read in order to learn the proper oratorical techniques, plus a discussion of educational principles that stress the importance of heroic revolutionary role models and a "sublime" speaking style.[1] It is a new kind of pro-Reconstruction text, the novel-as-syllabus, a more radical "freedmen's book" to replace those published by Lydia Maria Child and the American Tract Society. The author traveled in black communities throughout the South, selling copies of his novels door to door.

The lengthy paraphrases and samples of oratory in *Imperium in Imperio* play a dramatic role, advancing the plot and demonstrating the fruits of the protagonists' education, modeling for Griggs's readers how to *move* an audience with sound reasoning and powerful rhetoric. Ultimately, though, Griggs's novel does not function by providing its readers with idealized black leaders to imitate. Rather, the novel serves as a sobering cautionary tale about the dangers of demagoguery. Hence the educational model that it demonstrates is a liberal arts one more than an imitative one. The novel's labyrinthine twists and turns, not to mention the shadowy depths of the human psyche that it explores, teach attentive readers to be skeptical of appearances, a polished oratorical manner, binary oppositions, and the siege mentality—the demand for unity and conformity— that all forms of nationalist rhetoric exploit.[2]

## 1

Preceding the bravura displays of the best that can be thought and said in *Imperium in Imperio* is a rather humble scene of instruction in the opening chapter, "A Small Beginning." "'Cum er long hunny an' let yer mammy fix yer 'spectabul, so yer ken go to skule. Yer mammy is 'tarmined ter gib yer all de book larning dar is ter be had even ef she has ter lib on bred an' herrin's, an' die en de a'ms house." With characteristic hyperbole (Griggs's favorite figure of speech), the narrator explains that these actions by a "poor, ignorant Negro woman" "vitally affected the destiny of a nation and saved the sun of the Nineteenth Century . . . from passing through . . . the ugliest clouds of all its journey" (3). Never mind for now Griggs's cryptic allusion to his novel's ending; focus on his portrait of that "Mammy" figure. Aggressively attacking the plantation-fiction stereotype of a Mammy solely concerned about her rich white child's aristocratic status—such as the figure of Mammy Krenda in Thomas Nelson Page's *Red Rock* (1899) or in Joel Chandler Harris's stories—Griggs focuses on this black mother's devotion to her actual child, Belton Piedmont, who will prove to be the novel's hero. Just as important is Griggs's demonstration that the mass of newly freed slaves not only had a unshaken respect for book learning but also hoped to erase illiteracy within a single generation—a claim whose truth has since been validated by historians such as James Anderson and Allison Dorsey. The narrator's apocalyptic rhetoric alluding to storm clouds and blood—a kind of second Civil War at the end of the nineteenth century—stands in foreboding contrast to the woman's idealistic dream.

Behind Griggs's ambitious presentation of Reconstruction reforms, of course, stand Tourgée's heroes from *Bricks without Straw*, Eliab Hill, the man of intellect, and Nimbus Ware, the man of action. Both Tourgée and Griggs were more comfortable writing set speeches with multiple subheadings for their protagonists than developing more novelistic ways of revealing character in action.[3] Nowhere is Griggs's debt to and revision of Tourgée clearer than in Belton Piedmont's final speech, the one that leads to his execution by the Imperium, the black revolutionary organization he has joined. Belton dissents from the Imperium's plot for a black nationalist revolt by using arguments similar to those of characters in Tourgée's novels in favor of absolute equality but gradual reform. Like Tourgée (and, of course, a host of other contemporary writers, black and white), Belton assumes that Africa embodies savagery. He suggests that the horrors of the middle passage and slavery and war had one saving grace—the American descendents of Africans now have access to the English language and European Enlightenment arguments for liberty and equal rights. The goal of blacks ought to be through their behavior and their writing to *force* from whites acknowledgment of black rights and accomplishments. And to this end Belton is extremely critical of blacks' current behavior. Like Tourgée, he argues they are basically unprepared for freedom (235); he criticizes their use of the ballot and suggests that in some cases whites' angry reactions were hardly irrational (240).

Overall, Belton's speech is a masterful balancing act, juxtaposing a critique of white supremacy with a frank discussion of the debt blacks owe to "Anglo-Saxon civilization" (the locution is Belton's, but hardly unusual for the time), plus the need for black self-critique and self-reliance. As well as sounding like Tourgée, Belton's rhetoric borrows liberally from Patrick Henry, Frederick Douglass, Alexander Crummell, Booker T. Washington, and others. Belton holds up Enlightenment ideals as a universal model for all races, and the English and American Revolutions as inspiration for all later movements for reform. The reconstruction of the constitutional flaws of the American republic, for him, must be complete, not piecemeal, allowing full civil liberties and economic and educational opportunities for all races. If these reforms are blocked, blacks under the Imperium will colonize Texas (taking it over from its current settlers) and make it an alternative imperium, a new black nation.[4]

The Imperium's revolutionary reconstruction plan ends in ignominy and martyrdom, reproducing rather than vanquishing the disaster that had become Haiti's dream of an independent black state. Written during the height (or depths) of Jim Crow, the novel's history of how ideals of black progress are betrayed surprisingly focuses not on whites but on blacks—blacks whose anger turns on each other, making martyrs of their own best and brightest. Although Griggs's novel seems packed with straightforward diatribes and set pieces, and the narrator repeatedly commends to his readers the positions on black uplift outlined by the various protagonists, Griggs's own "position" in the text is not easy to deduce, nor is it easy to state the moral of the Imperium's self-immolation. Borrowing a relevant later phrase from Carter Woodson, we might say that Griggs's novel could be subtitled "The Mis-education of the Negro." Like Woodson's text, though in the form of a novel, *Imperium* details the disastrous consequences of an education built on idealistic intentions but false principles and methods.

## 2

The novel's villain, Bernard Bertrand, is the double of its hero, Belton Piedmont. Bernard receives an even "better" education than Belton did; he was Belton's classmate but then attended Harvard, followed by rapid success in both the U.S. government and the secret black government, the Imperium, where he is elected president. Griggs does not give us a clear explanation of how Bernard becomes fixated on power and vengeance; indeed, one of Griggs's most subtle touches in this sometimes unsubtle novel was to leave mysterious the precise causes of Bernard's flaws. We can argue with equal plausibility that Bernard's vices are shaped by U.S. violence and hypocrisy or by his white father's rejection of him as an illegitimate child or by the fact that Bernard was always pampered in school, whereas his equally brilliant but more steady companion Belton was not.

Griggs's tragedy of the hero-as-traitor turns on the fact that the black men who are executed as traitors to their race turn out to be its champions, while those proclaimed race heroes hide an evil side. Bernard's Imperium ironically comes to mirror the obsessions of another invisible empire, the Ku Klux Klan. Bernard's methods of combating white supremacy lead him to adopt its nationalistic rhetoric of violence and also its determination to keep free of pollution the racial and cultural purity of the black body politic. Consider the subplot involving Antoinette Piedmont's alleged adultery, awkwardly interwoven by Griggs into the main story. So influential has been the Imperium's rhetoric of blood purity that Belton plans to divorce her because she has given birth to an apparently "white" child; he suspects adultery and has his wife ostracized. But as the child ages, its skin color darkens and his father's features in the child suddenly "develop," until at last Belton is able to not only see the skin color as "Negro" but see himself in his child's face (256). But Belton still demands photographic proof of the color changes "taken at various stages of its growth" (258). A baby's "color" may indeed change in the months after birth. Griggs here alludes to the "one-drop" rule that so obsessed whites, making one's racial identity fetishistically connected to skin color, but also concedes that skin color was not definitive—one could have a strain of "blackness" yet appear "white." Belton demands visual proof of "true" blackness, yet the evidence he requires paradoxically documents how the signs of racial identity can change and also be misread. Further, by placing this episode immediately after Belton is condemned to death, Griggs is rather heavy-handedly connecting two parallel examples of race-traitor rhetoric, one involving beliefs and the other blood and sex, one associated with the "male" sphere of politics and the other with the "female" sphere of home and womb.

Bernard has his own crises of identity. His white father, a U.S. senator, funds Bernard's education but refuses to recognize his son in public (he even threatens suicide if their connection is too soon revealed) until after his son achieves success in the white world (90–94). Bernard's focus on fame and power follows his father's model, yet he is never able to obtain his father's recognition of kinship; he is always still too "black." Bernard's obsession with measuring up to the standards of whiteness slowly mutates into hatred. Bernard's father tells his son that he wants his success to "make it possible for me to own you ere I pass out of life" (93), yet such a use of the word *own* exemplifies Bernard's double-bind: his father primarily uses it to mean recognize as an equal, but Bernard feels he is a mimic-man "owned"—enslaved—to his father's (and the white world's) double standards. Eventually, he resolves to use all its "gifts" to construct his revenge. Bernard's race logic and methods have ironic parallels with Thomas Dixon's. Not only does he see he is fated to remain merely an "educated Negro" in whites' eyes, but—precisely anticipating the "logic" of Dixon's *The Leopard's Spots* (1901)—Griggs's educated Negro Bernard Belgrave is resentful and envious of whites and thus the most dangerous to them. Bernard doesn't lust after white women, it is true, as Dixon's worse blacks invariably do, for Bernard instead demands the utmost "black" purity in his mate (and inspires the suicide of a light-skinned woman not black enough for him). If Dixon locates black lust and anger in genetics, Griggs's critique stresses how Bernard's demons of blackness are cultural foster-children of white society and its obsessions.

## 3

The fate of a third key character in *Imperium*, Berl Trout, also casts light on Griggs's critique of a compensatory black nationalistic rhetoric of racial purity. A member of the firing squad that executes the "traitor" Belton Piedmont, Trout later guiltily has second thoughts. Trout himself proves a much more deadly traitor to the Imperium than Belton ever threatened to be—he reveals its existence to whites at the worst possible moment, thus causing its collapse. Trout's confession begins and ends the novel and demonstrates how he moves from a rhetoric obsessed with revolution and violence to repentance, guilt, and abjection. Trout remorsefully figures his own black body as an abomination, a source of deadly pollution for his race: "Those who shall be detailed to escort my foul body to its grave are required to walk backwards with heads averted ... to warn all generations of men to come not near the air polluted by the rotting carcass of a vile traitor" (1). Trout's diction grotesquely turns upon *himself* Bernard's vow of revenge upon whites: "Make my father ashamed to own me, his lawful son; call me a bastard child; ... exhume Belton's body if you like and tear your flag from around him to keep him from polluting it!" (263).

Trout's confession is so placed in the novel to reveal that the "traitor" Belton is proven instead to be a heroic martyr, one who, despite his flaws, died upholding ideals that the black community most needs as it struggles against internal and external racism—reason, moderation, honesty, courage, ambition, and the ability to tolerate dissent. Trout ends up agreeing with Belton that acts of scapegoating make victims of everyone, including those for whose purity such acts are perpetrated. Trout's confession ends not with self-hate but with a vision of being blessed for what he has done by those of all races (2).

Trout's status as either traitor or hero in *Imperium* is ultimately undecidable. No eloquent speech definitively resolves the question of who betrayed the Imperium and who was its hero. Griggs so constructed his novel that his readers had to debate among themselves these crucial issues. Much of the novel vividly portrays the temptation for black communities to place their education and fate in the power of Moses-like liberators and interpreters. *Imperium* contains hardly a single scene representing education as a communal process—though one might concede that such a possibility is vaguely suggested by the mother's speech in the opening chapter or the occasional references to black adult discussion groups like those chronicled in Elizabeth McHenry's study, *Forgotten Readers*. Again and again in *Imperium*, one person brilliantly performs before an enthralled crowd, not merely persuading but cowing them into unanimity. Even Belton's concluding remarks, which urge moderation and balance praise and criticism, are described in violent terms: "like dynamite, [it] blasted away all opposition" (247). The heroic models of speech in *Imperium in Imperio* thus represent an insoluble problem for Griggs, for he is both enthralled with such rhetoric—and such leaders—yet deeply suspicious of both.

Berl Trout at first does what he is told but then later, privately, repents and asks why. Fittingly, although the novel's most dramatic scenes are dominated by long speeches in which the audience is told what history means and what the future will bring, the novel's beginning and end reveal that the most daring acts occur in private. Trout wrote the story of Belton and Bernard while he was jailed awaiting execution, so that his readers may learn of the difference between a leader and a demagogue. Finding a public space to express private doubts and suggest alternatives remains an elusive goal, yet the novel's preface and conclusion demonstrate that Griggs understood such acts of independence to be absolutely necessary for building a healthy black politics and community. The novel's preface and conclusion speak from such a private space of conscience, and the book wants us to hope that such writing done privately may eventually transform the black public sphere.

## 4

A final point regarding Griggs's brilliant and flawed novel: Trout's tale opens with a short announcement by one Sutton E. Griggs. Like Nathaniel Hawthorne, in his "Custom-House" essay introducing *The Scarlet Letter*, and Ellen Ingraham in *Bond and Free*, Griggs says that the novel the reader holds was given to him or her by someone else. *Imperium* allegedly was written by Trout and merely edited by Griggs. Griggs reduces his act of authorship to authenticating the honesty of another's character and the veracity of his text: "There are other documents in my possession tending to confirm the assertions made in this narrative. These documents were given me by Mr. Trout, so that, in case an attempt is made to pronounce him a liar, I might defend his name by coming forward with indisputable proofs of every important statement" (ii). By phrasing his "authentication" of the narrative in this manner, though, Griggs is gesturing not so much toward Hawthorne as toward other authors and narrative traditions operating in the antebellum United States—the ex-slave narrative written by blacks and usually "validated" for truthfulness by white authorities in the book's prefaces. Obliquely making this connection between his novel and the ex-slave narrative tradition, Griggs suggests that his book is best understood as an updated narrative of enslavement and freedom. And as in the earlier ex-slave narratives, Griggs focuses on the crucial role literacy must play in helping citizens judge the difference between unjust power and freedom. Griggs's novel should be understood as a tragic parable of the dangers of blacks' *re*-enslavement—not only by bounty hunters or the Ku Klux Klan but by blacks themselves, in the name of liberation. Griggs also helped his readers see that identifying the difference between good and evil is not always as simple as it may appear.

Ironically, *Imperium in Imperio* seems at first a tale where good and evil and "progress" and the value of "education" are all easily representable in narrative by positive or negative role models. But the novel's plot shows the opposite, that the true ideals of representative government (as opposed to tyranny) are dangerously *un*representable in fiction—at least by parables constructed using exemplary characters. Griggs's novel does indeed educate powerfully—by leading its readers right into a moral labyrinth regarding the proper definitions and methods of black schooling and black citizenship and leadership. Courageously, *Imperium* shows that solutions to a society's profoundest needs cannot be dictated to the masses from on high. Nor can they be found via an educational model that stresses rote imitation and the absolute authority of role models. Instead, they must be puzzled out in a variety of educational forums, by minds capable of handling irony, complexity, and contradiction, using two of the three B's—Berl and Belton, not Bernard—as exemplars but also as cautionary tales. In short, Griggs's novel courageously anatomizes the failures of education when skepticism and criticism are allowed no public forum. By the novel's conclusion, we have become spectators to the apocalypse threatened at the novel's beginning, forced to view both the un-making of reputations and the destruction of community. And all this occurs with no stable omniscient narrator to guide the characters or the reader as we try to survive our mistaken choices and learn from harsh experience.

To counteract Jim Crow, many blacks turned in compensation to a culture of uplift, hero worship, and sameness. Such a worldview treated those who dared criticize black leaders as traitors to the race. In diagnosing both the attraction and the fatal flaws of such a strategy of black resistance, Griggs's *Imperium* explored difficult issues in building an imagined community of *diverse* blackness, not a monolithic black empire. The novel was, both in conception and in execution, a text that modeled liberal arts values by putting them to the severest of tests. In doing so, Griggs provided a powerful precedent for later writers, including W. E. B. Du Bois, James Weldon Johnson, Wallace Thurman, George Schuyler, Carter G. Woodson, Zora Neale Hurston, Ralph Ellison, Melvin Kelley, and Chester Himes.

# Chapter Five

# Lynching and the Liberal Arts

The black southern educator and writer George Marion McClellan (1860–1934) has mostly been written out of U.S. literary history—not that he was really ever in it to begin with. Primarily a chaplain, educator, and high school principal who was trained at Fisk University and worked in Alabama, Kentucky, and Tennessee, McClellan also wrote fictional prose, poetry, and literary criticism that he privately published between 1895 and 1916. McClellan's fiction has received much less attention than that of other black prose writers who have recently been rediscovered and returned to literary history, such as Frances Harper, Pauline Hopkins, or Sutton Griggs; yet like those writers McClellan was doing innovative work and writing for a primarily black audience using small press publishing. McClellan's eclipse is partially due to Sterling Brown's and Robert Bone's surveys of black fiction, for they both assigned McClellan to the netherworld of being a genteel and sentimental writer of very minor stature during a time of transition. But such a depiction of McClellan's fiction is oversimplified. His one story collection not only provides the most complex portrait of a consciously interracial romance in New South fiction of the 1865–1920 period, but also renders an in-depth history of one of the new postwar southern black schools for advanced students, plus what may be the first portrait in fiction of late nineteenth-century black vaudeville performers.[1]

The only critic to treat McClellan's fiction with any attention is Dickson D. Bruce Jr. Consider his comments on "Old Greenbottom Inn":

> At the heart of the story's distinctiveness is the fact that, although Daphne is in many ways a typical sentimental heroine, her relationship with Joseph and her pregnancy bespeak a view of love—interracial or otherwise—that was far from common in turn-of-the-century sentimental writing, black or white. . . . In McClellan's story, passion is an important characteristic of

83

love; and the author did not openly condemn either Daphne or Joseph for succumbing to it in their love for each other. . . . Joseph comes to understand the evil of prejudice. McClellan was thus not using racial mixture as a literary convention to expose simple white perfidy in contrast to black virtue. The possibility of true love across racial lines is something he treated as natural and normal. (*Black American Writing* 142)

Yet two decades after Bruce's intriguing reassessment, not a single article on McClellan's fiction has appeared in literary journals.

I would like here to make a case for this invisible man's importance as a writer of short stories, on two grounds: his innovative subject matter and his ambitious, richly literary style. McClellan's *Old Greenbottom Inn and Other Stories* (1906) collects all of his fiction, with the exception of the late story "Gabe Yowl." The volume contains five stories set in the South, principally rural Alabama, middle Tennessee, and Kentucky, though there are also episodes in New Orleans, Baltimore, and other places, plus an introductory page-long "Proem" that presents McClellan's theory of tragedy and his claim that such literary conventions are necessary to tell the full dimensions of the black experience in the postwar South.

McClellan tells us in an introductory note that the first three stories were inspired by tales told to him about the Old Greenbottom Inn in northern Alabama, once a plantation and after the Civil War a school for Negroes, based on McClellan's own experience with the "Industrial and Normal School" in the northern Alabama town of Normal (renamed "Buena Vista" by McClellan). "For Annison's Sake" is a tragic romance and suicide that ends with a miracle; it is the weakest story in the volume. "The Creole from Louisiana," while fascinating both as a brief portrait of Fisk University and as a character study of its three major figures, is in the end marred by its sentimental romance convention that the patient love-martyr will win out in the end. The best and most ambitious stories in the collection are "Essie Dortch" and "Old Greenbottom Inn." After a general discussion of some of the distinctive features of McClellan's style and sense of black cultural history, this chapter will conclude with a more detailed reading of the volume's title story.

McClellan is hardly a prose artist of the stature of Twain or Chesnutt. His most congenial literary predecessors are Harriet Beecher Stowe of *Uncle Tom's Cabin* (1852), William Wells Brown's versions of *Clotel* (1853–), and Lydia Maria Child's attempt to update "tragic mulatta" narratives for postwar America in *A Romance of the Republic* (1867). Ida B. Wells's anti-lynching writings were no doubt important to him as well. But the source with which McClellan's *Old Greenbottom Inn* may be most thoroughly engaged is never directly named, though it was published just three years before: W. E. B. Du Bois's *The Souls of Black Folk* (1903).

Like Du Bois, McClellan undertakes a critique of Booker T. Washington's strategies for Negro progress and Negro education, particularly his emphasis on "practical" skills taught by rote imitation, though McClellan is more indirect than Du Bois. *Old Greenbottom Inn*, like *Souls of Black Folk*, places the great hope for the race's future in its new institutions of higher learning, especially universities like Fisk and the new Normal schools for training teachers. All of these schools feature a liberal arts model for education, combining practical skill instruction with courses of reading in the humanities and the natural sciences.

Rhetorically, McClellan's style is as ambitious, if not as accomplished, as Du Bois's own—densely allusive and unashamed to display references drawn from all realms of knowledge, from science to religion to art, from Europe to the African diaspora, ancient to modern, "high" culture to popular culture. It presents itself as a working example of the fruits of a liberal education. Both authors imply that only such a complex, mixed literary style can truly give voice to the souls of black folk and their rich history. Although McClellan's primary subject is the new life that blacks were trying to build in the South after the Civil War and the dismantling of Reconstruction reforms, he never portrays a simplistically unified black community heroically struggling against odds. His stories zero in on the contradictions of the new black middle class in the South, small as it is, and also tensions between older blacks who survived slavery and the new generation of blacks who were being raised in the postwar period.[2]

McClellan's stylistic ambitions are most noticeable because of the allusive richness of his style—its range of reference is even broader than the new arts and sciences curricula being offered in the early twentieth century at universities such as Fisk or Vanderbilt.[3] A page of McClellan's prose may contain allusions to astronomy and classical European music, religion and pastoral painting, and literature from the Greeks to the English classics. He wants to apply classical paradigms derived from pastoral and tragedy to black history and, indeed, opens *Old Greenbottom Inn* with a short disquisition on key elements of tragedy's origin in Greek satyr plays and their relevance for contemporary literature. (These astute comments on Greek tragedy well reveal McClellan's experience as a schoolteacher. They will be discussed in more detail in the conclusion.)

Yet throughout McClellan's fiction there is also a deep appreciation for the complex, layered ways in which African American history as become a part of *American* culture in places such as rural Buena Vista, Alabama, or New Orleans or Nashville. Despite McClellan's worship of "high" art, he has no easy contempt for popular culture; rather, we are offered in his stories brief but relatively detailed descriptions of Negro funeral traditions or the program offered by touring Negro vaudeville troupes. McClellan is hardly an uncritical viewer of black American popular culture, but he was also a good deal less condescending toward many of its cultural productions than was Du Bois. The tale "Essie Dortch" in *Old*

*Greenbottom Inn* is proof. Three years after W. E. B. Du Bois in *The Souls of Black Folk* singled out the Fisk Jubilee Singers as a paradigm of the cultural contributions of the New Negro, McClellan audaciously approached the topic of the role of the popular arts in black cultural progress from another angle entirely—he chose for his focus not singers of spirituals sponsored by a respectable university, but a commercial black touring vaudeville troupe with a comically inflated name, the Wilson and Watkins Grand Opera Company.

## 1

"Essie Dorch" may be our first portrait in literature of the black performance companies that toured the country to enthusiastic audiences in the late nineteenth and early twentieth century, competing with white "blackface" organizations in offering songs, dances, comedy routines, history lessons about black "progress," juggling and acrobatic acts, and, not incidentally, sales pitches for all kinds of patent medicines.[4] As such, McClellan's tale is an invaluable historical document. But it also functions as a work of literary art: in it, we can see the narrator struggling to make sense of the audacious newness of black popular culture. In other words, the narrator in this tale plays a dramatic role; the subject of the story is not just black vaudeville, but also the limitations of how black popular culture was represented and understood in 1906. Highly educated, McClellan's narrator finds that his elite models for what "culture" should be do not always work when confronted with the new. As we see him alternating between irony, condescension, bewilderment, and wonder, we see him working toward a much more capacious understanding of why black popular culture is so strong. McClellan's narrator discovers that black vaudeville was in many ways quite avant-garde: traveling performance artists such as the one featured in "Essie Dortch" were central in creating and celebrating a mélange of different performance styles crucial for the emergence of new forms of popular culture in the twentieth century. Best of all, McClellan is able to undertake his cultural analyses without reducing his subject to an abstraction; he makes this black vaudeville show come alive again for his readers, as the audience and the performers might have experienced it—and then he uses his narrator to add a new, more reflective and ambivalent way of understanding performance art. Recently, a number of academic studies of the history of African American dance have appeared—such as Jacqui Malone's and Nadine George-Graves's—that give us crucial new information about the importance of the period between the Civil War and World War II. But none of these studies cites McClellan's story, although it appears to be a crucial piece of contemporary evidence in our ongoing reconstruction of the history of U.S. popular culture.

The primary plot of "Essie Dortch" is rather conventional: it focuses on the love affair of the titular heroine with her dancing partner, and then her eventual betrayal by him. Although Essie has some fire in her, McClellan's portrait of her for the most part is quite conventional and sentimental; the narrator's phrasings are full of clichés. The originality of the story lies elsewhere, in its depiction of black vaudeville in action. It is in those scenes that her character and the story come most to life.

McClellan's narrator opens "Essie Dortch" by commenting on the lack of respect black performers receive in the United States from both black and white cultural elites. He then contrasts such disdainful treatment with Antonin Dvorak, who praised Negro songs as "'the only native American music.'" "They call them 'coon songs,'" the story begins, and then mentions that this term appears even in respectable dictionaries (167). But the narrator also hints that Dvorak, for all his respectful praise, could not really understand this new art form either because he could only define it by what it is not—European grand opera: "the perform- ance of the Wilson and Watkins Grand Opera Company would be another thing [Dvorak] could not define musically in any relation to grand opera" (168).[5] As the story makes clear, this "Opera Company" is an American music-and-dance per- formance company, not a troupe performing excerpts of European grand operas. Neither racist condescension from white audiences nor Dvorak's sincere praise with its troubling assumptions prove adequate. So what? The narrator shrugs: "But then it does not matter. Wilson and Watkins were a grand success. . . . The cake walk was fine. The buck dancing was superb" (168). Here, McClellan wryly hints that one American standard for measuring success—financial—perhaps overrides all others. Even so, American audiences, like Dvorak, need the "sanc- tion" of high European art to justify their enjoyment of vaudeville shenanigans: the troupe must name itself a grand opera company, as if in compensation for the "coon songs" and other "low" cultural materials it features.

Like the King's and the Duke's extravaganzas in *Huckleberry Finn*, Wilson and Watkins's show features a series of pitches for medicines interspersed with the musical numbers and skits. This troupe's wily pitchman is named Diamond-stone Kitt. "He understood human nature well. For instance, he would sell medicine for rheumatism for just so many minutes, and after that he would not sell the medi- cine for ten times its price. . . . [T]hose who had not been able to get to him in time to get the medicine for rheumatism would buy the medicine for the next evil" (175). McClellan's eye and irony are sharp too when he considers how even nar- ratives of black cultural progress since slavery are shamelessly commodified when they are appropriated as part of a vaudeville show: interrupted by sales shills, such narratives help sell the show's sponsors' products by legitimizing them.

Sexy dancing works similarly. At first the narrator is ironic and conde- scending about what the story's heroine brings to the troupe: "In all the Negro advancement which the company set forth, they had not got him up to skirt dancing, so that Essie in her art was ready for the stage at once" (171). But as the narrator watches the performance of Essie and her partner, he begins to be won over by the brio and skill of their dancing. He also notices that their perform-ance is profoundly *cosmopolitan*, a celebration of black mobility via a variety of urban and rural dance styles: "'Buck and wing dancing' suggest[s] ... free air, shady groves, saw-dust and all the jollity of country life and picnics ... youthful vigor, good health and strong animal life.... But the waltz is another thing.... When ... Essie with her partner began to move in the sensuous maze of its rhythm there was the impression all around that she had a part in another life than that of the village to which they all belonged" (178). The show is so popu-lar with both black and white audiences because it gives them a pleasing mix of several different modern identities that can be enjoyed together—country and cosmopolitan, pre–Civil War and contemporary, black (the "buck and wing," which blended both African and African American dance traditions) and white (waltzes imported from Europe, where Strauss was the rage, then given distinctly American touches).[6] In a nation that by 1906 had become profoundly segre-gated, not to mention divided by class lines, there is something heady about a stage show that ignores all such cultural dividing lines or refers to them in order to cross them. And it does so by rejecting an earlier performance style that was also famous for its cultural mixture: Essie and her partner do not wear blackface, though there appear to be blackface routines in other parts of the opera compa-ny's show, such as its "coon songs". Essie's stage persona is romantically urban and urbane and *new*, yet it also allows her to reconfigure elements of her rural past identity, not reject them.

The vaudeville "Opera" show as a whole is even more eclectic than its leading star: acrobatics and singing, dancing and sales pitches, "high" instructional goals about black history and "low" appeals to the audience's desire for pleasure and newness. McClellan's narrator can be rather arch, elitist, and befuddled as he tries to absorb the lively confabulation of materials that make up black vaudeville; he sometimes sounds rather like a blushing principal or minister who is afraid he was noticed in the audience. But at key moments of the story the narrator comes round and becomes much less self-conscious and standoffish. His elaborate men-tal dance as he tries to comprehend the new cultural phenomenon of vaudeville is as vividly rendered and entertaining as Essie's own moves. In short, McClellan's "Essie Dortch" argues that black vaudeville's very vulgarity and vitality, its mixed style, celebrates the diversity of black popular culture and the force of black aspirations for progress. Indeed, McClellan is much more liberal or generous in his appreciation of the popular arts than cultural elites of the era normally were. His generous curiosity about the new operates without ceding his right to critique or to place current events within a historical perspective. McClellan pays tribute to black vaudeville's diverse performance styles by inventing a chronicler-narrator who himself embodies a diversity of voices and views and modes of understanding. The story expresses liberal arts values even as it describes them in action.


## 2


The overall tone of *Old Greenbottom Inn and Other Stories* is reflective melancholy, not exuberance. This tone can certainly become overly sentimental, but this tendency of McClellan's is often counterbalanced by his skeptical intelligence, sharp eye for the revealing detail, a broad sense of history and irony, and a fine talent for making his settings and landscape function as dramatic presences, not mere background. At its most complex, McClellan's tragic sensibility is deeply stoic and ironical—and it places its stories about the fates of particular people within provocative social and historical contexts.

In the volume's title story, for instance, the narrator provides us with a stunningly succinct two-page summary of Civil War history before giving us specific examples of how these faraway events affected the lives of both black and white characters in rural Alabama. Here is an excerpt:

> On the second day at Gettysburg, the South, represented by Gen. Lee, was confidently in a few days expecting in Philadelphia or New York to dictate terms of peace. But on the night of that second day, troops on both sides kept arriving all night and taking their places on the battlefields in the moonlight for the awful death struggle that all saw must take place the next day. And the great battle came. It was the American Waterloo. In it Lee's army, the strength, the pride, the flower of the South, went down and with it the Southern cause. From that time on, beginning the next day with the fall of Vicksburg and the immediate appearance of the Monitor at Hampton Roads, the Southern Confederacy went downward step by step, without a single upward move, till it came to its bitter end. (24)

Historians may quibble with the passage's suggestion that the end of the war was never in doubt after Pickett's Charge, but there is no denying this passage's conceptual power and dignity of phrasing. Consider also this vivid and shrewd description of a juggling act in "Essie Dortch": "He was a sight to see as he stood in the glow of the lamplight in his green scale-bespangled tights. His pitching the glittering balls and dangerously sharp knives in mid-air with such rapidity and dexterity amazed beyond words those slow-moving farm-worked men, who were only accustomed to handle the plow, the hoe and the rake with leisure-like movement" (176).

It is certainly true that McClellan's narrators can sometimes guide their tales with an overly pushy hand, using clichés and mistrusting a reader's ability to make conclusions: "Ambition was tugging hard at her heart, and what was more pitiful, love was growing in her breast for the rake who was playing false to her innocence and ignorance" ("Essie Dortch" 171–172). But contrast such a moment with the following portrait of an old black woman named Rhoda reacting to the lynching of her child:

> By and by the moon came up over the mountains and sent a shaft of light into the cabin making more silvery an old head already white with the toil of slavery and the sorrows of many years. The mid-night passenger train on the Memphis & Charleston road came past Mercury with a shriek, leaving behind it a trail of sparks and smoke. It turned the curve at Ferns and began ringing the bell for Buena Vista, where it stopped for a moment. But the engine was heard to roar on as if impatient for the race onward. With a mighty snort the great iron steed sped on and on to its terminus, bearing its freight of human life, bending, leaning and twisted in all positions asleep. ("Old Greenbottom Inn," 81)

Comparing a steam engine to an iron horse is hardly original, but what is remarkable here is how McClellan uses the train to add a new dimension to his portrait of inconsolable grief. The train embodies American violence and energy, the compulsions driving its dreams of progress. And yet this older woman, a survivor of the Civil War, is in her own way as dominant a force as the train; she remained on the old plantation and earned wages as a cook for her former owner with one goal in mind—to educate her son for a new future. Her dream of progress has just been ended by a lynching, whose brutality is powerfully reconfigured in the above passage by the description of the locomotive. McClellan has taken a familiar icon of civilization's "race onward" and given it a suggestion of regression into savagery.

Furthermore, juxtaposed against the old woman's sleepless night is the brief description of the train passengers carried through the landscape in the different poses of sleep, all oblivious to this black woman's story. This seemingly extraneous detail may be the most extraordinary feature of all. Through it, McClellan conveys at once both how unknown to the majority Rhoda's tragedy is and how any single person's story is connected to the larger scene, the deeper history. The energy of the passing train cannot be made solely to symbolize American violence; it also represents an old black woman's equally American dream of travel and escape. The passage suggests the way in which trains for blacks enduring Jim Crow began to have the same association with a flight to freedom that ships had for Frederick Douglass in his *Narrative*.[7] Although Rhoda may be oblivious to the power of this train symbolism, many of McClellan's readers in the new generation, fed up with just the dream-destroying viciousness that is chronicled so well in "Old Greenbottom Inn," were not. Indeed, Rhoda's reaction to her son's murder vividly captures black despair in the South: it shakes her faith in God to its foundations. Once "the chief shouter in revivals and a rebuker of sinners at all times," Rhoda is now "in the dark. She had lifted up her face to pray to her God, but he was gone from his throne. He was swaying to the breeze with hemp and death in the gray dawn over the bridge at Moore's creek" (82).

"Old Greenbottom Inn" is unequivocally McClellan's best as well as most ambitious story. Eighty pages in length, it really should be classed as a novella. McClellan's tale goes well beyond earlier pro-Reconstruction fiction in its representation of the history of black schools in the South, for it focuses not on the early years of Reconstruction and reaction, but on black achievements in advanced education—against great odds—at the dawn of the twentieth century.

The story's focus is an Industrial and Normal School enrolling four hundred Negro students, located in the fictional town of Buena Vista in the mountains of northern Alabama near the Tennessee border. The boardinghouse for the teachers at this school is the former Old Greenbottom Inn, which has a history leading back into slavery times, when it was an inn on the property of a working plantation. McClellan's tale accentuates the site's sharply layered history, once an integral part of the plantation system (used to house visiting slave traders) and now a local center of black hopes for freedom.

McClellan begins in the present, early in the twentieth century, with an affectionate and somewhat dreamy portrait through a teacher's eyes of everyday activities at the school one Saturday just before 4:00 p.m. Done with their lessons for the day, some students are listening to a band play a John Philip Sousa march; others are on the move so they won't be late for roll call in industrial workshop classes in blacksmithing, broom-making, and other skills; others are preparing for a marching drill (like the males enrolled at Tuskegee, who had caps right for a military marching band as part of their official uniform). Oxen pulling a heavy load of meal, pork, and molasses make their way up toward the commissary, while three girls with a load of the teachers' laundry are also seen (7–8). There is also an amused account of several students and their place of punishment, giving the impression that the school regulates behavior strictly but not harshly: the eight boys sentenced to work in the nearby quarry for late-night shenanigans reflect that what "had been such fun the night before seemed a very stupid affair" now as they break rocks (9).

As one of the teachers relaxes on the ground near the bandstand and dreamily reflects on the scene and the mountain vistas beyond, he self-consciously turns both its present and its past into a sweetly melancholic pastoral fantasy, almost like a scene from a poem by the eighteenth-century pastoralists Thomas Gray or James Thompson, or a French painting by Claude Lorraine or Corot, except for its touch of southern color: "The flocks were browsing along the hillside and slowly wending their way to the folds. . . . The smoke was curling over the kitchen chimney of the Teachers' Home, heralding supper. In a flash I saw Greenbottom Inn in all its glory of ante-bellum days, and a beautiful quadroon girl who used to watch the coming of the cows and meet them with milkmaid songs and caressing names" (13–14). The narrator's pastoral fantasy about "the glory of ante-bellum days," though, is rudely interrupted by a different voice heard in his head: " 'A beautiful, innocent child indeed! She's a nigger brat, and she'll bring disgrace and ruin along her track as her mother has done' " (14). The rest of "Old Greenbottom Inn" is thus cast as a dark, involuntary meditation on this vicious voice from the past. Whereas the present Normal school represents "new life and new hope in the new order of things" (87), the slurs of racist prophecy rudely interrupt such idealization. Is the girl's life to be "only a memory" unconnected to the school's present, "not a story to pass on," in Toni Morrison's phrase at the end of *Beloved*? Or must a troubling confrontation with the most disturbing elements of the past be a crucial part of black children's and black teachers' education, giving them a sense of history that can be the only firm foundation on which to build?

McClellan's tale provides only an ambiguous answer. There is no suggestion that the complex history of Greenbottom Inn is being taught at the new school, where more "practical" skills and an optimistic narrative of black progress seem emphasized, along with military drills and uniform-wearing along the lines advocated by Booker T. Washington. Yet McClellan's tale asks the question of what role a deep and critical sense of American history is to play in black education—and, even more importantly, whether an appreciation of tragic complexity must be in a curriculum worthy to be part of black education. The story raises precisely the cultural issues (including a criticism of Washington's vision for Negro education) that W. E. B. Du Bois addressed in *Souls of Black Folk* just three years earlier, in 1903. Indeed, *Old Greenbottom Inn* may be read as the first important response to Du Bois's masterpiece by a black American writer. If in "Essie Dortch" McClellan was even more audacious than Du Bois in using black popular cultural forms (vaudeville rather than sorrow songs) to state his deepest themes, in "Old Greenbottom Inn" he joins Du Bois in offering a profound defense of the value to the black community of a liberal arts education strong in the teaching of history and literature.

"Old Greenbottom Inn" excavates the deep history that occurred on the site of the Normal school, a history about which its present students doing laundry and military exercises seem largely ignorant. The voice from the past that interrupts the narrator's fantasy of black progress so rudely with the cry of "nigger brat" introduces us to a girl named Daphne. She was never a student at a school such as this. Her story, briefly, is this. Before the Civil War, a slave owner named

Mrs. McBride, who owns the property that would later become the Buena Vista school, wants Daphne and her mother sold away because they are her husband's daughter and mistress. But Mrs. McBride is able to force the sale only of Daphne's mother, who leaves cursing the McBrides and all their land. (The scene as rendered by McClellan is a small masterpiece of understated power: the mother refuses to adapt her step to the departing coffle's rhythm and eventually has to be bound and carried away in the luggage cart.) Mrs. McBride later makes Daphne be her daughter's lady's-maid. After the Civil War, which to Mrs. McBride seems like the curse come true, a Negro school is established by northern white teachers near the property, while Mrs. McBride is reduced to poverty—the curse acting a second and third time. The cook, "Aunt Rhoda," has stayed on the plantation and is now paid wages; she has also become a kind of surrogate mother for Daphne and is determined to enroll both her and her son, John Henry, in the new school. When her former mistress objects that education "does nothing but spoil" Negroes, the narrator drily comments: "In nearly all things Mrs. McBride's opinions were taken as law and gospel by Aunt Rhoda as completely as in slavery days, but in this one point . . . Aunt Rhoda took her freedom. In her heart she had one great ambition and that was to see John Henry a gentleman and that too after the Southern notion of a gentleman. To this end Aunt Rhoda cooked, washed, scrubbed and served 'Miss Celia' with slave devotion" (26). Consciously revising the "mammy" stereotype of the minstrel stage and anti-Reconstruction fiction, McClellan's Rhoda continues to serve her old owner while keeping her eye on the prize—a new identity for the next generation. But Rhoda's aspirations will have tragic consequences.

The primary action of "Old Greenbottom Inn" takes place in 1875, just at the time when, in Alabama and elsewhere, what few reforms Reconstruction brought to the state were being dismantled. John Henry is twenty, Daphne sixteen. Mrs. McBride's daughter is being courted by a young white gentleman, Joseph Cramer, whose southern family is still rich enough to support his ambition to be a new kind of southern aristocrat—a world traveler and painter who questions inherited social mores and roles and lives instead for beauty, especially in art and music. Cramer is a character type that rarely appears in black fiction before the 1920s, though he is familiar enough in the contemporary works of Henry James. We may trace Cramer's genealogy in American fiction back to the work of earlier anti-slavery white writers such as Lydia Maria Child and Harriet Beecher Stowe, for both *Uncle Tom's Cabin* (1852) and *Romance of the Republic* (1867) feature gentlemen-aesthetes who in different ways become entangled in the color line. McClellan's Cramer, predictably enough, falls in love with Daphne while visiting the plantation to court Mrs. McBride's daughter. Daphne becomes pregnant. John Henry (who is himself in love with Daphne) confronts Cramer and a fight ensues, in which Cramer, for all his supposed cosmopolitanism about

race, suddenly acts and sounds very much like an older version of a white southern gentleman determined to exercise his privilege to demean black men (62).
Cramer is accidentally killed in the fight and John Henry is pursued and caught,
in a scene that may be the most powerfully dramatized lynching in American literature until Jean Toomer's *Cane* and William Faulkner's *Light in August*.[8] Both
Daphne's and Rhoda's lives end up destroyed as well. Daphne goes mad and, after
giving birth, mutters to her child the same words Mrs. McBride used about her:
"She's a nigger brat with poison in her blood" (86). Daphne's mother's curse on
Mrs. McBride has done its work, but its circle of devastation ends up including
far more than she ever intended.

Daphne, John Henry, and Joseph Cramer, for all their education, prove powerless to stop this tragic train of events; indeed, their training is strongly implicated by McClellan in helping cause the disaster. During Reconstruction all three
have learned to question social roles and have acquired new skills and powers
that upset the racial status quo. Without her new educational opportunities,
Daphne would not have learned to sing European art songs in a way Cramer
finds irresistible, and Cramer himself might not have appealed to her as a figure
representing the allure of worlds beyond the one she has known. Similarly, John
Henry's lynchers make it clear they kill him not just because of Cramer's death
but because he has become an articulate and educated leader in the black community. For his part, Cramer has traveled widely enough to affect a bohemian's
belief that he may live and act above or beyond society's injunctions, though the
narrator also stresses somewhat abstractly that as far as seducing Daphne goes,
Cramer "knew he was following an inclination in the very nature of the case
impossible, without the likelihood of harm to come" (54).

So is McClellan's tale in agreement with those who implied that with blacks a
little liberal arts education is a dangerous thing? Hardly. It is crucial to emphasize
how complex his story is, in ways that cannot be well captured by the plot summary necessary to introduce readers to this narrative. It is no mere cautionary
tale condemning interracial romance, or suggesting that Daphne, John Henry,
and Joseph Cramer were corrupted by their fancy education and forgot their true
"place" in southern society. Nor does it idealize the three characters simply as
martyrs to southern barbarism. All the protagonists are complexly drawn, despite
the narrator's occasional lapses into cliché; the tale contains no simple villains,
not even Mrs. McBride, and no simple moral regarding the education of blacks,
the temptations of crossing the color line, or the right response to evil.

When the book learning that Rhoda has laboriously paid for causes her son to
doubt God, for instance, McClellan stages a complex debate between mother and
son on how God will manifest himself in a world where it seems only the Devil
prospers. John Henry cites a white mob's recent looting of black-owned stores
and cooperatives in a nearby town, along with the murder of sixty-two black

citizens, and concludes, "'God may love the Negroes as he does the white people, but I don't believe it!'" His less educated mother refuses to believe that God has abandoned blacks:

> "Chile, I knows de Lawd lets some cur'ios things go on, but I knows he loves me 'cause I carries de witness in my breas' and I is a cullud person. Den de Bible pintly says, 'De Lawd ain't no disrespecter uv persons.'"
>
> "No, mother, the Bible does not say that. It says, 'He is no respecter of persons.'"
>
> "Well, ain't dat de same thing?" said Aunt Rhoda, with rising wrath.
>
> "No, mother, it is not the same thing. I think He must be a great disrespecter of some persons if He is righteous Himself." (37–38)

This discussion alludes to several famous passages in the Bible that use the phrase properly quoted by John Henry to stress the equity of God's judgment according to every person's actions in life. Here are three instances:

> Then Peter opened his mouth, and said, "Of a truth I perceive that God is no respecter of persons: But in every nation he that feareth him, and worketh righteousness, is accepted with him." (*King James Bible*, Acts 10: 34, 35)

> But he that doeth wrong shall receive for the wrong which he hath done: and there is no respect of persons. (Colossians 3: 25)

> And if ye call on the Father, who without respect of persons judgeth according to every man's work, pass the time of your sojourning here in fear. (I Peter 1: 17)

In his anger, John Henry asks for immediate evidence for the kind of intervention described in Colossians; seeing no evidence of God actively "disrespecting" the wicked, he suggests God has abandoned the world. His less-educated mother's black vernacular misquotes the King James English but infallibly understands the *spirit* of these biblical passages: God will never abandon those with faith; punishment for the wicked will eventually come.

McClellan was a Sunday school teacher as well as an educator, but here his text does not preach. Neither does it give us easy choices and urge us to take sides. Who are human beings to judge whether God's "respect" and "judgment" will be revealed in this life or the next, or how they will manifest themselves? The mother's and son's tragically divergent readings of the Bible's textual and spiritual mysteries both fit their characters and raise difficult questions—just the kind that should be part of a liberal arts curriculum—about how to interpret and respond to the power of evil in the world. This brief dialogue becomes all the more moving when we later learn that John Henry's lynching causes Rhoda to doubt what she so eloquently trusts here, the "witness" of God's love in her breast.

3

In McClellan's introduction to *Old Greenbottom Inn and Other Stories*, somewhat portentously entitled "Proem," he gives a brief and learned history of tragedy in Western literature and announces his own ambition to use tragic catharsis to know and then possibly redeem southern history. Responding to Aristotle while drawing on him, McClellan argues emphatically that tragedy does not require solely aristocratic characters. He notes that the struggles against fate by common people are usually thought to be "too insignificant for notice in a conception of tragedy"; when their deaths come, unlike Lear's or Hamlet's, it is not called tragic but merely cause-and-effect, "a natural consequence of vulgarity, sin." McClellan stresses his ambition to show that tragic catharsis—in other words, a *deep* education, not merely a "normal" education in industrial and other practical arts, however important that may be—may be found in southern sites, such as the Old Greenbottom Inn in Alabama, which unfortunately have their full share of "sublime sorrow and grand crimes" and characters who heroically struggled against their fate.

McClellan's introduction concludes with two key sentences. The first uses a biblical mode to prophesy a stellar future for black American literature: "By and by, that one from among us who is coming, who has not yet arrived, but whose heralds are already heard in the distance proclaiming his sure coming, will tell our stories." (The context makes it certain the "our" refers to black southerners, the South's "darker subjects," though McClellan's references to Aristotelian tragedy also make clear he is claiming as well universal relevance for such stories.)[9] McClellan's final sentence stresses tragedy's redemptive power with Emersonian cadences: "And then the great heart of all our vast domain, which ever responds to great sorrow when it is touched, and, notwithstanding its multitudinous contradictions, is ever working towards right and justice to all—will make many things better concerning which now exist only silence, unbelief, and indifference." Such a redemptive faith is obviously in tension with the tale's exploration of the delusions fostered by Daphne's, John Henry's, and Joseph Cramer's education in the arts, and with the narrator's caustic "art exhibit" demonstrating scenes from the lynching. But this tension propels the tale and also adds complexity to McClellan's own tendencies toward aestheticism and narratives of progress. In proclaiming more clearly than other writers of the time (Mark Twain and Charles Chesnutt excepted) that southern U.S. history contained the stuff of Greek tragedy, McClellan in 1906 prophesied much of the best southern literature to come.

96

Given McClellan's beliefs, and the complex achievement of *Old Greenbottom Inn and Other Stories*, our contemporary ignorance about his fiction is profoundly distressing. We need hardly overstate this author's accomplishments—one short-story collection is, after all, a narrow foundation for a lasting reputation—to assert that any list of important U.S. fiction from the late nineteenth and early twentieth century should include George Marion McClellan's. The problem of the twentieth century was not just the problem of the color line, but also that on this topic we still read too narrow a canon of authors.

Along with Griggs's and Harper's novels, the title story in McClellan's collection provides a key piece of the puzzle as we try to understand how black fiction at the turn to the twentieth century attempted to represent the democratic possibilities inherent in black schools, but also the dangers those schools and their students faced. Despite their varied approaches and outcomes, all the fictions considered in part 1, except Woolson's, embrace the vision that the goal of black schools should be to create citizens, not subjects. How well they vivify this ideal is, of course, a different question. Despite the increasing pessimism these works chart as we move from 1867 to 1906, the belief that the United States could and should evolve into a multiracial, egalitarian democracy remains unvanquished. These authors' obdurate faith in education, the strength of black popular culture, and democracy—a faith affirmed even as the grip of Jim Crow tightened on the throats of black communities throughout the South—is most profoundly enacted by the ways in which their texts' readers are led forth (the root meaning of education, after all) to becoming engaged and independently thinking citizens. Like McClellan's narrators in "Essie Dortch" and "Old Greenbottom Inn," they muse on local and national spectacles of U.S. history in action and learn to see not only tragedy and farce but also hope.

# PART II

# Jim Crow Colonialism's Dependency Model for "Uplift"

## PROMOTION AND REACTION

Part 2 focuses first on a broad story: how the history of Reconstruction was rewritten by the New South and national Progressivist intellectuals and leaders in the 1890s and after to endorse U.S. colonialist expansion abroad. They linked disfranchisement and Jim Crow segregation at home with the apparent expansion of democratic rights in the new colonies—and called both progress. To chart this mess of historical contradictions, I have chosen as key variables the specific ways in which Reconstruction-era discourse regarding voting rights and proper educational models for southern blacks was adopted and revised to apply to new tropical colonials. Brief anatomies of the origin and development of Samuel C. Armstrong's and Booker T. Washington's educational philosophies are used to build my case that Reconstruction-era modes of creating subjects rather than citizens return in striking new configurations in the post-Reconstruction period. The Hampton and Tuskegee Institutes received huge amounts of funding from whites and served a small minority of blacks, while Reconstruction-era plans for a network of modern public schools funded by taxes to serve blacks were largely abandoned. Meanwhile, after 1898 U.S. government officials drew up ambitious plans for educating the masses of colonial subjects in the new overseas territories—hiring many teachers, building new schoolhouses, creating the necessary administrative resources. Of course, private philanthropy supporting schools was welcomed in the South and abroad. But when it came to the education of people of color, what was said to be inappropriate for the federal and state governments in the South was seen as indispensable in Hawaii, the Caribbean, and the Philippines: tax-supported, government-supervised public schools.

The contradiction between the U.S. government's role in education in the South versus in the colonies is striking and requires explanation. It parallels similar anomalies in voting: after 1898, there were many national discussions about when and how to give the new colonial subjects in Hawaii, the Philippines, and Puerto Rico limited voting rights, while simultaneously in the South massive numbers of blacks were being disenfranchised. In the midst of all the heterogeneity in U.S. educational and voting policies toward people of color, however, one unifying factor emerged: dissimilar policies at home and abroad were justified using the rhetoric of carefully controlled tutelage and uplift—Progressivism's supposedly rational response to the alleged limitations of a people's character and culture.

These developments in late nineteenth- and early twentieth-century Progressivist public policies occurred against a backdrop of rapidly changing discourse about racial difference. As numerous scholars have shown, the most important identifiers of racial difference moved from mapping visible characteristics to a model stressing inner *character*, the hidden potentials and limits for a person's and a racial group's development. Behavior and culture were now seen by many as the crucial racial markers, the most reliable way the workings of biological inheritance would be revealed and known. With the new discourse stressing racial behavioral differences came new arguments for nurturing those differences, making them properly prominent. For whites, providing proper models of superiority was necessary. For people of color, Progressivism prescribed disciplinary training: a "raising" to natural limits that was also a containing. Violence and other forms of repression were certainly used to enforce new forms of social stratification as well, including public segregation and lynching, but, in general, violence was not sanctioned by the power elites; they much preferred to describe these social changes using language that stressed their own benevolence and realism. Such discourse was most well known by its slogans about "uplift" and taking up the "white man's burden." It is this nexus in U.S. Progressivist domestic and colonial policy that I dub Jim Crow colonialism—a term that is relevant throughout part 2, but whose evolution is given particular attention in chapters 6 and 7.

Although policy elites defining what black education should be appropriated the most idealistic language of Reconstruction to speak of creating black citizens and entrepreneurs, the educational methods they endorsed emphatically followed a more regressive model. They contained the ambitions of a new generation of people of color and accommodated the many whites who wanted minute economic advancements for blacks in exchange for an agreement not to agitate for citizen's rights. The rapturous reception of Booker T. Washington's "Atlanta Compromise" speech in 1895 is the best-known example of such a trade-off. This sharply selective and revisionist appropriation of Reconstruction's legacy in the field of education and politics was paralleled in other fields, most notably historiography; chapter 6 will also demonstrate parallels between claims used by historians of the "Dunning School," who in the late nineteenth and early twentieth centuries re-wrote Reconstruction history to justify white rule in the New South, and common contemporary arguments in favor of U.S. colonial projects abroad.

A key phase in the transition from Reconstruction to the new U.S. colonialism occurred when white plantation-owners and other elites were promoted as the experts best left in charge of providing education for rural blacks, on the grounds that they supposedly knew "their" blacks best. This argument was commonplace in public policy declarations by New South elites and others in the 1880s and 1890s, but it also appeared in fiction, in what has become known as the "plantation school," with Joel Chandler Harris and Thomas Nelson Page as its most influential exemplars. (Constance Fenimore Woolson's hugely popular short stories, discussed in part 1, may be understood as a precursor to the rise of this school.) Since the ideological commonalities of plantation-school writers have been much discussed by literary historians, I focus instead on a novel that should be better known because early in the 1880s it explicitly made the case that, when it came to rural black schools, southern plantation owners knew best: Ellen M. Ingraham's *Bond and Free* (1882). Along with the Tuskegee and Hampton models, planter paternalism provided a key index for how later U.S. colonial education systems would work. Indeed, as we shall see, there is a good deal of convergence between arguments in favor of "modern" (slavery-free) plantations that stressed how well they trained their workers and the two most famous black schools supported by northern philanthropy, Tuskegee and Hampton.

Part 2 then turns to chapters focusing on how representative writers of imaginative literature in the post-1898 era—Marietta Holley, Mark Twain, and the Philippine playwright Aurelio Tolentino—give us insights into the volatile contrast in Jim Crow colonialist discourse between its surface arguments and its inner tensions. Holley's narrator, "Josiah Allen's wife," wants to believe in both the splendors of the St. Louis World's Fair of 1904 (including its "Philippine Reservation" exhibits) and the virtues of the U.S. colonial adventures abroad. But doubts keep intervening, in part because of Holley's distant memories of Reconstruction. Twain's notorious diatribe, "To the Person Sitting in Darkness," of course takes a very different approach, exaggerating as vigorously as he knew how the hypocrisies and inconsistencies of U.S. colonial discourse. Twain's slash-and-burn technique handling "white man's burden" clichés is worth comparing to the Philippine playwright Aurelio Tolentino's response to the contradictions of U.S. policy. Tolentino's play, which was performed in Manila for just one night in 1903, damns U.S. activities yet affirms U.S. ideals of freedom. It also literally represents the voice of a person sitting in darkness: the play was deemed seditious and shut down by U.S. military authorities, its author imprisoned. Tolentino gives an incisive portrait of the cruelties of Spanish rule and expresses the sharp disappointment many Filipinos felt when they understood that the independence they thought had been promised by the United States would not be forthcoming. Yet such are the archival and documentary ambitions of colonial empire that the full text of the play was translated and annotated by a U.S. bureaucrat, as part of an extensive survey of cultural developments in the new colony. Reading the ways in which the bureaucrat's editorial comments both translate yet also try to contain and revise the meanings of Tolentino's protest provides an even more vivid demonstration than Twain's text of how colonial discourse is not coherent in itself as it "answers" the voice of the native, but is itself *constituted* by contending voices and its own inner contradictions.

The final chapter in part 2 focuses on Thomas Dixon and Owen Wister and tests my premise that when racial identity is understood to be acculturated, not given, whites must learn their superiority by following proper role models. Dixon's novels in his Reconstruction Trilogy are case studies in the psychosis of lynching, whereby white manhood can be constructed only via narratives of black dismemberment before enthralled white spectators. Despite Dixon's role in providing the source-text for D. W. Griffith's movie *The Birth of a Nation*, however, his novels have not been interpreted with an eye to how cinematic tropes function in Dixon's narratives to hypnotize whites with images of black savagery and white virtue. Dixon's fascination with lynching, cinema, and other forms of mob spectacle represent the most demonic application in *Sitting in Darkness* of the imitative model of education for shaping human behavior. Dixon's ambivalence regarding the U.S. colonial experiments also receives some attention in chapter 9, for his doubts about the justifications for massive colonial uplift projects vividly explain one reason why those policies troubled so many, including white southerners.

Equally racist, Owen Wister was nevertheless a much more ardent supporter of U.S. regime-change policies in its new colonies. While his best-selling novel, *The Virginian*, focuses on the frontier West, not the Caribbean or the Pacific, his text contains key colonial references, not to mention a narrative depicting how an ex-Confederate named "the Southerner" redeems himself as an American role model by imposing civilized order on savagery. Indeed, one of the ways to understand the long-standing popularity of the Western is that it provides a universal model for white heroism that its audience understood could be applied anywhere—not just in barely settled Western frontier spaces that most readers well knew were disappearing by the 1890s, but also in the new colonies. Narrated not by the Southerner but by an awe-struck and rather less manly easterner, Wister's novel, like Dixon's, exemplifies how the imitative model of learning behavior could be applied to whites. The final passages of *The Virginian*, however, also encode Wister's doubts about the wisdom of uplift or civilizing narratives, intimating that in the modern world the Southerner may prove more a martyr than a model of success.

Both the paternalistic discourse justifying Jim Crow colonialist policies and the anguished doubts about these policies from authors such as Dixon contrast markedly with the majority of works discussed in part 1. However shadowed their fiction's themes became, Child, Griest, Tourgée, Harper, Griggs, and McClellan struck one shared ground-note: the United States can and should become a multiracial democracy, not an empire with vast wealth and civil liberties disparities, a tiny middle class, and a global plantation system supplying raw materials to an centralized industrial economy. For these dissidents, only a liberal arts education could grow the middle class and create a responsible, critically engaged citizenry. They well knew that the liberal arts model was a necessary but not a sufficient condition for building democracy; it was not a panacea and could easily be adapted to justifying undemocratic values, such as elitism and racism. But both Twain's rage and the unkillable idealism in Tolentino's suppressed play have much to teach us too. Regardless of our color, unless we learn the difference between democracy and empire, as well as the ways in which these two political systems have historically been connected, citizens can be little more than subjects.

# Chapter Six

# Ghosts of Reconstruction

SAMUEL C. ARMSTRONG, BOOKER T. WASHINGTON, AND
THE DISCIPLINARY REGIMES OF JIM CROW COLONIALISM

We, who are a trifle progressive, are called "imperialists," because we are not going to allow the poor Filipinos to vote. Probably we are not going to allow them to vote until we are satisfied they can vote intelligently; but, just as certainly, when the time comes that the islanders are qualified to exercise the right of suffrage they will get it. In all human probability they will secure it sooner than some of the negro population in some of the Southern States. Gentlemen of the South, gentlemen of Dixie—some of us imperialists do not blame you at all for taking all possible legal measures to protect your cherished rights. Will you not forgive us, if we pursue the same policy with regard to a new and untried race?

... The people [of the Philippines] are intelligent and kindly and are imbued with republican principles. To say that we want to enslave these people is a slander. To say that we shall not improve their condition is to contradict history.

—CHARLES DENBY, "What Shall We Do with the Philippines?"

The effectiveness of disfranchisement is suggested by a comparison of the number of registered Negro voters in Louisiana in 1896, when there were 130,334, and in 1904, when there were 1,342.

—C. VANN WOODWARD, *Strange Career of Jim Crow*

"Be sure not to forget what your grace promised me about the ínsula; I'll know how to govern it no matter how big it is."

—MIGUEL DE CERVANTES, *Don Quixote*

Southerners were among the U.S. citizens advocating expansion into the Caribbean, Mexico, and other areas, and they also played a central role both before and after the Civil War in the debates about whether an American empire was an inevitable expression of—or a threat to—a healthy democracy. Before the war many southerners envisioned making new slave states of territories such as Cuba to help displace northern dominance in Congress. The so-called Young

Americans group of the 1840s united a younger generation's banking, mercantile, railroad, and political interests, including Stephen A. Douglas of Illinois, George N. Sanders of Kentucky, and Judah P. Benjamin of Louisiana, with visions of Cuban sugar marketed throughout the United States and U.S. wheat, pork, and other products finding a ready market south of the border. Long before 1898, U.S.-based partisans tried to overthrow Spanish rule in the Caribbean, such as Narciso López's three invasions of Cuba between 1849 and 1851 aided by Mexican war veterans, Sanders, and one Jefferson Davis.[1]

After 1865, U.S. expansion into the Caribbean proved a potent temptation for figures who held widely differing views over the Civil War and Reconstruction. J. D. B. De Bow enthusiastically promoted a U.S. tropical empire in the Caribbean, hoping his adopted city of New Orleans would play a major role in this imagined source of growth for a postbellum South, while many Radical Reconstructionists, especially Charles Sumner, vehemently opposed U.S. expansion in the Caribbean on the grounds that it suppressed black rights for nationhood. Frederick Douglass, however, broke with Sumner and allied with Ulysses S. Grant over the issue. Douglass argued, "When the slave power bore rule, and a spirit of injustice and oppression animated and controlled every part of our government, I was for limiting our dominion to the smallest possible margin; but since liberty and equality have become the law of our land, I am for extending our dominion whenever and wherever such extension can peaceably and honorably, and with the approval and desire of all the parties concerned, be accomplished" (*Life and Times* 417). Douglass tried carefully to qualify this 1881 statement regarding the United States' right of "dominion": "To me [annexation] meant the alliance of a weak and defenceless people, having few or none of the attributes of a nation, torn and rent by internal feuds, unable to maintain order at home, or command respect abroad, to a government which would give it peace, stability, prosperity, and civilization, and make it helpful to both countries. To favor annexation at the time when Santo Domingo asked for a place in our union, was a very different thing from what it was when Cuba and Central America were sought by filibustering expeditions" (*Life and Times* 416–417).

Douglass hoped that Santo Domingo might eventually become the first U.S state with a majority black population. Later in *Life and Times*, when Douglass denounces the collapse of Reconstruction and the rise of Jim Crow, he considerably complicates his portrait of the postwar U.S. as a dominion bringing freedom. Analyzing the causes of the betrayal of Reconstruction in the U.S. South, Douglass's language shifts and sounds positively anti-colonial. For U.S. southern rather than Caribbean blacks, dreams of citizenship have been betrayed by "strangers, foreigners, invaders, trespassers, aliens, and enemies" (513). Given the era's events, it is hardly surprising that Douglass had trouble acknowledging, much less solving, this contradiction in his life and times.

U.S. dominion in the Caribbean proved so attractive a possibility after the Civil War that it brought under its sway not just Douglass but white southerners who had been firmly against both abolition and Reconstruction. Indeed, as the historian Moon-ho Jung has shown, Chinese laborers were imported to work the sugarcane fields of Louisiana following Caribbean plantation models; it was felt that the Chinese racial mixture of docility and industry would serve as a competitive role model to blacks, whose work ethic whites believed would otherwise degenerate in freedom. With the rise of the New South in the late 1870s and the 1880s, it is true that many southerners strongly opposed U.S. expansionism for racist reasons, arguing that the last thing the body politic needed was responsibility for even more "colored" dependents. But key southerners before and after the heady victories of 1898 supported further links between the U.S. South and the Caribbean and the South Pacific, in part because they felt the southern economy, especially cane and cotton growers and mill owners, would directly benefit.

As colonial trade and cultural uplift became central elements of Progressivism at the turn to the twentieth century, public discourses advocating democratic rights and economic development in nascent colonial republics protected by U.S. power clashed with policy-makers' determination to control the economies and politics of the newly owned territories. Theodore Roosevelt shaped a new understanding of the Monroe Doctrine so that it now meant that the United States had a right to ensure that European colonial rivals did not use debt problems or trade monopolies to gain undue influence over any country in the hemisphere or the Philippines. He also generally agreed with white southerners that the mistake made during Reconstruction was giving blacks voting rights too soon. Progressivist arguments for expansion quickly found support from Republicans like President McKinley, independents like Roosevelt, and key southern Democrats. It was a southern Democrat, Woodrow Wilson, after all, whose presidency simultaneously instituted Jim Crow segregation as standard government procedure in the nation's capital while vigorously extending U.S. colonial domination abroad. Wilson continued support of a U.S.-friendly Nicaraguan government set up in 1911; made Haiti a protectorate in 1915; and directed the invasion and military rule of the Dominican Republic in 1916 and Cuba in 1917, among other events. By 1920 the United States had 120,000 troops stationed in eight overseas territories (Heffernan 119). These interventions were justified as strategic self-interest, but also invoked were arguments stressing altruism—the white man's burden to export democracy and modernity to barbaric peoples.[2]

White supremacism in this era was as explosive as dynamite, Alfred Nobel's recent invention; it did not necessarily bond easily with arguments for empire that conceded empire might be difficult and white rule would not go unchallenged. Kipling's poem that made famous the phrase "the White Man's burden," after all, was as much a warning as it was a challenge. But it did memorably suggest that the United States would never enter adult maturity as a nation unless it realized its destiny as an imperial power: "Take up the White Man's burden/Have done with childish days." Promoters of U.S. expansionism had to work mightily to prove that acquiring colonies would be beneficial to whites both at home and abroad, and would allow the United States to compete successfully with European empires across the globe. They also had to demonstrate that any changes instituted in the new colonies in the name of modernization would give people of color limited political and economic rights but not threaten the status of whites in charge.

In striking such a delicate balance in U.S. imperial discourse, the example of the New South played an absolutely crucial role. In the post-1898 period, Reconstruction was frequently invoked as both a key precedent and cautionary tale for the new colonialism. If Reconstruction was so roundly rejected by so many by 1877, how can we explain this curious afterlife? Beginning in the 1890s, after the rise of the New South, there was a huge surge of new studies of the postwar period published by academic historians. What connections might we find between these new revisionary histories of Reconstruction and the contemporary debates over expansionism abroad? Another large question: How can we explain that just as the limited civil rights legislated for blacks during Reconstruction were being curtailed in the 1880s and 1890s, U.S. expansion abroad was justified in part because it would *bring* democratic rights to oppressed peoples abroad? Was this contradiction merely an example of hypocrisy, a dissonance that went willfully ignored? Or did pro-expansion Progressivists try to explain such anomalies by claiming that peoples of color at home and abroad were not denied civil rights, but rather were being tutored how to *gain* such rights and enter modernity?

Critiquing how the white man's burden was understood in the United States, we must understand that the creation of citizens-as-subjects also involves the subjection of people of color, the attempt firmly to delineate limits within which they may exercise their newly created political and economic power. To comprehend such a paradox in action we must think historically, which means returning to the history of Reconstruction, the first self-consciously national program in the United States designed to construct new citizens of color fit for democracy. As we do so, we may want to remember that John Philip Sousa moved without missing a beat from composing the "King Cotton" march for the Cotton States Exposition in Atlanta in 1895 to writing "El Capitán" —which, after its Broadway debut in 1896 in a comic operetta satirizing Spanish colonial rule, became so popular it was played on board Admiral George Dewey's flagship as it steamed into Manila Bay in the Philippines in 1898.[3]

1

When C. Vann Woodward in 1951, in the midst of the Cold War, linked the disfranchisement of black voters throughout the South to U.S. colonial policies in the tropics, his analysis was as correct as it was daring. But it was also perhaps too narrow, lacking the emphasis on irony for which *Origins of the New South* justly became famous. Woodward's claim of a link between disfranchisement and colonialism also had a contradiction at its heart that has not been analyzed closely enough.

Woodward suggested that the "Second Mississippi Plan" for un-registering black voters gained notice throughout the South in the 1890s after the scare of Populism, but that it was only after Booker T. Washington's "Atlanta Compromise" speech of 1895 and the Supreme Court's endorsement of the Second Mississippi Plan in 1898 that the majority of ex-Confederate states, plus Texas, Oklahoma, and Arkansas, followed suit (321–323). "In the meantime," Woodward pointed out, "the North had taken up the White Man's Burden, and by 1898 was looking to Southern racial policy for national guidance in the new problems of imperialism resulting from the Spanish war" (324). Here Woodward implied that southern practices restricting black voting had become a unified "policy" by 1898 and *only after that date* were adopted as a model for U.S. colonial rule.

Yet elsewhere Woodward stated that in some cases the southern states' new suffrage restrictions used emerging U.S. colonial policy in Hawaii as a model, not just Mississippi. The relevant passage is worth extended quotation:

Commenting on the Supreme Court's opinion upholding disfranchisement in Mississippi, the *Nation* pronounced it "an interesting coincidence that this important decision is rendered at a time when we are considering the idea of taking in a varied assortment of inferior races in different parts of the world" —races "which, of course, could not be allowed to vote." Senator Morgan of Alabama was chairman of the committee of the Hawaiian Commission that framed the voting restrictions for one "assortment of inferior races." To reject the property and literacy tests recommended for Hawaiians, reported the Senator, would be to "turn the legislature over to the masses" and "deprive the more conservative elements and property owners of effective representation." Senator Morgan's advice was also sought by the white-supremacy advocates of his own state who were currently debating additional franchise restrictions for Alabama. A speech in defense of American imperialism by George F. Hoar "most amply vindicated the South," said Senator John L. McLaurin of South Carolina.

He thanked the Massachusetts statesman "for his complete announcement of the divine right of the Caucasian to govern the inferior races." The Boston *Evening Transcript* reluctantly admitted that the Southern way was "now the policy of the Administration of the very party which carried the country into and through a civil war to free the slave."

Events in the Philippines soon indicated that the Mississippi Plan had become the American Way. (*Origins of the New South* 324–325)

In other words, before the Mississippi Plan to control voters of color spread throughout the South, it was first reconceived as a valid national or American plan. For this to occur, the Mississippi Plan was field-tested, so to speak, in a new U.S. colony abroad. Versions of Mississippi's tactics may well have been adopted by the entire South without the acquisition of Hawaii or a war with Spain: several cities in Tennessee, for example, had experimented with a plan to reduce voter rolls in the 1880s. But many voting districts in the South still had large numbers of black voters as late as 1898, and the sudden acquisition of overseas colonies and national debates about limited suffrage in the colonies transformed how Jim Crow disfranchisement tactics were understood and justified.[4]

Given the ambiguity about the Mississippi Plan's origins in Woodward's *Origins*, perhaps we should briefly revisit the issue of suffrage in the colonies and not focus so exclusively, as Woodward does, on instances of North/South agreement on black disfranchisement. Instead of using a narrative that assumes policies regarding voting rights were internally coherent and worked out in one domain before applied to another, I want to explore whether new "domestic" and "colonial" policies regarding citizens' rights were *mutually constitutive*, emerging together in the crucial period of the late 1890s. What precedents and arguments were used to validate Mississippi-style tests for voters? What does it mean that public forms of racial segregation were adopted for newly occupied colonial cities such as Manila or Havana *before* they were instituted throughout the South? When we investigate answers to such questions, we notice immediately that whites' experiences during Reconstruction were repeatedly invoked to justify these developments, bolstered by quotations about the white man's burden and the clash of civilizations. We also will quickly notice that U.S. colonial policies—especially regarding education and voting rights—were not homogeneous or internally consistent from colony to colony. In part this was because the policies developed incrementally. But we may also understand that the internal contradictions in imperial policies and discourses are similar to those in both Reconstruction and the post-1877 New South—the nation's first and second large-scale programs for regime change and citizen making.

A complex Progressivist narrative of discipline and uplift, not outright exclusion, was used to justify the white man's burden toward people of color at home and abroad. For this reason, I suggest the term "Jim Crow colonialism" as being most appropriate for these and related policies. Highly paternal, Jim Crow colonial policies stressed the strategic use of both violence and other forms of punishment *and* narratives of patient nurturing that presented U.S. goals as being altruistic and innocent as well as pragmatic. But by making racial segregation a key practice of U.S. colonial policy, a new dimension was introduced: Jim Crow effectively became national policy after 1898, not merely regional and southern. Further, this new, more explicitly codified form of segregation in public places was understood as just one element in the United States' plans for the proper uplift and development of backward peoples. Just as their economic, educational, and political systems would be hauled into the modern era, so too would their race relations. Jim Crow colonialism, in short, was a key constituent of Progressivism.[5]

Recently a number of scholars, most notably Amy Kaplan, have stressed the ways in which the United States' new imperial discourses positioned the new colonies in a liminal space that was both "belonging to" and "not a part of" the U.S. proper. Reading the Supreme Court decisions now known as the Insular Cases, Kaplan unpacks the paradoxes involved when discourses of the "domestic" and the "nation" are dependent upon their antitheses: the justices "repeatedly conjured an image of Puerto Rico as a 'disembodied shade' that lurked around the edges of the embodied nation" (*Anarchy of Empire* 5). I will take a complementary approach here, stressing the ways in which both the New South and the new colonies were seen as necessary *correctives* to the failed program of Reconstruction that nevertheless retained many of Reconstruction's large ambitions. In my approach the stress is not so much on liminality as it is on centrality. For Jim Crow colonialists, Reconstruction's attempts to build a modern democratic citizenry and economic infrastructures would be repeated both in the South and abroad—but this time the United States would get it right. Progressivist social policies—especially those involving political rights and education reforms—applied models of development to both the South and the colonies, assuming close parallels, not fundamental differences, between the future of the re-annexed South and that of the newly acquired tropical colonies. Yet just as federal Reconstruction was not a single government policy and was full of contradictions—as historians such as Woodward, John Hope Franklin, Eric Foner, and Saidiya Hartman have shown—so too U.S. colonial policies in the 1890s and beyond were defined not by a single discourse but by a set of competing narratives that proved impossible to synthesize. No matter how disparate, however, such narratives did find one point of agreement: the postwar U.S. South provided both models and cautionary tales for U.S. colonial development.[6]

2

One representative example of how contemporary debate linked New South and colonial development is Charles Denby's article "What Shall We Do with the Philippines?" excerpted as an epigraph for this chapter. It appeared in 1899 in the *Forum*, a major public policy journal of the Progressive era. Alluding to the vigorous anti-imperialist debates of the time, Denby downplays their arguments that the conquered lands deserved independence, not U.S. supervision. He invoked white rule in the United States after Reconstruction as a valuable precedent and then, revealingly, focused on both Jim Crow and U.S. colonialism as policies of improved Reconstruction—policies that fixed Reconstruction's excesses and, this time, gave a properly controlled education in self-government to peoples who had suffered enslavement and cultural impoverishment. The U.S. South's "peculiar institution" and Spanish colonial rule were cast as similar villains (both caused broad cultural degeneration, though they partially "civilized" Africans). With the overthrow of slavery and colonialism both territories were seen by Denby as being liberated into the light of modernity and progress. Denby, it should be added, also qualified his vision of the supervised progress of the colored races in an important way, suggesting that because blacks were the most inferior race their rate of advance might be slowest.[7]

To examine further the ways in which late nineteenth-century U.S. racial discourse, including colonialism, legitimized itself via allusions to Reconstruction and the post-1877 South, let us turn to John W. Burgess's *Reconstruction and the Constitution* (1902). A leading public intellectual of the time, Burgess had two goals in publishing *Reconstruction:* to validate the New South's revisionary history of Reconstruction, and to invoke this corrected and modified version of Reconstruction, now embodied in the New South, as a precedent for U.S. global power. The praiseworthy aim of Reconstruction, in Burgess's words, was "to secure the civil rights of the newly emancipated race, and to re-establish loyal Commonwealths in the South" (vii). "Two ways were open for the attainment of the end sought": the first was to place "political power in the hands of the newly emancipated"; the second Burgess termed "the nationalization of civil liberty by placing it under the protection of the Constitution and the national Judiciary, and holding the districts of the South under Territorial civil government until the white race in those districts should have sufficiently recovered from its temporary disloyalty to the Union to be intrusted again with the powers of Commonwealth local government" (vii–viii). In Burgess's view, Reconstruction made the disastrous first choice, giving too much power to the newly emancipated, while the New South proved the wisdom of the alternative. Note how in Burgess's description of what that proper alternative is in the quotation above, he glides in mid-sentence from stressing the importance of a strong federal government to lauding the return of white rule.

Burgess believed Reconstruction was the most significant transformation of federal power in U.S. history, after the 1787 Constitution itself. He argued that this new power had been tragically misapplied, in effect colonizing white southerners, but that the new federal power assumed during Reconstruction was not in itself malicious. In fact, it would prove absolutely necessary in the postwar global era where strong nations must undertake "imperial enterprises." The United States is learning "every day by valuable experiences that there are vast differences in political capacity between the races, and that it is the white man's mission, his duty and his right, to hold the reins of political power in his own hands for the civilization of the world and the welfare of mankind" (viii–ix). Reconstruction as corrected by white southern rule, then, was a rehearsal for new empire, an example of military rule yielding to a political order installing carefully delimited democracy. Burgess did have later reservations about the compatibility of democracy with empire, most notably developed in his study, *The Reconciliation of Government with Liberty* (1915). But others did not, including Burgess's colleague at Columbia, the sociologist Franklin Giddings, and a professor at Princeton named Woodrow Wilson.

In a 1901 article in the *Atlantic Monthly* entitled "The Reconstruction of the Southern States," Wilson repeated the by then conventional analysis of the "dark chapter" of black rule but, like Burgess, found a positive element too: federal Reconstruction was the first imperfect expression of a new national consciousness in the postwar nation. For Wilson the reunion of North and South unleashed feelings of new patriotism that inevitably expressed themselves in expansion abroad: "Undoubtedly, the impulse of expansion is the natural and wholesome impulse which comes with a consciousness of matured strength; but it is also a direct result of that national spirit which the war between the states cried so wide awake, and to which the processes of Reconstruction gave the subtle assurance of practically unimpeded sway and a free choice of means."[8]

Franklin Giddings's *Democracy and Empire* (1900) assumed that the final stage in the evolution of democracy was expansion and a new form of empire: not the conquest of territory but benevolent dominion over less developed states as they are tutored to make as much of a transition as they are capable of doing from still-feudal postcolonial states to modern democracies. He recognized that for a constitutional democracy, difficult polity and ethics issues were involved in governing any colonies it acquired. Pro-imperialists had some difficulty explaining colonial resistance to U.S. rule, particularly in the Philippines, where U.S. troops' bloody battles with an insurgent army fighting for independence received much coverage in U.S. newspapers. Was it right to educate an unwilling people in U.S.-sanctioned democracy without their consent? A particularly revealing chapter is Giddings's

"The Consent of the Governed." "Consent is more than submission," Giddings stated; "it implies that the consenting person, with full apprehension of the facts, has agreed to a certain conclusion or policy, through an act of his individual reason" (259). But such rational, informed consent was hardly possible, at present, for the population of the Philippines: "if a barbarian people is compelled to accept the authority of a state more advanced in civilization, the test of rightfulness . . . is to be found not at all in any assent or resistance at the moment when the government begins, but only *in the degree of probability* that, after full experience of what the government can do to raise the subject population to a higher plane of life, *a free and rational consent will be given* by those who can come to understand all that has been done" (265, Giddings's italics).

Masquerading as rational, with deep concern for the free interaction of autonomous subjects, Giddings's rhetoric is, of course, circular doublespeak and demonstrates the opposite of what it claims. Filipinos in the above scenario can claim their rights as citizens rather than subjects only by ceding the definition of those rights to the United States. Their rights at present are thus *alienable*, not inalienable, and "free" consent can only be given at an unnamed future date, "after full experience" of the U.S. colonial experiment in disciplinary democracy. Giddings's rationale for the white man's burden was echoed by many, including Woodrow Wilson, who, when lecturing at Columbia in 1907, said in reference to the Philippines, "Self-government . . . is a form of character. It follows upon the long discipline which gives a people self-possession, self-mastery, the habit of order and peace. . . . No people can be 'given' the self-control of maturity. Only a long apprenticeship of obedience can secure them the precious possession" (*Constitutional Government* 52–53).[9]

Giddings's and Wilson's disquisitions on how to interpret the Declaration of Independence's phrase "the consent of the governed" have an intriguing prehistory, for to create their arguments they drew not just on the history of Western political philosophy but also on Senate debates and cartoons about the new colonies appearing in the popular press. The idea that the "consent of the governed" really meant "the consent of *some* of the governed" was famously Senator Orville Platt's. Against senators who argued that constitutional rights applied to the territories, Platt in 1898 sharply distinguished between the rights of inhabitants of states and those in territories; he claimed the latter were governed by the laws of Congress but not the Constitution: "Where is the limitation in the Constitution on the right to acquire? Where is it said in the Constitution that the territory acquired by conquest must be held by the United States for the purpose of admitting States?" Citing various Supreme Court justices, including Chief Justice Bradley, the author of the majority opinion in the "Civil Rights" cases of 1883 that were a crucial step in the Supreme Court's destruction of the Fourteenth and Fifteenth Amendments, Platt stressed Congress's absolute authority; it may not only abrogate laws of the territorial legislatures, but it may itself legislate directly for local governments.

Replying to Senator Hoar's question whether "governments derive their just powers from the consent of the governed," Platt answered, "from the consent of *some* of the governed." Platt then made his key point: "I admit that whenever we stipulate in the acquisition of territory with the country from which we acquire it that we will admit it as a State or States into the Union, we are in honor bound, in the performance of that contract, to do everything we can in a preliminary way to fit that Territory and its people for admission as a State. But when that clause is wanting in the treaty [as with Alaska, Hawaii, Puerto Rico, Cuba, and the Philippines], I deny that there is any constitutional or moral obligation to fit the Territory for statehood." Such reasoning nevertheless asserted Congress's legislative authority over the new colonies, just as it had ultimate authority over territories in the West that were not yet ready for statehood, and just as it had exercised legislative dominion over the southern states after Reconstruction until they were ready to be re-admitted to the Union with rights equal to those of the other states. Platt's suggestion that the white man's burden was in part a pedagogical one was quickly picked up in the popular press, as the Louis Dalrymple cartoon "School Begins" (illustrated and discussed in the introduction) cogently demonstrates. Dalrymple's graphic was especially shrewd in its linkage of federal colonial policies of dependency with Reconstruction, where the southern states were governed "without their consent until they [could] govern themselves."[10]

If southern whites proved capable of joining (or rejoining) the "some of the governed" who properly understood the responsibilities of self-governance, others were thought to be less capable. Consider the wording of the 1898 Supreme Court decision validating the Mississippi Plan: "Under section 244, it is left with the administrative officer to determine whether the applicant reads, understands, or interprets the section of the constitution designated" (*Williams v. Mississippi*, 170 U.S. 213). The Court claimed such tests were racially neutral because some whites took them as well as blacks. Its legal discourse stressed neither exclusion nor coercion toward those who failed, but rather a gradual and sometimes painful education in their future constitutional rights. The Fifteenth Amendment, however, could not have been more plain: "The right of citizens of the United States to vote shall not be denied or abridged by the United States or by any State on account of race, color, or previous condition of servitude." Progressivist racial discourse in the 1890s adeptly translated the "privileges and immunities" guaranteed citizens by the Fourteenth Amendment and the right to vote guaranteed by the Fifteenth Amendment into *rights that could be managed by racial superiors until the distant future moment when they could be understood and claimed.* Rights evolved and had to be earned and understood through proper education and disciplining; they were not inborn. Hence they were not being "denied or abridged" by *Williams v. Mississippi*, according to the Court; they were only being nurtured under beneficent but firm rule. Like "culture" itself,

Fig. 6.1. "[Made Anglo–Saxon] By Act of Congress"

in fact, civil rights in the Progressive era could either progress or degenerate and be lost.

The Progressive era's stance toward blacks treating them as schoolchildren being tutored in democracy had its most immediate precursor in Reconstruction's massive plans to help blacks make the transition from ex-slaves to citizens. But Reconstruction's discourse of uplift and disciplinary tutelage, of course, has an earlier history as well; in the first half of the nineteenth century, similar assumptions were articulated to justify official U.S. policy toward Indians. The most famous instance is Justice John C. Marshall's argument in *Cherokee Nation v. The State of Georgia* (1831) describing the Cherokees being displaced from Georgia to the Oklahoma Territories as "domestic dependent nations" in a "state of pupilage." Despite clear differences in the circumstances Indian nations and ex-slaves found themselves in relation to the United States government, especially its military and legal systems, in the nineteenth century, Marshall's concept of a people as a "ward" with the state as "guardian" (Prucha 59) proved fungible after 1898, particularly with both the *Williams v. Mississippi* Supreme Court decision and emergent U.S. colonial polity.

Given the perceived failures of Reconstruction, there was an obvious tension in Jim Crow colonialist rhetoric between teaching citizenship and maintaining subjection. Fears that blacks (or colored colonials) would "misunderstand" the privileges conferred by the Reconstruction amendments to the Constitution as applying to the present, not the future, found their way into contemporary humor, such as the cartoon (see fig. 6.1) in *Puck*, 7 September 1898, a New York satiric journal that also frequently indulged its readers' taste for minstrel-style portraits of blacks in the New South in the context of pro-imperial rhetoric.

The cartoon's caption reads:

By Act of Congress.

Mr. Johnson — I'se in favor ob de Anglo-Saxon alliance eb'ry time!

Mr. Black — G'wan! Yo' ain't no Anglo-Saxon.

Mr. Johnson — Cou'se I is! We's all Anglo-Saxons sence de Fifteent' 'Mendment wuz passed.

## 3

John Carlos Rowe, Oscar Campomanes, and others have persuasively argued that U.S. expansionism has a long history of justifying itself as anti-colonial or anti-imperial.[11] Allegedly, it builds independent republics, never colonies, by tutoring territories under its sovereignty to enter modernity. Such claims were very common at the turn to the twentieth century in particular, when debate over what having an "empire" would do to the United States as a democracy was vociferous. Like many expansionist movements before it, Progressivism asserted that the United States would be "exceptional" and exempt from the decline of past civilizations if the new U.S. power formations corrected the errors of previous empires and ruled by trade and education and "influence," not coercion. In addition, one of Progressivism's distinctive contributions to the U.S. discourse of imperialism was to follow Frederick Douglass's lead and synthesize the most powerful reformist rhetoric of the antebellum United States—that of abolitionism—to the late Victorian discourses of evolution and progress. It was a powerful mix. Here is Theodore Roosevelt in 1901: "It is our duty toward the people living in barbarism to see that they are freed from their chains."[12]

Roosevelt's recycled abolitionist rhetoric was hardly unusual. Kristin Hoganson has explained why even before 1898 many white Americans supported mixed-race Cubans against Spain: U.S. newspapers cast the struggle for independence as an adventure-filled chivalric romance, temporarily overriding negative racial stereotypes (45). After 1898, though, Americans saw themselves, not the Cubans, as the heroic knights. The 1898 photograph on the cover of Nina Silber's *The Romance of Reunion: Northerners and the South, 1865–1900*, shows a Rebel and a Union officer clasping hands in front of a young girl representing Cuba, whom they have united to liberate. In a classic pose adopted from antebellum abolitionist iconography, the ex-captive raises high an arm holding her broken chains. If abolitionism focused on liberating blacks, the new imperial rhetoric of the 1890s claimed to liberate peoples of all colors from their benighted cultural imprisonment. But the new colonialism was arguably also intent on liberating *whiteness*. It is no coincidence that the "Cuban" girl in Silber's cover photograph is blonde, or that countless new imperialists, most notably Rudyard Kipling and Theodore Roosevelt, stressed how colonial activism re-energized and matured white males. The imperial trope of reinvigorated whiteness had long been a staple of colonialist/settler discourse, most notably in the captivity narratives that were best-sellers in the eighteenth and early nineteenth centuries. But Progressivism's innovation at the end of the nineteenth century was to redefine the melodrama of white identity under siege. Anti-Reconstruction literature of the white South had portrayed white southerners enslaved by savages, victims of a demonic reversal of proper colonialism who were emancipated only by the rise of the white-rule "Redeemers" of the New South. At their most melodramatic, the new Progressivist arguments for expansionism abroad also exploited white rescue narratives in order to spike popular support. In this way, Progressivist imperialism under Roosevelt and others stripped away the careful qualifications Frederick Douglass had attempted to apply to his arguments for the United States' right of dominion abroad. Unlike Douglass, the United States no more dreamed of allowing independent states ruled by people of color in its territories abroad than it had allowed blacks to keep power long in the former Confederate states. The alleged fiasco of black rule during Reconstruction made such new colonial policies appear rational and prudent, even as they were also cast as inheriting all the moral righteousness of the anti-slavery movement. Revising Reconstruction history, Dunning, Giddings, and their followers made a powerful case for limiting suffrage in the colonies and closing down the questions of whether colonial subjects could vote in U.S. national elections, or whether colonies could eventually become states.

As the United States in the late nineteenth and early twentieth century rearticulated itself as the vigorous new scion of a centuries-long tradition of Anglo-Saxon civilization-building, a crisis in the very definition of race became unavoidable—not just among race theorists in biology and anthropology, but also in U.S. political and literary discourse. By the turn of the century, contradictions and inconsistencies mounted in studies attempting to define racial difference in physical terms. "Scientific" works attempting to ground race in skull, hair, skin, and even fingerprint differences had not disappeared, but increasingly after 1880 they had to compete for authority with studies arguing that the primary differences among the races were matters of character and culture, history and learning ability. Many Progressivists accepted the new scientific skepticism regarding efforts to define race in terms of quantifiable biological difference (blood, skull shape, etc.), in favor of an emphasis on group differences defined in part by blood but mostly by acculturation—by "character" shaped by a group's cultural history. As Walter Benn Michaels has helped us understand, such "race-into-culture" discourses hardly resolved the issue of whether allegedly "racial" characteristics were innate or learned. But they did assume that individual and group character were not fixed but could develop and mature—within certain limits—or degenerate. One example is the anthropologist Franz Boas's *Changes in Bodily Form of Descendents of Immigrants* (1912), a study funded by the U.S. Immigration Commission. Boas debunked racial phenotypes as a reliable system of classification, in part because "bodily form" did not remain stable from one generation to the next, particularly with intermixture of racial and ethnic types in the United States. Instead, Boas promoted anthropometric studies of culture and behavioral traits. Although many of his contemporaries hardly agreed that "race" was an illusion, much less were accepting of his thesis that U.S. history charted the gradual amalgamation of Indian, Negro, and white, Boas's emphasis on observable "character" being more reliable than visual signifiers was widely shared well before 1912. Such shifts in the meanings of "racial" difference had a pronounced impact on U.S. Progressivist policies both at home and abroad—especially those foregrounding the importance of education.

"Character" in the late nineteenth-century context, as Cathy Boeckmann has demonstrated, meant the ability to govern one's immediate desires in order to achieve long-term goals. One racial group—Anglo-Saxons—allegedly had an abundance of this talent for deferred gratification, and only this group was thus fit to rule over others for their own good or to incapacitate them by competition. In moving racial difference even partially and incompletely away from visual signs that could be read toward a set of interior characteristics that were learned and then performed, however, such discourses made whiteness rather unstable. Whiteness became not a firm racial essence but a characteristic that could be lost if performed poorly or stolen and worn as a mask. It was no longer a status biologically guaranteed, but a heritage, a quality of behavior, and a set of rights that could be betrayed or learned.[13]

Furthermore, by tying racial difference more closely to character than it had ever been, Progressivist race discourse linked it to the development and modernization of a nation managed by enlightened white rule. For if race defined an individual's and a group's potential, then racial identity could be properly or improperly nurtured by one's environment. Whites were assumed to be superior, but they could only be properly trained to their role by a modern racial state governed in their interest. However we define it, Progressivism was replete with paradox. One way to think of Progressivism was as a discourse of social engineering helping different groups progress at different rates determined by their inner destiny. But by the late nineteenth century, the fate of racial identity paralleled that of rights: neither was inalienable; like character, they had continuously to be performed and claimed.

Nancy Cohen's recent study of Progressivism and its precursors has added important nuances to our understanding of the contradictions in the "free labor" ideology that undergirded both abolitionism and Reconstruction. As both Eric Foner and Saidiya Hartman have shown, free labor ideology stressed how only wage labor could create the self-discipline necessary for responsible citizenship. In "A Civilizer's Errand: Southern Man, the Politics of Free Labor, and the 'Race Question'" in *The Reconstruction of American Liberalism, 1865–1914*, Cohen asks why many white northern supporters of Reconstruction during the crucial 1865–68 period favored free labor contracts for the freemen, but not land redistribution. Her answer: the northerners' free labor ideology claimed that saving one's wages from fairly negotiated labor contracts would best educate former slaves in the responsibilities of citizenry, not gifts of confiscated land. The majority of white supporters of Reconstruction never campaigned openly to prevent many confiscated southern farms and plantations from being returned to their original owners or other white claimants. Further, Cohen rightly stresses that such attitudes were classically colonialist: the "colonialist character of the Northern project reached its most refined development among Radicals who opposed land redistribution. Economic transformation, accomplished through political and military domination, would remake the people of the South, and civilization would thus be implanted in the dark corner of the nation" (65).[14]

By the 1870s, as northern support for Reconstruction waned, northern liberals and New South Democrats came to agree that it had been a disastrous mistake to give freedmen suffrage. They also agreed that it was naïve to believe contract labor would quickly erase the bad habits of slavery. Summarizing the arguments in James S. Pike's *The Prostrate State* (1874) and Charles Nordhoff's *The Cotton States in the Spring and Summer of 1875* (1876), two important texts legitimating the northern retreat on Reconstruction, Cohen says, "Pike and Nordhoff agreed that a long apprenticeship as agricultural laborers would do the best good for the free person's chance at evolution. Both waffled, however, on whether the old Southern planters or a new breed of superior Northerners would make the best trustees. This ambiguity marked the contradiction of forging a colonial model of development for a region within the territory of a liberal nation-state" (83–84). Over the next decade and more, the New South's solution to that contradiction consisted in having it both ways—further encouraging northern capital's presence in the South while simultaneously stressing southern independence and a supposedly modernized plantation staple-crop economy employing labor that euphemistically was said to be "share-cropping."

Cohen did not consider the question of how central such discourses of disciplinary reform were to Progressivist colonial policies abroad. In the new colonies, what would the new schools for democracy teach? How would the teachers be taught? It is time now to examine briefly new discoveries by historians concerning the most influential example in the New South and Progressivist periods of constructing an "education in modernity" for people of color—the Hampton/ Tuskegee "industrial education" model. Here too we will find New South and colonial histories inextricably convolved—and both haunted by Reconstruction's earlier, more ambitious dreams of school and citizen building.

4

Consider first some startling facts. Booker T. Washington's Hawaiian-born mentor, Samuel Chapman Armstrong, used a model of missionary education in Hawaii for his Hampton Institute in Virginia for educating blacks, founded in the height of Reconstruction, in 1868. Later, Armstrong also enrolled students from Cuba and Puerto Rico, though not without numerous discipline problems, and also Native American students; indeed, Hampton was an important model for Richard Henry Pratt's Carlisle Indian Institute in Pennsylvania. Some black leaders, most notably William S. Scarborough of Wilberforce University, argued that U.S.-born blacks were uniquely qualified to elevate the backward peoples of the Orient and Africa. The U.S. Federal Bureau of Education and the Hampton educator Thomas Jesse Jones promoted Booker T. Washington's Tuskegee Institute to the British for their educational efforts in Africa, while Germany recruited Tuskegee experts to demonstrate advances in cotton cultivation in its African colonies (Anderson 257, Gatewood 296–297). José-Manuel Navarro has described the influence of the Hampton/Tuskegee model of manual education on reforms instituted in Puerto Rican schools during the first decade of U.S. control—many of them supervised by U.S. government officials who had extensive previous work with the Freedmen's Bureau after the Civil War.

With the rise of poststructuralist and postcolonial criticism, the careers of Samuel Chapman Armstrong and Booker T. Washington have received renewed attention. Two notable examples are Robert Engs's biography of the former and Houston Baker's meditation on the latter. Baker stresses the Foucauldian aspects of Washington's Tuskegee as a modernized plantation for the control, not the freeing, of black labor. Armstrong's life, as discussed by Engs, unforgettably demonstrates ties between the reformist agendas of Reconstruction, Christian missionary efforts, and emergent U.S. colonial policies. Samuel Armstrong's father, Richard, was a Baptist missionary in Hawaii, where Samuel spent his boyhood, and he passed on to his son a devotion to making people of the colored races respectable through educational methods that built character by teaching the manual skills necessary for farming and other trades. But, as Engs points out, few natives became independent farmers in the mid-nineteenth century after such schooling; increasingly, Hawaiian land was owned by the families of European and U.S. missionaries and businessmen, who established cattle ranches and sugar cane and pineapple plantations. The efforts of Richard Armstrong, "no matter how well intended, were not so much training the indigenous population for self-sufficiency as preparing them for labor on white-owned lands" (Engs 21). Other schools sprang up in Hawaii that were run on the Armstrong model, such as Uldrick Thompson's Kamehameha School for Girls and Boys (discussed in the introduction), which trained its students for non-plantation labor. But these schools, too, focused on job training, not liberal arts instruction.

Richard Armstrong's son Samuel went to Williams College, fought at Gettysburg, led a Negro regiment, and then was a Freedmen's Bureau agent stationed at Hampton, Virginia. As early as 1866, he began appealing to northern philanthropists to support his vision of black education, described in his essay "Lessons from the Hawaiian Islands" as follows: "deficiency of character is the chief difficulty[;] ... to build up character is the true objective point of education, ... largely on a routine of industrious habit" (Engs 74). This educational model became the keystone for the Hampton Institute.

Experiments in a "practical" rather than liberal arts education for blacks began in the eighteenth century with Thomas Jefferson and were a feature of several schemes proposed by abolitionists and others in the antebellum years. But in the nineteenth century the most influential version of this educational ideology was the so-called Hampton/Tuskegee model, a joint product of Colonel Samuel Chapman Armstrong at Hampton and his one-time pupil Booker T. Washington in Tuskegee, Alabama. Called "industrial" education to give this educational method the caché of modernity, this approach trained blacks for only a limited number of professions, and many were hardly what we would call industrial. Its agricultural course sequence followed the Hawaiian model most closely, stressing "farming and market gardening" skills. Other course sequences were commercial (bookkeeping, business letters and contracts, some commercial law) and mechanical (sewing machines, penmanship, drawing, printing). Canning and meat-packing and sawmill skills were taught, to be sure—in fact, Hampton's financial agent opened a meat-packing and canning factory on the institute's grounds in 1879, using cheap student labor. Most of the skills taught at Hampton, however, could properly be called pre-industrial, such as farming, blacksmithing, and shoe-making, plus classes in how to wait tables and wash dishes for the men and, for the women, sewing, clothes repair, gardening, and cooking, but not stenography or typing. Further, enrolled students repeatedly protested that their classes did not accomplish their goals. The carpentry classes at Hampton, for instance, may have focused on building window frames, not whole houses (Anderson 59–60). And the school's vision of social change did not address the question of what carpenters or other construction workers would be allowed to build after they graduated, or whether they could open independent businesses and become self-employed "free" labor.

Training teachers was emphasized as much as any other work. As a promotional pamphlet for Hampton assembled by Helen Ludlow proclaimed, "Since 1868, the school's graduates have taught more than 150,000 children in eighteen states in the South and West" (last page, unnumbered). Although Ludlow boasted vaguely that "almost every one" of Hampton's graduates became land-buyers (11), those who know the Jim Crow South may be more skeptical.[15] What Ludlow's statistics do reveal is that dropouts (called "ex-students") far outnumbered graduates: over 5,000 versus 1,101 (last page). If the Hampton/Tuskegee model can indeed be properly called industrial, it is only because of its machine-like efficiency in generating donor money and good publicity.[16]

As James D. Anderson convincingly has demonstrated, ex-slaves wanted training and employment opportunities in all practical professions. At the same time, though, resistance to such a narrowly industrial or vocational model of education was consistent, as measured by the broad spectrum of black community opinion; many wanted the stronger presence of a liberal arts curriculum as an option, funds to support an extensive and modern public school system (not just select privately run schools like Hampton), and educational results that would increase social mobility and black community prosperity rather than legitimizing stratification. True, most students at Hampton took some courses in English, with particular emphasis on spelling, grammar, composition, and elocution; geography; mathematics; history (English and American, but also "Universal History"); some classes also in natural science; and the "leading principles of mental and moral science, and of political economy" (Engs 78; see also 104–105). So the basics for a liberal arts curriculum were in place. But these proto-liberal arts courses received much less emphasis than vocational training at Hampton.

Even though some of the privately funded colleges, universities, and Normal (teacher-training) schools had stronger versions of a liberal arts curriculum, schools following the Hampton/Tuskegee model were consistently the best funded in the 1890–1920 period, often receiving considerable support from both white religious organizations and white businessmen. Northern religious support for the freed slaves and their children tended by the late 1870s to focus increasingly on a few select black colleges, unlike the interest in primary and secondary education immediately after the Civil War—thus in effect leaving black communities to fend for themselves to educate their children. Northern philanthropic intervention financially supporting select, high-status black schools in the South like Hampton and Tuskegee must be understood as a response to the subversion of other means through public policy for funding a well-organized, universal school system with a diverse curriculum for blacks. A limited number of grades and a focus primarily on practical education were assumed by the vast majority of whites in debates about black education well into the 1930s.[17]

Because the Hampton Institute was seen as a valuable generator of trained hands to meet job needs in those parts of the economy deemed appropriate for blacks, Armstrong's institution received land grants from the white power structure in the state, and as it grew its dominant center building remained a rehabilitated and refurbished "Big House" from a former plantation. In the end, Armstrong and Washington may have promoted their work as creating self-employed entrepreneurs and citizens, not dependents, but what they actually *produced* in their schools were laborers on spec for demands set by others. Washington's 1895 "Atlanta Compromise" speech at the Cotton Exposition validated trading away not just black voting rights but also blacks' ability to choose a liberal arts education—all in order to create a trained manual worker pool that he said would better allow southern white employers to compete against cheap immigrant labor in the North and West and in the new colonies.[18]

## 5

As the United States moved into the new century, Armstrong's and Washington's dependency model for black education was chosen to guide official U.S. colonial educational policies in Puerto Rico and the Philippines. These policies preached the creation of a self-sufficient citizenry through "Americanization," yet produced graduates trained to match the caste divisions and labor needs of the new colonial societies. The fullest study documenting the influence of the industrial education model on U.S. colonial policy makers is José-Manuel Navarro's *Creating Tropical Yankees: Social Science Textbooks and U.S. Ideological Control in Puerto Rico, 1898–1908*. Official government reports by the "Porto Rico" and Philippine Commissions to President McKinley in 1899 and 1900 were full of paternalist optimism reminiscent of the heady early days of Reconstruction.[19] The Puerto Ricans and Filipinos were seen as recently liberated victims of a decadent and pre-modern Spanish social system who needed to be taught values of education and modernity that could only come from the United States. "Put an American schoolhouse in every valley and upon every hilltop in Porto Rico, and in these place the well-fitted and accomplished American schoolteachers, and the cloud of ignorance will disappear as the fog flies before the morning sun" (53; quoted in Navarro 35). A flock of white American women migrated to the island to teach in the regular and teacher-training schools, much like the many white northern women who went South to teach after the Civil War. Furthermore, those in charge of colonial educational policy were often key figures in the Civil War and Reconstruction—such as General John Eaton, who before heading the Bureau of Education in Puerto Rico had extensive experience as a Union officer, a supervisor of seven hundred thousand ex-slaves following the Union armies, and a Freedmen's Bureau agent organizing schools throughout the Mississippi valley (Navarro 44–45).

Charles De Garmo's life encapsulated this pattern. A professor of education at Cornell University, De Garmo issued an educational progress report at the request of the new president, Theodore Roosevelt, that not only argued for an industrial education model; it explained precisely how and why such new and improved Reconstruction policies should be adapted for Puerto Rico:

> For a long time after the close of our civil war it was thought that all we needed to do to make the former slaves self-respecting, self-supporting, and self-governing was to train their minds in the same way that the sons of ministers and college professors were trained in the North. The idea did not occur to us that Latin would not have the same transforming influence upon the mind of the black men.... It is only now, after some thirty or more years of experiment, that we are fitting our education to the social and economic needs of these people, and it is a striking fact that the best type of education to-day is found in the colored and Indian schools for industrial training.... Porto Rico is in a position to profit by this long and extensive experimentation in the United States. (*Report of the Commissioner of Education*, 1903; cited in Navarro 73–74)

A better example could probably not be found of how a revisionary and selective history of Reconstruction grounded post-1898 U.S. colonial policies, especially when education was concerned. Notable underneath De Garmo's pseudo-scientific language and smooth complacency is his assumption that pragmatism involves recognizing mental differences caused by race, not just "social and economic needs." As in much of the rhetoric associated with both Reconstruction and Progressivism, De Garmo preaches the social construction of economic and civic independence while signaling that these will be trumped by racial limitations requiring dependency and supervision, training for the manual labor needs of the new U.S.-dominated colonial economy.

Despite the lofty discourse about building an island-wide public school system that would "Americanize" Puerto Ricans and open the doors of opportunity to those with a strong work ethic, the statistics tell another tale. In 1902 and 1903, there were 427 public common schools with eight grades in Puerto Rican towns, but these were only 25 percent of the total in these areas, and in the countryside 75 percent of the schools had no more than three grades (Navarro 72–73). Admittedly, this fledgling school system in Puerto Rico—unlike that in the post-Reconstruction South—was seen as a *federal* as well as local responsibility. What had been deemed inappropriate for U.S. blacks was now validated for new colonial subjects as official U.S. government policy. Historians have concluded that the new education system in Puerto Rico largely reinforced rather than challenged local employment patterns, caste divisions, and poverty, though some individual graduates certainly were unprecedented success stories. Its effects thus paralleled those of new schools for children of color in Hawaii and in the U.S. South, though the Puerto Rican system was federally mandated and maintained.[20]

Let us now turn to works of imaginative literature to see how such works might test this chapter's thesis that Reconstruction's dependency model for black education morphed with the rise of Jim Crow colonialism into new forms of uplift-bondage and perpetual sitting in darkness. We will find that interpreting the phrase "the consent of the governed" proves a more complicated and morally ambiguous task than Senator Orville Platt or Frankling Giddings assumed. Writers such as Albion Tourgée or Sutton Griggs or Frances Harper or George Marion McClellan would certainly not have been surprised at De Garmo's revisionist reading of the meaning of Reconstruction; they would have recognized it as part of an emerging national, not just white Southern, consensus—one that also elevated Booker T. Washington to being *the* sole black voice with national authority to speak about the educational needs of blacks. Nor would those writers discussed in part 1 have been deaf to a certain degree of unintended irony in the quotation with which this chapter began, Charles Denby's "Gentlemen of the South, gentlemen of Dixie—some of us imperialists do not blame you at all for taking all possible legal measures to protect your cherished rights. Will you not forgive us, if we pursue the same policy with regard to a new and untried race? . . . To say that we want to enslave these people [in the new colonies] is a slander. To say that we shall not improve their condition is to contradict history" ("What Shall We Do" 50–51). For sometimes history presents its own contradictions to those like Denby or De Garmo who would presume to speak for it.

# Chapter Seven

# From Planter Paternalism to Uncle Sam's Largesse Abroad

ELLEN M. INGRAHAM'S *BOND AND FREE* (1882) AND
MARIETTA HOLLEY'S *SAMANTHA AT THE ST. LOUIS
EXPOSITION* (1904)

Tourgée's early fiction sold so well it made him rich. It also brought him even more enmity than his previous work as a Yankee Reconstruction judge in North Carolina. For those who disagreed with his interpretation of Reconstruction as "the greatest political experiment in modern civilization" despite its flaws (*Fool's Errand* 142), they had to provide counterexamples to his influential characters and his narratives. Those ripostes in fiction came thick and fast, by Ellen M. Ingraham, Thomas Nelson Page, Joel Chandler Harris, Thomas Dixon, and even George Washington Cable, among others.[1] These writers differed in temperament and ideology: Ingraham, Cable, and Harris, in general, promoted limited rights for blacks as citizens, while Page and Dixon were unapologetic white supremacists. Where Tourgée had rethought his education models, particularly in *Bricks without Straw*, to give blacks more agency, intelligence, and responsibility, however, the majority of white novelists and other authors who followed him systematically attacked his vision and, not surprisingly, emphasized a model for education that stressed black dependency and white benevolence. Even a northerner like Marietta Holley, who lamented the nation's rejection of Reconstruction, saw no reason to question that blacks had to be tutored in the fundamentals of democracy.

Early in the 1880s, Reconstruction revisionism in New South fiction presented itself to the world not as a complete repudiation but as a more realistic continuation of certain Reconstruction goals, particularly the general ideal of black uplift. Constance Fenimore Woolson may have adumbrated what such a revisionary paradigm could look like, but for a full understanding of New South revisionist strategies in fiction we must look to the next decade. One obvious indication of how patchy New South literary history remains is the neglect of Ellen Ingraham's 1882 novel, which draws precisely zero references in the MLA Bibliography, even though the text of this work is readily available on a well-known Web-site archive, the University of North Carolina's Documenting the American South. It turns out that this novel exemplifies par excellence the New South strategy of promoting planter paternalism when it came to the issue of black schools in rural areas. The image of the benevolent planter well loved by his black servants for rescuing them from the chaos of the Reconstruction era became a mainstay in what has become known as the "plantation school" of New South fiction by whites. This narrative of white southerners' benevolence in tutoring their charges in the fundamentals of democracy and a market economy then becomes very useful after 1898 for those defining a moral imperative and a method for U.S. policies toward its new colonies. Planter paternalism toward blacks, now morphed into "Uncle Sam's" good will toward the natives in his new colonies, becomes a central theme in Marietta Holley's account of her visit to the Philippine exhibit in the St. Louis Fair in 1904.[2]

## 1

Primarily known in her day as a painter, not a writer, Ellen Ingraham was born in 1832 in New Haven but lived and taught painting in Indianapolis from 1865 until her death in 1917. She exhibited work in New Orleans in 1885 and in the Women's Pavilion of the Columbian Exposition in Chicago in 1893 (Petteys 364). In *Bond and Free*, her only novel, Ingraham presents a denunciation of slavery that would have been very familiar to northern and southern postwar readers: the country was well rid of slavery because it was demonic, encouraging miscegenation, greed, hypocrisy, and violence. But Ingraham's portraits of slave owners could have been excerpts from any pro-slavery antebellum tract; if slavery as an institution for her was notorious, some of its primary beneficiaries mysteriously resided unscathed within its moral ruins as paragons of virtue. Set mostly in Virginia before and after the war, *Bond and Free* tracks the fortunes of the Templeton family, including Oscar and his sister Letitia and their slave, then loyal servant, Madison. Ingraham not only adopts the romance mode but features in the first half of her novel a plot favored by anti-slavery novelists such as William Wells Brown and Lydia Maria Child: the melodrama of a light-skinned woman with a "trace" of black blood sold into slavery. When Letitia is sold into slavery, Oscar Templeton rides south to rescue his sister. Her owner, on being convinced she was sold illegally, says, "It will afford me great pleasure to sign my name to her emancipation, and rejoice with you in her restoration of family ties" (132). The man even gives his departing ex-slave-girl money as a going-away present.

Once Letitia is restored to her rightful place at the top of the plantation hierarchy, her slave experience paradoxically makes her an exemplary slave manager and plantation owner. Both she and her brother represent so many Enlightenment virtues that they are positively dazzling. Letitia's slaves love her so much they refuse her offer of emancipation (147), and Oscar has to settle not for freeing Madison but for reforming his character from sluggard to a model of black entrepreneurship. Ingraham was one of those liberal authors who believed blacks' "laziness and stupidity" (as the narrator so delicately puts in on page 124) was not inborn but the product of slavery: the "responsibility of self-ownership had never once occurred to [Madison]" (121). Lest readers be uncertain as to the relevance of her portrait of slave-owner generosity to the postwar era, Ingraham drove her point home: "Had he not still felt that he could lean on his young master for aid and guidance, Madison would have been as much the object of pity as thousands of those who were liberated at a later day, and left to rise or fall in their own helplessness" (125). We may call this the "mastering freedom" paradox of Reconstruction revisionist fiction. It suggests that, given blacks' limitations, tutoring them to be responsible was best done in the schoolhouse of slavery or, after emancipation, under their former master's caring gaze.

During Reconstruction, instead of relying on forty acres and a mule from the government, the Templeton blacks are able to acquire all these—and seed too!—because of the kindness of their former owners. Letitia dispenses kernels of advice along with her oral work contracts: "When you get money for your crops, you must pay me what you shall then owe. Try to be saving, and not buy anything to waste, so that you may have money left, and save up enough to buy land and mules of your own. Would you not be pleased to do so?" (175). Letitia indeed runs her postwar plantation as a model factory-school of free labor efficiency. And one of her best products is the reconstruction of black character. Letitia not only administers food, clothing, medicine, and self-help bromides, but encourages regular church-going and runs the "only school-house" in the area for blacks, personally hiring the teacher herself (243). (A separate school is later set up for white children in the neighborhood.) Madison the ex-slave goes into business selling and renting horses and mules. Eventually, he is able to save enough money to buy an inn that not only can thrive without selling liquor, but is run by a white man who has no problems having a black boss. Ingraham meant to leave no doubt that "Free Labor" solved all postwar problems: this heroic phrase is the title for her first post-emancipation chapter.[3]

Ingraham's vision of plantation schoolhouses supervised by planters conforms to the kind of advice that was frequently dispensed by postwar southern journals and newspapers. From the very start, most white southerners were adamantly opposed to having black children learn anything more than the most rudimentary skills in reading, writing, and ciphering—if that. Schools were attacked and even burnt to the ground, schoolteachers and children were harassed, and much prose filled with threats and castigations appeared in publications throughout the South. So powerful was this prejudice that an editorial in the *American Freedman* in 1866 advised that teachers in the new schools should carefully avoid "the discussion of the vexed issues of the past." An article in an 1867 issue of *Flake's Bulletin* put the anxiety of southern elites succinctly, if rather euphemistically: "Besides teaching the freeman to say his a b c's, these teachers from abroad put foolish notions in his head, and destroy the usefulness of his labor. . . . Every planter who can find on his place a white or black person, intelligent enough to teach reading and writing, will avoid a world of perplexity by establishing the school and by not waiting for the government to send one who may perhaps inculcate notions not exactly in concordance with our social customs."[4]

Dangerous northern teachers apparently came from a world so distant that it could be described as "abroad," as if from a foreign country overseas. By the time Constance Fenimore Woolson published her story "King David" in 1878, the Freedmen's Bureau had been dismantled and Reconstruction rejected, though northern missionary societies continued to send teachers south. With the publication of Woolson's story, such idealistic would-be educators of blacks could be seen not just by southern whites but by her many national readers as not a threat so much as a comic butt, an idealist gone wrong. Woolson hinted vaguely at a solution to her national readers, one thoroughly in line with what southern elites had been recommending all along: the planter and other white elites should be put in charge of black education. But to make such a solution seem effective for readers, fiction needed to create such a heroic type—and needed to have such a figure not only represent the best of southern virtues, but accede reasonably to some key Reconstruction educational ideals, so that the transition from Reconstruction to white rule in the New South could appear seamless, inevitable, and just.

This is where Ellen Ingraham comes in. Her novel *Bond and Free* hardly rejected the primary assumptions of some white Republicans that inspired key Reconstruction programs, especially their belief in black dependency. She just did Reconstruction one better and made her reconstruction southern, homegrown, and privatized. And in her portrait of Letitia, she tried to create a type that would have wide national appeal. Like many heroines in abolitionist literature, Letitia was sold into and then rescued from slavery. But as Ingraham draws her, she now becomes the very model for how white plantation owners in the New South after 1877 should get control of rural schools, positioning themselves as the compassionate, practical, and *enlightened* corrective to Freedmen's Bureau and northern missionary society mistakes. True, Letitia's good deeds confuse a few old-fashioned planters and anger white racists who try to cause trouble. But in Ingraham's fictional world true virtue is unstoppable—its moment of historical destiny has arrived.

There is just one slight problem with Ingraham's New South heroine. Letitia is mixed-race. The novel tries to convince readers that this is an inconsequential issue, suggesting that "black" blood is not that apparent in her heroine, even while also claiming that the New South has freed itself of its old anti-black prejudices. In making such moves, Ingraham deploys a shrewd strategy indeed: she appropriates the light-skinned protagonist central to many popular anti-slavery and pro-Reconstruction writings and then rewrites her to be the heroine of the white New South's rise.[5]

Needless to say, today's historians of the postwar South might find a few points of disagreement with Ellen Ingraham. As a group, planters were somewhat less than enthusiastic about black education, unlike Letitia Templeton. They well understood that controlling labor meant suppressing education; illiterate or poorly literate workers could easily be put at a disadvantage through vagrancy laws and written labor contracts (which quickly became standard after slavery). In 1866, the Freedmen's Bureau education superintendent, John Alvord, documented a few instances where planters financed schools or even shielded them from white violence because labor was scarce and their workers needed incentives to stay. But Alvord also noted that schools on the plantations were normally financed by the ex-slaves themselves.[6] One result of literacy was that ex-slaves began demanding that the right to attend school be recognized in work contracts, or even that the planter help finance local schools. The education historian James D. Anderson stresses that valuing literacy and education was "rooted deeply within [the ex-slaves'] communal values," not something learned from northern whites and certainly not from planters (9). By 1860 about 5 percent of the slaves had learned to read, and many of these became leaders in their postwar communities. In the case of Virginia, where Ingraham's novel is set, its twenty-five black delegates to the Constitutional Convention of 1867–68 were indispensable for mandating a public education system supported by corporate and property taxes (Du Bois, *Black Reconstruction* 657–658). Earlier, a mixed-race woman, Mrs. Peake, worked with the military governor and the American Missionary Association to convert an all-white school into the beginnings of Hampton Institute for blacks, before it was taken over by S. C. Armstrong (Du Bois, *Black Reconstruction* 642). Toward all this history *Bond and Free* is blind. Or, if not oblivious, then intent upon obscuring such facts with a different narrative arguing that stable reforms in black education could only come from enlightened planters and other white elites.

In defense of Ingraham's novel, one might argue that her mixed-race heroine's enlightened views of black education represent a courageous ideal model of what planters and others *should* have been doing in the South, not a picture of what actually occurred either during Reconstruction or after. Ingraham's text does reveal that Letitia's actions are highly unusual and controversial. Perhaps readers were meant to conclude that the heroine's experience as a slave made her more sympathetic toward ex-slaves' hopes for education. Overall, Ingraham's narrative logic is consistent with the free labor ideology that motivated many northern white liberal reformers both before and after the war. Schools and fair contracts (and free medical care dispensed by Letitia herself) make her plantation's workers the most productive in all postwar Virginia, according to the narrator. Yet Letitia's individual success functioned in the post-Reconstruction era as a brief *against* extensive state or federal involvement in black public education, including the use of taxes to support black schools.

Ingraham italicized this subtext to *Bond and Free* by having the novel ostensibly authored by the plantation school's white teacher, Grace Lintner. Erasing the history of black activism and the most radical elements within Reconstruction and the Freedmen's Bureau, Ingraham implies that enlightened planters like Oscar and Letitia Templeton, guiding white teachers like Lintner, were the only appropriate forces for positive social change in the postwar South. Her novel's readers could very reasonably conclude that planters and their workers saw their interests as fully compatible—that enlightened ex-slave owners encouraged blacks to value education and that the share-cropping system was as fairly and mutually negotiated as Letitia's oral promises to her workers.

As Ingraham's Letitia Templeton says to the schoolteacher she hires, "When I am led to realize their [blacks'] dependence, ... it seems as if it must be the work of this generation of masters and mistresses to prepare the black race for leading lives of independence" (186). Historians can easily fault the novel's "facts," but we also need to account for the power of its revisionist paradigm. Changing Letitia's meaning, we might say that "realizing" black dependence was indeed the ideological work undertaken by Ingraham's *Bond and Free*. Her discourse of nurturing worked hand in hand with other harsher New South measures that Ingraham's text erases—such as extensive jail sentences for minor convictions, land-sale fraud, convict labor leases, and lynchings—that were used to control black labor and suppress black resistance. Another way to make this concluding point would be to say that Ingraham uses all the resources of fiction to validate the most conservative disciplinary regimes associated with Reconstruction—such as those detailed in Jared Bell Waterbury's tract *Southern Planters and the Freedmen* (1865).[7] Ingraham, too, demonstrates how elites may refashion a sense of obligation in their subordinates and call it freedom. But she makes her text representative of the white New South, not Reconstruction—key to the 1880s, not 1865. Perhaps we should call Ingraham's novel *Free, Then Bond*.

Published by an obscure press in Indianapolis, *Bond and Free* appears to have had little national circulation—certainly nothing to match a nonfiction work such as *Southern Planters*. Many more such projects justifying the return of white rule in the New South were soon to come in fiction: authors such as Joel Chandler Harris, Thomas Nelson Page, and Thomas Dixon did receive wide national readership. The shrewdness of Ingraham's fictional strategies would be confirmed by much of the New South short fiction and poetry published in popular magazines in the 1880s and 1890s, especially those featuring postwar blacks as affectionate servants and budding entrepreneurs happy to give their earnings to their white benefactors. By the late 1890s and after, other New South texts by whites would appear that treated black schools and black activism with a much harsher light—the light of flames.

## 2

In 1904, Marietta Holley, a U.S. humorist at the time almost as well loved as Mark Twain, published a little book called *Samantha at the St. Louis Exposition, by Josiah Allen's Wife*. Chapter 14 featured a trip by the narrator and her family to the Philippines exhibit. The St. Louis Fair was one of the first to expand the well-tried spectacle format of such fairs celebrating domestic progress to incorporate the new tropical colonies.[8] The "Philippine Reservation"—revealing term—was the largest exhibit in the fair, covering forty-seven acres of re-created jungles, lagoons, and native villages complete with huts, costumes, and live villagers; it also included a life-sized replica of part of the walled city of Manila. Holley's language was part satire and part boosterish tour brochure. She reveled both in narratives of progress and those of noble or not-so-noble savagery, sometimes admiring how like "they" can be to "us" and other times making nervous jokes about cannibalism. She celebrated blow guns and native crafts, yet also the Native Boy Scouts who marched as "smooth and even" as modern machinery.

Marietta Holley's representative American family also fully understood that colonial power turns all it possesses into a spectacle in which the unknown and the new can be safely known and made "ours." "What wuz the use of travelin' so far to see our new possessions" in the South Pacific, when they can come to St. Louis? Throughout, Holley expertly translates elite Progressivist colonial rhetoric into familiar, down-home paternalism:

I thought it a first rate idee to show off to the world the almost limitless wealth as well as the hard problems that face Uncle Sam in his new possessions, for like a careful pa he will see that they learn how to take care of themselves before he sets 'em up in independent housekeepin'. . . .

The big normal school building in Manila is handsome enough for any American city, and the smaller district and industrial schools are doing jest as good work. Our Government sent five hundred and forty teachers there in 1901, and now we have about seven hundred there. I took comfort in seein' the great work they have done.

The entire exhibit was meant to illustrate the civilizing triumphs of U.S. colonial policies abroad, plus the basic principles governing the new science of anthropology, as described by Louis Henry Morgan and other academics. According to Morgan, all human societies displayed one of the four stages of human progress: barbarianism (with no ability to progress), savagery, civilization, and enlightenment. The fair's Philippine Reservation included villages for the Negritos, who represented the hopeless lowest group; three Igorot groups, who represented primitives with some limited ability to rise; and finally the villages of the Visayan, who were thought to have the most fully developed culture and optimistic future.

In the Philippines the Igorots, which means "mountain people," were farmers and miners. While in St. Louis, several Igorots showed an interest in the American presidential election of 1904 and asked to cast ballots. In response, two polling places were established in the reconstructed Igorot village. Photographs of the two candidates, Theodore Roosevelt and Alton B. Parker, were placed over Igorot gongs, and beans served as ballots. Roosevelt won, eighty-three to two (see fig. 7.1). An Igorot election in the midst of a fair on the banks of the Mississippi was meant to display colonialism bringing democracy and civilization to the islands—yet in 1904 in the rest of the United States, apart from this Philippine Reservation, people of color were mostly completely disenfranchised and unable to vote, for Jim Crow policies were taking over the land and within a decade would become de facto national policy as well. And, of course, colonized subjects who owned property in the Philippines might receive the franchise, but U.S. policy allowed them only to vote locally, not in U.S. elections. The voting rights of the Philippine Reservation thus existed in a strange liminal state, neither within the Philippines nor within U.S. law—a fictive franchise that, like much of the fair itself, was a spectacular but also spectral demonstration of freedoms that did not exist outside of the theatrical space in which they were projected and celebrated.[9]

Such contradictions, predictably enough, were elided by Marietta Holley. Halfway through Josiah Allen's wife's meditations, though, her tone changes, for she realizes that her excitement at the "progress" demonstrated by the Filipinos becomes haunted. Holley contrasts the colonial uplift agenda for Uncle Sam's new "step-children" with a previous obligation: the narrator says Uncle Sam should "do as well by his steal children, the dark complexioned ones stole away from their own land to be slaves and drudges for his white children." The narrator's comment initiates an argument with her husband, in which they both play out in shorthand vernacular the classic arguments for and against Reconstruction. These arguments come to diametrically opposite conclusions, yet share the same assumption that blacks are children. Holley's narrative tries to end on a comic and positive note, as the narrator marches to "the music of the future" only she can hear. But mixed into her Progressivist parade are "louder" discordant notes and memories that, despite her assurances about a free conscience, cannot be

Fig. 7.1. "Igorot Voting." Photo used with permission from St. Louis Public Library.

blended to make the last chord of her chapter sound harmonious. I quote the chapter's ending:

> It sings of an ignorant, oppressed race changed into an enlightened prosperous one, this great work done by our own country, this song comes floatin' into my ears over the wide Pacific. And another louder strain comes from nigher by made tender and pathetic by years of oppression and suppressed suffering that could find expression in no other way than this heart searching pathos. And blending with it, ringing over and above it, triumphant happy echoes telling of real freedom of mind and conscience, the true liberty.

For other writers who were Holley's contemporaries, such as Mark Twain in the United States and Aurelio Tolentino in the Philippines, finding a harmonious concord between U.S. constitutional ideals and its developing Jim Crow colonialist policies proved more difficult. These authors turned with particular vengeance upon Progressivist claims that, as Woodrow Wilson succinctly phrased it, "self-government . . . follows upon the long discipline which gives a people self-possession, self-mastery, the habit of order and peace. . . . No people can be 'given' the self-control of maturity. Only a long apprenticeship of obedience can secure them the precious possession" (*Constitutional Government* 52–53).

Chapter Eight

# Counter-statements to Jim Crow Colonialism

MARK TWAIN'S "TO THE PERSON SITTING IN DARKNESS"
(1901) AND AURELIO TOLENTINO'S
*YESTERDAY, TODAY, AND TOMORROW* (1905)

Where might we look in cultural history for what Marietta Holley called that other "strain," critiques of the United States' turn-of-the-century discourses of a civilizing mission justifying colonialism? In general, U.S. historians have tended to focus on only one area in the cultural spectrum, the writings of Boston's Anti-Imperial League. Like their opponents, these figures were white cultural elites who had access to the most widely distributed public newspapers and periodicals. Many were northerners and once supporters of Reconstruction, but eventually there were branches of the League in other areas of the country, such as Minnesota. The Anti-Imperialist League's most prominent members were Mark Twain and Andrew Carnegie; Carnegie even offered to buy the Philippine Islands from the United States and give them their independence.

The League's key objections to U.S. policies in the Philippines were that U.S. power should be used to create independent states, not U.S. colonies, and that administering an empire would eventually destroy democratic institutions. In the words of the League's 1899 platform:

> We hold that the policy known as imperialism is hostile to liberty and tends toward militarism, an evil from which it has been our glory to be free. We regret that it has become necessary in the land of Washington and Lincoln to reaffirm that all men, of whatever race or color, are entitled to life, liberty and the pursuit of happiness. We maintain that governments derive their just powers from the consent of the governed. We insist that the subjugation of any people is "criminal aggression" and open disloyalty to the distinctive principles of our Government. We earnestly condemn the policy of the present National Administration [of President McKinley] in the Philippines....

We denounce the slaughter of the Filipinos as a needless horror. We protest against the extension of American sovereignty by Spanish methods.[1]

The League's definitions of justice were inspired by the Declaration of Independence, the Constitution (especially the Bill of Rights), and the Fourteenth Amendment, which specified that no citizen should be deprived of equal protection before the laws. What was remarkable in the League's declaration was that it explicitly extended at least a healthy portion of such rights to "any people" in their dealings with "American sovereignty." As David Healy and others have shown, however, persistent racism and xenophobia fueled some of the League's writings, even as members raised astute questions about the effects of military empire on U.S. democracy and were adamant about colonized peoples' inalienable rights to self-determination.[2]

Progressivist public officials and intellectuals who promoted colonial expansion, such as Elihu Root, Charles R. Denby, Franklin Henry Giddings, and the Reverend Josiah Strong, knew they had to neutralize the arguments of the League. They did so by assuring the public, first, that expansion was absolutely necessary for U.S. economic and political strength and, second, that the United States would tutor the Philippines in democracy and help them set up democratic institutions, eventually leading to complete independence. The task of charting the transition from military rule to civil rule was the particular charge of the First and Second Philippine Commissions, composed of U.S. civilian experts headed by Judge William Howard Taft. Root helped draft a charter for the Philippine Islands that, like his Platt Amendment for Cuba, defined independence as the goal but made dependence on the United States the reality. At times, the language of the 1900 *Report of the Philippine Commission to the President* made it sound as if the Philippines might follow the model of many U.S. territories and eventually become a state, not a protectorate in perpetuity: "the commission recommends that in dealing with the Philippines this vast power [of the U.S. Congress] be exercised along the lines laid down by Jefferson and Madison in establishing a government for Louisiana, but with the deviations in the direction of larger liberty to the Filipinos" (anonymous 1: 112). But the commission's summary statement struck a very different note: "The Filipinos are wholly unprepared for independence, and if independence were given them they could not maintain it." Admiral Dewey himself is quoted dismissing the rebel Aguinaldo's claim that the islands were promised independence by the Americans as "a tissue of falsehoods." The report's final words on the matter are unequivocal: "The men of property and education, who alone interest themselves in public affairs, in general recognize as indispensable American authority, guidance, and protection" (1: 121).

Willard B. Gatewood Jr.'s study of the role played by the black press in these debates found similar contradictions in both its pro- and its anti-imperialist statements. Although editorials in black-owned newspapers sharply criticized the growth of Jim Crow–inspired discrimination and violence in the colonies (and at home), the majority also lauded the "civilizing" goals of empire and steered away from any sustained criticism of U.S. imperial projects. Black journalists confronted the challenge of U.S. expansionism no better than did Frederick Douglass in his *Life and Times* two decades earlier—except that U.S. black newspapers spent much less time than Douglass envisioning a black-run colony becoming a state in the Union: with the consolidation of Jim Crow in the South, that prospect seemed much more remote in the early twentieth century than it had for Douglass in 1881. Kevin Gaines (in "Black Americans' Racial Uplift Ideology as 'Civilizing Mission'") has shown that colonialist discourse involving a "civilizing mission" at home and abroad also imbued the work of most black reformers of this period, including Pauline Hopkins and Ida B. Wells-Barnett, even as they sharply criticized Jim Crow.[3]

Other stories of complicated responses to U.S. imperial discourse have not been told. We need fully comparative, *transnational* histories of critiques of U.S. expansionism during the Progressive era, not ones focusing primarily on elites in Boston and New York with occasional glances elsewhere. We need to juxtapose what might be called the United States' "imperial colonization" of the meanings of Reconstruction and the Fourteenth Amendment to other interpretations of what was and could have been. Why is there no comparative work on W. E. B. Du Bois and the Philippine writer José Rizal, for example? Rizal anticipated in the late 1880s many of the key anti-colonial arguments that would move to the foreground after 1898, particularly with W. E. B. Du Bois's "To the Nations of the World" statement at the 1900 Pan-African Conference in London, his later manifesto at the 1919 Pan-African Congress, and other relevant writings of his from the first two decades of the twentieth century. Yet both writers made assumptions about how to measure "development" or "civilization" that were hardly free of the colonialist rhetoric they were trying to question. U.S. cultural historians have really just begun the much-needed project of assessing statements made by, say, Philippine independence leaders—or those fighting for Cuban, Puerto Rican, or Hawaiian rights, or José Martí's *Our America* (written in New York City)—as primary players in turn-of-the-century anti-imperial discourse, including the ways in which those critiques were often laced with contradictions, their own enactments of elitism, racism, and other problems. In general, we should increasingly look to anti-colonial traditions "outside" the United States in order to reassess patterns of resistance "within" the United States. To pick just one example, little work has yet been done on the degree to which Ida B. Wells-Barnett understood her anti-lynching and anti-racism writing as reversing the central tropes of colonial discourse, exposing the savage acts perpetrated in the name of civilization.[4]

Ada Ferrer's fine article, "1898: Rethinking Race, Nation, and Empire," focuses on Cuba and provides one example of recent innovative approaches to postcolonial U.S. cultural history for the 1898–1920s period. Ferrer demonstrates that U.S. actions in Cuba during that period must be understood not only as attempts to control Cuba's economy, particularly its sugar production, but also as a systematic campaign to disarm the "fragile anticolonial and antiracist promise of the nineteenth-century Cuban revolution" (42)—all done while proclaiming its goals to be Cuban independence and progress. The Cuban independence movement was itself hardly free of racism or classist bias. As Ferrer shows, some rebel leaders had enough fears of lower-class and black dominance to lead them to explore the possibility of allying with the United States against Spain before the war actually broke out. After the U.S. victory over, first, Spain and then the anti-colonial resisters, the United States not only disarmed the rebels, but introduced Jim Crow practices to the island that were far more explicitly delineated than the subtle class and color hierarchies that distinguished Spanish colonial Cuba. According to Ferrer, the new rulers of the island stressed the value of Cuban independence and suffrage, but they immediately set about limiting access to electoral power by imposing literacy and property restrictions on Cuban voters similar to those that were being adopted in Hawaii and throughout the South and had just been upheld as constitutional by the U.S. Supreme Court in *Williams v. Mississippi*. U.S. officials in Cuba tended to empower "white" Cubans who had been educated in the United States, and they repeatedly asserted that to prove their readiness for freedom Cubans had to remain peaceful, orderly, and respectful of property and U.S. visitors. Recent reinterpretations of the career of the Cuban writer José Martí demonstrate the inadequacy of simple binaries like pro- versus anti-colonial in assessing the historical roles played by both colonizer and colonized.[5]

Some attention has been given to the ideological role played by fiction published in the United States during this imperial period, most pointedly articles by Amy Kaplan and Andrew Hebard studying the popular romances of imperial adventure, such as Richard Harding Davis's best-selling *Soldiers of Fortune* (1897). In this chapter, I will look at the role played by other genres—satire and drama—as they seek not to justify the expansion of empire but to critique it. Kaplan's and Hebard's claims are worth paraphrasing briefly first, though, for they provide a paradigm for the ways in which we may understand that literature—even without referring to historical events directly—may be complicit with how those events are interpreted and justified.

In "Romancing the Empire," Kaplan posits that a gendered double discourse involving bodies governed both popular romances and U.S. political debates about the new colonies. American males could have their physical and mental masculinity affirmed in adventures abroad, but America itself would not rule over the body of a geographical empire; rather, it would project a sphere of influence through the power of its ideas, products, and economic, political, and cultural institutions. Hebard, in "Romantic Sovereignty: Popular Romances and the American Imperial State in the Philippines" (2005), argues for an even more intricate confluence between U.S. fiction and U.S. polity. In his view, both historical romance fiction and imperial administrative discourse designate a world or representative milieu as intelligible and governable, using a mix of what is marked as "ordinary" versus "extraordinary." Just as popular novels such as Davis's cycle between realistic and wildly fantastical episodes, so too did U.S. rule combine a mix of civil and military actions: the former use the regulative norms of bureaucratic discourse to govern the islands; the latter rely on explicit forms of violent intervention. Such complementary modes of state action occur together, though, in general, U.S. policy also assumed after the defeat of Aguinaldo's insurgents that there would be a gradual evolution from military to civil rule in the Philippines, first with Americans in charge and then, later, an increasing percentage of Filipinos. U.S. dominance of the islands would not fade; rather, it would change its modes of operation.

The paradoxes of power management deployed so suavely by best-selling U.S. romances in the period indeed came to pass in history as well—both during the early phase of colonization, when the U.S. military had to suppress a guerrilla insurgency, and in later phases, when various forms of civil order were imposed. Under the direction of President Woodrow Wilson in 1916, for instance, the next phase of "Filipinization" of the government occurred under the so-called Jones Autonomy Act of the U.S. Congress. Under this act, more native Filipinos voted in elections and more were certainly appointed to positions of power within the administration, courts, and government bureaucracies than had been the case in the 1900–1916 period. However, U.S. military presence in the islands grew rather than diminished; U.S. economic interests dictated even more firmly the primary workings of the Philippine economy; and what Wilson's limited transfer of power accomplished was to turn the government into an oligarchy with power primarily in the possession of a few native elites who controlled voting and appointments. Carefully managed forms of "autonomy" in the colonies served the interests of both U.S. and native elites. In Hebard's apt formulation, Filipinos were "situated as both subjects and citizens" occupying "ambivalent legal territory" (812). When Twain satirized U.S. colonial policies in the Philippines, he targeted just such a paradoxical understanding of autonomy, as well as Jim Crow colonialism's staple narrative that colonization must sometimes employ violence, but only to move resisting peoples to a sustained period of tutelage before they can understand the virtues of full independence. At this point in *Sitting in Darkness* we should be able to recognize the provenance of such a colonial tutelage narrative: it has deep roots in the contested historical terrain of Reconstruction, particularly dependency models of education.[6]

Part 3 of volume 1 of the 1900 *Report of the Philippine Commission to the President* catalogues the deplorable state of education in the islands under Spanish rule, complete with charts, statistics, and personal testimonies. The critique turns on a pernicious mixture of incompetence and what is taken to be the corrupting influence of the Catholic Church on Spain's colonial administration. The tone of the report suggests the light of reason and accountability is finally being cast on the dark gap between promises and achievement: "The Spanish regulations provided that there should be one male and one female primary school teacher for each 5,000 inhabitants, instruction being given separately to the two sexes. This wretchedly inadequate provision was, as a matter of fact, never carried out" (1: 17). The fervency with which the educational inadequacies are described, not to mention the data tables, are nothing if not reminiscent of a representative Freedmen's Bureau report detailing the problems encountered and the proper solution proposed for those problems, a system of public schools. The ghosts of Reconstruction can be heard, too, circulating beneath the statements of purpose and method made by the Philippine commissioners—as illustrated by this passage from a 1913 memoir by the 1900 commission's secretary, Daniel R. Williams: "The question is, How far are we justified in forcing our ideas and ideals upon these people, and how far should we sacrifice and delay what we believe is best in order to meet the viewpoint, traditions, desires, and prejudices of the local output? Our government has deliberately chosen the harder task; it has elected to become a guide rather than a master, to teach and train the people rather than attempt arbitrarily to force them to our ways" (287).

Both the Freedmen's Bureau and the Philippine Commission solutions involved the importing of massive numbers of schoolteachers to run the new schools. In one particularly spectacular example of migration, in August 1901 a converted cattle ship, the USS *Thomas,* sailed from San Francisco carrying over five hundred male and female schoolteachers to the Philippines to begin instruction in English in a new school system administered by the U.S. colonial government.[7] Many such efforts were managed by religious organizations, including the American Missionary Association. Another clear parallel with Reconstruction lies in the fact that U.S. administrators on the islands felt under siege once their program of reform had begun to be implemented. Those that they were helping, U.S. commissioners believed, were profoundly grateful, but the administrators received nothing but grief from local elites and from many back home. Here again the memoirist Daniel R. Williams is worth quoting at some length:

So far as can be judged, the mass of the Filipinos are satisfied at this time with what we are doing for them, though there is a growing tendency to clamor for more privileges and perquisites than the most liberal policy justifies. Our course is roundly criticized by the American press of the islands, and by most of the resident foreigners, as being altogether visionary and dangerous, while we are castigated at home by various highly-sensitive individuals of Boston and thereabouts [a reference to the Anti-Imperial League] for "oppressing a patriotic people."

Referring to the American papers in Manila, they have been anything but a help to us thus far. From the very beginning they have antagonized and obstructed the work of the civil authorities. The confidence expressed by the Commission in the people has been ridiculed, and its appointment of natives to office denounced and condemned. They have attacked everything Filipino, called the natives treacherous, untrustworthy, etc. . . .

As to the papers, their circulation is largely an army one, their revenue being derived in great part from that source and from the advertisements of companies whose trade depends upon supplying canteens and army commissaries. The larger the army of occupation, and the longer it remains, the greater their profits; hence their advocacy of military [rather than civilian] government. (287–288)

Parallels between Reconstruction and Philippine colonial efforts must not be over-stressed. In the case of the Philippines, the sharpest criticism came from white elites who wanted the military to *continue* its role, not to withdraw—just the reverse from the U.S. South in Reconstruction. And those elites were hardly native. But in several other respects the similarities between the dilemmas faced by Bureau and commissioner administrators are striking and significant—especially how their work is obstructed and resisted. We might want to call this moment in the new colonies Reconstruction redux, for narratives of uplift facing much resistance unite both historical moments, and both also result in many more people of color ascending to power with the help of the U.S. government. Yet given that this experiment in reconstructing the Philippines occurs just when people of color are being stripped of power and rights back "home," we must more properly speak of Reconstruction revised and exported. Reconstruction's ghosts, its violated ideals, still circulate. Regarding the brute ironies involved, both Twain and Tolentino will have trenchant comments, so I will refrain from more analysis here. Let us turn now to both these writers, for in them that other "strain" that Marietta Holley listened for—a critique of Jim Crow colonialism—lives strongly.

# 1

Mark Twain's "To the Person Sitting in Darkness," perhaps the most famous anti-imperialist satire written by a U.S. author in the early 1900s, was published in the *North American Review*, February 1901. It has remained a touchstone for all historians of the Anti-Imperialist League. Much debated in its day, the essay was not usually recognized as a key part of the Twain canon until the efforts of Jim Zwick and other scholars recently made it once more impossible to ignore. Yet the "position" of this "anti-colonial" text is more unstable than first meets the eye, and these complications in Twain's text have not been as fully discussed as they should be.

Twain's target was the language of liberation used to support U.S. colonialism. But the essay's sense of outrage may be so fiery because Twain was a rather late convert to anti-imperialism. As recently as 1898, despite doubts about colonialism expressed in *Following the Equator*, Twain admitted to a friend that he believed the United States' war with Spain was exceptional: "It is a worthy thing to fight for one's freedom. It is another sight finer to fight for another man's. And I think this is the first time it has been done" (quoted in Zwick, "Mark Twain's Anti-Imperialist Writings" 40). "To the Person Sitting in Darkness" seethes with Twain's fresh sense of betrayal. In particular, he zeroes in on published arguments justifying recent massacres of Filipinos as unfortunate necessities when civilization-building is attacked.[8] Well before George Orwell invented the term "doublespeak," Twain used the art of parody and collage to show its workings. Twain skewers clichés about the white man's burden marketed by elites whom he calls the "Blessings-of-Civilization Trust," which functions more as a corporation operating for profit than government policy created by the consent of the governed. He also parodies American exceptionalism (including the self-assured belief that U.S. traditions and ideals ensure that "our" influence abroad will be progressive, selfless, and successful). For Twain, such rhetoric is the latest American patent invention, demonstrating our unmatched ability to delude ourselves and harm others in the name of progress:

> Shall we . . . go on conferring our Civilization upon the peoples that sit in darkness, or shall we give those poor things a rest? . . . Would it not be prudent to get our Civilization-tools together, and see how much stock is left on hand in the way of Glass Beads and Theology, and Maxim Guns and Hymn Books, and Trade-Gin and Torches of Progress and Enlightenment (patent-adjustable ones, good to fire villages with, upon occasion), and balance the books, and arrive at the profit and loss, so that we may intelligently decide whether to continue the business or sell out the property and start a new Civilization on the proceeds? (60–61)[9]

Twain's rhetorical pairings above first appear dangerous because they expose the *link* between "bad" motives and "good" ones—greed versus religion, murder versus hymn singing, etc. But Twain's lists do more than link, they merge. Helping involves hurting. Simple greed and complex "civilizing" ideals in colonial

142

history prove inseparable—both selfishness and selflessness are really different outcomes of the same new "patent invention," a newfangled Enlightenment torch with many uses, from burning down villages to holding itself aloft as a beacon of liberty for those living in darkness. And throughout this passage's multiplying figures of speech, the master trope is that of corporate capitalist accounting: not just a straightforward calculus of profit or loss, but an infinitely malleable ledger that allows losses to count as profits, liabilities as assets. When one rationale for colonial civilization-building fails, another can be quickly inserted in its place.

The target of all this imperial speculation, the "Person Sitting in Darkness," emerges from Twain's text not as a barbarian but as a sober truth-teller or accountant. Quietly shadowing all imperial gestures, this colonial, unlike his colonizers, doubts rather than believes and speaks in plain English rather than fancy flourishes. And yet, of course, this figure supposedly remains in darkness rather than "light." Twain marks his opinions as hypothetical, something guiltily imagined and then suppressed by colonialist bookkeeping: "The Person Sitting in Darkness is almost sure to say: 'There is something curious about this—curious and unaccountable. There must be two Americas: one that sets the captive free, and one that takes a once-captive's new freedom away from him, and picks a quarrel with him with nothing to found it on; then kills him to get his land'" (64).

The imperialist response to this challenge, according to Twain, is this: "We must arrange his opinions for him" (64). Twain ends his satire with the Blessings-of-Civilization Trust speaking in a frenzied first-person-plural monologue, desperate to erase all doubts about the "Game" and the "Business" of freedom on the march: "There have been lies; yes, but they were told in a good cause" (67). Twain's final acid irony is twofold. First, the real person in darkness is the colonizer who thinks his motives are "enlightened." Second, no matter how skeptical of imperial discourse Twain is, he cannot find a way to step "outside" the prison-house of its assumptions and rhetoric; this is why the person sitting in darkness in his satire remains in the shadows and speaks only hypothetically.

If, as Kaplan and Hebard suggested, popular romance fiction elided the differences between violence and nurturing by deftly placing both kinds of "heroic" American actions within a narrative of the progress of civilization-building, Twain's diatribe may be said to do the opposite. Satire ruthlessly exposes the gap between words and actions and between one narrative mode and another; it highlights incompatibilities rather than smoothing them over—indeed, it makes the contradictions unbearable, so that the only response is tears and laughter, and perhaps action. And instead of giving us endlessly varied ways of rendering the world "intelligible" and the protagonist's powers invincible (whatever his temporary setbacks), as Hebard shows is endemic to the action of romance, satire brutally dismantles claims that the world can and should be made transparent and the savage civilized. Indeed, Twain's satire finds the most disturbing forms of savagery in the "patent-adjustable" narratives positioned in the name of furthering freedom and civilization.

2

Just a few years after Twain's word-bomb caused such a ruckus, Aurelio Tolentino's play *Kahapon, Ngayon at Bukas* (*Yesterday, Today, and Tomorrow*) had its premiere in Manila, in 1903. It resulted in no less of a stir. In fact, its performance, though in Tagalog, so angered Americans in the audience that they stormed the stage before the final act, tore the set apart, and shut the play down. The author was soon tried, convicted of sedition, and jailed.[10] Colonial power, however, works in mysterious ways. Though deemed so dangerous that it could not be performed, Tolentino's manuscript was collected and translated soon afterwards by a U.S. government bureaucrat and incorporated into a volume entitled *The Filipino Drama*—complete with critical and historical introductory remarks and footnotes—that was part of a mammoth project mandated by the Philippine Commissions of 1900 and after to document, evaluate, and make intelligible to U.S. citizens all known elements of Philippine "culture" past and present. This tiny sample of the U.S. colonial archive well exemplifies how the discourses of colonialism try to absorb and catalogue even the most critical comments about their enterprise. But such endeavors, no matter how massive, cannot contain the ironies of history.

Originally edited by the bureaucrat Arthur Stanley Riggs and published in Manila in 1905, then reprinted again in the Philippines in 1981, *The Filipino Drama* has never officially been published in the United States, much less been considered a part of U.S. literary history of the early twentieth century. Those interested in reading the translation must find one of the rare libraries that have a copy, or use inter-library loan to borrow the volume in possession of the Philippine Embassy library in New York City. There is a photo of Tolentino (see fig. 8.1), accompanied by Rigg's annotation, "Aurelio Tolentino y Valenzuela, 'Blue,' the greatest of the present-day Filipino dramatists, now in Manila Penitentiary for his seditious plays."

Tolentino's *Yesterday, Today, and Tomorrow* presents the Spanish colonialists as "blind with eyes open" and the Americans as distinctly untrustworthy liberators. The Americans appear on the scene only in the final act, immediately after an episode in which Spain, after forcing some natives to be buried alive, is vanquished by Filipino fighters outraged at Spanish barbarism. The Americans insist that the Filipinos not form a republic now, but agree to be protected by America until they may earn independence at some unspecified future date. Tolentino clearly alludes here to post-1898 Progressivist claims about the long-term beneficial aims of U.S. global power. Neither a display of the miraculous forces of the Philippine army, nor

Aurelio Tolentino y Valenzuela,
"The Blue."
The greatest of the present day
Filipino dramatists, now in
Manila's Penitentiary for
his seditious plays
(Courtesy of Col. W. S. Scott, P. C., Manila)

Fig. 8.1. Aurelio Tolentino

the pleas of children on their knees—nor even the American military commander's nightmare of a dying eagle and ghosts rising from their graves—are enough to stop the Americans from claiming the islands as theirs to protect. At the play's climax, a character representing the Philippine people gives an impassioned speech that—even in Riggs's stilted 1905 translation—reads like a medley of impassioned U.S. orations from the Revolutionary, abolitionist, and Radical Reconstructionist periods: "The liberty which I long for thou didst also long to obtain from him who was thy master.... Canst thou deny to us that which thou didst desire so much? That which is bad for thee thou shouldst not do to another.... [God] has created men to be free, and he who voluntarily enslaves is an executioner of the rights of his fellowman.... Think and do not forget the sorrow of our people.... We love thee dearly. Why doest thou then disturb us and interfere with our desired rights?" (Tolentino 332). After this speech, Philippine children reappear and kneel before an American, presenting a large book, "the record of our unhappy people." The American rejects the book and drops it, but from out of the text a huge banner swirls and fills the stage—the blue, white, and red flag of the free Philippine Republic (332). It was at this point that Americans in the audience shut the play down (Tolentino 332–333n38; *Manila Cable News*, 9 December 1903).

In gathering a translation of *Yesterday, Today, and Tomorrow* and other plays into a publication sponsored by the U.S. government, Arthur Stanley Riggs designed the

collection both to show the natives' guilt and demonstrate the enlightened benefi-
cence of U.S. rule. Riggs boasts of preserving an archive of Philippine cultural
history even as it intervened and irrevocably altered that history. Further, Riggs's
unctuous introduction and his sometimes contentious footnotes seek to prove that
Tolentino was both a dangerous subversive and impossibly naïve when it came to
the craft of play-writing. Riggs's claims, like the larger U.S. colonial enterprise of
which he is a part, are replete with ironies and contradictions. Riggs asserted that
Tolentino's play bored its Philippine audience because it was too political and
untraditional—yet elsewhere his footnotes record spirited Filipino participation,
including hissing the American figures and cheering the rebels (cf. 325n34, 332n38).
A long footnote added from the sedition trial transcript proves beyond a doubt
how dangerous the Americans found the play's effects on its mixed audience—yet
this same footnote also preserves an eloquent speech by the play's author at his trial
on the universal right to liberty (327-328n35). A further irony is that the final scene
of the play—never performed—contains the speech that puts the U.S. in the best
light, as her soldiers finally relent and give the Philippines what it has asked for,
earning a concluding chorus of praise for the United States (333).

In that final scene, the Filipina heroine says America will be her "mirror" as
she realizes liberty and wealth in independence. But the play demonstrates more
forcefully that Tolentino understood the Philippines to be a mirror *for the United
States:* only when the United States accedes to Filipino desires for freedom will it
re-validate its own originary ideals and valor in the glass of contemporary colonial history. If it does not, it will void those ideals and dishonor its name.

Read with Tolentino's play in mind, Daniel Williams's supercilious words
quoted earlier cannot but become laced with irony Williams hardly intended: "The
question is, How far are we justified in forcing our ideas and ideals upon these people, and how far should we sacrifice and delay what we believe is best in order to
meet the viewpoint, traditions, desires, and prejudices of the local output? Our government has deliberately chosen the harder task; it has elected to become a guide
rather than a master, to teach and train the people rather than attempt arbitrarily to force them to our ways." Such a reversal (or deformation) of "mastery" may
also be a consequence of the colonial archive. Texts and other forms of evidence
are constantly interpolated by and placed in subordination to other texts in that
archive—Tolentino's play encased in Arthur Stanley Riggs's interpretive apparatus,
not to mention his English, for example. But the archive is not stable. Texts and
meanings may not forever remain in subjection; nor do all forms of supervision
remain superior.

*The Filipino Drama* volume, Riggs's contribution to the U.S. colonial archive
cataloging the Philippines, should be understood as designed to displace a *competing* archive, the "book" referred to in the Filipino/American confrontation
scene described above. In Riggs's translated words, that book is "the record of our

unhappy people" (332) and also the secret storage place for the illegal flag of the free Philippine Republic. Tolentino's play thus takes care to stress the *textual* sources of Philippine rights that the flag symbolizes. It does this via both the dialogue's many quotations and allusions to texts like the Declaration of Independence and the declaration that the Filipino appeal to justice; their demand to be recognized by the Americans as free *citizens*, not colonial wards, grows out of a long record of abuse under Spain. In the face of U.S. claims between 1900 and 1905 that it will build schools and slowly guide a premodern people toward understanding what freedom means, Tolentino counters with this scene's image of the Filipinos already being a people of the *book*. The play demonstrates that the Filipino children not only know the book of freedom by heart but understand the ideals inscribed therein better than the American adults who confront them and assume them to be illiterate.

In the case of the U.S. colonial archive, as shown by the 1900 *Report of the Philippine Commission*, much emphasis was made on the fact that U.S. experts were correcting—re-inscribing—and expanding an archive incompetently done by the Spanish. There is much emphasis on quoting what the Spanish wrote to be their education goals and then exposing how those goals were never realized. The *Report* promises that for the first time readers will have access to an accurate accounting of the state of the school system, or the present condition of "the Filipino drama," etc. Jesuit surveys on the islands' geography, etc., are also redacted, translated, and incorporated, along with Spanish administrative records, so that the U.S. archive is actually an archive of archives, with the U.S. contributions outdoing all its predecessors'. Remarkably absent in this drive to encyclopedic comprehensiveness, however, are the voices of the Filipinos themselves. When their views were solicited in interviews conducted by others, these were frequently paraphrased rather than quoted directly. The few written records by native Filipinos that existed—such as certain subversive plays written by dangerous agitators—were understood to be exceptional, requiring commentators to use utmost care to frame how such views are read and interpreted. Tolentino's play reverses that process. At least for one moment on stage—a moment never fully performed, and therefore hypothetical—the alternative archive is presented directly to the Americans and dictates the terms of their interchange in this colonial contact zone.

An analogous situation in Hawaii should help make the point that the U.S. colonial archive is always already re-inscribing other archives that may include records of democracy, not primitivism, in action. Many leading Hawaiian citizens of color created anti-annexation petitions and sent a "Memorial" letter to President McKinley in 1897 protesting U.S. actions in Hawaii between 1893 and 1897 and hoping for redress. These texts show a deep understanding of the large ethical and constitutional crises caused by recent events, especially the coup of 17 January 1893, instigated by U.S. businessmen and other figures with cooperation from the U.S. military, and the debates in the 1897 U.S. Congress regarding the so-called Organic Act covering Hawaii and the ratification of a treaty formally annexing the islands as U.S. territories.

The Hawaiians argued that the "Republic of Hawaii" set up after the 1893 coup was a sham because it overturned a duly elected government and was grounded in a new constitution created by a convention composed of self-appointed members and a few delegates elected by a numerically insignificant minority of white and aboriginal male citizens. Citizens' groups were organized and anti-annexation petitions signed and delivered all the way from Hawaii to Washington. These petitions stressed that the Hawaiian people were fully accustomed to participating in constitutional forms of government, in the election of legislatures, in the administration of justice through regularly constituted magistrates, courts, and juries, and in the representative administration of public affairs, and that they fully understood the principle of majority rule. Here is an excerpt from one such petition, of many available on the World Wide Web:

The Abermarle Hotel
New York, July 24, 1897

HON WILLIAM Mc.Kinley,
President of the United States;

May it please your Excellency to find accompanying this letter two petitions, of which I am the duly commissioned bearer from three societies of patriotic associations therein mentioned. These organizations represent the people of native or part native birth, who to the number of forty thousand are still opposed to any loss of their independence and in favor of the restoration of their Queen; Her Majesty Liliuokalani.

It was their wish and my own to present these to you during the first week of your administration, and to this end a letter was written to your Excellency and delivered by me at the Executive Office. To this no reply whatever was received, and after waiting nearly a week, I wrote to your Secretary simply inquiring if it had reached your hands.

Upon being informed by him that it was under consideration, yet still receiving no response, I delayed the delivery of the within documents and communicated the facts to my fellow-citizens at Honolulu.

By them, I have been recently advised to send to your Excellency these papers without further delay, which I now do, hoping for myself and for that great number of my countrymen and countrywomen who are denied the exercise of their rights at home and the privilege of any representation abroad, that the United States Government in whom Her Majesty and her people have alike trusted will never consent to any Treaty or protect any Hawaiian Rule, without a full recognition of her constitutional rights and those of the aboriginal people of the Hawaiian Islands. Commending this to the consideration of Your Excellency, in whose kindness of heart and strict sense of justice, we have every reason to trust, I have the honor to remain.

Most respectfully yours,
[signed] Joseph Heleluehe

Secretary, Her Majesty Liliuokalani, and Commissioner of HUI KALAIANA—and also of the AHAHUI HAWAII ALOHA AINA and the WOMEN'S PATRIOTIC LEAGUE

For various reasons, most of them having to do with internal Senate politics, the Senate failed to ratify the annexation treaty in 1897. The whole issue became moot in 1898, however, when in the midst of war fever, in July 1898, another annexation measure easily passed the U.S. Senate and Hawaii officially became a colony. Joseph Heleluele, the secretary for the Queen of Hawaii, was kept waiting for an entire week in New York without being allowed even to present his petitions and his case to the newly elected U.S. president. His materials eventually were accepted, but then buried in U.S. government files; the Web site notes uncertainly that the source for this particular scanned document is "U.S. State Department files (?)." Ignored the petitions may have been, but a counter-archive of both their arguments and the treatment Hawaiian representatives received was created and preserved and eventually became part of a collection maintained by a network of Hawaiian institutions as varied as community colleges to state university branches. With the advent of the World Wide Web in the twenty-first century, a sampling of these materials has been made available to the world via an archive site run by the University of Hawaii at Manoa, "The Annexation of Hawaii: A Collection of Documents."[11] The facts of annexation remain unchanged (though not well enough known), but the interpretations of the meaning of these facts have shifted greatly between 1897–98 and the present. History winds in mysterious ways.

### 3

Aurelio Tolentino was convicted under U.S. Congressional Act No. 292 (1901), which made advocating Philippine independence a crime. That Philippine Sedition Act became a legal precedent for the U.S. Sedition Act of 1918, the first anti-sedition legislation applied to residents of the United States since 1798. Under the authority of this 1918 act, as well as the Espionage Act of 1917, the notorious Palmer raids against citizens and aliens were conducted, which resulted in the U.S. Attorney General Alexander Mitchell Palmer and other authorities working for President Woodrow Wilson holding detainees without legal counsel indefinitely, in legal limbo, until many were tried, convicted, and either deported or imprisoned. By 1920, Palmer and a certain enthusiastic assistant named J. Edgar Hoover had rounded up at least ten thousand individuals, the largest mass arrests in U.S. history. The reason why such extreme measures against the U.S. populace were deemed necessary was because the country was in a state of war against a surging socialist movement at home and Kaiser Wilhelm's Germany abroad. What had once been an instrument important for the proper functioning of "civilizing" measures against colonial subjects had now morphed into a tool that, it was claimed, was necessary for the United States government to use—along with wiretaps, brutal interrogation, and other extra-constitutional measures—against its "home" inhabitants, citizens as well as non-citizens.[12]

One counterpart to Twain's imprisoned rage or Tolentino's imprisoned idealism is what postcolonial scholars such as Sarah Sarita See have called colonial melancholia—a persistent, haunting sense of ennui, bodily injury and dismemberment, displacement, memory loss, and mourning mixed with anger. Such a set of symptoms certainly marks Tolentino's play, both its production and publication history and the text itself—and it marks Twain's "person in darkness" as well. Colonial melancholia as defined by See is the set of symptoms suffered by the victims of colonialism, both its physical acts and its acts of representation and interpretation, its forms of silencing and its claims to speak "for" those who are colonized. Such a state should be distinguished from imperialist melancholia, i.e., the guilt, shame, and other feelings held by some (not all) of those allied with colonizing powers. Elites may be troubled with such feelings regardless of whether they are pro- or anti-imperialist, foreigners or natives. Amy Kaplan well defines imperialist melancholia in the complicated case of Mark Twain: "a form of blocked mourning for both the victims of imperial violence and the lost privileges of imperial power, which for [Twain] were intertwined with the loss of slavery" (*Anarchy* 57)—and, I would add, the loss or endangerment of the colonist's sense of superiority, the firm sense Twain once had that his country was fighting in the Philippines "for another man's [freedom]. And I think this is the first time it has been done."[13]

Until *Yesterday, Today, and Tomorrow* and other archival material like it are read not just as examples of Filipino or other "native" literature but also as colonial constituents of the literary history of the United States, these anti-colonial voices will remain hidden wounds, beings sentenced to sit in darkness in the midst of the "canon" that is American literature. Pairing Tolentino and Twain should also encourage us to rethink the dynamics of the entire Jim Crow colonial period, precluding any premature boundary-drawing we might make between the U.S. South, the nation, and the nation's new colonies.

# Chapter Nine

# Educating Whites to Be *White* on the Global Frontier

## HYPNOTISM AND AMBIVALENCE IN THOMAS DIXON AND OWEN WISTER (1900–1905)

> There are certain hideous sights which when once seen can never be wholly erased from the mental retina. The mere fact of having seen them implies degradation. Whoever . . . has ever taken part in lawlessly putting to death a criminal by the dreadful torture of fire must forever have the awful spectacle of his own handiwork seared into his brain and soul.
>
> —Theodore Roosevelt, 1903[1]

In *Invisible Empire* (1880), Albion Tourgée's history of the rise of the Ku Klux Klan, he commented on the postwar financing of the new public schools in the South, citing Mississippi as a representative case: "Mississippi State law (after Reconstruction) established separate public schools for white and for colored children, and directed their support as to come from a common school fund consisting of the proceeds of certain land sales, penal fines, license taxes, &c.; and the State Constitution levied in aid of this fund a poll tax. . . . Both the assessors of these taxes, and the teachers employed, fell under the violent displeasure of the white population" (58–59).

Such displeasure was vividly confirmed in many anti-Reconstruction novels published in response to authors like Tourgée, especially Thomas Nelson Page's *Red Rock, A Chronicle of Reconstruction* (1898) and Thomas Dixon's Reconstruction trilogy: *The Leopard's Spots, A Romance of the White Man's Burden—1865–1900* (1902), *The Clansman, An Historical Romance of the Ku Klux Klan* (1905), and *The Traitor* (1907). Both these authors vilified Reconstruction black schools—not just as bad uses of taxpayer's money, but also as sites where blacks and traitorous whites plotted revenge and insurrection against responsible white leadership. Focused on the rise of blacks into power in the immediate post–Civil War period, and then on the white supremacist victories in the 1870s that led to the collapse of Reconstruction in the South, these novels also become crisis-filled allegories for the new forms of racial struggle emerging in the South in the 1890s, when in response to economic depression and other perceived threats, whites consolidated their power via laws mandating public segregation and black disfranchisement, among other measures, and public lynchings became more virulent than ever before. Dixon's and Page's novels imperfectly tried to meld whites' views of the turmoil of the immediate postwar period with those of the New South crises of the 1890s. Yet far from representing white power as the solution to all the South's problems, Page, Dixon, and other apologists for New South Jim Crow in their fiction suggest that whiteness is under siege, confused about its aims and uncertain of its racial and cultural genealogy.

Page's and Dixon's historical fantasias of white supremacy reborn in the New South appeared at a moment in U.S. literary history when historical romances of all kinds were best-sellers. As chronicled by Amy Kaplan's "Romancing the Empire: The Embodiment of American Masculinity in the Popular Historical Novel of the 1890s," authors such as Richard Harding Davis, Charles Major, George Barr McCutcheon, Owen Wister, and Mary Johnston featured chivalric rescue narratives in which a beleaguered white hero rediscovers his self-confidence and sense of historical mission by saving a primitive frontier territory under siege, often with the aid of a heroine who finds a new social position for herself by aiding and eventually marrying the hero. These romances' settings may be as diverse as medieval Europe, the South Pacific, the American West, colonial North America or Latin America, or mythical kingdoms far in the past. They all struck a chord with the reading public because, in the midst of the "closing" of the Western frontier and debates over U.S. expansionism abroad, they provided generally optimistic narratives about how the Anglo-Saxon virtues of American whiteness could be rejuvenated.

Much more work needs to be done collating the ideological parallels and differences between popular historical romances of the 1890s and after depicting the U.S. South and those set in other geographies and other eras. In what ways can these texts be read as allegories of contemporary U.S. history? How is whiteness defined? And in what ways, if any, do such novels express ambivalence or doubt about their heroic narratives?

The post–Civil War language of white supremacy in the United States may be best understood as a developing and often unstable discourse, not a fixed and stable one, nor one operating only via overt expressions of racist hate and white superiority. White supremacism wielded tremendous cultural authority, true, but it also proved to be immensely insecure, in need of constant reiteration and reformation and boundary-drawing, not to mention violent purgations and reaffirmations of its own virtuousness. It thereby revealed itself not to be a given, but to be something that had to be learned and reinforced. If there is one trend that marks the development of the study of the languages of race, nation, and empire in the 1990s and the early twenty-first century, it is that discourses of power are no longer treated as simply monolithic and repressive or terroristic, though at times they can be all these. Discourse networks fracture and speak in many voices, including apparently beneficent ones; and they operate in multiple public and private arenas, developing over time patterns that are more like a matrix of vectors than a concrete solidity. To investigate what whiteness meant in the United States at the turn to the twentieth century, legislative and judicial debates and actions are obviously important, but so too are other records of activity in the public sphere, from discussions of education and citizenship that may appear inclusive, to public spectacles, such as demagogic speeches and lynchings, that are clearly meant to put non-whiteness forcefully in its proper place. New South novels, though fictional, are crucial to consider in such an investigation because they actively helped shaped the dynamism in the public sphere of the time; they did not merely reflect it. Further, because of its multivocal and symbolic registers, fiction tends to reveal with great clarity the contradictions in public discourse. Its attempts to manage and resolve these contradictions are equally instructive. Both the surface narratives and the subtexts of novels can mark anxieties and fantasies that often cannot express themselves, except from behind a mask. These ironies are particularly notable when we look at heroic representations of white superiority in fiction.

Two best-selling U.S. authors from the early twentieth century, Owen Wister and Thomas Dixon, bring all of the above concerns sharply into focus. Both were obsessed with rehabilitating southern white male heroism by making it recognized as an *American* resource, no longer a threat to national unity. They also in different ways link healing the United States' North-South divide with a new and even more heroic phase of history, the United States' emergence in the 1890s as an industrial, imperial power on the global stage. Their fictions promoting these rescue narratives, however, are also besieged by doubts over whether whiteness would indeed emerge triumphant.

Wister's indelibly influential Western hero in *The Virginian* (1902), "the Southerner," has an effect much like hypnotism on both his admirers—particularly the novel's narrator—and his enemies. Wister sets his novel's action within North America but signifies that it is also to be interpreted as an allegory creating a new Anglo-Saxon hero for America in its post-1898 imperial era—one very much modeled on Theodore Roosevelt's ideal of the rough rider, the manly man. Yet Wister's novel—particularly its ending—also implies a turbulent ambivalence about the fate of the racial and moral values his hero is meant to embody and others to imitate.

Like Wister, Dixon fantasized about how to make mesmerizing white heroism in action, and he too was particularly concerned with rehabilitating southern white manhood. The section on Dixon will broaden the schoolhouse theme of *Sitting in Darkness* in order to accommodate what is the most important and dramatic scene of instruction in *The Clansman*, which takes place in a cave whose shadowy drama morphs in Dixon's rendering into a *cinema-house* for the inculcation of white supremacy. Dixon's portrait of black schools in the novel is basically unnuanced and negative; but his depiction of how whites need to be schooled to adopt white supremacy is filled with fascinating tensions. If much Progressivist educational practice prescribed an imitative model for educating people of color to be subjects, not citizens, Dixon's most gripping scene in *The Clansman* applies that discourse to *whites*: they must be tutored what white supremacist acts to copy and what black behavior to abhor. Of course, Dixon intended that such scenes of instruction would validate whites' fitness for rule. But the white crowd scenes in the novel actually do the opposite, depicting anything but an enlightened citizenry confident in its genetic superiority to reign over others. Whites must not only discover their whiteness and understand its power through the new legal measures of Jim Crow segregation and the old arts of demagogic rhetoric; a powerful new technology, the cinema, must be brought to bear as well, whose affect on its audience is to hypnotize them into believing that only they are destined to be free. At such moments in *The Clansman*, Progressivist dependency models of education take a powerful new turn, one replete with unintended ironies. Dixon desperately wanted to believe that the new visual language of the cinema—as well as public spectacles like lynching—would work wonders in stabilizing and shaping white solidarity. But what his texts reveal in practice is how troubled and turbulent such spectacles are as means of codifying whiteness and its destiny. Wister's and Dixon's visual tropes hope that the ideals of whiteness their novels promote can be made permanent and irresistible, but their narratives also tell a different story.

# 1

Philadelphia-born Owen Wister, obviously, was not a southern author, nor is his novel *The Virginian*, strictly speaking, about the South. It is set in the frontier West, mostly the Wyoming territory before statehood. But Wister's best-seller did not just single-handedly establish the Western as a key genre for twentieth-century U.S. fiction. It took a significant narrative line from popular white postwar fiction about the South—the marriage (usually) of a northern man to a southern woman as a sign of the fruits of national reunification—and revised this North-South narrative axis into an East-West one, contemplating the consequences of uniting cultured East with rugged West. Narratives set in the ever-receding "Western" territories had been popular and influential in the United States since before the Civil War, of course, with James Fenimore Cooper as the most important example. But only after the rapid growth of immigration and urbanization in the East, Midwest, and West Coast, the "closing" of the frontier in the continental United States, and the acquisition of colonies overseas in the 1890s, did Westerns celebrating cowboys in the open plains and mountains really begin to take hold in U.S. popular culture, from "Wild West" shows, nickelodeon shorts, feature films, and dime novels to more "legitimate" fiction promoted by prestigious New York publishing houses (in Wister's case, first *Harper's Magazine*, then Macmillan).

This northerner's Western is also significant because it invented a new way to make a southerner a national epic hero. As David Blight and Nina Silber have shown, in the South in the 1880s and after the new Decoration Day holiday honored Confederate veterans; Lost Cause nostalgia throughout the South reimagined them as tragic heroes who fought for independence, not to preserve a slave system. After the Spanish-American War, Union and Confederate soldiers were increasingly honored together, rather than in separate ceremonies. And in popular narratives, veterans from both sides of the War between the States were increasingly depicted as figures who later worked together to help conquer the West and defend U.S. interests overseas. Wister's *The Virginian* played a crucial role in this rehabilitation of southern whiteness into an action hero embodying American global, not regional, power. In the complicated aftermath of the victory over Spain, when U.S. forces had to fight insurgents in Cuba and the Philippines, Wister created an instantly famous cowboy hero who could tame savagery with the same sure hand he used to train horses. As well as being the most influential Western in the young century, Wister's *The Virginian* portrayed an idealized hero for the epic of U.S. expansionism abroad that many U.S. citizens desired, including Theodore Roosevelt, to whom the book was dedicated with glowing praise. But unforeseen ironies kept intruding into Wister's narrative, even though irony was a mode for which his hero had no use—not to mention the unmistakable symptoms of imperial melancholia.

From the very first chapter, the hero of Wister's *The Virginian* is anonymous, known only as "the Southerner" or "the Virginian," not as the "ex-Confederate" or the "Rebel," even though we learn that he lost two brothers and his father in the Civil War. This southerner is seen not as an outsider figure needing to be reintegrated into what is acceptably "American," but an epic hero whose acts revivify American maleness itself. He can deflate eastern pretensions and the various kinds of decadence that come with civilization, thus providing an antidote to it. He has a streak of animal primitivism, something eternally beyond being civilized or feminized. He is fully conversant and comfortable with modernity—knowledgeable about capitalism, technology, eastern institutions, and even the subtle differences between New York and Philadelphia restaurants (128). However, though he desires to be made more "civilized" by women, he retains the right to make dry remarks about all forms of culture, especially those that seem poorly adapted to their rough western surroundings.

By Wister's design, the Southerner is an epic hero of his time but also somehow outside of time. The Wyoming territories become a mythic space where character is tested and revealed and Good battles Evil. But recent criticism by Richard Slotkin, John Calwelti, Jane Tompkins, and Amy Kaplan has persuasively argued that such transcendental and mythic tropes in the American Western mask how time- and culture-bound they are. Indeed, Wister's Western is an imperial romance, wherein domestic spaces are re-purified through the invigorating violence of a hero's encounters with barbarism at the edges of the "civilized" world. A tale of how a southerner becomes American now also becomes a story of how America itself may be tested and strengthened in its core by what occurs on its global "frontiers."

We first glimpse the book's hero from a train, as a group of cowboys try to lasso a feisty horse in a corral near the tracks. As yet wholly unknown, the man catches the narrator's eye because his body moves "with the undulations of a tiger, smooth and easy, as if his muscles flowed beneath his skin" as he effortlessly moves to subdue the horse. Once captured, the animal becomes completely tamed, walking "with a sweet, church-door expression" (3–4). This man is first called "the giant" by the narrator, as if he is larger than life, and then "the Southerner" after the narrator hears his accent. When this same figure is discovered mercilessly teasing an overdressed and effete old man, the narrator, picking up the Southerner's sense of humor, calls him a horse "combed and curried to a finish" by so-called civilization (5). Unmatched in his power to subdue and civilize, the Southerner also apparently moves apart from civilization, able to see it with an irreverent, critical eye. To the eastern-bred narrator's eyes, it is almost love at first sight. Homoerotic energy between the narrator and his ideal of masculine prowess runs remarkably strongly as an undercurrent throughout the novel, but never more than in the first chapter, when the narrator at one point even says, "Had I been the bride, I should have taken the giant" (5). The only figure who perfectly balances animal strength and refined culture, cunning and morality, seriousness and wild humor, the Southerner is portrayed both as a force of nature and the very model of Jeffersonian natural aristocracy, a "gentleman" through and through even though he sports jeans and boots covered with trail dust (10).

If the Virginian embodies a regional accent and its mores, he also in the narrator's eyes quickly becomes robustly national, American. He sings with gusto love ballads or southern minstrel songs, including one about beating up a "Car' lina nigger" named Jim Crow (139).[2] Yet Wister's hero is far more than a regional hero morphing into something national, and this extra quality is not merely mythic or transcendental. It is transnational or, more properly speaking, extra-territorial or colonial. It embodies the nation and its values but may exist outside of its territories, beyond them. The space of the West as it is developed in this novel allows this hero continuously to circulate outside of strict community and national boundaries, yet always also to reinscribe them. Wherever the Southerner walks or rides, in the narrator's awe-struck eyes he brings "America."

In an early sketch called "The Evolution of the Cow-Puncher" on the allure of the cowboy, Wister wrote that such a figure would be an attractive hero for the postwar nation because he represented the "slumbering untamed Saxon" virtues of self-reliance and resourcefulness that the United States needed. In itself, the Anglo-Saxonism in Wister's essay is hardly remarkable; it is wholly a part of the racialist rhetoric of the times, as Reginald Horsman and others have described it. In *The Virginian*, written several years later, Wister's genealogy of his imagined hero still implicitly praises Saxon virtues, but it is also intriguingly specific, delineating a southern identity that can now claim to be the American Everyman:

> I am of old stock in Virginia English and one Scotch Irish grandmother my father's father brought from Kentucky. We have always stayed at the same place farmers and hunters not bettering our lot and very plain. We have fought when we got the chance, under Old Hickory and in Mexico and my father and two brothers were killed in the [Shenandoah?] Valley sixty-four. Always with us one son has been apt to run away and I was the one this time. I had too much older brothering to suit me. But now [out West] I am doing well being in full sight of prosperity. (239–240)

Here defeated Rebel is resurrected as archetypal American, with a plain and honest (and endearingly unpunctuated) prose style to match. Wister dedicated his novel to his hero, Theodore Roosevelt, well aware that in his Southerner he had created the very model of the rough-riding, Saxon heroism Roosevelt extolled as necessary if a newly prosperous America were to remain in fighting trim and rise to its imperial destiny. Wister's Southerner to some degree was also modeled after Kipling's heroes, as Roosevelt himself noticed (Wister, "Preface" xxxv).

Amy Kaplan has pointed out that the original title for Wister's essay on why U.S. fiction needed such a hero was "The Course of Empire" (*Anarchy of Empire* 119). Wister's first title plotted a single trajectory aligning medieval chivalry, the regeneration of manliness in the American West, and the testing of it in the United States' new empire in the Caribbean, Latin America, and the Pacific. In Wister's eyes, his western hero was a plain American translation of the medieval concept of *translatio studii*—the idea that the destiny of being the world's leading civilization has continually passed westward, from Greece to Rome to Europe.[3] The more mythic and timeless *The Virginian*'s western setting, then, the more potent its historical references and resonance could be to U.S. readers in the post-1898 era.

Wister registered his interest in having the American West signify something far beyond itself at the end of the very first chapter in *The Virginian*. As the narrator comically stares forlornly after the east-bound train that has left him without his luggage in the middle of nowhere, he says, "I stared after it as it went its way to the *far shores* of civilization. It grew small in the unending gulf of space, until all sign of its presence was gone" (7, italics mine). This is our first taste of the Western sublime in *The Virginian*, just as we have had a first taste of western humor a few pages earlier. That is, Wister's West is not just a geographical space but a territory offering a cultural and metaphysical upheaval and revelation. It is a world of complete openness and newness, where all the signs of civilization are made infinitesimally small and one is now on one's own confronting the new and the strange. (Thus, it qualifies as a version of the sublime, that aesthetic category that mixes profound beauty with danger, strangeness, unpredictability, and spiritual immanence.) But Wister's West is also clearly marked in the above quotation as a space beyond the "shores" of American civilization, as if out in the far Pacific colonies.

Another way to understand the broad cultural significance of the Southerner is via Wister's interest in the historical novelist Walter Scott. John Seelye has commented shrewdly on Wister's indebtedness to Walter Scott and James Fenimore Cooper for their use of landscapes as well as their plots and their epic ambition. To put it another way, what Wister does is use basic Scottian narrative devices to rehabilitate southern whiteness and make it national and heroic once again. The traditional Scott hero mediates between two cultures, neither of which he fully belongs to; he achieves his destiny by sacrificing himself to become the agent of a historical synthesis that could not occur without him. The landscape of the majority of Scott's historical romances was generally the borderlands between Scotland and England—or, in the exception that is *Ivanhoe*, between Anglo-Saxon and Norman medieval England. In the case of *The Virginian*, Scott's borderlands became the American West, his knights and other heroic figures the American cowboy. But which two cultures in *The Virginian* clash and synthesize in this liminal territory, via the agency of the Southerner? Vermont and Virginia? Civilized East and lawless West? Experience versus book learning? Anarchic cattle rustlers versus law-abiding cowboys allied with the institutions of civilization, from ranches to railroads and court systems? Female spheres versus male spheres? Ranching culture succeeded by that of railroading and mining and politics? Perhaps all of the above. It also should be stressed that the Southerner's eventual bride, Miss Mary Stark "Molly" Wood from Vermont, is almost as important a figure for negotiating culture clash as the book's male hero. In making his heroine a rebellious yet mediating figure, here too Wister was following Scott.[4]

Another obvious and successful Scottian motif in *The Virginian* is the epic confrontation between Good and Evil. The Southerner's verbal and gun duels with the cattle rustler Trampas were as popular in the early twentieth century as Ivanhoe's jousting and sword fights were in the nineteenth. Like Ivanhoe, the

Virginian is nursed back to health from a near-death experience (chapter 27) before he has his climactic battle (chapter 35). In contrast to *Ivanhoe*'s epic battle, though, *The Virginian*'s gun duel is calculatedly anti-climactic; after a long, suspense-filled lead-up, it is over in a second. Wister's prose even makes the gunfight seem a minor natural event: a bullet fired at the hero is described as "[a] wind seemed to blow his sleeve off his arm." The hero's cool calm under pressure could not stand out more strongly in contrast to the frenzied crowd: "'I expect that's all,' he said aloud" (310). Here Wister wholly changes his model Scott; whereas Ivanhoe is rather reticent, Scott's narrator is verbose and Latinate and his fight descriptions go on for pages. In *The Virginian* Wister invented a new vocabulary for male heroism, a mixture of infinite inner strength, casual ease, and a taciturn distrust of language—an ideal later immortalized by the Hemingway hero and the phrase "grace under pressure." Such a hero exercises violence reluctantly and only after repeated provocation. When he does unleash it, it is intensely controlled and implacable, yet handled with an air of nonchalance.

Before the Southerner's confrontation with Trampas, he debates the ethics of what he is about to do with a bishop and Molly, his wife-to-be. Both urge him not to fight, citing first religious principles such as the Ten Commandments and then the claims of a more secular civilization's laws and manners. The Southerner concedes their claims but says he cannot change his own frontier ethics, which rely on manly honor not accountable to church, state, or wife. Both the bishop and Molly wind up conceding that, by his lights, the Southerner is right to do what he has to do. In *The Virginian*, Wister thus appears to posit two mutually exclusive ethical spheres co-existing simultaneously—one appropriate for the frontier and the other for civilization. But this dichotomy is rather too simple. *The Virginian*'s actions and words suggest that the "civilized" world actually follows after the state of nature and is therefore indebted to it. Without the Southerner battling the forces of evil after sundown, there could be no town, no bishop, no wife out West. He is apart from civilization ethically, yet his actions establish the ground on which lawful society and ethics may be built. At least, this is the calculus Wister's novel proposes. As the narrator comments at one point, the Southerner "had lived many outlaw years, and his wide knowledge of evil made innocence doubly precious to him" (292).

Wister also shows that this hero's confrontation with evil must occur continuously—it is not a one-time battle. And it is staged not only on the far boundaries of what is taken to be civilization, but also in its heart. Thus the climactic shootout in the novel takes place not in the mountains but in the small settlement's main street, thereby establishing the paradigm used in countless Westerns that followed. Before this battle, both the bishop of Wyoming and the Southerner's wife-to-be push him to choose between barbarism and civilization. But the hero knows better: he knows that his courage allows them the luxury of their fine ethical distinctions. This paradox linking violence with a new phase for civilization's growth is a Scottian theme expertly and originally handled by Wister.

Neither the Virginian's nor Trampas's frontier codes of conduct, strictly speaking, are anarchic, part of a state of nature, though both are outside the bounds of civilized behavior as defined by the town's proper citizens. Both men have their own frontier ethics—once they give their word or make a threat, they have to back it up or their honor will be gone. There is thus a social or communal sense to the savage world they inhabit; it is not merely a world of every man for himself. Furthermore, both the rustler Trampas and his cowboy-rancher antagonist, the Southerner, are competing for the same cattle markets. Trampas represents the essence of anti-social behavior and perhaps even Evil itself. But he is also portrayed by Wister as just a bad market speculator who is neither as knowledgeable nor as self-regulating as his adversary. Wister represents Trampas as a more primitive stage of capitalism at work, a man whose time and methods are rapidly becoming outdated. Both these dimensions—the historical and the transcendental—make Trampas the effective villain that any epic conflict requires to be worthy of its name.

A central episode in the novel's long build-up to the Virginian's decisive act of violence proves that Wister wanted his hero read as an agent of modernity, not just a noble savage. Molly Stark and Judge Henry debate whether there is a moral difference between lynchings in the South and the cowboy hero executing a man in the frontier without a trial. Wister stage-manages the debate so that the judge decisively wins:

> "I see no likeness in principle whatever between burning Southern negroes [sic] in public and hanging Wyoming horse-thieves in private. I consider the burning a proof that the South is semi-barbarous, and the hanging a proof that Wyoming is determined to become civilized. . . . We are in a bad way, and we are trying to make that way a little better until civilization can reach us. At present we lie beyond its pale. . . . And so when your ordinary citizen sees this, . . . he must take justice back into his own hands where it was once at the beginning of all things. Call this primitive, if you will. But so far from being a defiance of the law, it is an *assertion* of it—the fundamental assertion of self-governing men, upon whom our whole social fabric is based." (280–282, italics Wister's)

Such arguments are quintessentially Progressivist, of course, precisely paralleling the kinds of claims that justified whites' "controlled" use of violence to pacify western territories or plant civilization in Caribbean and Pacific colonies. Progressivist figures like Roosevelt saw lynchings as a barbaric embarrassment, while Roosevelt justified wielding violence against insurgents on the frontier or in the colonies as integral to the civilizing mission.

In Ida B. Wells-Barnett's anti-lynching campaigns, which were contemporaneous to Wister's novel, she explicitly resisted the kind of reasoning articulated by Wister's judge (and Theodore Roosevelt) that would sharply distinguish between lynchings and the violence used to civilize. In her "Lynch Law in America" essay of 1900, for instance, Wells-Barnett makes a point to chronicle lynchings throughout the continent, not just in the U.S. South. She records that in 1892 there were 9 lynchings in the Wyoming territory, the locale of Wister's *The Virginian*, as well as 241 nationwide. For Wells-Barnett, anyone justifying lynching and other forms of mob violence would use arguments for their necessity very similar to those of Wister's judge. While recognizing the implicit critique of homegrown violence embedded in Wells-Barnett's use of statistics, however, we must also acknowledge the complex *colonialist* aspects of Wells-Barnett's anti-lynching discourse. In order to increase her appeal for justice at home, Wells-Barnett linked her anti-lynching activities to the reform projects of U.S. colonialism that she believed her audience endorsed: "Our nation has been active and outspoken in its endeavor to right the wrongs of the Armenian Christian, the Russian Jew, ... the Cuban patriot. Surely it should be the nation's duty to correct its own evils!"

As we will see in a moment, those who sought to justify lynching, such as Thomas Dixon, challenged the judge's reasoning by taking a different angle. For them, lynching was an assertion of the rights of a self-governing people, not a proof of barbarism. As much an admirer of Theodore Roosevelt as Wister was, Dixon would in his fiction directly challenge Roosevelt's claim that lynching was a sign of savagery. Dixon defended such acts not just as essential to the "social fabric" of civilization, but also as a spectacle creating a sense of racial unity among whites that would not exist without it. Racist discourse certainly drives *The Virginian*, but except for certain moments it operates more as a subtext than a primary theme. In Dixon, though, white supremacism moves to the foreground and becomes indispensable to any proper understanding of modernity.

After Trampas is shot dead and the rustlers routed, the Southerner and his bride retreat to an island for a honeymoon spent camping (chapter 36). It is as if they have returned to the Garden before the arrival of the snake. Wister's prose in this chapter is never more like Mark Twain's, particularly Huck's descriptions of Jackson's Island and the raft in *Huckleberry Finn*. But by the novel's end we learn that once Wyoming Territory became a state in 1890, others cleverer than Trampas's gang in the ways of corruption not only gained control of most of the ranches but ran the newspapers and most of the state's new institutions (323). This decidedly downbeat and ironic ending to *The Virginian* may be interpreted as an urban easterner's call for Progressivist reforms in the new states out West. But Wister's conclusion also has all the symptoms of imperial melancholia—regret over what was lost after "progress" was made.[5] Wister's rather ambivalent ending to *The Virginian* did not influence the early Westerns that followed, for they brim with the righteousness of colonial victors. But its equivalent may certainly be felt in later Westerns (such as the movies *Broken Arrow* or *The Misfits* from the 1950s, or the recent Border Trilogy of Cormac McCarthy) that contrast the loss of a supposedly open frontier with the barbarism that passes for civilization.

In sum, much can be made of *The Virginian* as a quasi-colonial narrative in which the hero's carefully controlled violence applied at the boundaries of "civilization" allegedly regenerates its values and proves its moral and cultural superiority. I have followed historians like Richard Slotkin, Jane Tompkins, and Amy Kaplan in skeptically examining the ideological role of such an action hero. But we should not ignore the antinomy: the concluding paragraphs of *The Virginian* (and scattered earlier moments) are profoundly elegiac and dystopian. Wister never questioned that his hero embodied all that is good, but his novel's ending makes illusory any simple victory of civilized values over barbarous ones. If we press a critique of *The Virginian* and its Kiplingesque post-1898 colonial warrior-hero, as we should, then we must also admit that the book asks (however quietly) whether the hero's victory was really that successful. The Edenic island vision of the West the Southerner defended has evolved into what the narrator calls a "broken country" (323) run by thieves. The only thing that saves the Southerner's ranch and lets him teach his boys to ride horses is a railroad that gives the coal he mines access to the markets of the industrial East. So Wister's paradigmatic Western in the end waxes ambivalent about the fate in an industrial age of its Progressivist frontier-colonial paragon. But the novel's concluding sentence tries to turn away from such doubts, back to the vision of a hero who will "live a long while" (323) in some mythic space apart from, yet dependent upon, a world he abhors.

## 2

The classic example of an intellectual who gravitates toward the powerful by giving them an image of themselves they yearn for, Thomas Dixon tried to embody in his first novel the main ideals of Progressivist imperialism then taking shape. Subtitled *A Romance of the White Man's Burden, 1865–1900*, *The Leopard's Spots* (1902) casts the white southerners as America's new visionaries, while its northerners merely know how to manufacture wealth. In the view of Dixon's heroes, abolitionists forced to South to secede, but secession was a disaster because "we collided with the resistless movement of humanity from the ideal of local sovereignty toward nationalism, centralisation, solidarity" (335). One influential figure does warn that America is threatened by a demonic version of national oneness: "'You cannot build in a Democracy a nation inside a nation of two antagonistic races. The future American must be an Anglo-Saxon or a Mulatto'" (387). But, in general, the novel tries to be optimistic that Anglo-Saxons will prevail. Other

characters promote a solution to the "Negro problem" that does not involve erad-
ication or export; rather, a new, improved form of bondage will be created via
agricultural labor contracts and sharecropping and a ban on blacks in other jobs,
such as mill work—all very much like what was actually being instituted in the
South under Jim Crow at the time (cf. *Leopard's Spots* 463–464). The climax of
the book comes at the Democratic political convention, when the hero, inspired
by the victory over Spain, expounds on the "world mission" of whites in language
that is half Hegelian, half Teddy Rooseveltian:

> "The Old South fought against the stars in their courses—the resistless tide
> of the rising consciousness of Nationality and World-Mission. The young
> South greets the new era and glories in its manhood. He joins his voice
> in the cheers of triumph which are ushering in this all-conquering Saxon.
> Our old men dreamed of local supremacy. We dream of the conquest of
> the globe.... We believe that God has raised up our race, as he ordained
> Israel of old, in this world-crisis to establish and maintain for weaker races,
> as a trust for civilisation, the principles of civil and religious Liberty and
> the forms of Constitutional Government." (*Leopard's Spots* 439)

The Dixon hero means to prove to his audience that the white South's wounded
masculinity will be healed by joining the national consensus in praise of the
new colonialism, which works first by force and then in the name of Anglo-
Saxon generosity and constitutional principles. The language with which the
task is described here and elsewhere, however—most markedly, "In this hour of
crisis, our flag has been raised over ten millions of semi-barbaric black men in
the foulest slave pen of the Orient" (439)—suggests immense anxieties swirling
amidst all Dixon's paeans to white reunification under the banner of colonialism. The vexing racial conflicts of the Old and New South, he fears, may now be
re-enacted on a global stage. In *The Leopard's Spots* the U.S. national unconscious
seethes so hysterically with uncertainty about the "race question" at home and
the new imperial ventures abroad that it may be swayed "from laughter to tears
in a single sentence" (443) by a demagogue posing as a democrat.

Dixon's first novel remains controversial for its venomous racist rhetoric,
which, like much of the discourse of the time, veers back and forth from biological essentialism to judging blacks by their supposed lack of "character" and
cultural accomplishments. But Dixon becomes trapped into using the same racial
discourse with all its contradictions to proclaim *whites'* destiny as well. Anglo-
Saxons can achieve their role as the new Israelites only if they recognize the fundamental racial unity that strengthens their world mission. To a great extent,
Dixon's sense of Anglo-Saxonism is congruent with many prior authors who
stressed the heterogeneous sources yet powerful synthetic bio-cultural forces that

fused to make hyphenated Anglo-Saxonism into "Aryan" or "white." Witness, for instance, the following point made by a famous European theoretician of Aryan racial supremacy, Herbert Spencer, interviewed in the *New York Times* in 1882: "From biological truths it is to be inferred that the eventual mixture of allied varieties of the Aryan race forming the population [of the United States] will produce a more powerful type of man than has hitherto existed."[6]

Yet when Dixon's hero in *The Leopard's Spots* attempts to catalogue all the "allied varieties" that constitute the new improved Anglo-Saxon emerging in the United States, his rhetoric of varied "linear" descents converging into synthesis quickly spirals out of control: "The courage of the Celt, the nobility of the Norman, the vigour of the Viking, the energy of the Angle, the tenacity of the Saxon, the daring of the Dane, the gallantry of the Gaul, the freedom of the Frank, the earth-hunger of the Roman and the stoicism of the Spartan, are all yours by the linear heritage of blood" (446). Each subgroup remains locked within its characteristic "trait"—many of which comically just happen to alliterate with the subgroup's name—and so instead of newly discovered white unity, what the speech actually enacts is infinite hyphenation determined by blood-cultural difference. The passage is anything but "linear."

Such a textual aporia exemplifies how in white racist discourse *whiteness* persistently resisted coherent definition. Was it the same as Anglo-Saxon, or, more broadly still, Saxon or Aryan? Even an emphasis on northern European roots for whiteness started to intertwine with other tribal rhizomes, as Dixon's catalogue of sources for whiteness moves inexorably south and east, through France and Italy toward Spartan Greece. Looming unnamed are the Caucasus themselves, those mountains in south-central Asia (in what is now Chechnya) that yielded a skull whose features Johann Friedrich Blumenbach in 1775 gave the name "Caucasian." By the nineteenth century, Caucasian had become a much disputed synonym for "white" or even Anglo-Saxon—yet by locating the origins of whiteness outside of Europe proper, Caucasian made incoherent the competing geographical, cultural, and genetic/biological influences that were to be synthesized into "white" identity. For similar reasons, white racial genealogy emerges from Dixon's *The Leopard's Spots*—indelibly—as spotted.[7]

Dixon's *The Leopard's Spots* embodied better than he knew the doubts and internal divisions regarding Aryan identity that made white supremacist rhetoric so vitriolic. As he moved from the exposure and denunciation rituals of his first novel to the orgiastic violence against blacks in *The Clansman*, Dixon conceded that an abstract conception of world-conquering destiny, however noble, might not be enough to fuse "whites" into race unity. A bloody bonding ritual involving public scapegoating and the clear demarcation of the *difference* between black and white would be necessary.[8]

In the New South of Dixon's era blacks could be lynched for being too successful as well as for being accused of a crime such as rape.[9] They could be strung up for speaking or refusing to speak, burned for looking where they "shouldn't" look or for just appearing in a way that was taken to be offensive and threatening—such as requiring payment for completed work before contracting to do more. But most often their crimes against whiteness were heightened by being made out to be crimes against white womanhood, the threat of a black seed defiling the purity of a white womb and fathering a host of children who might pass. Butchering a scapegoat in a public space, the ritual of lynching has a paradox in its dark heart: it is not just a black body that is dismembered, but black communities at large that are targeted and changed. Lynching was meant to terrorize the body of the black community as a whole—but especially any members of an emergent black middle class. Many such acts against individuals were accompanied by white riots that focused on property, not just black bodies, destroying black-owned businesses, homes, and other possessions in order to scarify an entire community on the rise. The Wilmington, North Carolina, white riot of 1898 is just one of many notorious examples. Statistics gathered by Ida B. Wells-Barnett as well as by contemporary scholars show that the number of lynchings spiked in periods of most economic and social tension, with the 1890–1910 period—during the imposition of Jim Crow segregation, black disfranchisement, and numerous economic crises—being the deadliest for blacks, only excepting the immediate postwar years, 1865–1870. Blacks were not the only people lynched in the postwar period, of course; Chinese and Italians were also frequent victims. But they were decidedly in the majority, and not just in the U.S. South. In 1892, for instance, when Wells-Barnett recorded 241 lynchings, 160 involved black victims: 4 in New York, Ohio, and Kansas, the rest in the South, including 29 in Louisiana, 28 in Tennessee, 25 in Arkansas, 22 in Alabama, and 5 in Dixon's North Carolina. The vast majority of those lynched in 1892—155 out of 160—were men.[10]

Important as it was as a terroristic threat against blacks, lynching also acted to re-enforce and purify the boundaries of the white body politic (as well as the particular body of a white woman whose penetration by blackness was the most frequently alleged "reason" for lynching). James Allen's *Without Sanctuary: Lynching Photographs in America* reveals that many lynching postcards do not prominently feature lynched black bodies, though some of course do. In these others one must search hard to find the corpse. What instead is front and center in many photographs is a phalanx of whites, often staring proudly but also somewhat anxiously into the camera lens.[11]

Lynching may ultimately be understood as a kind of demonic version of the Christian sacrament of the communion ritual commemorating the crucifixion. The lynched black body was not merely disfigured, dismembered, castrated, burnt, or otherwise scarified and erased; it was symbolically *consumed* in its violated state by whites as a sign of their renewed white unity and power. Yet in this twisted version of the sacrament, it is the white community of spectators that is to be resurrected, not the figure on the "cross." Lynchings were thus a kind of demonic Last Supper enacting the trials and resurrection of whiteness. Whites bought picture postcards of lynchers and spectators posing together near the corpse(s) and sent them to friends, thus widening the circle of participants. Actual body parts from lynchings would sometimes be displayed in white communities too, such as the blackened knuckle bones W. E. B. Du Bois described in the window of an Atlanta store right alongside the latest brand-name consumer commodities. Many lynchings took place in barren sites outside of a town or city, but others occurred near town centers or key buildings or bridges. The ritual was thus understood as an act that affirmed, not shamed, white power as civilized and modern and progressive—and a rite of acculturation and bonding. How otherwise to understand the frequent jokes made on the back of postcards treating lynchings as picnics or barbeques? We might even more darkly call lynchings the church socials sponsored by the gospel of whiteness.[12]

Such an analysis stressing cannibalism and communion may seem extreme, but only ritual and religion can explain the visceral power that lynching rituals held for those who instigated them and those who traded in their images and signed messages joking about consuming them as one would a tasty barbeque. They were simultaneously an informal social festival and a scene of instruction, full of deadly seriousness teaching what it means to be white and how white "purity" must be defended. They were improvised yet thoroughly scripted as to their outcome; informal yet pedagogical, even pedantic; thoroughly secular, with a focus realigning sex and status and economic differences, yet ultimately mystical and Dionysian while striving to be Christian as well.

The same may be said for Dixon's best-selling narratives, which functioned for a broad audience of readers in the United States not unlike lynching postcards. They are meant to unleash frenzies of fear and anger and then resolve them cathartically, as melodrama does; yet they also frequently interrupt the swirling action for stentorian lectures on history and politics. Furthermore, like lynching's enthusiastic adoption of the modern arts of mechanical reproduction, Dixon's The Clansman would have its readers become members of a new consumer community, repurified and made modern and vigorous in its whiteness. Captured by his feverish plots, visually striking imagery, and apocalyptic rhetoric of whiteness under siege, whites could envision participating vicariously in righteous racial revenge and the rebirth of white pride. In no novel is the blood sport of lynching more important for the formation of whiteness than The Clansman. Yet the novel (like many lynching postcards) does not show the dead body directly; what Dixon is most fascinated with is the lead-up and the aftermath, the means by which the leaders of the mob stoke its members into a frenzy of lust for revenge. No doubt Dixon yearned for some of the same absolute control over his white audience's responses as his heroes had over theirs.

And for Dixon the new mechanical art that offered him the most tempting power to bond whites together was not the mass-produced postcard but the moving pictures of the cinema.

Although Thomas Dixon's *The Clansman* is well known as the source for D. W. Griffith's *The Birth of a Nation* (1915)—arguably the most influential U.S. movie in ideology and cinematic technique until the release of another movie indebted to Dixon, *Gone with the Wind* (1939)—Dixon's own obsession with tropes of hypnotism and cinema in his early fiction has been much less discussed.[13] *The Clansman*'s Dr. Cameron does not just believe in hypnosis; he believes that he may with sheer willpower (and strength of gaze) overpower an inferior's sense of identity and rewrite it to conform to what he believes is that person's "true" identity: Dr. Cameron "transfixed [his former slave Gus] with his eyes, and in a voice, whose tones gripped him by the throat, said: 'How dar you?'" (228). Dixon thus grants Dr. Cameron the power to project onto blacks' retinas and brains moving images of their abjection before white supremacy—a kind of demonic *kalokagathy* that would make blacks' interiors always legible and writeable to whites.[14]

Dr. Cameron believes he has similar powers over whites. In a later scene, the doctor explains to his skeptical son that his knowledge of how to control a person's self-image is aided by his investigations into how the eye's retina retains images while transferring them to the brain. In the case of Mrs. Lenoir, who commits suicide with her daughter after both have been raped, Dr. Cameron believes that if he examines her retina with a doctor's microscope "the fire-etched record of this crime can yet be traced"—her corpse will retain the image of her attacker, as if on a photographic plate (313). Based on his investigations, the Ku Klux Klan arrests Gus as her rapist. Neither the doctor's complicated theories, nor measurements matching the rapist's footprints and Gus's, however, are persuasive enough to convince Ben Cameron and his fellow KKK members of Gus's guilt. This causes a problem for Dixon, who feels he cannot have his heroes lynching a man before his guilt is definitively proved, even if he has the "heavy-set neck of the lower order of animals" (216). Therefore, during an inquest held before the Klan Dr. Cameron uses his hypnotic powers to get Gus to reenact the crime before a white audience, thereby providing them with what they take to be convincing proof of his guilt.

This notorious scene—book 4, chapter 2—takes place in a cave, the Klan's hideout. Dixon represents Gus's memories as if they are a motion picture reel stored inside his brain, with Dr. Cameron rewinding it via verbal commands and then having Gus re-enact the images in his head before the fascinated and horrified audience. "The negro [*sic*] began to live the crime with fearful realism—the journey past the hotel to make sure the victims had gone to their home. . . . Now they burst into the room, and with the light of hell in his beady, yellow-splotched eyes, Gus gripped his imaginary revolver and growled. . . . Gus . . . started across the cave as if to spring on the shivering figure of the girl." A "single fierce leap" follows (322–323). Ordinarily, popular theatrical metaphors might be enough for Dixon to stage such a reenactment. But Dixon's emphasis on hypnotism and light-etched images seems to speak more strongly to the new mass entertainment technology of the era, the "moving pictures." Mrs. Lenoir's retinas indicted Gus because they contained photographic evidence of his guilt. But Gus's brain, as manipulated by Dr. Cameron, dooms Gus because it contains a cinematic record of his evil deeds that can be replayed on command. And, astoundingly, Dixon's cinematic "reality" (as acted by Gus) comes complete with dialogue—twenty-some years before motion pictures could talk. Curiously, though, for all of Dixon's visual obsessions, his narrative tropes concede that crucial evidence of Gus's guilt cannot be seen, cannot even be described. His viewers must imagine (or project) the victims' presence; otherwise, Gus springs at nothing. The critical paragraph describing supposedly conclusive visual evidence of rape is filled with "as if . . . as if" phrases (323), highlighting the fact that in the end it is not so much Dr. Cameron's powers but the spectators' imaginations that create the moving picture of Gus's guilt.

The effect viewing this scene has on the audience is certainly not hypothetical. They react so violently that they threaten to interrupt the performance before the crucial moment; Dr. Cameron repeatedly has to calm them, to no avail: "Strong men began to cry like children. 'Stop him! Stop him!' screamed a clansman, springing on the negro and grinding his heel into his big thick neck" (323–324). As Sandra Gunning has rightly noted, "the Klansmen are feminized" by such an assertion of black power, experiencing "the live Marion's violation as their own" (43). Dr. Cameron is in effect a director getting his helpless actor Gus now to imprint his audience's retinas and emotions with the indelible image of black bestiality. And Dixon takes pains to show that the audience reacts as one: no skeptical voice is heard, unlike earlier (314). They howl like they are simultaneously eye-witnesses to and degraded victims of the rape.

From this moment underground, the Klan rises re-masculinized to avenge all atrocities against Anglo-Saxon civilization. The ensuing scene in *The Clansman* describes a ritual meant to signal the Klan's emergence from hiding to re-purify the blood of the two violated women and, by analogy, that of the whole white race. This scene too is obsessively concerned with light in the midst of darkness— a "Fiery Cross, extinguished in sacrificial blood" burning in the night (326). This moment later links to the final passage of the novel, where lights symbolizing the heavenly dispensation of Anglo-Saxon civilization have finally extinguished the hell-fired imagery that tormented the white South's retinal memory: "Look at our lights on the mountains! They are ablaze—range on range our signals gleam until the Fiery Cross is lost among the stars!" (374). Dixon's goals as an author are thus similar to Dr. Cameron's as a hypnotist: he will use all the power of his art to inscribe on the mind's-eye of his readers fire-written, indelible images of Negro savagery and heroic white resistance. Once that is accomplished, he believes, the course of U.S. history will be redirected. Dixon's book was not merely a source-script for D. W. Griffith's even more influential epic glorifying the Ku Klux Klan as the savior of American civilization. *The Clansman* indeed can be said to prophesy and enact some of the very techniques for shaping mass audience response (including close-ups and reaction shots) that Griffith's movie so exploited.[15]

Theodore Roosevelt, one of Dixon's heroes, of course interpreted the fire-wrought retinal imagery of lynching in a rather different way. The quotation used as an epigraph to this chapter was taken from a private 1903 letter of Roosevelt's denouncing lynching that was soon made public in the *New York Times*, where Dixon read it. Roosevelt stressed that the memory of lynching in whites who participated would not inscribe racial pride at all, but rather shame: "Whoever . . . has ever taken part in lawlessly putting to death a criminal by the dreadful torture of fire must forever have the awful spectacle of his own handiwork seared into his brain and soul." Much earlier, Edgar Allan Poe used the phrase "mental retina" to describe memory, so Roosevelt's trope was perhaps not wholly uncommon.[16] But Dixon in *The Clansman* seized on Roosevelt's figure of speech, literalized it, and then rewrote its meaning to signify not white shame but white rebirth. Indeed, Dixon's *Clansman* plot implies that such a spectacle of trauma and revivification is *indispensable* for white unity to envision itself and believe in itself. Lynching for Dixon becomes a sacrament by which the white race reenacts its crucifixion by the powers of blackness, then transforms that moment of abjection into unity and victory via the sign of the burning cross—a crux that reduces the threatening black body to ash while resurrecting the body of whiteness. Without such a blood rite, "whiteness" in *The Clansman* might be merely howling in a darkened cave, a diverse congregation of clans at odds with each other and ignorant of their shared destiny. In short, although Dixon idolized Roosevelt, he wasn't afraid to take him on regarding the issue of lynching. He made lynching quintessential to Progressivist modernity, not a barbaric aberration of it.

Stressing the symbolic meanings of lynching as a kind of demonic sacrament resurrecting the body of beleaguered whiteness must *not* be understood to imply that lynching and its related activities did not have real, physical effects. As stressed above, many acts of lynching attacked blacks who were seen to have transgressed their place, especially in terms of class and property status as well as race: it was an act of terrorism to take away property and status, not just lives. But to understand the workings of terrorism we must not reduce its meanings solely to its material effects. Lynching can be understood as the demonic underside of Progressivist rhetoric about uplift and gradual citizen-building for all, the great NO countering Progressivism's highly qualified YES, the noose that drew the color line tauter.

Aside from his powerful screenplay for lynching, Dixon used other techniques for hypnotizing his white reader. As well as focusing on black outrages, *The Clansman*'s plot depicts the struggles between two sets of whites with different visions of the United States' destiny. One set, centered around Austin Stoneman, are traitors to the race and actively plot to turn the United States into a multiracial democracy. The other, a diverse group of northerners and southerners, work to create the white-ruled New South as a model for everything that in Dixon's eyes the national Progressivist movement ought to stand for. Hence, although Dixon set *The Clansman* in South Carolina in 1865–70, he cleverly and anachronistically appropriated various harangues against tyranny popular in the 1890s and the early twentieth century and associated with Progressivist policies. One inveighed against the tyranny of black rule and was particularly associated with South Carolina's governor and then senator, "Pitchfork" Ben Tillman. Others were by Dixon's calculation national, not regional, in their appeal. Canonizing the martyr Lincoln as a "Friend of the South," in contrast to the conniving Andrew Johnson and Thaddeus Stevens, the discredited Senate leader of the Radical Republicans, was one effective tactic for gaining the sympathies of all whites for Dixon's southern heroes. Another tactic was Dixon's anachronistic appropriation of Teddy Roosevelt's popular rhetoric against corporate monopolies—all of which was more appropriate to 1905 than to the years immediately following the Civil War, when *The Clansman* ostensibly takes place. Dixon's propagandistic stroke of genius was to connect the alleged corruption of Reconstruction to all the elements that his readers did not like about modernity in the 1900s—including robber barons and corporate capitalism, economic recessions and social upheaval. In turn, these forces of corruption were linked to an even earlier form of evil, the tyranny of the English king over the North American colonists. As a result, whole sections of *The Clansman* read like a heady mix of Progressivist anti-monopoly rhetoric, Tillman's "populism," and the Declaration of Independence's tactic of listing the grievances that justify rebellion. This potent brew sold to Dixon's readers as quickly as a cure-all potion at a country fair, where part of the spiel was to list all the deadly diseases of modern life it would miraculously cure:

> The first great Railroad Lobby . . . thronged the Capitol with its lawyers. . . .
> The Cotton Thieves . . . had confiscated unlawfully three million bales of cotton hidden in the South, . . . the last resort of a ruined people. . . .
> The Whiskey Ring has just been formed. (153)

Countering such plagues in *The Clansman* is a Jeffersonian vision of capitalism in moderation, supposedly now being modeled in the reborn New South.

Thomas Jefferson's adulation of yeoman farmers as the chosen people of God in *Notes of the State of Virginia* was expanded by Dixon to include mill owners: "The old Eagle cotton-mills had been burned during the war. Phil organized the Eagle & Phoenix Company, interested Northern capitalists, bought the falls, and erected two great mills, the dim hum of whose spindles added a new note to the river's music" (278). Dixon knew that the best way to refute charges that the New South was governed by a corrupt, feudal oligarchy was to provide a heroic counter-example. Thus he imported the northerner Phil—the son of his villain Austin Stoneman, no less—to marry Dr. Cameron's daughter and populate the (white) American future. Phil's mills are not satanic, but musical machines in the garden that is to be the mixed (rather than primarily plantation-based) economy of Dixon's New South. Phil treats his white workers like family because he's learned from his southern friends how they treat their "good" Negroes on the plantations; evil mill cities run by greedy capitalists would never be his model. It is Jefferson's vision of the yeoman farmer retooled to fit Progressivism—though the dim hum of those stream-side mills would no doubt have the scion of Monticello turning like a spindle in his grave. Dixon's concluding vision of the New South in *The Clansman* is an Eden with a lynching tree guarding its borders.

Effective as Dixon's scripts were in inducing his audience to racist outrage, bonding, and, eventually, optimism, Dixon's projected images of white unity and black demonism do contain a central blind spot or contradiction: his white characters admit several times in *The Clansman* that "democracy" and "civilization" are incompatible. Dixon was hardly alone in 1905 in being uneasy with "hordes," black or not, asserting the right to vote and other privileges and immunities of citizenship; a similar point was made by the sociologist Franklin Giddings in *Democracy and Empire* (1900). But of all the binary oppositions that drive Dixon's melodrama, the tensions between "democracy" and "civilization" were the most destabilizing and dangerous, as they were indeed for Progressivist discourse in general, as I argued in chapter 6. Dr. Cameron alludes to many racist arguments of the post 1898-era and earlier when he demands that voting rights must be strictly limited because the only force that will save democracy from decadence is "the genius of the race of pioneer white freemen . . . , the purity of this racial stock" (291). But for such a genius to emerge, whites had to be taught to *identify* as white, to see their destiny and then seize it. To accomplish this, the visual language of mass culture was needed, and both the best-selling novel and the new form of the movies had a central role to play.

In short, for Dixon the technology of image manufacture and discourse manipulation was as important as Phil's mills, white supremacist legislators, a vigilant Ku Klux Klan, Progressivist reforms at home, and a vigorous program of U.S. expansionism abroad if the only redeemed white civilization in the Americas was finally to realize its potential. But lurking in Dixon's Progressivist Eden, this empire of white rule, would always be the fear that lynchings and military force in themselves would not be enough to usher white supremacy into the destined new phase of its power. That voice of doubt speaking to the Democratic convention in *The Leopard's Spots* could never be satisfactorily stilled: "In this hour of crisis, our flag has been raised over ten millions of semi-barbaric black men in the foulest slave pen of the Orient," the Philippines (439). Why would not the vexing rebellions against white rule in the Old South be re-enacted on a global scale after 1898, in both the New South and the new U.S. colonies?

## 3

Wister's influence on the Western was as broad as the Great Plains, as deep as prairie loam. Aside from D. W. Griffith's *The Birth of a Nation*, Dixon's influence on U.S. culture is more difficult to measure. His work can be said to cast its shadow whenever melodramas of beset whiteness play across U.S. popular culture, with their signature mix of fascination and loathing toward the scapegoats such narrative patterns seek. Flipped upside-down, however, Dixon's hysteria and earnestness regarding race can make fecund fodder for satire. Consider the wry deconstruction of Dixonian rhetoric by the Harlem Renaissance writer George Schuyler in his 1931 novel *Black No More*, when blacks can purchase a special scientific treatment that allows them to pass for white:

> The great mass of white workers . . . had first read of the activities of Black-No-More, Incorporated, with a secret feeling akin to relief but after the orators of the Knights of Nordica and the editorials of *The Warning* began to portray the menace confronting them, they forgot about their economic ills and began to yell for the blood of Dr. Crookman and his associates. Why, they began to argue, one couldn't tell who was who! Herein lay the fundamental cause of all their ills. Times were hard, they reasoned, because there were so many white Negroes in their midst taking their jobs and undermining their American standard of living. None of them had ever attained an American standard of living to be sure, but that fact never occurred to any of them. So they flocked to the meetings of the Knights of Nordica and night after night sat spellbound while Rev. Givens, who had finished the eighth grade in a one-room country school, explained the laws of heredity and spoke eloquently of the growing danger of black babies. (81)

Schuyler's text not only dissects how race antagonism was used to prevent black and white workers from uniting against the economic conditions that kept them impoverished, but also savages the KKK's and Dixon's obsession with genetic versus cultural markers of racial difference, the "Mulatto-ization" (cultural and racial) of America, and other irresistible targets. Schuyler even alludes to lynching as a demonic sacrament of the church of whiteness, in which black body parts are consumed (as souvenirs) to reaffirm God's divine sanction for whiteness. But, outrageously, he plays the novel's climactic lynching scene for farce, not melodrama. Intended for readers of all races, Schuyler's lampooning of the United States' phantasmagoric racial nightmare gave a wake-up call to all those who had been hypnotized.

# The Dark Archive

EARLY TWENTIETH-CENTURY CRITIQUES OF JIM CROW
COLONIALISM BY NEW SOUTH NOVELISTS

Both those who reviled Reconstruction and those who revered it acknowledged that it greatly enlarged the powers of the U.S. government and, in doing so, transformed the nation. Proponents of Jim Crow colonialism, such as John W. Burgess and Woodrow Wilson, well understood that without Reconstruction's expansive redefinition of federal powers the United States would not have been able to envision post-1898 imperial projects abroad, much less coordinate the military, bureaucratic, and corporate forces that supported these enterprises. True, not all who supported Jim Crow at home endorsed colonial enterprises overseas; such critics saw no reason why the racial conflicts of the South would not be reenacted in the tropics with even more explosive results. Indeed, they feared that the very programs for uplift that in their view had gone awry after 1865 would become dangerous boondoggles in the new century too, and for the same reasons. But for many Progressivist intellectuals, their expansive assertion of federal regulatory and managerial powers represented Reconstruction done right, with its dangerous errors corrected and its "scientific" methods for social reform now applied properly both at home and abroad. Just as Jim Crow laws were understood by those who favored them not to be acts of repression but rather examples of proper tutelage and boundary-drawing, so too U.S. expansionist policies outside of the country were seen to be fundamentally non-coercive, except when necessary. If administered correctly, so the thinking went, our policies would teach our colonial subjects a model of education that—in Woodrow Wilson's words—would be "the long discipline which gives a people self-possession, self-mastery, the habit of order and peace" (*Constitutional Government* 52). Whether these same colonized subjects would ever graduate from tutelage, of course, was an open question.

Still other Americans felt that Reconstruction's limited programs for voting, education, and a new start toward prosperity had been sabotaged, not saved, in their new incarnation as colonial policy; this made their original betrayal even bitterer to swallow. Writers like Albion Tourgée, Frederick Douglass, and John Roy Lynch argued that the potential powers Reconstruction legislation had given the federal government—military, legislative, and judicial—had tragically never been properly used to protect the Reconstruction Constitutions across the South against assault after 1865. Those same activists saw a similar betrayal of civil rights unfolding again in the 1890s and after, as more and more states formally or informally adopted Jim Crow practices—even as there were earnest discussions in national forums about voting and other rights being extended to new U.S. colonial subjects. Yet such was the insidious double bind of U.S. imperial rhetoric that figures who castigated U.S. violence and hypocrisy at home had trouble defining the grounds upon which they could criticize U.S. projects abroad. Ida B. Wells-Barnett and George Washington Cable, for instance, conceded that the United States had the right and even the duty to promote freedom and development abroad; they just wished that such federally funded reforms would be as ambitious at home.

The three writers included in the final section of *Sitting in Darkness*—Walter Hines Page, W. E. B. Du Bois, and George Washington Cable—all found themselves struggling to cut through Jim Crow colonialism's double bind, its sinister Gordian knot. In key ways, they all rebelled against a color line that severed equal rights at home while endorsing a paternalist ideal of disciplinary tutelage for other societies the United States was interested in seeing "develop." Exposing and challenging the criminal inconsistencies in "uplift" narratives proved difficult. Page criticized American racial policies and educational inequities, yet was a strong supporter of Woodrow Wilson's foreign policies, including his strong-arm tactics in Latin America. One of the key characters in Cable's *Lovers of Louisiana* suggests that the United States should follow England's colonial model in Bermuda, where people of color had limited voting rights but no chance to institute dangerous forms of "social equality" at the expense of proper racial and ethnic hierarchies. And right in the midst of some of the most anti–Jim Crow and anti-colonial rhetoric in Du Bois's *Darkwater*, he reverts to the colonialist discourse of disciplinary uplift for Africa.

Nevertheless, Page, Du Bois, and Cable in their imaginative writings stage actions that threaten to cut through Jim Crow colonialism's double bind. Page's Nicholas Worth, Du Bois's Zora Cresswell, and Cable's Philip Carleton give significant speeches lauding a liberal arts model for universal education for blacks and whites that would eventually move a divided United States toward genuine multiracial democracy and greater economic and political equity. And in their private lives and public interactions with others, all these characters create social spaces where a critique of imperial hypocrisies and bloody mistakes may emerge, though often veiled and carefully camouflaged. These fictional characters' efforts are aided and abetted by the complex moves made by the narrative voices that Page, Du Bois, and Cable deploy. Whether in first person or third person, a single voice or a medley, the story-telling devices these authors use all engage with the standard narrative assumptions and rhetorical structures undergirding Jim Crow colonialism. Such strategies hardly free these authors from the contradictions of their historical moment. But they do create imaginative spaces within this difficult history where doubts can be voiced and alternatives imagined.

The analyses in part 3 thus continue the expanded definition of "education" that was initiated in parts 1 and 2. That is, they broaden the topic to include not just schools for students of color and the theories of education that organize them, but scenes of instruction for *all* citizens—the education of the nation and beyond. Visits to black schools play key roles in all the texts considered in part 3, but all also demonstrate that the *local* concerns of schoolhouses in the U.S. South are inextricably connected via a network of imaginative spaces to the *global* aspirations of oppressed people for freedom. Inspired by the contents of a bookstore kept by one of the most intriguing characters in Cable's *Lovers of Louisiana*, the ex-slave Ovide Landry, I call this hidden network of fictive spaces a dark archive, a set of counter-memories and alternative interpretations resisting, nobly if imperfectly, the dominant discourse of Jim Crow colonialism that claimed to be "real," not fictional. The texts discussed in this section are not that archive's only contents; Page, Du Bois, and Cable may be linked to earlier writers who were socially progressive in their views and experimental in their literary work—including Child, Griest, Tourgée, Harper, Griggs, McClellan, Twain, and Tolentino. But a careful study of the early twentieth-century texts that are the focus of part 3 can be definitive proof that an archive of imaginative resources for resisting racism was encoded into certain fictional texts published about Reconstruction and the New South in the post-1865 period—a canon whose emergence and integration into the literary history of post-slavery and postcolonial societies is long overdue.

# Chapter Ten

# The Education of Walter Hines Page

A GENTLEMAN'S DISAGREEMENT WITH THE NEW SOUTH
IN *THE SOUTHERNER: BEING THE AUTOBIOGRAPHY OF
"NICHOLAS WORTH"* (1909)

Walter Hines Page's one published novel, *The Southerner: Being the Autobiography of "Nicholas Worth"* (1909), may be a novel of ideas, but it cannot be adequately understood merely by summarizing its plot or Page's critique of the New South. It is set in the 1880s in a fictional southern state that closely resembles Page's native North Carolina. Although ideas and arguments about needed New South reforms live vividly in the book, they are expressed in the novel's narrative texture with a complexity and nuance that so far has eluded the book's few but earnest commentators. Literary critics have tended to ignore the novel, while historians and biographers have cited it respectfully as a pseudonymous roman à clef presenting the Progressivist views of Page, an influential southern-born editor, journalist, publisher, and reformer who later became (under Woodrow Wilson) a respected diplomat and ambassador to England. Page's best biographer, John Milton Cooper Jr., has rightly judged that the novel suffers from too much didacticism, with Page's fictional double, Nicholas Worth, serving as a "mouthpiece for his creator's ideas about southern problems," particularly those involving public education (200). According to Cooper, Page was at his best in position papers, letters, and editorials addressed to a familiar audience; when he had to imagine an anonymous audience, as in fiction, his writing became less vigorous.

But what if, conceding some of these limitations, we take Page's novel of ideas as a *novel*, not simply as a mouthpiece or a blander synthesis of all of Page's editorials and articles? To what degree did Page use anonymity to create a fictive space in *The Southerner* in which he could critique both New South verities and his own beliefs with vigor unavailable to him in his "real" identity? After all, Page had done something similar via the use of a pseudonym at the very beginning of his career, in the notorious "Mummy" letters of the mid-1880s criticizing southern conservatives blocking educational reforms and other progress. Could this novel be Page's wry version of a bildungsroman, chronicling Nicholas Worth's education through error?

Beginning in 1881 with an article on the southern educational problem, a series of essays flowed from Page's pen to the major periodicals of the day. Page supported educational reforms for blacks and whites, expressed unease with black disfranchisement, and after 1898 lauded U.S. imperial adventures abroad. Some of the best of these articles were reprinted in the one book published under his own name in his lifetime, *The Rebuilding of Old Commonwealths* (1902). What tied together these disparate topics was Page's Progressivist belief in the state's responsibility to educate all its citizens for responsible modernity. Deeply influenced by Charles D. McIver, a crusader for North Carolina education, and by Booker T. Washington's work at Tuskegee Institute, Page believed that a tax-supported public school system in the South might have reversed the growth of slavery and was crucial to the postwar recovery of both blacks and whites from slavery's blight. In Page's native state of North Carolina in 1890, 26 percent of whites were still illiterate (J. Cooper 143). Page exemplified twentieth-century Progressivist white southern social-reform attitudes, just as his writing and editing for the *Forum*, the *Atlantic Monthly*, and then *World's Work* helped create the concept of a modern national newsmagazine of ideas, opinion, and investigative reporting (J. Cooper 150, 179–188). Page's later diplomatic work in Europe for Woodrow Wilson sought to apply the essential ideals of *Rebuilding* to the old commonwealths of Europe wrecked by the First World War, all the while turning a blind eye to the racism delimiting Wilson's Progressivist reforms at home. Such contradictions in Page the reformer and diplomat could not be evaded as easily in his one attempt at fiction. There was something about wearing a mask that allowed Page to explore deeply his own (and his region's, his nation's) capacity for doublespeak.[1]

The neglect of the literary qualities of *The Southerner* is perhaps understandable, since Page's forte clearly was not plotting. The less said about the novel's main romantic subplot, for instance, the better—except to note that Page's activist heroine, Louise Caldwell, was perhaps a model for Mary Johnston's Hagar. The novel features a number of memorable characters, however, or perhaps we should say character types, since figures such as Uncle Ephraim, Nicholas's servant; Professor Billy, one of his sources for reformist ideas; and Colonel Stringweather and Senator Barker, two of Nicholas's nemeses, are sharply if conventionally drawn, each with his own distinctive speech. The novel's namesake, Nicholas Worth, is far more than a simple, self-righteous crusader; he may have ambitious plans for social reform, but his persona contains large doses of modesty, skepticism, and ironic humor that leaven his high-mindedness. He needs such leavening because he proves more anti-hero than hero: he fails as a schoolmaster, then as a college professor, then as a politician. After basically retreating from public life two-thirds of the way through his story to write a history of his home state, Nicholas considers himself inadequate as a historian and memoirist as well. It may be that neither affirmation of eternal values nor reformist ideals about the building of new commonwealths are at the heart of the novel's vision, but rather a complicated and rather inward sense of alienation and skepticism toward all forms of identity that deny complexity and contradiction.

In *The Southerner*'s conclusion, the hero reaffirms the central role in southern life played by the values represented by his family's "Old Place" homestead. Yet the ending also chronicles the secret, multiracial history of that same family, one that cannot be publicly acknowledged. As an ironic bildungsroman, a novel of education, the text reveals the many ways in which its hero's sensibility and ways of knowing *cannot* be integrated into the emerging New South social order marked by Jim Crow. Ignored *The Southerner* may be, but its blend of reformist zeal and ambivalence approaches that of other contemporary experiments in mixing autobiographical, fictional, and historical genres, such as Booker T. Washington's *Up from Slavery: An Autobiography* (1901, published by Page); W. E. B. Du Bois's *The Souls of Black Folk* (1903); James Weldon Johnson's novel, *The Autobiography of an Ex-Coloured Man* (also published pseudonymously, in 1912); and Henry Adams's *The Education of Henry Adams* (1918).

I approach Page's *The Southerner* from three directions. First, I evaluate it seriously as a novel of ideas: in fact, one of the most eloquent responses to the long tradition of pastoral republicanism in southern letters that has been identified by John W. Grammer and others. Page's work, however, adds several significant new elements to this Jeffersonian tradition. The first is a rather utopian argument that a healthy New South economy must be based on a mix of urban and rural, industrial and agricultural, and black and white enterprise. The second reflects Page's admiration for Booker T. Washington and other reformers attuned to the values of industrial capitalism.

In the middle section, I argue that Page's novel represents a key example of how the New South's vision of reunification among northern and southern whites in effect provided a new paradigm for *nationhood* for the United States during a time of racial and economic upheaval at home and imperial expansion abroad. I consider this topic in what is perhaps a surprising way, by focusing on Page's appropriation and rewriting of key ideas in W. E. B. Du Bois's *The Souls of Black Folk*. Paradoxically, Page applies Du Bois's concept of double consciousness to white southerners, using their response to victimization as a way for them to reclaim membership in a modern, expansive nation-state. Yet Page's trope of how white southerners are shadowed and disinherited resonates with meanings that his book's nationalist theme cannot successfully contain.

This chapter's final section takes up the theme of unsuccessful containment and shifts the focus to *The Southerner* as a novel full of textual ambiguities, not just a set of compelling arguments about modern education and citizenship. That is, I contemplate key ways in which the various projects of reform advocated by characters in the book are enriched by the novel's haphazard structure and the narrator's pervasive sense of irony, contradiction, and hidden meanings. The narrator's sensibility is much more that of an exilic anti-hero and skeptic—and a keeper of secrets—than it is the man of action and speechifying that best suits a conventional "novel of ideas." What effect such textual and structural complexities have for the "argument" of *The Southerner* will be explored through readings of several key chapters near the novel's attention to changes that Page made between his 1906 *Atlantic Monthly* serialization of the novel and its 1909 publication as a book, and a concluding meditation on the novel's use of bildungsroman conventions. Though to some degree my method in the conclusion of the Page discussion contradicts that employed in its first two parts (since it focuses on inner subtleties rather than broad themes), I intend all three to make the strongest reasonable case for giving Walter Hines Page's novel renewed attention.

1

John Grammer's study *Pastoral and Politics in the Old South* focuses on five Virginia politicians with literary talents who were central figures during the decades before the Civil War in inventing "the South" not just as a distinct region but also as a set of alternative values. Grammer names this intellectual tradition pastoral republicanism. Rooted in Jefferson's wariness of centralizing federal power, pastoral republican thought had a number of features that are thoroughly relevant for understanding Page's *The Southerner*.

The locus classicus of pastoral republicanism is Jefferson's famous "Query 19" in *Notes on the State of Virginia*, which tried to counter fears about the effects of slavery raised in "Query 18" by arguing for a vital link between small landowner-farmers, the education of the new republican citizen, and the civic virtue of the state. Henry Grady, Charles McIver, Booker T. Washington, Walter Hines Page, Thomas Dixon, and other promoters of a New South modified Jefferson's distrust of merchants and cities, choosing instead to stress that republican virtue necessarily relied on a properly mixed economy of small farms (not large plantations), factories and mills, and a public school system that trained the male citizens to thrive in such an economy.[2] Despite the sometimes caustic and comic portraits of New South hypocrites and mummies retarding progress, Nicholas Worth tries to be as optimistic as possible regarding the South's prospects. His will to believe is thoroughly in line with the millennial optimism John Grammer stressed as one crucial aspect of the southern republican tradition. Nicholas's brother manages a successful cotton mill and a housing development for its workers called Millworth. Such a social vision makes the ideals of pastoral republicanism an achievable future goal, not a lost past. It is also Progressivist in its faith that changes in technology and education and a more centralized economy may be harnessed (to use an agricultural metaphor) for democratic change—that is, for creating new social arrangements allowing wealth and power to be shared by many rather than few. Page's pastoral republicanism in *The Southerner* thus proves a pedagogical device for the training and molding of the ideal democratic citizen—much as it had been for Thomas Jefferson or Benjamin Rush during the republican era, but now updated by Page to suit a much larger and more mixed agricultural-industrial economy. Page also envisioned that, with a reformed public education system, the South would finally return to being a major source of economic and political leaders.

Booker T. Washington played a role at least as important as that of Henry Grady and other New South spokesmen for Walter Hines Page's vision of education's role. Washington's influence on and friendship with Page is well documented and extends far beyond the fact that Page's firm of Doubleday Page published *Up from Slavery*.[3] Like *The Southerner*, *Up from Slavery* is an autobiography of a representative man, a blueprint for social progress by many, not one. Washington's vision of the proper fit between healthy educational systems and economic systems receives a most eloquent voice in U.S. fiction in *Nicholas Worth*, where the hero visits Negro secondary schools and the Hampton Institute and espouses educational ideals quite similar to Washington's.

Intriguingly, though, Nicholas's political platform is a good deal more radical than Washington's could afford to be. Nicholas makes no "Atlanta compromise," Washington's decision to press for white support for educational and economic advancement while turning away from protesting the voiding of black voting rights throughout the South. Worth openly campaigns for the Negro vote throughout his state and stresses black political rights in no uncertain terms. At such moments, Nicholas Worth and his creator are much closer to two other white southern "race traitors," Albion Tourgée and George Washington Cable, than he is to Washington, Grady, or other proponents of mainstream New South discourse. For such a stance, Nicholas Worth loses not just the election but also his position as a professor of history at the state university; he is insulted with impunity as a race traitor and worse both in public and in private.

In Washington's and Page's vision, not only do southern farmers market their products to the nation and its colonies, but their work represents standards of efficiency that have distinct parallels with those being created for workers in mills and factories. In *Up from Slavery* and *The Southerner*, the pastoral is not so much natural as engineered. Washington's goal was to determine the best solution for all major needs in an agriculture-based economy, from harness making to cotton growing, and then to train black students en masse for each of those jobs. Similarly, in Page's text tax-supported state schools teach the most productive farming methods for all crops, and farmers' land cooperatives give away unimproved land to any male citizen (black or white) willing to follow the approved techniques. "Every man here may have as many acres, up to twenty, and he and his family can cultivate to the required standard—free of charge, to become his as soon as he brings it to that degree of culture which your own committee requires," says Worth at one point in a speech promoting his scheme, adding that "all these things were supervised by the superintendents and experts of the coöperative farms' company" (402–403). Jefferson's idealized independent farmer is here organized into a vast complex that defines the rights of ownership in terms of conformity to a proper, rational model of productivity. In this essentially modernist vision, the rural countryside is little different in terms of structural organization from a late nineteenth-century industrial corporation. The millennial rhetoric at the heart of Old South pastoral republicanism has, in these two leading New South reformers, Washington and Page, become corporate and national, even international. In doing so, they demonstrate how Thomas Jefferson's continental empire of liberty contained a theory of replication wherein the universal idea of what a republic could be would fabricate iterations of itself in Cuba or Mexico, just as it had in territories that eventually became states.

Ironically, although Nicholas Worth loses his election battle he largely wins the cultural war. The politicians who do win eventually have to promote his key ideas in education and economics, so greatly have the population's expectations been changed. The great exception is black voting rights. John Grammer has rightly emphasized the strong strain of nostalgic pessimism countering pastoral republican optimism in the South. Despite Nicholas Worth's faith and the popular success of many of his reforms, such a strain inflects his voice and vision throughout his memoir, but especially at its end. It is quite proper to stress the novel's corporate Progressivism as well as its witty and acerbic satire of the anti-modernist forces holding back southern development, personified by charming villains such as Colonel Stringweather, the Daughters of the American Revolution, and others. But Nicholas in the end feels very much like an exile in his southern homeland, his ideas partially victorious but his person and his honor battered, dismembered, misunderstood.

Nicholas retreats to the privacy of a small circle of family and friends, to continue with his unfinished revisionist history of the state and begin the very memoirs that we are presumably reading. The tone of the book, especially at its beginning and end, is one of equivocal bittersweetness—and this certainly has many parallels with the Old South Virginians whom Grammer studied, especially John Taylor. But Nicholas Worth also remains determinedly hopeful, akin to the northerner Ralph Waldo Emerson as represented in that masterpiece of ambivalence, his essay "Experience." Worth's last words to his audience in *The Southerner* include the following: "Therefore to you who read this, if you believe (as I do) that our American ideal is invincible and immortal and that men may in truth govern themselves and give fair play and abolish privilege and keep the doors of opportunity open—even here where fell the Shadow of the one Great Error of the Fathers—we who have toiled where doubt was heaviest now send good cheer" (424).[4] Such a mixed tone is quite congruent with the pastoral republican ideals that animate Page's entire novel.

## 2

Despite the fact that many of Nicholas Worth's enemies consider his position on black education and voting rights to disqualify him from membership in the white race, Worth in public in the South strictly adheres to the rules of Jim Crow. It is easy from a twenty-first-century perspective to notice Nicholas's paternalism and condescension in race relations, his unfailingly elitist tinge of noblesse oblige. But let us now turn to a different way of contextualizing *The Southerner*. Page's work may be read as a response not only to Washington's *Up from Slavery*, but to W. E. B. Du Bois's *The Souls of Black Folk* (1903). This aspect of Page's novel has been ignored by commentators yet is crucial. Admittedly, Page's novel appears to align itself most closely with Washington's, not Du Bois's, vision of both education and limited social reform. Both assume that the ex-slave is a burden on the South, fundamentally untutored in the essentials of democracy and independence; both agree whites' proper role to be that of benevolent patriarchs; and (despite Nicholas's veneration of the Greek classics) both stress vocational over liberal arts education. But Page's novel arguably engages as fully with Du Bois's key ideas as it does with Washington's. At first, this may be surprising, since Page was one of many readers who were offended at Du Bois's forthright criticism of Washington's strategies for reform in chapter 3 in *Souls of Black Folk* (J. Cooper 218). But Page and Du Bois shared a number of other assumptions, including that the problem of twentieth-century American democracy was "the problem of the color-line," to use Du Bois's immortal phrasing. Both men also believed that public intellectuals had to think and work iconoclastically and independently for any social advance by their society.[5]

Page's *The Southerner* stands as the first work of fiction in U.S. literature by a white writer to respond seriously to Du Bois's *Souls of Black Folk*. (It thus pairs eerily, and sadly, with George Marion McClellan's now equally obscure *Old Greenbottom Inn*.) Page's novel engages with Du Bois on the most basic level by taking up figures of speech as well as arguments that are central to his vision. Some of most famous lines from Du Bois's *Souls* echo throughout Page's novel, but with their context and meanings altered in ways that reward close attention.

One chapter that well exemplifies this pattern comes near the conclusion, "My Journey to Boston" (chapter 29). Nicholas is asked to give an address on the South at Boston's Midweek Club, whose members include many philanthropists (businessmen and clergy) sponsoring Negro schools and other improvements in the South. Nicholas decides to be confrontational, to make the northerners question their perception of moral superiority and the practical effects of their actions. The scene was wholly revised between the 1906 and 1909 versions of the novel and very much improved. What Nicholas had earlier summarized generally and dispassionately in the third person is in the revised version rendered dramatically, as a vivid debate about means and ends. Page constructs a kind of symposium or national debate about northerners' and southerners' responsibilities, one that vividly demonstrates the dramatic, intellectual, and ethical possibilities a novel of ideas may have for stimulating critical thinking in a democracy—particularly on the much debated issue of the role of public education in citizen building.[6]

Du Bois's tropes of "behind the Veil" and the "shadow" are well known in *Souls of Black Folk*. In the "Forethought" and the first chapter, "Of Our Spiritual Strivings," they appear in a number of variations, from intimations of hidden history and pride ("The shadow of a mighty Negro past flits through the tale of Ethiopia the Shadowy and of Egypt the Sphinx" [*Souls* 6]), to frustration caused by the betrayal of Reconstruction ("the shadow of a deep disappointment rests upon the Negro people" [7]). Equally famous are Du Bois's definition of "double-consciousness"—"this sense of always looking at one's self through the eyes of others, of measuring one's soul by the tape of a world that looks on in amused contempt and pity" (5)—and his wry exposure of the unasked question he feels whites are usually too ashamed to ask directly of blacks: "How does it feel to be a problem?" (3–4).

In the 1906 version of Page's *The Southerner*, the hero's trip to Du Bois's home state of Massachusetts prompts this reflection: "But in the South there was ever the shadow of the Problem. What did I owe the Negro, or the Negro owe me? . . . Oh, free men, wherever you live and toil and think, you who believe in the triumph of our democracy, my fellows and I do not ask your pity; but we do ask your sympathy and your understanding,—we of the post-bellum South, who had nothing to do with its old misfortunes, but whose lives must be spent in the struggle out of the shadow of them" (*Atlantic Monthly*, October 1906, 475). Like Du Bois's, Page's main character here raises dangerous questions that must be faced if any sanity is to be achieved on the race question. The "shadow" for Page, as for Du Bois, is the blighted legacy of slavery and racism, one lying over both blacks and whites. Nicholas Worth sees it as the South's tragic flaw, the problem that shriveled not just its economic development but also its entire social and cultural life. It is also in his view the tragic inheritance of all Americans lodged in the heart of the Constitution—"the one great error of the Fathers" Nicholas calls it in the 1909 version (384).

Page's revised 1909 version of Nicholas's speech in "My Journey to Boston" extends such Du Boisian tropes even more thoroughly—a sign that Page wanted to underline their importance. A crucial passage is worth quoting at some length so we can trace the ways in which Page both extends and refashions Du Bois's main metaphors.

"I will make a confession to you that every candid Southern man must make—of a shadow that follows him.

"I do not myself, of my own will, carry or feel any sectional consciousness. It is the community that will not let me lose it—the present community, the past, and the shadow of the past, the whole combination of forces that we mean when we speak of 'The South.' For instance, I try to study the large problems of the Republic and I adjust myself to them precisely as I would if I had been born and lived in Boston or in San Francisco. But, while men in Boston and San Francisco may think their thoughts and express their opinions and work out their problems without a sectional consciousness, I may not.

"And the fault is not mine. It is first my community's fault. When I hold an opinion that differs from the dominant formula, I am asked if I have forgotten that I am a 'Southerner.' ... Now a Southerner is a proper and proud thing to be, but (here comes the sorrowful paradox) I cannot be the Southerner that I should like to be, because of the presence of this must-be 'Southerner'—this self-conscious 'Southerner' that is thrust upon me. If it were not for this self-conscious 'Southerner' that must become a part of every public Southerner's self, better men would enter public life from these States.

"This shadow 'Southerner' is a dead man which every living man of us has to carry. He is the old defensive man.

"... If you, you who live in New England in particular, would regard us who now live and work in these Southern Commonwealths as citizens of the Republic, your regarding us so would help to make us so. So long as we are regarded as a problem we must play the part of a problem, whether we will or no.

"And thus we carry an unfulfilled ambition that gives a deep seriousness to our lives, an ambition for these States and these people as a part of the Union. The ambition that men felt in the time of Washington, of Jefferson, of Marshall—this is what I mean. ... *In our own fathers' house, we are yet disinherited in a certain sense, disinherited because of the shadow 'Southerner,' whom you help to keep alive.*

"Do you wonder that we are become weary of being a problem?" (389–391, italics mine)

This eloquent speech ought to be as well known as Henry Grady's famous 1886 oration about the New South's birth after Reconstruction, also delivered to a northern audience.[7] But one is hardly surprised to learn from Nicholas Worth that his analysis is not received with the tears and applause that greeted Grady's encomium to progress and reunion (and, not incidentally, white rule). The Yankees expect Nicholas to be defensive and apologetic, but he refuses.

I would like to make several further points about the moves Nicholas's rhetoric makes. First and most obviously, Page's text borrows Du Bois's central tropes of the "shadow" and the "problem" but sharply revises them. Du Bois ironically appropriated whites' discourse calling blacks a "problem" in order to shift the focus to the real difficulty—white supremacy. Page keeps Du Bois's suggestion that the problem is really in the eye of the beholder, but he applies Du Bois's ironic language of victimization not to blacks but to all southern whites, particularly the elites who aspire to leadership in the reborn Union. In Page's account, it is southern whites who are victimized by double consciousness, or what he calls "sectional consciousness"—being forced to see themselves through the eyes of those other whites who hate or pity them.

Du Bois's solution to the problem necessitated both a confrontation with white racism and a re-evaluation of the black cultural traditions that constitute the soul of a people. Page's Nicholas Worth identifies a different problem, southern whites' victimization, and then offers a markedly different solution—white reunion, predicated on the possibility that northern whites will at last treat southern whites as equals. But the very language Nicholas uses to envision postwar white reconciliation is borrowed from the most progressive black writer then publishing. In other words, Nicholas Worth's most eloquent tropes defining white southerners' ostracism and their claims for rejoining the national community were first penned by a northern-born black man trying to define the dilemmas of black American identity. Was such intertextual irony intentional or unconscious on Worth's part, or on Page's? Or should we just call it stealing? I believe it is impossible to say. Perhaps Page just found Du Bois's concepts so eloquent that he couldn't resist appropriating them to very different ends.[8]

A final comment about Nicholas Worth's speech must be made. For all of the borrowed eloquence Page gives his hero, Nicholas Worth remains apart from both his northern and his southern white peers, essentially unknown and confusing to them, his private self and opinions perpetually behind a kind of veil—especially when it comes to the matter of race relations. Nicholas's speech completely fails to win over his audience, who pepper him with skeptical questions. Nor does Nicholas feel at home in the South when he returns. No longer perceived as a direct threat, he is still seen as an unregenerate reformer and radical, one who must be shunned though not driven into exile. Yearning for union and inheritance, Nicholas's voice in the novel achieves its greatest eloquence when it expresses his ironic consciousness of disinheritance, distance, difference, and contradiction. This is hardly the position he strives for—"We ask that we be regarded in a normal way," he pleads to the Bostonians (391)—but a form of exile behind a veil is nevertheless the position Nicholas inherits, the one that best suits his sensibility. We miss the irony of this if we focus solely on blaming Nicholas (or Page) for stealing Du Bois's language and then using it to claim a place in a white man's nation. Elsewhere in the novel Nicholas also uses the concepts of the color line and his hero's double consciousness, though the language Page gives him is not so markedly Du Boisian. In these instances, when Nicholas deploys the idea of double consciousness and a veiled identity, it should be interpreted not so much as a strategy to claim whiteness, but as a disguise for his rejection of Jim Crow.

In such key scenes, the "shadow Southerner" who most haunts Nicholas is that part of himself which cannot abide the color line, which works for black civil and educational rights and realizes, consciously or unconsciously, that the Worth family's genealogy is part "black"—black like the identity of his nation and the very texture of his prose with its hidden Du Boisian strains. In a moment, I will give some details regarding Nicholas Worth's rebellion against Jim Crow, but first it is worth meditating on the paradox here. To tell *this* story of disinheritance and difference within the Worth's family's whiteness, Nicholas must somehow find other words than the borrowed Du Boisian idioms he sneaks into his Boston speech. *The Southerner* turns out to be the autobiography of this "shadow" self as well as Nicholas's public self; we might even think ahistorically for a moment, for the sake of a pun, and, alluding to James Weldon Johnson's masterpiece, call Page's book *The Southerner: Being the Autobiography of an Ex-White Man*. Certainly most of Nicholas's opponents would not object to that title for Nicholas's story, if they only knew his secrets.

3

A close reading of portions of two of the novel's best chapters may provide keys to other important and subtle elements in the text: the understated dignity of its narrative voice and the novel's fascinating tension between melancholic nostalgia and impatience for experiment and reform, between Nicholas's public performances of "white" identity and his private subversion of its norms behind a veil. Not coincidentally, these two chapters feature the private Nicholas Worth more than the public one. The nuances generated by close reading can be further enhanced by comparing the two versions of these chapters (and relevant passages from others) in their 1906 and 1909 variations. For these textual shifts reveal how Page reconceived his narrative to publish it in book form.

The first chapter on which I will focus is 23, entitled "With Ulysses by the Sea" in 1909. It portrays Nicholas Worth's retreat to a seaside resort with his trusted black servant "Uncle Ephraim" after the stinging defeat of Nicholas's candidacy and his educational reform platform in a statewide election in the 1880s. The tone of the chapter is one of genteel retreat, a turn from the politics of New South demagoguery and vote stealing to the healing presence of what Nicholas thinks are the eternal truths represented by nature and the Greek classics, especially Homer. Homer's epic heroes reaffirm for Nicholas the virtues of "self-mastery" in times of bitter disappointment. Such long perspectives give Nicholas the strength to see humor in how he was slandered as an enemy of "white supremacy" merely for arguing that improvements in Negro schools would benefit all the states' citizens, not just blacks. He also finds amusement in how once he is safely defeated he becomes a gentleman again to the very newspapers that slandered him: "A month ago I was a vile enemy of social order. Now I was a scholarly ornament of society" (303).

The chapter's most intriguing element is its portrait of "Uncle Ephraim," whom Page's first biographer, Burton Hendrick, has called "perhaps the best-drawn character in the book" (*Life and Letters* 92). (No, Nicholas is, but Hendrick is right that the servant is indeed memorable.) On the one hand, it is easy to chronicle the ways in which Uncle Ephraim fits neatly into the conventions of the loyal ex-slave servant—"Yer 'umble sarvant, suh" (299)—so central to the "plantation school" in New South fiction.[9] On the other, Page uses but also re-shapes the stereotypical figure of the loyal black servant in several significant ways. He updates the portrait to be not merely a representative of pastoral plantation harmonies and "family"-like bonds, but a working model of Booker T. Washington's ideals of black self-improvement and social service within the boundaries of Jim Crow. That is, Ephraim embodies the proper New Negro approved by both Washington and the white leaders of the New South: he is industrious yet humble, with no desire to change his social sphere. Not only does Ephraim manage the Worth family plantation, the "Old Place," with alacrity and efficiency, training the ex-slaves in specific skills and a work ethic as efficiently as Washington ever did (and perhaps more so). Ephraim also holds legal title to and farms many acres of his own land. His social position thus stands in marked contrast to the vast majority of blacks in the New South who sank deeper and deeper into debt every year as sharecroppers on white-owned land. None of the loyal servants in racist New South fiction by Thomas Nelson Page or Joel Chandler Harris has anything like the power, stature, and wealth possessed by Uncle Ephraim in *The Southerner*. Furthermore, like his "master" Nicholas, Booker T. Washington, and other progressive spokespersons for the New South, Ephraim is emphatically in favor of improved new schools for blacks. The second half of the "Ulysses" chapter features a speech of Ephraim's praising a black school—an episode not present in the serialized 1906 draft of the novel. It is a most Tourgée-like moment.

In addition, we should note that Ephraim's and Nicholas's relationship and ideas do not conform to New South models for a proper master-servant relationship. Their challenge to Jim Crow is particularly notable in the original 1906 version of the "Ulysses" chapter, which contained details that Page later suppressed. These reveal that Nicholas's and Ephraim's living arrangements violated rules against "social equality" between blacks and whites. In both versions of the text, Page includes Nicholas's caustic reflections on race-baiting and political mudslinging—how in corrupt southern political discourse white racial fears are exploited to block needed social and economic changes. "Everybody knew that I had never thought for a moment of proposing or of practicing 'the social equality of the races.' Yet men (thousands of men) voted against me, and thousands of women regarded me as a sort of social ogre, because these oratorical phrases 'social equality,' 'white supremacy,' the 'bottom rail on top,' and the like, were repeated thousands of times" (303, 1909 edition). In the original version of *The Southerner*, though, Ephraim and Nicholas engage in a reversal and parody of Jim Crow rules that rather belies the above statement.

Nicholas and Ephraim have journeyed together to a beach resort (on North Carolina's Outer Banks?) because both are feeling "poo'ly." At first the servant needs to be instructed in how they will live together: "'You are going to sleep in the room next to my room. A waiter is going to bring your meals to you, and I am going to wait on you myself. I am bringing you down here to rest. When you feel like it, you can go out and walk under the pines; or you and I will go and look at the ocean.'" Ephraim initially protests this arrangement, but then quickly adopts Nicholas's spirit of imitation and inversion of the rules of Jim Crow. "'Don't you forget, you've got to be my old servant—my venerable family servant,'" Nicholas said. "'I ain't gwine to forgit nothin',' said the old man with a chuckle" (*Atlantic Monthly*, September 1906, 318). Both Nicholas and Ephraim share a laugh as they violate the color line while appearing to affirm it. Of course, such an inversion of master/servant roles is merely symbolic and temporary. It is also done in secret, not affirmed in public. But once it becomes highlighted in Nicholas's memoirs, it begins to take on a more subversive and public status as a symbolic action directly challenging the color line, in however small a way. Page edited out this entire exchange in the 1909 version, perhaps sensing that he had indeed crossed a line. All these private subversions of Jim Crow rules in Ephraim and Nicholas's relationship remain rather deeply buried by the 1909 version of the novel. On the surface, to his conservative countryman's eyes Nicholas's master/servant relationship with Ephraim is easily the most normal thing about this dangerous reformer. But there is more.

The last chapter of *The Southerner*, as its title tells us, is set "Twenty-Five Years After"—in short, not in the early 1880s but around 1906 to 1909, precisely when Page was writing. Like the rest of the novel, it is animated by a tension between its reverent tone and its edge of irony, its concern with traditions of the past as well as its attraction to future reforms. The continuities that are celebrated are explicitly patriarchal: "My brother and I have kept the Old Place, to which another generation learned to make pilgrimages of childhood. We often went there with our children in pleasant weather for a night of story-telling. . . . Their great-grandfather and Uncle Ephraim thus took places in their minds (as I was glad to see) among their heroes. . . . We all hope, indeed, that the Old Place will be kept by Nicholas Worths yet unborn" (417, 423). Page's concluding chapter also seeks to pass on Nicholas's worthy virtues of honor, optimism, ironic humor, openness to change, modesty, patience, and a sense of citizenship. There is talk of the possibility of selling the Old Place to strangers, but it is all light hearted. The chapter concludes with a valedictory address toward sympathetic future readers who are, figuratively, welcomed to join the Worth family circle and share its beliefs. All the novel's revised ideals of pastoral republicanism are thereby maintained and passed on.[10]

The final chapter's bittersweet mixture of irony and encomium, however, is interrupted by the arrival of a stranger, a Mrs. Wheelwright of Pittsburgh. Her name is Julia and she is a mixed-race woman light enough to pass for white. She is the granddaughter of Ephraim, but her father was a nearby member of the white aristocracy, Tom Warren, Nicholas's conservative vanquisher in the elections long past. Once forced by Ephraim and Nicholas to acknowledge his paternity, Warren "'fought fair'" (421) as a gentleman should and sent Julia money for an education and her escape into the anonymity of the northern middle class. Julia too is participating in a private pilgrimage to the Old Place, though unlike the Worths' migration hers must be shrouded in secrecy. She has come to visit her grandfather's grave.

After Julia updates her story for Nicholas, here is his reaction: "I sank into as deep a reverie as ever overwhelmed a man. This had been her home, and there was no human being but me to whom she could tell so simple a fact without risk of wrecking her own life and her husband's life. She had stolen away and made a long journey to see it once more. Even to her father she dared not reveal herself for her own sake as well as his. He had other daughters now—very like her, I noticed" (422–423). Nicholas's celebration of pastoral and patriarchal continuities in the book's final chapter is therefore also shadowed with an example of slavery's and racism's legacy, its publicly unspoken stories. Nicholas later alludes to the woman's visit when others return, but he changes her story so that it becomes merely the inquiry of a white "Yankee" woman about whether the Old Place was for sale. "They looked up with wonder at so absurd a question, and we passed from the subject with a laugh—as we pass by many dark tragedies that lurk just behind the hedges of our lives" (423). Although Page here alludes to the tradition of the tragic mulatta in American fiction, he is revising that tradition, for Julia is hardly a tragic figure in *The Southerner*, whatever her losses. Her fate is explicitly different than that of the mulatta in William Wells Brown's *Clotel* (1853) or Charles W. Chesnutt's heroine in *The House behind the Cedars* (published with the help of Page at Houghton Mifflin in 1900), both of whom die. Yet Page's hero also acknowledges that this woman's story is a part of his family's history that *cannot*, because of Jim Crow, be publicly mentioned.

In the 1906 version of this episode, Page's hero violates the rules of Jim Crow in an even more explicit way: "At dinner time,—we still have dinner in the middle of the day,—we sat down and ate together, the servants wondering who she was. When they were present we talked guardedly" (*Atlantic Monthly*, October 1906, 488). Such an act represents the height of Nicholas Worth's rebellion against the color line, one practiced not at a remote barrier island, as was his experiment in living with Ephraim, but in the Old Place's dining room. His readers (if not his white family) know what he has done. In his own way, Page's hero here enters forbidden territory shared by only a few other contemporary writers, including Mark Twain, Joel Chandler Harris in the final story in *The Chronicles of Aunt Minervy Ann* (1899), Frances Harper, Pauline Hopkins, and Charles W. Chesnutt. Nicholas's rebellion remains secret, and thus we must not exaggerate its effect. Nicholas's self-silencing also proves deeply contradictory to his oft-expressed hope that in a reborn South all topics may be discussed publicly in open and honest debate. Nicholas's repression may be realist, but it also shadows his chapter's celebration of family continuities—a fact compounded by Page's silencing, via revision, of his hero's own most dangerous act acknowledging Julia as kin, and Page's refusal in either 1906 or 1909 to acknowledge that he was the author of *The Southerner*. Yet by marking the grave of Julia's story, so to speak—by indicating that it has been silenced and passed over—Page gently forces his readers to make their own pilgrimage to that story's burial place. Julia's disinheritance becomes as fully a part of the southern history the Old Place embodies as the public career of the Worth family.

### 4

Twenty-first-century readers may rightly feel that Nicholas's frequent retreat into private and ironic meanings inscribes not a genuine challenge to the social order so much as the elitist privilege of withdrawal. Yet we must not underestimate the powerful repercussions caused when a work of fiction marks private doubts, ironies, and a different sense of history from the majority view. In doing so, novels create a space, a language, out of which future social change may be imagined and then created. In a small way (admittedly made somewhat smaller by the deletions discussed above, and by Page's publishing his novel under the mask of anonymity), Page's hero *publicly* educates his attentive readers to the lies of the color line. He uses the Du Boisian concept of a veiled identity not to reclaim a privileged state of whiteness (as in the Boston speech) but to mark white family identity itself as shadowed, interwoven with "blackness." Only in the hidden yet public spaces created by fiction may such truths find utterance. Once they do, they indeed provide an education, and they prophesy a future—a truly new New South—toward which the region would only gradually and painfully evolve.

Walter Hines Page's New South version of pastoral republicanism modifies not just its vision of a homogeneous economy and culture, but also its naïve assumption that its leaders would exhibit no contradiction between their outer and inner selves. Although *The Southerner* follows the pattern of a bildungsroman by chronicling the education of its hero and concluding with his (partial) re-integration into his society's social structure, the novel also traces the story of that representative man's exilic shadow-self, a "problem" that cannot yet be publicly acknowledged, much less resolved, in either the U.S. South or the nation. The hero's abiding ambivalence remains behind a veil, as unspeakable as the history of his disinherited double, Julia Wheelwright. Further, Page's hero's secrets are comparable to those shared by two of the main figures in Griggs's *Imperium*, Beryl Trout and Belton Piedmont, and by the narrator in McClellan's "Old Greenbottom Inn." That is, none of these figures can easily speak in public the truth of their actions or their understandings of recent history in which they were directly involved. They all remain behind a veil: Beryl voicing a cautionary tale about black leadership; McClellan's narrator, a complicated black history that "industrial" education in black schools largely silences; and Page's hero, a rebellion against whiteness that dare not speak its name.

# Chapter Eleven

# Anti-colonial Education?

W. E. B. DU BOIS'S *QUEST OF THE SILVER FLEECE* (1911)
AND *DARKWATER* (1920)

Aesthetically speaking, W. E. B. Du Bois's first novel, *The Quest of the Silver Fleece* (1911), is a bale mixing together weevil-damaged and good cotton. Du Bois hoped to make his economic and social analyses acceptable to a broad reading audience by employing melodramatic narrative and character conventions from popular fiction of the era. He gambled that if such formulas created huge popular successes for Thomas Dixon or Albion Tourgée, why not for his own fantasy about a multiracial Farmers' League revolt led by an intrepid heroine? Ironically, though, it is the *white* characters (particularly John Taylor, Mrs. Vanderpool, and Mary Taylor Cresswell) who come across as somewhat complex and unpredictable in Du Bois's narrative, while Du Bois's black protagonists, in general, are the most two-dimensional. Du Bois had inveterate problems giving life in fiction to southern working-class blacks. Especially egregious are his attempts to describe his black heroine, Zora Cresswell, as a combination of nymphet, labor organizer, swamp-queen Earth mother, and victim of voodoo. (Du Bois's "knowledge" of voudun presented in the novel is pure bunkum.) Scenes in elite black society in Washington, D.C., and elsewhere fare somewhat better, particularly those involving Bles Alwyn and Carolyn Wynn, for their social identities and inner lives are rendered in knowledgeable detail.[1] But Du Bois's relative success portraying the dilemmas of the black elite causes a problem for his novel as a whole, for he wanted his working-class black characters, particularly Zora, to be the driving force for change in his narrative. She is that, but her portrayal is schizophrenic. In many scenes Zora is divided and confused, constantly needing reassurance from various mentors and protection from those who would prey on her, while in other scenes, especially in the latter half of the book, she is superhumanly self-confident. The causes for such a transformation are never convincingly narrated. Further, it doesn't help matters that the text constantly moves the melodramatic plot forward with dialogue that is not merely wooden, but petrified: "You are going to marry the man that sought Zora's ruin when she was yet a child because you think of his aristocratic pose and pretensions built on the poverty, crime, and exploitation of six generations of serfs" (180).

As a whole, then, *The Quest of the Silver Fleece* is considerably less than the sum of its parts. But it has scenes that are absolutely fascinating and successful, most notably the confrontations between antagonists that allow Du Bois to anatomize how both whites and blacks, working class and elites, are trapped within a New South economy dependent upon transnational cotton markets. Even the South's main hopes to break such dependency—a new system of public schools for workers' children and farmers' cooperatives that will give them greater bargaining power—prove vulnerable to outsiders with greater power and greater capital. Further, it is crucial to see the novel's ideas about how change happens in history within the context of Du Bois's evolution as an intellectual who placed U.S. developments within the context of world history. Between the publication of *The Souls of Black Folk* in 1903 and *Darkwater* (1920), Du Bois increasingly became involved in international efforts against colonialism, and as he did so he came to understand the plight of sharecroppers and small landowners in the U.S. South as an anti-colonial struggle. For Du Bois in his pre-Marxist phase, this meant the farmers' fight to be able to compete in international markets on fair and equitable terms, as free agents. *Quest of the Silver Fleece* thus marks a key phase in Du Bois's thinking as he begins to conceptualize the U.S. South's economic and racial problems in transnational terms, as symptoms of a great global struggle to make multinational capitalism more democratic and less monopolistic.[2] This chapter will use two key texts—*Quest of the Silver Fleece* and *Darkwater*—to chart a crucial phase of Du Bois's evolution in the second decade of the twentieth century, as he shifted his focus from U.S. problems escaping the legacy of plantation slavery to how to attack those problems by undertaking a global history of how colonialism has shaped modernity.

1

Following the lead of novelists like Frank Norris and journalists like Ida Tarbell, who had tackled the workings of corporate capitalism, Du Bois decoded the postwar southern plantation not as a pastoral alternative to race, gender, and class strife—the way in which it was often portrayed in New South fiction by whites—but as a single, life-sapping component in a transnational capitalist economy. If the cotton gin mechanized the removal of seeds and the production of bales, contemporary economic forces, in Du Bois's view, were acting in an analogous way on a much larger scale throughout the New South—consolidating the industry vertically by weaving together cotton fields, processing plants, mills, and finance and marketing into a single industry, allowing greater control over production and prices: "a vast trust of cotton manufacturing covering the land" (62), modeled on the oil and steel conglomerates forged as postwar capitalism in the United States entered a decisive new stage.

Du Bois's novel further demonstrates how such reorganization in the rural South was forced by the systematic generation of debt and dependency all up and down the line of cotton production—except at the top, of course. Black farmers (both sharecroppers and landowners) were the most obvious victims, slipping into permanent financial bondage to white landowners and storekeepers. But southern white cotton producers and processors themselves usually also became enmeshed in debt, to northern financial syndicates that cornered and manipulated seed and cotton prices. If they fleeced farmers using crop liens, they in turn often were gouged by financiers. A wide variety of scenes in *Quest* demonstrate how any threat of uniting against such a system could be undone, offering token concessions and appointments while also engineering sharp drops in cotton prices, bookkeeping fraud, race and class antagonisms, or imprisonment or murder. One meaning of Du Bois's novel's title is clearly ironic, for the Jasons questing to control cotton's silver fleece are the southern planter Colonel Cresswell and the northern financier John Taylor, hardly epic heroes. But the broadest referent for Du Bois's irony was the quest of global capitalism itself. *Silver Fleece* shows how the U.S. South's cotton fields must be understood as part of a transnational plantation economy increasingly controlled by southern elites and urban financial centers far from the South. Against such fleecing networks of power, the novel's primary heroine, Zora, struggles with heroic inventiveness.

Another key element in Du Bois's deconstruction of the cotton economy is the role played within it by black schools. When the issue is education, for Du Bois the focus always should be whether a school system functions to reinforce social inequities or to change them. For all its flaws, Du Bois's novel has something approaching genius in the way that it synthesizes and critiques the views of black schools, northern philanthropy, and competing educational models that were published in prior fiction and nonfictional discourse after 1865. Three white women and one black woman have primary roles involving black education: Mrs. Grey, Mary Taylor (later Cresswell), Sarah Smith, and Zora Cresswell. Du Bois's novel scathingly explodes myths of benevolent planters or northerners supporting the best possible black plantation schools in the South. Planters in *Quest* try to destroy or impoverish rural schools because they know educated blacks will be more resistant to manipulation: "the Cresswell domain . . . lay like a mighty hand around the school, ready at a word to squeeze its life out" (131). Sarah Smith's school gains two hundred acres because of a dispute between poor and rich whites, but then white landowners counterattack by refusing to let their tenant farmers send their children to the school. They hope to drive the school into bankruptcy by forcing it to buy off black farmers' "debts" and move them to its own land in order to get students. They have considerable resources on their side because they control the only bank in the area that may lend money. Du Bois pointedly juxtaposes his portrait of the black school trying to get a fair mortgage to raise money for improvements with a sketch of "Uncle Jim," Jim Sykes. Barely literate, Sykes thinks he owns a deed to land and has been paying good wages for more. But his deed is no more than "a complicated contract binding the tenant hand and foot to the landlord," while his written records of his payments prove merely "blind receipts for money 'on account'—no items, no balancing" (136, 135). Both school and sharecropper are trapped in the New South's new methods for shackling black labor, with impoverished black schools producing a whole new generation of black laborers who may be readily exploited.

In *The Quest of the Silver Fleece* Du Bois continues his longstanding dispute with Booker T. Washington and other promoters of "industrial" education.[3] The financier John Taylor sometimes suggests that the Darwinian energies of capitalism will eventually dissolve the South's fetish for caste distinctions reinforced by unequal schools: like many northern industrialists, he believes black education's primary goal should be to create more reliable workers (cf. 397–398). But Taylor's daughter, Mary, is drawn by Du Bois to demonstrate the dangerous delusions of the Progressivist uplift discourse so popular with industrialists and volunteer white teachers in black schools: "[She] believed it wrong to encourage the ambitions of these children to any great extent; she believed they should be servants and farmers, content to work under present conditions until those conditions could be changed; and she believed that the local white aristocracy, helped by Northern philanthropy, should take charge of such gradual changes" (130–131). Until a dramatic conversion scene at the end, Mary is one of the book's cautionary tales. Well-meaning but gullible, she is duped into educating her black students for a lifetime of servitude. Some of the novel's most effective satire involves a grim parody of sociological "experts" advising the teacher Sarah Smith on the best ways to give students piecemeal and mediocre "practical" education—leaving them fit to be only sharecroppers or servants. Furthermore, a loan might solve many of the school's problems and allow it to expand, but those who lend the money will also control the school: "One condition is that my friend, Mr. Cresswell here, and these other gentlemen, including sound Northern business men like Mr. Easterly, shall hold this money in trust, and expend it for your school as they think best" (178). When a group of such philanthropists inspects the school they propose to help, one of them gives a pompous sermon to the children in favor of subservience and silence, while another takes notes about skull shapes and inferior deportment. They assess the children as if they are on a kind of slave-auction block: "splendid material for cooks and maids ... and plough-boys" (177). The children's response is to sing a sorrow song, a "soft minor wail" that "wavered on the air and almost broke, then swelled in sweet, low music" (176).

The woman in charge of the school, Sarah Smith, shocks her benefactors by rejecting this devil's bargain of a loan with strings attached. Through her efforts, and Zora's, to make the school independent intellectually and financially, Du Bois presents his own alternative vision of the role such schools—and women schoolteachers—could play to challenge the entire southern social order. *Silver Fleece* should be considered part of a stirring series of texts by Du Bois analyzing the problems and possibilities of black education, from *The Negro Common School* (1901), *The Souls of Black Folk* (1903), and "Reconstruction and Its Benefits" (1910) through *Darkwater* (1920)—particularly the chapter "The Immortal Child"—and *Black Reconstruction* (1935) and other works. Under Sarah's and Zora's guidance, this model school not only frees itself from its "sponsors" and efficiently teaches the three R's to children of former sharecroppers, but also becomes the nerve center of a multiracial community farming cooperative that challenges the control of southern cotton production by white planters and merchants and northern financial elites.

Through charity and savings and Zora's help, Sarah Smith's school develops a small fund and provides incentives for sharecroppers to move so that the children can attend the school and they can have some land of their own to manage. Many do, for they quickly recognize a fairer system where their children will be well educated, they will be able to raise subsistence crops on their own plots, and on twenty acres of cleared swamp land they will collectively raise a large cotton crop whose profits will be shared by all. It is a kind of mini-Reconstruction program. As soon as this alternative cotton plantation and school show signs of success, Colonel Cresswell tries to sink the enterprise with one scheme after another. A partner of Zora's, for example, has to outmaneuver the Colonel's attempt to force the cooperative to buy a year's worth of supplies at inflated prices. When Zora's group deposits their harvested cotton in a Farmer's League warehouse, the Colonel tries to attach their crop for fictional unpaid debts. But Zora successfully defends the cooperative's right to their profits in court. Acting as her own lawyer (is there nothing she cannot do?), she exploits longstanding resentments toward planters felt by town whites, including the judge (402–417). Like Frances Harper's Iola Leroy, Zora proves unstoppable.

Zora's economic struggle enters a new phase when it is redefined by some whites as a racial revolt. In a scene worthy of Albion Tourgée, a white mob attacks the school while Zora, Sarah, and others defend it with a protective ring of bonfires (420–425).[4] The local sheriff provokes the riot because he fears the school is the germinating seed of a multiracial community violating the race and class lines structuring the New South: he sees "white children in the Negro school and white women, whom he knew to be mill hands, looking on" (420). In the end Zora and the Farmers' League are victorious. If they cannot yet change the transnational system through which cotton is financed, priced, and marketed, they have nevertheless created a small alternative economic base. Their new economic unit contains many elements of the old plantation system—Zora and others still think of the farmers as "their" tenants (408)—but it also represents an attempt at capitalist vertical organization and economies of scale so as to be competitive in larger markets. At the novel's end, sounding like a union labor organizer, Zora says the fight has only just begun: "'Think of the servile black folk, the half awakened restless whites, the fat land waiting for the harvest, the masses panting to know'" (430).

Before setting Du Bois's odd, idealistic first novel aside, it is worth concluding by stressing how much of Du Bois's economic and social analyses of the New South cotton economy have been confirmed by recent historians. Both C. Vann Woodward and Edward L. Ayers—to name just two—have shown how regional and national farmer's alliances tried to combat the ruinous crop-lien system used by planters and merchants, which kept many small landowners and all sharecrop farmers in debt, poverty, and low production. To counter such bondage, the so-called Macune business system for farmers spread from Texas to other southern states in the late 1880s before collapsing. In the 1900s, white Farmers' Union cooperative enterprises sprang up, uniting gins, warehouses, stores, fertilizer plants, flour mills, and alternative banks using an organizational logic that is mimicked by Zora's plantation and the Farmer's League in *Quest of the Silver Fleece*. Zora's organization, however, appears to be multiracial, though blacks are much in the majority. Her group also receives its key cash reserves from charity and earnings, not a farmers' bank; by the end of *Quest* it is still at a much earlier stage of development than the historical Farmers' Union. It is also quite small in the transnational scheme of things, with only a handful of families on several hundred acres.

Historically, farmers' alliances were concerned with far more than giving farmers fair interest rates and more leverage in marketing their crops. They sought educational reform and labor laws governing white children working in mills, and they elected legislators and governors supporting their agendas in key southern states. Farmers' groups in general were strictly segregated, however. Woodward reports that in 1890 the Colored Farmers' Alliance had over a million members, though this date appears to have been near the peak of its power as well as membership (*Origins* 220). Farmers' collective organizations must be central to any history of Populism and Progressivism including the rural U.S. South. Despite its focus on a highly unusual and idealized multiracial cooperative, Du Bois's *Quest* may depict the struggles of southern farmers' organizations more accurately than any other novel published in the New South period.[5]

Du Bois's novel was similarly incisive regarding the ways in which social reform movements and legislation could be co-opted. In chapters ironically titled "The Annunciation" and "A Master of Fate" (28 and 29), for instance, Du Bois records how blacks' agitation for more political appointments or black-white reform coalitions for education improvements and against child labor have their forces deflected by mill owners and politicians skilled at making small concessions in order to gain greater power. A southern senator's support for an watered-down education bill can be a bargaining chip to gain a prestigious ambassadorship. Du Bois's main black male protagonist, Bles Alwyn, is offered a highly visible but basically powerless position in the federal Treasury Department in exchange for undertaking a complete reorganization of southern school systems to put them firmly in control of whites. And southern mill owners create a Cotton Combine that is far more powerful than any coalition of workers Zora can put together. The Cotton Combine pushes through the U.S. Congress cotton inspection and tariff bills that are highly favorable toward plantation and mill owners, plus legislation that so dilutes child labor laws as to render them essentially meaningless, thereby achieving their goals of unrestricted labor conditions and high profits (308). Du Bois's mordant novel masterfully delineates the hundred different ways in which reformers of any race may be fleeced by those in power or tempted into making unethical concessions—all the while deluding themselves they have acted honorably and achieved significant advances.

Against such a panorama of failure and dishonesty, Zora stands out strikingly. She is tempted to sell out, as so many other reformers do, but in the end refuses to do so. As if to remind us that *Quest of the Silver Fleece* is ultimately a novel, not a work of sociology, DuBois suggests that Zora's freedom dreams come not from any legal deed or knowledge she learned in school, but from the Swamp, unfarmable land whose dark waters Du Bois makes seethe with both the forces of nature and the powers of resistance ever-present in black culture. Unfortunately, however, most of Du Bois's descriptions of the Swamp and earthy black folk culture in *Quest* are waterlogged clichés. Du Bois tried and failed to unite his most literary and "poetic" tendencies with his German intellectual heritage, especially Hegel and Marx. Zora's Swamp is clearly meant to represent that space in her and her race's psyche that can never be settled, colonized, or bargained away; it powers all of Zora's dreams of reform in the public sphere.

The fruit of all this mystical inspiration, Zora's Farmers' Cooperative and school, was intended by Du Bois to be a paradigm of world-historical importance that would supplant earlier, more inefficient and unjust rural economic systems. Zora's ultimate goal, and Du Bois's, is essentially Hegel's and Marx's: to realize freedom in a human social system. In short, *Quest* implies that a rural economy reformed along the lines imagined by its heroine would have a transformative effect on transnational capitalism itself, for all are linked. Du Bois consciously revised the history of the Colored Farmers' Alliances, which like other southern cooperatives struggled throughout much of the 1890s and after, to make that history more optimistic. He turned to fiction in order to write what he hoped would be a prophetic book about what could still be done. The novel was an attractive form for Du Bois because it dwelt in possibility—imagining what could be, not just confronting the tragedy of what was. But this first-time novelist was also determined to pack as much history into his book as it could bear. It is easy to enumerate the novel's flaws, which I've touched on rather lightly here. A far more worthy goal is to try to capture the power of the novel's critique and its undertone of sorrow song.

## 2

After *Quest*, the next key work in Du Bois's intellectual development was "The Roots of the African War," his seminal essay arguing that World War I was caused by European colonial powers fighting over the spoils of Africa, which Du Bois brilliantly read as signaling a crisis in capitalism itself. During the war Du Bois increasingly turned to understanding how U.S. racial and economic problems were part of a much larger history of colonialism and the struggles against it. Deconstructing the "civilizing" claims of white racism at home had to be combined with an ambitious historical analysis of colonialist discourse in all its manifestations. To undertake such analysis, Du Bois decided he needed a genre that was neither history, nor autobiography, nor fiction, but some kind of impossible, encylopedic mix of everything. Hoping, no doubt, for some of the inspiration his heroine Zora drew from the Swamp, Du Bois called his new experiment *Darkwater*. A heady brew of autobiography, sociology, history, parody, tragic prophecy, parables in both biblical and modernist modes, poetry and song, and apocalyptic vision, this text is nothing less than Du Bois's attempt to create an alternative historical memory in order to imagine a different future. *Darkwater* links a critique of New South hypocrisies and violence to European and U.S. colonialism, the emancipation of women, and the problem of how to increase the level of democracy in industrial societies and the developing world. Du Bois was skeptical that colonialism under enlightened leadership would eventually be self-correcting, building working democracies and modern economies in the U.S. South and in Africa, Asia, and elsewhere; instead, he saw it as a historical system sending all entrapped within it, regardless of their race, to disaster. *Darkwater* troubles the illusory coherence of the discourses of colonialism by assembling itself as a work acting out the unsolvable tensions in that rhetoric—its continual play of difference and contradiction. Doing so was not a bravura formalist exercise for Du Bois but a strategic move to open what he called "unusual points of vantage" leading to new insights (*Du Bois Reader* 497). Prophecy in the style of Jeremiah had to be full of many different voices, never a monologue.

Recently *Darkwater* has received splendid commentary by Arnold Rampersad, Eric Sundquist, and Amy Kaplan, among others.[6] Their discussions of the book's personal and historical circumstances, its brilliant de-formations of colonialist rhetoric, and its rich textual layerings mean that an extended exposition of the book's argument and structure is not needed here. Instead, by way of making a contribution to this nascent tradition of *Darkwater* criticism, I would like to explore why Du Bois has demonstrable difficulties responding to colonialism in ways that do not reproduce its insidious binaries of savagism and civilization, female and male. Educating readers about the connections between imperialism abroad and anti-democratic processes at "home" may have been Du Bois's goal, but the lessons taught by his primer may be somewhat different from his intentions stated in the text.

Historians of frontier colonialist fiction, such as Annette Kolodny, Jane Tompkins, and Amy Kaplan, have shown how such fiction imagines the frontier as a site where whites may renew potency and a sense of purpose lost in the decadent excesses of developed civilization. These stories of women and men on the frontier had curious parallels and differences. The frontier was hardly without its dangers for men, including being killed or, worse, regressing into a more primitive state. But, after Walter Scott, colonial borderlands were understood to be prime sites for successful epic romance—that is to say, where the hero may best discover how to remake his own and his society's identity. White women venturing into these spaces also had their mettle tested. By temporarily refusing to accept their "place" in the structure of their home society, like Owen Wister's Molly Stark in *The Virginian*, they renegotiated their relation to established society regardless of whether they literally returned to it or not. Colonial romance heroines claimed a newly defined aristocracy of character shaped by the frontier, not a fully traditional woman's role. Yet such narratives eventually tend to temper white women's frontier freedom, for generally the heroines make the transition from reckless independence to submitting to a white male's proper authority and, eventually, marriage.

If white women and men were both (within proper limits) masculinized on the colonial frontier, the "natives" themselves tended to be feminized and infantilized in colonial discourse. Like women or children, they needed benevolent white authority in order to discover freedom and modernity. Their alternatives were to die as a disgraced rebel or fade splendidly into the western sunset. Rebellious natives—those who refused to submit to the discourses of colonialism—were seen as hyper-masculine, regardless of gender. All parties in the colonial encounter, moreover, understood that a central feature of the struggle was for control over white women. Colonial borderlands narratives thus often offer as a subplot a dangerous alternative, the tale of a white woman who forgets whiteness and its responsibilities or becomes a victim of Native aggression; instead of leaving white society in order to be more strongly re-integrated into it after her borderlands experience, she becomes a cautionary tale. There was no surer way for a white male amidst sage-brush or jungle to renew his confidence than by rescuing a spirited compatriot who got herself in trouble.[7]

If one of the motifs of *Quest of the Silver Fleece* was figuring the exploitation of blacks in the South via sexual threats against his heroine Zora, in *Darkwater* Du Bois develops the rape analogy on a more global scale. *Darkwater* scathingly revises the rescue narratives and key catch-phrases of colonialism—such as the white man's burden, which he translates as "liquor and lust and lies" (510). He turns colonialist rhetoric back on itself—showing, for example, that the worst examples of barbarism in the world were all committed in the name of Western civilization, not its opposite. Given Du Bois's interest throughout *Darkwater* in linking women's liberation to colonial resistance, he appropriates the stand-ard colonialist scenario of white women being sexually threatened and then sharply revises it: now Africa becomes the rape victim. When Du Bois tries to imagine how Africa may be redeemed, he also uses highly gendered mystical language—first appealing to a vision of a long-suffering black Christ and then to the African queen Nefertari (510, 520). Note in particular how the following portrait of Africa shifts from depicting a prostrate victim to a figure posed rather like a pietà, a penitent and prayerful *über* mother: "Twenty centuries after Christ, Black Africa,—prostrated, raped, and shamed, lies at the feet of the conquering Philistines of Europe. Beyond the awful sea a black woman is weeping and wait-ing, with her sons on her breast. What shall the end be? The world-old and fearful things,—war and wealth, murder and luxury? Or shall it be a new thing,—a new peace and a new democracy of all races?" (520).

The parable that follows this scene to conclude "The Hands of Ethiopia" chap-ter, "The Princess of the Hither Isles," further heightens Du Bois's feminization of peoples of color oppressed by colonialism. It reads as a rather obvious morality tale: violence always lurks under whites' promises of benevolence. Most odd is Du Bois's portrait of the betrayed dark Princess: she literally offers the untrustworthy ruler of the world "her bleeding heart," as if when he pities her he will change his ways. But supplicants make easy targets; she is soon dodging his sword as well as his racist invective (522–523). Perhaps Du Bois intended this story to evoke sympathy. But aside from the clichés, it is disturbing how he has simply reversed, without revising, the colonialist narrative of uplift: in this retelling, the colonialist is seen in a different, darker light, but the posture of the Native remains suppli-ant. Her one act of rebellion is to commit suicide, leaping into a shadowy abyss. (Or is she making an impossible leap upwards toward the Sun, bypassing the King entirely?) A Zora Cresswell this Princess in *Darkwater* certainly is not.

By contrast, only two pages earlier, Du Bois had directed his readers *not* to inter-pret "the hands of Ethiopia" as "mere hands of helplessness and supplication": "rather are they hands of pain and promise; hard, gnarled, and muscled for the world's real work; they are hands of fellowship for the half-submerged masses of a distempered world; they are hands of helpfulness for an agonized God!" (520). Ironically, Du Bois's "timeless" parable feels more time-bound in its assumptions than the historically engaged materials elsewhere in *Darkwater*, such as the passage just quoted, or the trenchant "Of Work and Wealth" chapter, or the tales of women activists retold in "The Damnation of Women." The last thing Zora in *Quest* wanted was pity, though she too made many leaps of faith. Portraying colonized peoples as suppliant women was hardly the best way to argue for their rights. Similar supplicants, of course, have long been used to inspire those in power to engage in social reform without being unduly threatened. But *Darkwater*'s alignment here with earlier texts associated with Harriet Beecher Stowe and the abolitionist movement (which often focused on such supplicant figures) contrasts harshly with Du Bois's aspiration to write a jeremiad full of fiery indignation and prophecy—in the tradition of Douglass and Twain and others more than Stowe. Revising colonialist rape and rescue narratives did not address what Du Bois understood to be the central issue, which was how to critique the operations of power itself and posit historical forces that would need no miraculous rescue because they would shape their own outcomes. Still, these kinds of contradictions are endemic to U.S. reform traditions, and we should not assume Du Bois could magically escape their legacy.

Du Bois employed another narrative mode in "The Hands of Ethiopia" and elsewhere to argue that Africa would eventually become an agent of its own destiny, not a victim: the masculine, Hegelian language of state development. Such discourse, unfortunately, is also implicated in colonialist rhetoric, indeed is central to it. Du Bois sought to keep Hegelian ideals of development but to strip them of their burden of racism, which he implied was a vestigial inheritance of an earlier stage in Western development in which plantation slavery centrally figured. The twentieth century's key contribution to the history of civilization, for Du Bois, would be to demonstrate that realizing freedom in the form of a nation-state (Hegel's driving force in history) was an aspiration universally shared by all peoples. Racism—particularly, claims by Hegel and others that northern European civilizations developed at rates far superior to what any others could achieve or imagine—would be exposed by the processes of history as a philosophical error.

Writing after World War I, when the victors were debating whether or not to strip Germany and her allies of their colonies in Africa and elsewhere, Du Bois sided with the British Labor Party and other groups advocating the creation of independent states in Africa. He wanted those new states to have their rights recognized by an international body such as the newly formed League of Nations (see especially *Darkwater* 516ff). Yet *Darkwater*'s deployment of Hegelian development discourse is as full of contradictions as its use of rescue narratives. Although elsewhere in this text Du Bois acknowledges that complex social systems of tribal law in Africa were destroyed by the colonists (cf. 502), in "Hands of Ethiopia" Du Bois appears to adopt without qualification the colonialist dichotomy between savagism and civilization. His exhortations to "modernize" Africa sound rather like an ambitious colonial administrator's:

> Will it not be possible to rebuild a world with compact nations, empires of self-governing elements, and colonies of backward peoples under benevolent international control? . . .
>
> A curious and instructive parallel has been drawn by Simeon Strunsky: "just as the common ownership of the northwest territory helped to weld the colonies into the United States, so could not joint and benevolent domination of Africa and of other backward parts of the world be a cornerstone upon which the future federation of the world could be built?" . . .
>
> Obviously deleterious customs and unsanitary usages must gradually be abolished, but the general government, set up from without, must follow the example of the best colonial administrators and build on recognized, established foundations rather than from entirely new and theoretical plans. (517, 519)

It hardly seems possible to reconcile this rhetoric of disciplinary modernism with Du Bois's devastating critique of such rationales elsewhere in *Darkwater*. Du Bois assumes that if managed by a responsible world body rather than a corrupt and self-interested nation, such a system of "benevolent domination" would be benign, creating independent nations, not colonies. But, of course, turning "primitives" into wards and, later perhaps, into citizens was the stated justification for most colonialist policy, particularly in the United States. The excerpts just quoted could have been written by one of the colonialist administrators working for the British Crown or Presidents McKinley, Roosevelt, Taft, or Wilson. *Darkwater* at such moments is a broken mirror indeed.

In an eloquent passage in "Hands of Ethiopia" introducing the discussion of the future of Africa, Du Bois quoted various anti-imperialist English and U.S. organizations (including the American Federation of Labor) that were distrustful of whites' claims to be able to tutor others in democracy. "'No people must be forced under sovereignty under which it does not wish to live'"—a point that Du Bois glosses as follows: "In other words, recognizing for the first time in the history of the modern world that black men are human" (516). Like those authors discussed in chapter 6 who argued for or against expansionism, Du Bois struggled with but remained enmeshed within the belief that newly liberated colonies must be run by "the consent of some of the governed." Although he unflinchingly advocated universal democracy for industrial societies, for Africa he decided that benevolent outsiders managing its progress were necessary. It appears Du Bois even envisioned the African continent evolving as did the United States, with centers of "civilization" managing the transition of territories and peoples into recognized states that would eventually join a union. Such a stance treating the growth of the United States as a model cannot be reconciled with Du Bois's critique of U.S. social divisions along the lines of caste and color and its long history of violence against people of color claiming citizenship rights (such as the East St. Louis riot brilliantly analyzed in chapter 4 of *Darkwater*, immediately after "Ethiopia"). If U.S. ideals but not the realities of its history ought to be an example for Africa, how reliable a model was Du Bois choosing?

One has to ask whether *Darkwater*'s use of multiple genres heightens such contradictions in the discourses of development or simply glosses over them. If Du Bois's book was not as fully revisionary and prescriptive as its author hoped, though, it was at least encyclopedic. It fully mapped the history of European and U.S. colonialism as an ultimately self-defeating project for aggrandizing white power. In certain passages—not throughout—Du Bois's text also reproduced dangerous contemporary assumptions about what was "civilized"—thereby proving their insidious power. He assumed colonialist nations were necessarily corrupt but that an international body influenced by those same nations for some reason would not be. Yet if racism, not nationalism, were the real problem, as most of *Darkwater* eloquently contends, then why would an international body controlled mostly by white nations be a good guide for Africa's transition to democracy? This conundrum is never fully faced in *Darkwater*, much less resolved. Nor did Du Bois investigate the meanings of his terms *modern* or *civilized* with anything like the energy he devoted to showing the complex operations and euphemisms of white racism. He simply assumed that the ideals of modernity were universally valid and valued. Yet how could this be true if the concept of "whiteness" itself was a demonic and seductive invention of the modern era, as Du Bois proves in "The Souls of White Folk" in *Darkwater*?

*Darkwater* has a double ending that well captures its contradictory mix of utopian and dystopian rhetoric. After the world is obliterated by a comet, humanity seems to have a chance to begin anew, free of the obsessions of race, via the only two survivors, a black man and a white women who meet and help each other. But it soon turns out that it was only Manhattan whose history was erased. Soon crowds pour over the bridges back into the city, and the color line in all its forms is drawn again. Such a sardonic conclusion surely spoke to Du Bois's belief that the power relations of the Jim Crow New South had indeed taken over the entire nation, including its financial and cultural capital—not an inaccurate assessment of the state of the United States in 1920. But "The Comet" chapter may also be taken to signify the manifold ways in which *Darkwater* itself is divided and double voiced. Raising skeptical questions about *Darkwater* does not blunt the power of its critique of modern atrocities, nor its eloquent arguments for human rights, including a liberal arts education, nor its brilliant anatomy of U.S. race relations within a transnational context. Prophetic, indeed, Du Bois's comet of a book proved to be, both in its strengths and failures.

# Chapter Twelve

# Romancing Multiracial Democracy

## GEORGE WASHINGTON CABLE'S
## *LOVERS OF LOUISIANA (TO-DAY)* (1918)

George Washington Cable has been unfairly typecast as a major writer in a minor genre, the "local color" literature of New Orleans and the Old South. True, Cable's most influential literary works came early in his career, with *Old Creole Days*, *The Grandissimes*, and *Madame Delphine* (1879–81). Cable responded to acclaim with mid-career essays and speeches castigating New South racism and hypocrisy, collected in *The Silent South* and *The Negro Question* (1885–90)—work whose reception in the South made the author feel obliged to move to Massachusetts. Cable continued to write fiction between 1880 and the 1920s, but much of it is of such low quality that it strains the generosity of even Cable loyalists. Yet it turns out that at the end of his career, in 1918, Cable published another work that is astonishingly good—the novel *Lovers of Louisiana (To-Day)*. Cable's portrait of New Orleans and the United States in 1914 is an ambitious and largely successful attempt to merge his talent for fiction and skill in reasoned polemic, pairing an enjoyable romantic plot with a novel of ideas critically examining the New South, Progressivism, and colonialism. Although this text has received respectful if lukewarm appreciation within the narrow circles of Cable criticism, it may be that in the age of new historicism, postcolonial criticism, and the post–Hurricane Katrina devastation of New Orleans, the time for understanding the true importance of *Lovers of Louisiana* has finally arrived.[1]

The quality of Cable's fiction appears directly linked to his closeness to his family's adopted city of New Orleans: the fiction that made his name was written in the early years of his career before his exile to Northampton in 1885. But in 1909 and, especially, 1915, Cable was invited back to New Orleans for speaking engagements, and his warm reception there gave his writing unexpected new impetus, with his most ambitious novels in years, *Gideon's Band: A Tale of Mississippi* (1914) and *Lovers of Louisiana*, coming soon after those visits. As the subtitle to *Lovers*, *(To-Day)*, suggests, Cable's last novel sought to be emphatically modern and cosmopolitan—a study of contemporary southern manners and mores in the manner of William Dean Howells, Edith Wharton, Henry James, and Ellen Glasgow. Focusing on the multigenerational histories of representative New Orleans Creole, "Américain," and black families, the novel has a pronounced national and international reach, containing scenes in Atlantic City, Manhattan, and Bermuda, plus reflections on race relations, constitutional issues, British colonialism, World War I, and the United States' emergence as an imperial power. Although the work's first scene recalls the opening of *Old Creole Days* with its meditation on ornate New Orleans facades, most of the book's scenes take place not in ancient interiors but in a modern public sphere full of motion and change—trains, autos, boats, boardwalks, hotel lobbies, city streets, and places of commerce like banks and shops. In *Lovers of Louisiana*, Cable synthesized a lifetime of reflection and bitter experience. Despite the novel's occasional flaws and literary critical clichés about "the pen slows to a halt" (biographer Arlin Turner's unfortunate phrase about Cable's last decade), this work at the end of Cable's career has so much brio and optimism it is hard to believe its author was over seventy years old.

1

Before arguing in more detail for the novel's intellectual and artistic energy, I should pause for a moment to acknowledge the book's clear limitations. Aspiring to match Howells, James, or Wharton, Cable's prose is neither quite as witty nor as resonant as theirs, though it certainly makes pleasurable reading for fans of those authors. Unlike Cable's other important novel, *The Grandissimes*, which, as Richard Chase correctly asserted, drew its strength from its mix of genres, *Lovers of Louisiana* basically tries to modernize just one genre, the novel of manners. This genre traditionally takes as its subject the shifting caste divisions within an urban or rural elite, a focus that is, of course, tailor-made for Cable. But in *Lovers* Cable pushes the boundaries of the form by including repeated debates over political and racial matters that he tries to integrate into polite conversation and a romantic plot line.

An involved subplot with a corrupt cashier and a clairvoyant with a heart of gold was an unfortunate decision to include, for it is stuffed with stereotypes and coincidences. In the last third of the book, far too many chance convergences and interruptions are trundled forth to serve as plot devices to keep hero and heroine from uniting—not just children on a train or fugitives on a boat but also the sinking of the *Lusitania*. Most damaging of all for some readers will be the limitations of the novel's lovers, Philip Castleton and Rosalie Durel, and those of the principal elders, Philip's grandfather and Rosalie's father. Philip is understood by the Durels, one of the most respected Creole families in the city, to be a daring and dangerous young modern, disdainful of old New Orleans and the white New South's precarious racial and economic order. While Cable clearly wanted his romantic leading man to embody the bright future of the South (he is a newly hired professor of history at Tulane University, fresh from Princeton but also from a respected "Américain" family in the "new" New Orleans), Philip for many readers in 1918 may merely have seemed unromantic and needlessly provocative, especially on race matters.[2] For some contemporary readers, on the other hand, the professor will appear as just the opposite, fussy and fustian and rather like a "prig," a word he himself employs only half-jokingly (57).

Most if not all of Philip's "views" synthesize Cable's own yet also enact Cable's desire to be accepted by the very society he criticizes. Philip courts the good opinion of Monsieur Alphonse Durel even more assiduously than he does that of his daughter. The drama of this courtship is heightened by a latent Oedipal sub-plot that gradually reveals itself: Durel *père* was once in love with Philip's mother, thereby revealing that these two families from separate spheres of New Orleans society have a history of scandalous interaction that is revived by Philip's court-ship of Rosalie. Cable also adds to the plot the figure of Zéphire Durel, a middle-aged dandy also courting Rosalie; unfortunately, this figure is made as slimy as possible as a villain and rival to Philip, and when Zéphire and Philip interact the novel tilts toward melodrama's too-easy pairings of good and bad characters.

For all Philip's professed radicalism, his primary achievement is getting the Durels a new black servant (he rescues a girl from Zéphire's clutches), thus saving the elder Durel's finances and putting himself in position to marry into this most respectable of old Creole families. Similarly, with some crucial exceptions to be discussed in a moment, Philip's supposedly daring racial and political opinions represent standard New South and Progressivist ideology. His views may have been shocking to the elder Durel and other conservatives, but many of Philip's pronouncements were hardly unorthodox during this period for respectable white citizens to hold in the South. Philip denounces lynchings in favor of the rule of law; he laments New Orleans' and the South's isolation and backwardness and says that their fate is tied to that of the larger United States. In 1914, during the height of Jim Crow, Philip is asked to speak to the students and teachers at an unnamed, historically black New Orleans university near Tulane (Xavier?). In his talk, the professor promotes progress through good appearance and behavior, suggesting blacks be patient because they have supposedly already achieved sub-stantial rights. His most daring act in his speech is to request that his hearers for-get he is white—a suggestion that offends the few whites in the audience as being traitorous to his race, while being received with little enthusiasm by the many blacks in attendance. Many of today's readers will be skeptical as well, noting how Philip's comment about forgetting his whiteness assumes a free thinker can transcend race to speak in universal truths.[3]

Cable's novel as a whole, however, ironically refutes Philip's request by showing again and again with great subtlety how intellectual views are time and culture bound. It demonstrates that social change occurs not because of rarefied, transcendent truths finally realized, but because of what the text portrays as the constant and unpredictable friction of conservative and progressive interests in contestation in the public and private spheres. Such contrapuntal movements within the text's scenes are not easily captured by plot summary, and they offer a very different way of reading Cable's protagonist than simply as a man who heroically models all that Cable sees as right with the world, in confrontation with all that is irrational. The book as a whole may endorse Philip Castleton's counsel of patience, but it hardly validates his condescension.

A similar paradox relates to the book's treatment of colonialism. That is, at first glance its "radical" positions on colonialism may appear to a twenty-first-century reader as naïve, if well intentioned. Frequently in *Lovers of Louisiana*, Philip and another character, a Scotsman named Mr. Murray, appear to expound British colonialism as a model of enlightenment and development, "as democratic as she is imperial" (25), that both the New South and the entire United States would do well to follow. A key speech Murray gives early on typifies such reasoning and echoes the views of many U.S. expansionists:

> "Ah, you couldn't help that Philippine business, and I'm glad you couldn't," said the Scot. "It's profited the wurruld! Promoted its peace! Lifted it and the brown man on and up! Ye made that war in the fear o' God, so hold fast what he gi'es you. It paid ye in breadth o' mind. 'Twas so I talked to your Creole banker lawst night. 'The first founders of this nation,' says he, 'never set out to own Pacific islands.' 'Nor to buy Louisiana,' says I, 'but are you sorry 'twas bought?' Doctor Castleton, treat your Philippines as you may, no great people can ever be quite—or only—what they set out to be. Man, look at Britain?" (24)[4]

Philip is comically absent-minded during this harangue (he is thinking of his Rosalie). But Cable's signature touches of humor hardly deflect the ideological impact of the scene. Seamlessly and colloquially, Murray's argument unites both British and U.S. understandings of the meaning of manifest destiny and an Anglo-Saxon imperative to rule. Far from being dated, Murray's "uplift" rhetoric (minus the overt racial references) would appeal to some readers "to-day," in the twenty-first century—those who uncritically believe the United States spreads democratic values wherever its influence touches. Only a few times later in the novel will either Philip or Murray seriously question or complicate such easy talk of the white man's burden and destiny. But those few moments, arguably, are crucial.

2

Let us take a different approach toward both Philip's and Murray's "views" and the way the novel contextualizes them. Such an approach will not defend the flaws and dated aspects of the book conceded above, but it may be understood to present a different emphasis and assessment of what most matters. *Lovers of Louisiana* is a novel of ideas, not a tract advocating its author's views, and when we give closer attention to how ideas are espoused by characters and the narrator in specific scenes, we quickly notice that Cable's definitive mode is contestation and irony, not simple advocacy. Philip Castleton and Mr. Murray may "hold" several beliefs about the South and the United States demonstrably similar to those expressed elsewhere by Cable, but the novel's action does something far more interesting and complex than presenting the Creole Durels as old-fashioned foils to Philip's modernity.

First, key elements in Philip's arguments are indeed radical and—to a greater extent than in any novel by a white writer published in the period covered by *Sitting in Darkness*—they outline essential elements of the black civil rights movement during the 1880–1920 period and after. They also are in line with what critic Fred Hobson has called the "new critical temper" of a new generation of southern university intellectuals who began publishing critiques of the Jim Crow South at the turn of the century, in part inspired by older southern nonconformists like Twain and Walter Hines Page and Cable. Sadly, this New South novel that best captures their intellectual courage has been long out of print.

Cable's hero in *Lovers of Louisiana*, unlike Page's in *The Southerner*, stages his rebellion against Jim Crow publicly rather than privately. Some historical background should help make a properly limited case in favor of Philip Castleton's heroic radicalism. New Orleans had stronger support for Radical Reconstruction reforms, including black suffrage and penalties against Confederate government officials, than most southern cities. In it also resided the South's largest, most prosperous, and active free black community. In 1866, however, when a convention to adopt a new state constitution was convened, Radical delegates and their supporters were attacked by a white mob possibly organized by ex-Confederates in the police department. Three white Radicals and thirty-four blacks were soon dead and over one hundred were wounded. Cable had been a Confederate cavalryman during the war, but he also was employed as a clerk to General Nathan Bedford Forrest, and one of his tasks was to write manumission papers when Forrest freed his slaves. At the time of the 1866 riot, Cable was in New Orleans working as an errand boy, grocery clerk, and accountant (Butcher 23). He was also in the city in 1874 when armed white supremacists took over the statehouse, city hall, and arsenal until ousted by federal troops (Foner 551). Cable's shift to supporting the Radical Republican position on black rights took place slowly and gradually and was not publicly articulated until the 1880s, when hardly any whites in either the North or the South had the courage or foolhardiness to speak in favor of Reconstruction. As Wayne Mixon notes, in 1883 Cable chose a very public event, a University of Alabama commencement address, to counter the U.S. Supreme Court's 1883 "Civil Rights Cases" decision and argue that "white men were legally and morally obligated to assure the Negro protection of his civil liberties in the voting booth, in public accommodations, and in courts of law." Perhaps Cable hoped a new generation of southerners and university graduates would be open to his reasoning. If so, he could not have been more wrong. By 1890, now living in the North, Cable advocated federal intervention as a last resort to enforce the Fourteenth and Fifteenth Amendments (Mixon 99–100; Cable, "The Southern Struggle for Pure Government" in *The Negro Question*).

Cable's Philip Castleton may be the epitome of gentility, but with his spoken and published opinions he does take some risks, including public insult and losing the woman he loves. His position on black rights is essentially the same as Cable's. It also appears congruent with both the Radical Republican position during Reconstruction and with more recent intellectuals such as John Spencer Bassett of Trinity College in North Carolina, who published articles saying that intolerance of criticism and denial of black rights was impeding southern progress.[5] Philip argues repeatedly to his resistant listeners that the South is too isolated and defensive; that it ought to court criticism, internal and external, rather than fleeing from it; and that it ought to exemplify ideals expressed in the Declaration of Independence, the U.S. Constitution, and what Philip vaguely calls the "moral law." For Philip, this emphatically means rule by the "majority of the whole people"—which his listeners well understand means black voters as well as white. To advocate such views in the South in 1914 is, simply, heresy—made even worse because it is done in a public forum, not private moments of rebellion as in Walter Hines Page's *The Southerner*.

Provocatively, Tulane's new appointee in history demonstrates that the New South has all the symptoms of disease, not health. Using tuberculosis as a metaphor, Philip names all the ruses of Jim Crow voter disfranchisement—"grandfather clauses," "one-party elections," and "unwritten, unwriteable laws"—and calls these "spots in our political lungs" that have infected the entire nation's body politic (48). The narrator frequently seconds Philip's points, commenting, for example, on the "open chicanery" of Dixie's self-proclaimed "white-handed champions" who "disfranchised millions of [the Republican party's] rank and file, good, bad, literate, illiterate, taxpayers and hand-to-mouth poor, whose right of citizenship, wisely or unwisely, was written in the national constitution" in the Fourteenth and Fifteenth Amendments (58–59). Like his creator, who felt that a large number of "silent" southerners were also in favor of rational reform, Philip is confident that many more hold his views than will publicly admit it.

Nevertheless, stating such opinions in public and in print makes Philip well on his way to becoming a political outcast in New Orleans.

Cable handles all this drama with a deft comic touch, not a tendentious one. The discussion quoted above occurs on a train crossing the Mason-Dixon line heading south, and it is constantly interrupted by comic trivialities about chocolate creams, strikes, Hamlet, dog shows, whales, votes for women, and whelks (!). Indignant anonymous southerners who overhear Philip get the chapter's last, disparaging word. Rosalie, Philip's beloved, offers a decidedly ambivalent response, and the narrator, while appearing to support Philip, also compares the professor to Bottom wearing an ass's head in Shakespeare's *A Midsummer Night's Dream* (53). Cable's humor does not function to sugarcoat Philip's critique, but tempers his impatience with the narrator's Chekhovian sense of the tragicomic obstacles facing principled idealism. Such mixture characterizes the novel's best scenes.[6]

Equally worthy of commentary are several opinions Philip and Murray express linking the illusory stability of the U.S. racial order to Europe on the brink of World War I. Cable critics have suggested that Philip's race politics are rather tepid compared to the new generation of advocates for black suffrage and civil rights emerging around 1914, including the Niagara Movement and the NAACP (cf. Butcher 177n1). But no commentator has noticed that there are some striking similarities between ideas in *Lovers of Louisiana* and W. E. B. Du Bois's masterful essay "The African Roots of the War," which appeared in the May 1915 issue of the *Atlantic Monthly*, one year before Cable began his novel. Du Bois argued that the real cause for the war was competing imperial attempts by European nations to exploit African labor and natural resources as a way of enriching themselves and appeasing class conflicts and economic crises at home. He also prophesied that a conflagration worse than World War I would come if European civilization continued to refuse democratic rights to colonized peoples.

Compare the opinions expressed in Cable's novel by his two trouble-making protagonists. First, it must be conceded that most of Philip's and the Scot's opinions could hardly be mistaken for Du Bois's. As I said before, many of their claims and much of their phrasing sounds like apologies for the British empire's civilizing mission, and Cable's narrator even chides their discourse as "wearying" and predictable. In a long conversation with Monsieur Durel, Murray "cited the history of Britain's rule at home and abroad and dwelt on her blunders—the many missteps she had the courage to retrace and pay for—in her struggle to govern and serve, with equity and freedom, the throng of alien races, white and dark, of her far-stretched empire." But in the same breath, the Scot admits that the United Kingdom's conscience may not be as clear as he has just implied. Which "missteps" in Britain's colonial enterprise on the whole are honorable ones that are admitted and rectified and which are actions showing hypocrisy and brutal self-interest? The question of "equity and freedom," Murray stresses, is key for both Britain and the United States, and here he sounds his most recognizably Du Boisian note: "Ye can't *neglect* it to death; the neglect of all America can't kill it. It's in the womb o' the future and bigger than Asia, Africa, and America combined" (223, Cable's italics).

Philip Castleton is even more forthright on the contradiction between principles and practice. He praises U.S. ambition to play a greater role on the world's stage, but ties "our Southern doctrine of salvation" (which he defines as the Democrats' belief that "victory at the polls, fair or foul, is the only victory worth while") to the debacle of World War I, including the battle of the Marne raging as he speaks (101). Philip's implication is that American hypocrisy regarding its democracy at home will sabotage its ability to function morally as an international power. At present, he asserts, the United States cannot presume to defend democracy in Europe or in its colonies while condoning sham democracy at home, especially where black disfranchisement is concerned. Later, in a different conversation, Philip expands on the World War I theme with a most Du Bois–like point: "This European cataclysm was an awful warning against the risks hidden under the apparent harmlessness of all merely national, imperial, or racial standards of greatness or of a world's need" (318). That is a direct and incisive indictment of the standard justifications for Jim Crow colonialism.[7]

Any analysis of *Lovers of Louisiana* as a novel of ideas must also assess the roles played by Rosalie and her father, Alphonse Durel. They are far more complex than mere apologists for "tradition" and white rule who express standard southern doubts regarding Progressivist visions of empire. True, Rosalie's father is the quintessence of Creole class and racial elitism; he gets agitated when even the word "race" is used in polite conversation. But M. Durel offers also a tragic and ironic sense of history that not only stands as an effective counterpoint to Philip's Emersonian "self-assertion" (94) and idealism, but also articulates Philip's own inner doubts regarding the violence that can be done in the name of high principles. When Philip waxes on about the virtues of non-conformity, Durel reminds him of the unintentional pain rebellion may cause to others and himself; when Philip preaches moral purity, Durel demures: "all effective politics were inevitable compromises between what ought to be and what is" (101). Complex interplay and exchange make this novel live, not easy distinctions between progressive and conservative. So, too, the book's and the characters' high seriousness is regularly leavened with humor and self-deprecation.

In many scenes Rosalie Durel is too much a sounding board for Philip's ideas, while in others she is too simply resistant to them, as if conspiring on cue with Cable's other plot mechanisms to keep the lovers apart. Certainly Cable's Rosalie cannot hold a candle to Wharton's or James's best heroines. But Rosalie is surely one of Cable's better female protagonists. She is as mercurial and interesting as her father throughout the novel, and a decent case may be made that, for all Philip's posturing, the novel's heroine is the more daring and progressive of the two, at least in private. As a lady she risks more in crossing caste, color, and generational boundaries. A vivid chapter (21) on a ferry excursion along the New Orleans Mississippi waterfront reveals Philip as the more bookish, Rosalie as the true modern, the character most alive both to the city's history and its present vitality (132). Another scene involving tea with Philip's aunt hilariously exposes the self-righteousness and latent racism shared by all of Philip's family, making Rosalie's comparative lack of vanity and self-delusion shine by contrast (chapter 26). Rosalie questions her father's judgment at key moments (cf. 236) or leaves herself space to make what they both call, half-derisively, half-seriously, her "free American choice." Rosalie is not the passive or obtuse object of Philip's courtship, but embodies the book's pulse of life, its heady optimism that the best of the past can be preserved, its mistakes acknowledged and let go, and the future honorably met.

## 3

*Lovers of Louisiana* enacts the values of multiracial democracy by creating crucial spaces in the public sphere where citizens should be able to open themselves to new points of view and express unpopular opinions without fear of retribution or censure. Admittedly, such a vision is highly idealistic. But by refusing to give us easy answers in the numerous debates generated about issues of equity and freedom in the South, the nation, and the globe, Cable implies that it is in these modern spaces themselves that new answers are to be found. Most of the book's important conversations take place in the new liminal spaces mixing public and private spheres generated by urban, industrial civilization's needs for work, travel, and leisure. Such areas are never neutral and are always marked in one way or another by money, class, and caste, whether it be conversations by travelers on ferry or train, at leisure in Bermuda, or observing the significance of trash dumped in a public thoroughfare in the Vieux Carré. Cable's dramatic point is that such new social terrains promote (but do not guarantee) give and take, change, improvisation, and compromise. They create spaces in which democracy can work. Emergent public arenas are not immune from conflict or clashes of power or troubling exclusions and inequities, but are trustworthy sites in which to express and work through conflicts rather than repress them. As M. Durel says to Philip, they both, despite sharp political differences, can find a way to be friends, each bound up in self-interest but not reducible to that, engaging in forms of social interchange with room for patience, compromise, and the recognition of interdependency.

One of the most important sites marking imperfect democratic interdependency in *Lovers of Louisiana* is a secondhand bookstore on Chartres Street, New Orleans, run by a former slave of the Durels, Ovide Landry, and his wife. When we first hear of Ovide through the Durels, their account contains many elements of the standard New South narrative of a respectable "darkey" (36: the first word used to describe him). Offered his freedom, he refused it; during Reconstruction, he held political office but was not drawn into its supposed "cyclone of corruption" (39), a sterling exception to most of his race. But as Philip and Murray develop the theme, Ovide Landry's history comes to signify something different: "our old South could give him no worthy, no American freedom, . . . [and] the New South crowds him half-way down again to his old slavery" (41).

The first extended scene in which we can judge Landry for ourselves occurs somewhat later, in a chapter called "Raising the Dust." Landry, we learn, not only runs his store but heads a literary society associated with the nearby black university, and it is he who invites the young Tulane history professor to address them, in a gathering open to all races. The passage also stresses the "gentle dignity" with which this seventy-year-old activist "professed gratitude for an 'inner liberty' which his race's loss of much outward freedom could not destroy; a condition, he had said, far better than the outward liberty without the inner." Landry also believes that "in Europe, for a thousand years, unnumbered Jews, by this inner liberty, had got more out of life than the majority of their oppressors" (104). The rest of the chapter involves the men interacting as knowledgeable shopkeeper and customers, but also as citizens; they discuss Reconstruction and race relations from New Orleans to Mandalay, Burma. It is altogether an extraordinary scene that one wishes were longer.

Philip's ensuing talk at the black university, by contrast, seems tame almost to the point of insult; and, indeed, Cable's narrator dryly notes that one of the speaker's particularly glib assertions—about the "splendid rights you now enjoy"—draws merely faint applause (107). In such moments, Cable uses Ovide to mark the condescension not wholly disguised by Philip's race liberalism. The professor's "one great care had been to make clear that, whatever his convictions, his supreme sympathies . . . were for his own race" (108); and to Ovide afterwards he says, "Trouble is, it's harder than ever for even the kindest to take the colored race in earnest. Pardon me, but it seems a race of children." Landry's pointed rejoinder: "'Say, rather, a child race, professor, which every peasantry is, isn't it? But we're not all children and we claim the inalienable, individual right to grow up to such modern manhood as we individually can. Sir, our deprivation of that right is the rock our ship of freedom has struck on these fifty years [since Emancipation]'" (111). Close to his creator Philip may be in his opinions. But no one should read the above scene without sensing a sharp sense of self-critique on the part of Cable, aided by Landry. Such a move is consistent with the novel's unwritten credo, which is to leave no idea or opinion uncritically examined or historically unsituated. Readers may want to ask themselves, What other white author before Faulkner has created a black character as incisive?[8]

Landry's bookstore is an essential public space for a working democracy because it contains an archive of alternative histories of North America and the Caribbean. Philip's researches in family and Louisiana history draw him repeatedly to Landry's, where he discovers that the proprietor has compiled scrapbooks and done his own historical research work as well; he is no mere bookseller. In another, more minor work of fiction Cable published in 1918, *The Flower of the Chapdelaines*, Landry also plays a role. In that text, Cable not only juxtaposes antebellum tales of slave rebellion and escape with modern New Orleans. Texts about New Orleans' multiracial past that were once separated are united by Landry's archive, then read aloud to an enthralled audience, who experience them as living history, not the irrelevant past. Neither the content nor the structure of *Chapdelaines*, unfortunately, comes close to realizing the potential of Cable's conception. But what fails in this other text of Cable's allows us to see with particular clarity the importance of Landry's role in *Lovers of Louisiana*. As Cable well knew, by 1914 the history of Reconstruction and the New South had been so rewritten by white supremacists in fiction and nonfiction that few alternative interpretations of that past appeared possible—although Du Bois tried with *The Souls of Black Folk* in 1903 and "Reconstruction and Its Benefits" (1910), as did John Roy Lynch, the distinguished black Reconstruction legislator from Mississippi, in his 1913 memoir *The Facts of Reconstruction*.[9] Landry's shop and scrapbooks contain key suppressed and fragmented counter-narratives of the history of the South that there may be recovered, pieced together, and read anew. Given Cable's own embattled relationship with those New South elites who sought to manage southern memory to validate Jim Crow, perhaps Cable hoped that his own counterarguments to New South orthodoxies, including *The Negro Question* and *Lovers of Louisiana*, might find a home in an archive such as Ovide Landry's.

By the end of *Lovers of Louisiana*, Cable has so interwoven the family histories of the Castletons and the Durels—financially, socially, and emotionally—that the once separate worlds of Creole and American have become redrawn and intermingled. In such a Walter Scott–like merger of the clans, Cable has given us a history of modern New Orleans that to a large degree also replays the reunion of North and South in the fifty years after the Civil War. But unlike so many other narratives of the time (such as those discussed by David Blight and Nina Silber), Cable's does not create his fable of white union by subordinating blacks to the most minor and degraded roles possible in the polis and the nation. Instead, Ovide Landry, his family, and his store, though always strictly secondary, play indispensable roles in the novel's complex plotting of the financial and cultural interdependencies and changes that define Cable's decidedly different map of New South memory and the emerging nation.

Cable's attempt to use the novel of manners to imagine a more democratic future for his region and his nation had severe limitations he could not resolve. The form, in Cable's hands at least, had no way to portray social change occurring except when instituted by enlightened elites. The novel's plentiful sense of irony may constantly show how elites are self-deluding and self-serving, yet change is largely a subject of endless talk, not a matter of action. Philip Castleton, like Cable, fundamentally believes that once the right leaders are persuaded that multiracial democracy is morally just and practical for progress, then that will be enough; changes in opinion will lead to the reconstruction of society itself, reform flowing down from the elites to the masses.

Ovide Landry's role in *Lovers of Louisiana* may be a partial exception to this elitist vision of social change, but he too figures as an idealized figure, an impeccable leader. Like Murray and Philip, the novel overall is sharply critical of the violence and looting committed in the name of colonial "development" and shrewdly juxtaposes hypocrisies in the United Kingdom with those of Jim Crow Progressivism at home in the United States and in its new colonies. But Cable's text also assumes that the excesses of colonialism will somehow correct themselves through better morals and better management—in other words, through the governance of a more enlightened elite. Such a view is quintessentially Progressivist. Cable even has several late chapters set in Bermuda in order to offer that island as a counter-example to the benighted U.S. South regarding how colonial development and multiracial democracy are thoroughly compatible. A tourist's and an inveterate optimist's view of Bermuda, perhaps, but hardly accurate colonial or postcolonial history.[10] Ironically, the most subversive site in Cable's novel for imagining multiracial democracy and the complexities of history was a small secondhand bookstore on a New Orleans back street. From such an archive, we may trace a largely underground network of New South texts that critique Jim Crow colonialism and imagine what a multiracial democracy might actually look and sound like "to-day."

# Notes

A note on the notes: Only a portion of the manuscript's endnotes could be published in book form. For this book's complete notes, including both more extensive citations and analyses, see the author's Web page, where the organization and numbering follows the order presented here. Ellipses in brackets in the notes below indicate where further documentation may be found online. When a note does not have bracketed ellipses, that means the note as published in book form is complete. For clarity's sake, I occasionally add commentary in brackets in the notes below regarding the content of what has been cut.

This book's selected bibliography reflects key works cited in the printed text. My Web site publishes the book's complete bibliography to accompany the complete notes: www.swarthmore.edu/Humanities/pschmid1/scholarship.html.

## Introduction

1. The views described in *Sitting in Darkness* are the views of the author and do not represent the views or opinions of Kamehameha Schools, nor is there any approval or authorization of this material, express or implied, by the Kamehameha Schools.

2. This cartoon, from the *Literary Digest*, is part of an article on "The Third Battle of Manila."

3. I first discovered the *Puck* cartoon in the fine Web site set up by the Hawai'i State Archives, where it is dated incorrectly as 1898. Kahn Collection 37:39. [. . .]

The phrase "consent of *some* of the governed," including italics, was Senator Orville Platt's, spoken in Senate debate in 1898. Replying to Senator Hoar's question whether "governments derive their just powers from the consent of the governed," Mr. Platt answered, "from the consent of *some* of the governed." *Literary Digest* 18.2 (Jan. 14, 1899): 34. For fuller analysis of debates about colonialism, education, citizenship, and "consent," see especially chapters 1 and 6.

4. For a brief analysis of the design and ideological contradictions of the National Constitution Center in Philadelphia, see Vienne.

5. For recent historians' accounts of the Wilmington riot in a broad historical context, including some consideration of the role played by pro-colonial rhetoric, see Prather; and Cecelski and Tyson.

6. Historians focusing on the postwar U.S. South who are recognized as paradigm-makers for its social history include W. E. B. Du Bois, C. Vann Woodward, John Hope Franklin, Eric Foner, Joel Williamson, Edward L. Ayers, Nina Silber, David Blight, Nell Irvin Painter, Saidiya Hartman, and Steven Hahn—and many others obviously could be named.

7. For just several of many recent examples of the "transnational" in U.S. studies, see Shelley Fisher Fishkin's "Crossroads of Cultures"; Smith and Cohn's anthology *Look Away!: The U.S. South in New World Studies* (2004); Wai-Chee Dimock's *Through Other Continents: American Literature across Deep Time* (2006); or any of a number of recent issues of *American Quarterly*, the primary journal for the American Studies Association. See also the December 2006 special issue of *American Literature*, "Global Contexts, Local Literatures: The New Southern Studies," guest edited by Kathryn McKee and Annette Trefzer. [...]

8. [...] [More on Cleanth Brooks's construction of a timeless South.]

9. Wilson, *Public Papers*, v. 1. [...] [Further discussion of the claim that the short story was a distinctively American contribution to literature.]

10. The influential German model for a modern university was organized in Berlin according to the schema proposed by Wilhelm von Humboldt, but was relevant for other German cities as well, particularly Jena. See von Humbolt's "Theory of Bildung" and historical commentary in Westbury et al., *Teaching as Reflective Practice*, especially 55–107. [...]

11. For the full list of Reading Courses, topics, and organizational schema, see Alderman, Harris, and Kent, eds., *The Library of Southern Literature*, Vol. 16, Section 2, 1–226.

12. [...] [Further discussion of Pattee in context.]

13. [...] Jay B. Hubbell is an exception to my generalization about how anthologies from the 1930s through the 1950s and beyond followed Parrington and negatively treated almost all New South literature. Michael Kreyling rightly says that Hubbell "had probably done more than the pre–World War I anthologists to keep alive the literature of the South and fold it into the emerging mainstream of American literature," via his two-volume *American Life in Literature* of 1936 (*Inventing Southern Literature* 59). [...]

# Chapter 1

1. Quoted from the Land Ordinance of 1785, passed by the Continental Congress. Of course, the ordinance's Euclidean vision of property grids and schoolhouses was one thing, the reality that followed it another. For an excellent brief discussion of this piece of legislation as an Enlightenment prototype for the ordering of a continent, see Michael Gilmore, *Surface and Depth: The Quest for Legibility in American Culture*, 24–25. Also relevant is Richard Brown's *The Strength of a People: The Idea of an Informed Citizenry in America, 1650–1870*. For general background and the text of the Morrill Act, see usinfo.state.gov/usa/infousa/facts/democrac/27.htm. [...] One of the more compelling recent histories of the role blacks played in setting up a public school system in the postwar South is my colleague Allison Dorsey's *To Build Our Lives Together: Community Formation in Black Atlanta, 1875–1906*, especially chapter 4. The Emily Dickinson poem quoted is #657.

2. For a helpful anthology of recent scholarship on Reconstruction, see *The Freedmen's Bureau and Reconstruction: Reconsiderations*, Cimbala and Miller, eds. My brief synopsis also draws on W. E. B. Du Bois, John Hope Franklin, George Bentley, Eric Foner, Ronald Butchart, and James C. Anderson, among others. For the specific figures cited involving the number of schools created, see Foner, *Reconstruction* 144; and Bentley 176.

3. For an earlier study of postwar southern schools, see Du Bois's chapter 15 in *Black Reconstruction*, 637–669 [. . .]. [More on scholarship studying black and white southerner's attitudes toward public schools.]

4. My generalizations in the introductory paragraphs of chapter 1 summarize the work of the many historians cited in the text, but see in particular Charles Anderson, chapters five and six. [. . .]

5. Child's career has attracted fine new historicist scholarship in recent years, and *Romance of the Republic* has received invigorating readings by Carolyn Karcher, Bruce Mills (132–140), Shirley Samuels, and Dana Nelson, among others. For a succinct discussion of critical trends regarding Child's novel, see Dana Nelson's introductory essay to the paperback edition of *Romance*, especially notes 7–9. [. . .]

6. One invaluable recent discussion of the disciplinary restrictions placed on freedom as represented in Reconstruction-era Freeman advice tracts and other texts is Saidiya Hartman's *Scenes of Subjection*, chapter 5, "Fashioning Obligation," which also includes an extensive reading of the Helen Brown novel *John Freeman and His Family Scene* (1864) that was a predecessor to Child's.

7. Griest's *John and Mary; or, The Fugitive Slaves* was only briefly in print, but is one of the many texts about the South that have been digitally scanned and made available to all via the invaluable Documenting the American South Web site. For Griest's novel, see http://docsouth.unc.edu/neh/griest/griest.html.

8. Thanks to Christopher Densmore, head of the Friends Historical Library at Swarthmore College, and John Ward Willson Loose of Millersville University and the Lancaster County Historical Society, for valuable help with Ellwood Griest's life and historical context. Neither is responsible for any errors in my discussion.

9. All illustrations included in this chapter are taken from the anonymous *Harper's* "On Negro Schools" article, September 1874. For overviews of the history of Reconstruction and postwar black schools, see Franklin; Foner; Stampp and Litwack; R. Morris; Anderson; and the PBS documentary *The American Experience: Reconstruction* (2004) and its accompanying Web site, especially the Access to Learning materials: www.pbs.org/wgbh/amex/reconstruction/schools. The Digital History Web site also has excellent introductory materials on Reconstruction, including education issues: see www.digitalhistory.uh.edu/reconstruction/. The benchmark discussions of the rise of the New South on which I have most relied are Woodward's *Origins of the New South*; Gaston's *The New South Creed*; and Ayers's *The Promise of the New South*. [. . .]

10. For a history of the fate of the Fourteenth Amendment, see Epps. Useful discussions of the relevance of arguments of the *Plessy v. Ferguson* and related cases for literary history are in Sundquist, *To Wake the Nations* 225–270; Michaels, "The Souls of White Folk"; Pamplin; Fleischmann; Foreman; and especially three essays by Brook Thomas.

11. I thank Mark James Noonan for the Russell reference and for his expert analysis of plantation myth poetry and fiction, which I saw in draft form while working on this book. [. . .] Another indispensable source for the analysis here is MacKethan, "Plantation Fiction"; see also Schmidt, "Command Performances," on plantation fiction conventions. The Irwin Russell poem quoted is "Noverm People" (*Scribner's Monthly* 13 [January 1877]: 430) and is well discussed by Noonan.

12. For the Civil War in the U.S. national memory, see David Blight, *Race and Reunion*, especially chapter 3, "Decoration Days," 64–97; and Nina Silber's *Romance of Reunion*. Also relevant is Charles Reagan Wilson's *Baptized in Blood*, on the Lost Cause movement. [. . .] For analyses of the role the postwar magazine revolution played, see Hubbell 726–733; and Mott.

# Chapter 2

1. For overviews of Tourgée's life and work, see Edmund Wilson (529–548); Olsen; Hardwig; Gross; and Blight 216–221. Gross's comments on *Fool's Errand* and *Bricks without Straw* remain benchmark readings: 58–102. For Charles Chesnutt's comments in his journal in response to *A Fool's Errand*, see *Journals* 124–126, which mix both praise and criticism of the novel and ask where is the "colored man" who could write an even more incisive book about the South. But Chesnutt, like Tourgée, struggled over what role "fiction" should play in an arena where "hard facts" and truths, not lies, about the New South were paramount (126). [. . .] [On important studies of Tourgée in the context of *Plessy*.]

2. [. . .] [A discussion of scholarship on who taught in the new southern schools, and related matters.]

3. Tourgée's character Eliab Hill was based in part on an actual person, a Negro Baptist minister and preacher named Elias Hill in the South Carolina settlement of Clay Hill; his testimony is found in the *Report of the Joint Congressional Committee on the Ku-Klux Conspiracy*, vol. 5: 1406–1415 (Tourgée, *Invisible Empire* 62); for more, see Magdol. [. . .]

4. [. . .] As Tourgée emphasizes, black churches and schoolhouses were targeted by the KKK, as were teachers both white and black who instructed black children; white families who boarded teachers working in black schools were also harassed. See Allen Trelease, *White Terror: The Ku Klux Klan Conspiracy and Southern Reconstruction*; and Sandra Gunning.

5. Joel Williamson, in *After Slavery*, describes such a parade of blacks in Charleston, South Carolina, celebrating freedom and independence. [. . .] See Stampp and Litwack 211; and Williamson's chapter "The Meaning of Freedom" in *After Slavery*.

6. For instance, consider this key exchange between Nimbus, one of the black leaders, and Molly: "'Nimbus, I appoint you to keep order in this crowd until my return. . . . Do you understand?' 'Yes, ma'am, I hears; but whar you gwine, Miss Mollie?' 'Into the town.' 'No yer don't, Miss Mollie,' said he, stepping before her. 'Dey'll kill you, shore.' 'No matter. I am going. You provoked this affray by your foolish love of display, and it must be settled.' . . . 'But, Miss Mollie—' 'Not a word. You have been a soldier and should obey orders'" (157). See also Edmund Wilson's caustic comments on Mollie Ainsley's role in this scene (545). Wilson reads *Bricks without Straw* as "largely a repetition of its predecessor" (546), but he does develop a basic analysis of Tourgée's project for full public education.

# Chapter 3

1. William Still's *The Underground Railroad* (1872) remains indispensable for insight on how Harper's work and writing was understood by a contemporary (755–780). Frances Smith Foster has gathered many of Harper's poems and essays in *A Brighter Coming Day*, and for her overview of Harper's poetic ventures, see *Written by Herself* (Harper 131–153). The fullest account to date of Harper's postwar lecturing career in the context of other black women's reform efforts is Carla Peterson's (119–145 and 196–238); though see also Paula Giddings's important earlier overview of the period (17–131), in which Harper plays a central role. [. . .] [More on Harper scholarship.]

2. See, for example, Eugene Genovese, *Roll, Jordan, Roll*; Lawrence Levine, *Black Culture and Black Consciousness*; and Jacqueline Jones, *Labor of Love*. Barbara Christian was one of the first to point out

how astutely Harper here refutes stereotypes of loyal black servants that had recently become popular in fiction by Joel Chandler Harris and Thomas Nelson Page (29).

3. Dr. Latrobe, a white southerner, guardedly accepts the presence of some northerners in the South but adamantly states that "we Southerners will never submit to negro supremacy . . . [or] abandon our Caucasian civilization to an inferior race" (*Iola Leroy* 221). It is also worth noting the role played by Harper's sardonic narrative voice in "Open Questions." The narrator introduces Dr. Latrobe as follows: "It was a new experience to receive colored men socially. His wits, however, did not forsake him, and he received the introduction and survived it" (221).

4. Many of the opinions expressed in the conversazione scene in *Iola Leroy*—especially the condescension toward Africa—were commonly held among the postwar black middle class and shared by essayists of uplift such as Alexander Crummell, Anna Julia Cooper, and the early W. E. B. Du Bois. Even Thomas Dixon might have agreed with some of the points made.

5. On postcolonial elites, see Cheah (208–252), who gives a reading of both Cabral and Fanon; and also Chatterjee. See also Wilson Moses's classic study of black nationalism in the United States in the 1880–1920 period. Obviously, there are many differences between emancipated blacks in the United States and the citizens of newly decolonized countries. But slaves and their descendents arguably suffered the worst possible form of colonization and upheaval. After emancipation, as U.S. blacks tried to imagine new forms of community, they were divided between a nationalism that sought some form of secession from the United States and a nationalism that fought to claim the rights of U.S. citizenship, thus exchanging one form of nationalism for another. It is not wholly inaccurate to understand this dilemma within black political discourse as a postcolonial one.

# Chapter 4

1. "The teacher introduced [Bernard and Belgrave] into every needed field of knowledge. . . . There were two studies in which the two rivals dug deep to see which could bring forth the richest treasures; and these gave coloring to the whole of their after lives. One, was the History of the United States, and the other, Rhetoric. In history, that portion that charmed them most was the story of the rebellion against the yoke of England. . . . As part of their rhetorical training, they were taught to declaim. Thanks to their absorption in the history of the Revolution, their minds ran to the sublime in literature; and they strove to secure pieces to declaim that recited the most heroic deeds of man, of whatever nationality. Leonidas, Marco Bozarris, Arnold Winklereid, Louis Kossuth, Robert Emmett, Martin Luther, Patrick Henry and such characters" (*Imperium* 28–29).

2. [. . .] [Analysis of Griggs criticism and scholarship on black nationalism, light-skinned elites, and related matters.]

3. Griggs criticism needs to consider the Tourgée connection more thoroughly, though, of course, not at the expense of discussing crucial predecessors like Frederick Douglass, Martin Delany, David Walker, William Wells Brown, or Booker T. Washington.

4. For one history of debates on African colonization schemes, see Takaki, *Iron Cages* (36–55); for accounts that emphasize the history of black political thought and activism, see Pease and Pease, *Black Utopia*; Moses; Robin Kelley; and Porter, *Black Seminoles*. [. . .] [More on black Seminoles and Griggs's exploration of black nationalism.]

# Notes

## Chapter 5

1. I say a "consciously" interracial romance because there are several in fiction, such as Pauline Hopkins's *Hagar's Daughter*, in which the "black" identity of one of the principals is unknown. Sterling Brown writes on *Old Greenbottom Inn*: "subtler propaganda. Most of the stories tell of the pathetic love affairs of beautiful Negro girls, but there is some rewarding local color of the Tennessee Valley and of the earliest Negro schools" (*Negro in American Fiction* 101–102). Dickson Bruce's article on McClellan for the *Dictionary of Literary Biography* provides the best available biographical sketch of McClellan's life as well as survey of his poetry and prose. Bruce's later *Black American Writing* briefly summarizes one review *Old Greenbottom Inn* received in 1908, from *Alexander's Magazine* (143–144). McClellan describes a real Normal and Industrial school near Huntsviller, Alabama: see Richings 203–217. [ . . . ] [More on McClellan scholarship and McClellan's absence from recent anthologies of black literature.]

2. McClellan's difference from Washington makes it a mistake for Robert Bone to class McClellan as one of the "Washington" school of black writers active before the Harlem Renaissance. [ . . .].

3. For more on evolving literature curricula in U.S. universities at the beginning of the twentieth century, see the introduction, particularly footnotes 10 and 11.

4. There are portraits of individual post–Civil War black entertainers in Paul Laurence Dunbar's stories, particularly if we expand the term *entertainer* to include some of the new jobs in gambling and horse racing that became available to blacks after the war. Dunbar's tales "Schwallinger's Philanthropy," "The Race Question," "The Finish of Patsy Barnes" (all three about the horse-racing world), and "The Boy and the Bayonet" (about drill performers enrolled in one of the new colored schools in Washington, D.C.), among others, all broach new ground in terms of subject matter for black writing and were published in the early 1900s, before *Old Greenbottom Inn*. [ . . . ] Aside from Dunbar, McClellan's other predecessor for his portrait of "Essie Dortch" was possibly George Washington Cable's *Old Creole Days*, particularly a story such as "Tite Poulette," about a paid dancer, her daughter, and the antebellum New Orleans quadroon balls.

5. Dvorak is spelled "Davarak" in McClellan's 1906 text; I have adopted the more familiar spelling. I have also edited out a typographical error in my quotation above; in the original, a period is misplaced.

6. For Malone's description of the evolution of "Buck and Wing" dancing moves, see 222n12; see also Emery 89–90. For discussions of black and white performers in blackface minstrel shows, plus the nature of the various skits, characters, and the overall plots conventionally used to tie the skits together, see especially Lott's *Love and Theft*; and Lott's and Winter's essays in Bean et al., *Inside the Minstrel Mask*. These accounts also focus on the complex cultural politics of blackface, plantation nostalgia, and contemporary racism. Regarding black dance history, aside from the works already mentioned in the body of this essay, see also Lynne Fauley Emery's earlier study, *Black Dance* (1988); and Robert C. Toll's *On with the Show: The First Century of Show Business in America* (1976).

7. For a discussion of the relevance of trains to twentieth-century blues music, see Houston Baker's *Blues, Ideology, and Afro-American Literature*, especially 1–14.

8. [ . . . ] [On representations of lynching in fiction and nonfiction before McClellan, or contemporaneous with him.] For recent scholarly work on the cultural work of lynching as a scapegoat ritual and an initiation into "whiteness," see especially work by Hazel Carby, Trudier Harris, Gail Bederman, Sandra Gunning, and James Allen, plus the discussion in chapter 9.

9. McClellan planned a full-length study of American literature but, as noted in note 1, apparently never wrote it. He did publish one essay surveying American writing at the turn of the century

and giving a similarly sanguine forecast to this passage from "Old Greenbottom Inn." "The Negro as a Writer" originally appeared in a 1902 anthology of essays on black literature published in Naperville, Illinois; it has been reprinted in *Dictionary of Literary Biography* (1986)—where, however, McClellan is identified only as a black poet and critic, not a fiction writer (308). Presciently, McClellan's 1902 essay judges Charles W. Chesnutt to be the most important black fiction writer yet to publish in the United States.

# Chapter 6

1. My epigraph from Miguel de Cervantes's *Don Quixote* (Sancho Panza speaking to Don Quixote) comes from the fine new translation by Edith Grossman, 56. Although much recent work has been done on the history of U.S. expansionism in the late nineteenth and early twentieth centuries, I would like to stress the continuing importance of two classic histories by R. W. Van Alstyne and David Healy. A helpful introductory survey of some of the material covered in this chapter is David Southern's *The Progressive Era and Race: Reaction and Reform, 1900–1917*, which includes discussion of the complicated relations between African American reformists, southern Progressivists, and national figures such as Roosevelt and Wilson. A key omission in Southern's text, however, is analysis of Progressivist foreign policies for the new colonies in relation to Progressivist domestic programs, particularly regarding race relations. For more on southern Progressivists, see Grantham and Link. For a strong recent version of the argument that racism was antagonistic to the imperialist project, see Love.

2. For information and documents regarding Roosevelt's revision of the Monroe Doctrine to include economics as well as politics, see Gambone, 136–137; and Van Alstyne 168n2, which focuses on Robert Lansing's memo to President Wilson, endorsed by him, regarding key strategies for U.S. economic dominance in the Caribbean and Latin America, all in the name of protecting those states' economic and political independence. [ . . . ]

3. [ . . . ] [More on Sousa's "El Capitán," "King Cotton," and the Atlanta Exposition.]

4. For the brutal history of early white "Redeemer" activities to destroy Reconstruction in Mississippi (1873–75), see Lemann. On the later spread of voter disfranchisement tactics in Mississippi, Tennessee, and elsewhere, see Ayers, *Promise of the New South* 52–54, 146–149, 409–411. Particularly relevant is Mississippi's deployment of an "understanding clause" allowing officials to eliminate voters who, they claimed, couldn't understand well enough a selected passage from the Mississippi constitution. [ . . . ] [More on recent scholarship on disfranchisement.] The history of the U.S.-imposed Hawaiian voting plan is even more intriguing than Woodward allows. [ . . . ]

5. I favor the word *colonialism* because it foregrounds the understanding that colonies are dominated by but not incorporated into a nation. But in the 1890s and after, *colonial, imperial,* and *expansionist* were often used interchangeably and did not consistently mark differences between direct and indirect rule in the territories controlled by an empire.

In claiming that Jim Crow segregation became "national" policy after 1898, I do not mean that it was applied in the same form throughout the United States precisely at that date, or even throughout the South, but rather that it was justified in terms of national self-interest, and versions of Jim Crow spread far beyond the South in the early twentieth century. [ . . . ]

Only once in Woodward's *The Strange Career of Jim Crow* (1955) did he mention the relevance of the 1898 war with Spain: "As America shouldered the White Man's Burden she took up at the same time many Southern attitudes on the subject of race" (54). For more detail on this issue, consider the patterns discovered by Willard B. Gatewood Jr., who in his meticulously researched *Black Americans and the White Man's Burden, 1898–1903* notes how [...] trains heading south with troops for Cuba were segregated, as were troop ships bound for the Philippines, while "Whites Only" barbershops, restaurants, and brothels in Manila came quickly with U.S. rule (Gatewood 231, 282). [...]

6. For discussion of the ambiguities of the word "insular" (Latin for *island*) as they pertain to the Supreme Court Insular Cases involving colonial rights, see Amy Kaplan's *Anarchy of Empire*, the introduction. [...] An easily available introductory survey of these rulings may be found at the Island Law Web site: www.macmeekin.com/Library/Insular%20Cases.htm.

7. For a biographical sketch of Charles Denby, including his being raised in Virginia and France and his business interests in trade with the Far East, see Healy, ch. 10.

8. See Wilson, *Public Papers*, vol. 1: "College and State," 368–395; the quotations are from 388 and 394, respectively.

9. Wilson lectures were published in 1908 by Columbia University Press as *Constitutional Government in the United States*. My line of argument regarding the "tutelary aims of colonization" has been aided by Vicente Rafael's groundbreaking article and book; Rafael also discusses this particular Wilson citation on 215–216n8 of *White Love*. [...] [More on Wilson's conception of education and related matters, plus recent scholarship on Anglo-Saxon superiority discourse.]

10. "Consent of *some* of the governed": Sen. Orville Platt, quoted in *Literary Digest* 18.2 (Jan. 14 1899): 31–34; italics and brackets mine. I cite the Senate debate coverage in this popular, easily available publication rather than the Congressional Record because it was one of several ways that the majority of interested citizens could have followed the Senate debates on U.S. colonial policies.

11. Campomanes mentions William Appleman Williams as one of the first to identify the paradox, which he named "anti-colonial imperialism": see "1898 and the Nature of the New Empire." I especially recommend Sandra M. Gustafson's "Histories of Democracy and Empire" for an incisive overview of longstanding debates in Western political thought about how the terms "democracy" and "empire" have had their definitions shift as some theorists have argued that they are incompatible, while others have claimed that—as the history of Athens proves—democratic freedoms are often associated with some form of imperial state power.

12. Roosevelt quoted in Howard K. Beale, *Theodore Roosevelt and the Rise of America to World Power* 32 and 34; cf. Eric Cheyfitz, *Poetics of Imperialism* 4. For analyses of links between the New South and national Progressive movements, see Louis Gould, Nancy Cohen, William Link, Dewey Grantham, Steven Diner, and David Southern. For discussion of the anti-colonial colonialism paradox historically considered, see especially anthologies edited by Amy Kaplan (with Donald Pease) and John Carlos Rowe; Rowe's own book, *Literary Culture and U.S. Imperialism* 3–24; Walter Benn Michaels's "Anti-Imperial Americanism"; and the Gustafson essay mentioned in the previous note. Nina Silber's *The Romance of Reunion*, particularly her chapter "New Patriotism and New Men," has also been inspirational for my project here, though she focuses primarily on northerners who wrote about the South.

13. Key precursors to Boeckmann's analysis include Thomas Gossett; George Fredrickson; Reginald Horsman; Joel Williamson, *Crucible of Race*; Robyn Wiegman; and Walter Benn Michaels. I would like here the express my thanks to my colleague Kendall Johnson for helpful conversations on the convolutions in racial discourse in this period in U.S. history.

14. For more on the issues of free labor ideology and land redistribution, see Foner, *Free Soil*; and Foner, *Reconstruction*, especially chapters 3, 4, 6, and 8. An interesting related issue is raised by comparative history: the Dawes Act of 1887. [...].

15. Regarding black land-ownership, Edward Ayers asserts that in 1900 about one-quarter of blacks in the South owned the land they worked, though the proportion was far higher in the Upper South coastal regions than in the Deep South (208–209). [...] Such a statistic does not directly contradict Ludlow's 1903 pamphlet, but it does indicate a more complex picture. Another key piece of the puzzle is provided by W. E. B. Du Bois in his novel *The Quest of the Silver Fleece* (1911), one of whose major topics is blacks' control of land and the products of their labor. Du Bois notes that in the Jim Crow South, "no black man ordinarily can sell his crop without a white creditor's consent" (409).

16. A few other biographical details of the Armstrongs from Engs are worth footnoting, since they add layers of complexity and irony. Richard Armstrong moved away from strict missionary work and became minister of public education for King Kamehameha III in Honolulu, eventually establishing over five hundred schools in Hawaii that stressed agricultural and industrial training. He also fought a losing battle for land reforms so that more native Hawaiians could farm their own land rather than work for white-owned plantations. [...]

17. Two examples of black resistance to the industrial education model are Pauline Hopkins's 1900 novel *Contending Forces*, which includes two characters closely resembling Washington and Du Bois and stages several debates outlining the rationales for industrial versus liberal arts education for blacks (cf. 123ff and 166ff); and, of course, W. E. B. Du Bois's critique of Washington's rationale in *The Souls of Black Folk* (1903). Robert C. Morris's study of the education of freedmen in the South during the Civil War and Reconstruction contains extensive analysis of the textbooks used in the Freedmen's schools. [...]

18. Here is a key passage from Booker T. Washington's Atlanta speech, to provide proper context. Note that as well as making his notorious contrast between useful labor and liberal arts "geegaws," Washington places his famous plea to hire black labor within the context of *colonialism* and immigration: see my italics below. "Our greatest danger is that in the great leap from slavery to freedom we may overlook the fact that the masses of us are to live by the productions of our hands, and fail to keep in mind that we shall prosper in proportion as we learn to dignify and glorify common labour, and put brains and skill into the common occupations of life; shall prosper in proportion as we learn to draw the line between the superficial and the substantial, the ornamental gewgaws of life and the useful. No race can prosper till it learns that there is as much dignity in tilling a field as in writing a poem. It is at the bottom of life we must begin, and not at the top. Nor should we permit our grievances to overshadow our opportunities. *To those of the white race who look to the incoming of those of foreign birth and strange tongue and habits for the prosperity of the South*, were I permitted I would repeat what I say to my own race, 'Cast down your bucket where you are.' Cast it down among the eight millions of Negroes whose habits you know." My italics; quoted from www.historymatters.gmu.edu/d/39/, accessed October 23, 2006. My summary in this section of the chapter is indebted in particular to James D. Anderson, chapter 2. For more on the ironic parallels between plantation slavery and the Hampton/Tuskegee systems, see Baker, *Turning South Again*.

19. [...] [More on recent scholarship on Puerto Rican and Philippine education history under U.S. colonialism.]

20. One key difference between the U.S. South as a whole and the new colonies, of course, was the issue of language. [...] Reports concerning education in the Philippines show an analogous pattern to Puerto Rico. Judge William Howard Taft's *Report of the Philippine Commission* (1900) critiques and catalogues the deplorable state of education under Spanish rule and boasts that its work will be heartily approved by the Filipinos: a "system of free schools for the people—another American institution, it will be noted—has been an important element in every Philippine programme of

reforms" (vol. 1, 120); see also vol. 1, part 3: Education, 17–41. Later, in 1904, in the U.S. Bureau of Insular Affairs pamphlet *What Has Been Done in the Philippines*, statistics and growth rates for schools are charted and the natives' aptitude for education and Americanization lauded. But today's historians of the effects of the U.S. occupation on education tell a rather more complex tale: see for instance Canieso-Doronila.

# Chapter 7

1. Cable's *John March, Southerner* (1895) has been read by Butcher as an antiracist novel consistent with Cable's essays criticizing the New South's racial order (see especially 114–125). I think Butcher makes a decent case, but in the end I disagree. I believe instead that the novel's position toward both its hero and the New South is extremely muddled and contradictory, perhaps as a result of Cable's own mixed feelings toward the region in which he no longer felt welcome. Butcher feels John March is re-educated away from his typically New South prejudices over the course of the book, but I do not see convincing evidence of this. From the very start, March is extremely disdainful of black schools and black leaders, for instance, and never renounces such views. J. Harris's *Gabriel Tolliver: A Story of Reconstruction* (1902), like Page's *Red Rock*, treats the black school as a site for fomenting violence and black racial hatred. But Harris, typically, remains ambivalent about New South dogma about black monstrosity. Tolliver as a hero is sometimes drawn more toward black cultural spaces than white ones (see, for example, the scene in which he hides underneath the schoolhouse with Tasma Tid), even though at the end of the novel he ascends to power within the white New South hierarchy. Both these novels deserve new interpretations within a New South historical context.

2. On the Documenting the American South database, *Bond and Free* is listed under "Grace Lintner," a character in the novel who is the supposed author of the text, not Ellen Ingraham, its actual author. For other southern responses to Tourgée before Harris, Page, and Dixon, including William Royall, J. H. Ingraham (no relation to Ellen M. Ingraham), and N. J. Floyd, see Gross, *Tourgée* 84–86. For a general discussion of the "plantation school," see MacKethan.

3. Ingraham, *Bond and Free* 286. For more on the relevance of "free labor" ideology to the postwar period, see chapter 6. As a heroine, Ingraham's Letitia to some degree follows in the footsteps of some independent-minded heroines in prewar southern fiction, such as Caroline Hentz's *Eoline* (1852), whose title character flees her plantation home and an arranged marriage to become a teacher. Eoline eventually returns to the plantation to resume her rightful place at the top of the social hierarchy. See Karen Smith's discussion of *Eoline*, which suggests that by having her heroine be a teacher on the path to becoming mistress of a plantation, Hentz is pushing for a broader notion of acceptable women's responsibilities and identity (54). Such an expansion is part of the agenda of Ingraham's *Bond and Free* as well, even though Letitia is not, strictly speaking, a teacher; she hires one. But her path to becoming mistress of a plantation is certainly as extraordinary as Hentz's heroine's. Incidentally, immediately after the Civil War, southern planters were sometimes blamed by southerners for causing the South's poor level of social and economic development, including its lack of a public education system. One such example is D. H. Hill, an ex-Confederate general who published the *Land We Love* magazine in North Carolina in the late 1860s. Hill was an early advocate of widespread educational reform for whites, stressing the value of practical, not scholastic, education. For more on Hill, see Gaston 29–30. In Ingraham's *Bond and Free*, she suggests that planters were generally ignorant on matters of education, with her heroine, Letitia, the glorious exception.

4. Quotations from *American Freedman* and *Flake's Bulletin* (10 February 1867) are drawn from Bentley 176 and 181, respectively.

5. The mother of Oscar and Letitia Templeton was an octoroon and their marriage was recognized in New Orleans but not in their home state of Virginia. Unlike in Child's novel *Romance of the Republic* (1867; discussed in chapter 1), in *Bond and Free* the father apparently makes a will legally freeing his children, but his evil half-brother ignores it.

Ingraham's Letitia associates her black blood with sin, hardly an unusual reaction for the period, given attitudes toward miscegenation. What is far more intriguing, however, is that she also suggests traces of blackness can somehow be miraculously extinguished over a period of several generations, so that even though she is the daughter of a woman with one-eighth "black" blood, she now believes that not one drop of "blackness" remains in her to be passed on to her children. The heroine's concluding meditation is worth quoting for its immaculately contorted logic and its biblical metaphor of cleansing: "You can never realize how dreadful once seemed to me the thought of entailing upon children any trace of African descent, nor my happiness now in believing that in our family it is extinct. Even after this lapse of years, my mind will sometimes revert to the period when the transgressions of the fathers were visited upon me as a representative of the third and fourth generations, and my heart overflows with gratitude toward the love of a Saviour, whose blood 'cleanseth us from all sin.['] Is not that a beautiful picture?" (286–287). From the context, it is not at all apparent that Ingraham means for the reader to see her heroine's conclusions as naïve or incorrect.

6. Anderson, *Education of Blacks in the South* 22, citing Alvord 13.

7. For a fine analysis of Waterbury's text in the larger context of postwar ambivalence regarding black freedom, see Saidiya Hartman, 161–163 and 177–178.

8. For an expert recent analysis of this topic, see Paul Kramer, "Making Concessions: Race and Empire Revisited at the Philippine Exposition, St. Louis, 1901–05." Good study has been done on the matters of fairs or "world expositions," empire, industrial capitalism, and the uses of spectacle, including well-known books by Robert Rydell and Alan Trachtenberg, but here I would like to make special note of Timothy Mitchell's "Orientalism and the Exhibitionary Order." See also Rydell, "Rediscovering," who reproduces a stereoptic photograph of the Igorot Filipino village at the St. Louis Fair (58–59). Such photos were widely sold as fair souvenirs. In this one, ten Filipino men stand in the foreground wearing little clothing, while behind them on a row of benches sit white women spectators in voluminous skirts, blouses, and hats.

9. Photographs of the "Igorot Village," including of Igorots voting, were extensively distributed as publicity for and souvenirs from the St. Louis Fair. Sources for the facts about the Philippine Reservation include an online site set up by the St. Louis Public Library (http://slpl.org/slpl/interests/article240114133.asp); Rydell; and Clevenger. For the specific photograph of voting reproduced here, the URL is http://exhibits.slpl.lib.mo.us/lpe/data/lpe240023338.asp?Image=56593673, accessed 25 October 2006. Also relevant is Vergara's broader history of representations of the Philippines in colonial discourse.

# Chapter 8

1. Quoted from an Anti-Imperialist League archival Web site, http://www.civics-online.org/library/formatted/texts/anti-imperial.html, accessed 26 October 2006.

2. [. . .] [More on recent research on Carl Schurz and other Anti-Imperialist League members.]

3. Also particularly relevant to the issue of contradictions in both pro- and anti-imperialist arguments are two other articles in the *Cultures of United States Imperialism* anthology (edited by Kaplan
and Pease), by Walter Benn Michaels and Kenneth M. Warren. Pease and Kaplan's collection provides a
much-needed start for comparative and transnational perspectives on U.S. imperial discourse, but too
often writers from the Caribbean, Latin America, and the South Pacific are left out of the debates.

4. My request for more comparative and transnational work does not assume that U.S. writers
should always be central, but rather that bringing such perspectives to U.S. studies is an important
phase of the larger postcolonial studies project. For more on Rizal, see Campomanes, "1898 and the
Nature of the New Empire"; Rafael, "Nationalism, Imagery, and the Filipino Intelligentsia"; and Dizon.
[. . .] Sarah Sarita See has a fine essay arguing that white southerners' claims of being unjustly colonized
during Reconstruction must be understood in the context of legal arguments excluding Filipinos in
the U.S. from making analogous claims about the post-1898 period: see her "Southern Postcoloniality
and the Improbability of Filipino American Postcoloniality." [. . .] The 1900 and 1919 statements by Du
Bois on colonialism are discussed in Lewis's biography, vol. 1: 248–251 and 574–578. [The note concludes
with some discussion of the need for further scholarship on Du Bois, Wells-Barnett, and discourses
involving race, hemispheric citizenship, and the postcolonial condition.]

5. I read Ferrer in the context of other contemporary historians such as Amy Kaplan, Donald
Pease, John Carlos Rowe, Amritjit Singh, Louis Pérez, Oscar Campomanes, E. San Juan Jr., and Angel
V. Shaw and Luis H. Francia, among many, via books and essay anthologies such as *The Cultures of
United States Imperialism, National Identities and Post-Americanist Narratives, Postcolonial Theories and
the U.S.*, and *Vestiges of War: The Philippine-American War and the Aftermath of an Imperial Dream,
1899–1999.* For book-length studies of the paradoxes of the Cuban independence movement, see
Pérez and Helg. I have also immensely benefited from George Handley's fine analyses of the ideological
inheritance of plantation colonial discourse as it affects both U.S. and Cuban post-slavery writing,
including Martí's (chapters 1–3); Martí cannot simply be heroicized as a colonial resister. For another
complex postcolonial reading of Martí, see Irwin.

6. For much more detailed discussion of the paradox that in a colonial context the transition toward
native "autonomy" can serve the interests of both U.S. and Filipino elites, see *The American Colonial State
in the Philippines: Global Perspectives*, ed. Julian Go and Anne L. Foster (2003). This was articulated as early
as 1899 by President McKinley's secretary of war, Elihu Root, in his "Principles of Colonial Policy."

7. These teachers were known as Thomasites, after the ship; eventually over one thousand teachers
journeyed from the United States to the Philippines in 1901–02. Source: http://en.wikipedia.org/wiki/
Thomasites, accessed 26 October 2006.

8. Here is one representative justification of U.S. violence against the insurgents: "The Filipino, as
such, was little better than a dog, a noisome reptile in some instances, whose best disposition was the
rubbish heap. Our soldiers have pumped salt water into men to 'make them talk,' have taken prisoners
people who . . . peacefully surrendered, and an hour later, without an atom of evidence to show that
they were even insurrectos, stood them on a bridge and shot them down one by one, to . . . float down,
as examples to those who found their bullet-loaded corpses. It is not civilized warfare; but we are not
dealing with a civilized people. The only thing they know and fear is force, violence, and brutality, and
we give it to them." Correspondent for the *Philadelphia Public Ledger*; quoted in S. Doc. 166, 57th Congress, 1st Sess., 2. Cited by J. Slotkin, 859.

9. I quote from Twain's "To the Person Sitting in Darkness" as reproduced in the anthology *Vestiges
of War: The Philippine-American War and the Aftermath of an Imperial Dream*, edited by Angel Shaw

and Luis Francia in 1999, in order to underline the continuing presence Twain's satire has in contemporary postcolonial activism and cultural studies. For basic analysis of Twain's anti-imperialistic work, see Zwick.

10. All quotations from Tolentino's play are from Riggs's *Filipino Drama*, reissued in 1981. Riggs was a military medical officer attached to the occupying forces; he later had a flourishing career as a journalist and travel writer, among other adventures. Many of the standard historical studies of the United States' colonization of the Philippines are infected with Orientalism. As antidotes, I especially recommend Vicente L. Rafael's articles and book; Oscar Campomanes, "1898 and the Nature of the New Empire" and "The New Empire's Forgetful and Forgotten Citizens"; Ambeth R. Ocampo, "Bones of Contention," part of a special issue of *Amerasia Journal* on the United States and the Philippines (1998); Kimberly Alidio, "'When I Get Home, I Want to Forget'"; S. See, "*An Open Wound*: Colonial Melancholia and Contemporary Filipino/American Texts"; Epifanio San Juan Jr., *After Postcolonialism*; and Sharon Delmendo's *The Star-Entangled Banner*. Rafael has a excellent brief reading of Tolentino's censored play, *Yesterday, Today, and Tomorrow*, along with the colonial compilation *The Filipino Drama* by Arthur Stanley Riggs (1905), which features plays both in Tagalog and translated into English, citations from the Supreme Court sedition ruling, and Riggs's comments on the threats to U.S. rule that the plays posed (Rafael, "White Love" 208–209 and 217–218n6). For contemporary works treating Tolentino's play in its historical context, see Fernandez; and Dizon, especially "False Vision."

11. For the Hawaiian documents, see the libweb.hawaii.edu/digicoll/annexation/annexation.html address maintained by Hamilton Collection, University of Hawaii at Manoa (accessed 3 November 2006). [ . . . ]

12. For basic information on the Palmer raids, I have used Wikipedia: http://en.wikipedia.org/wiki/Palmer_Raids, accessed 30 October 2006. See also Howard Zinn's *A People's History*, "War Is the Health of the State."

13. Twain is quoted from a letter (Zwick, "Mark Twain's Anti-Imperialist Writings" 40). The Amy Kaplan quotation about imperialist melancholy is from her *Anarchy of Empire* 57; see also 51–91. For the foundational discussion defining what he calls "imperialist nostalgia," see Renato Rosaldo 68–87. For further work on race, loss, and melancholia, see D. Eng and S. See, who make the important distinction between imperial and colonial melancholy—the former involves regrets by those who benefit from the colonial enterprise; the latter, a sense of bereavement and dismemberment suffered by colonialism's victims.

# Chapter 9

1. The Roosevelt quotation in this section's epigraph was part of a statement deploring lynching written in a 1903 letter praising the governor of Indiana, Winfield T. Durbin, for sending state militia to break up a lynching. Roosevelt's comments were provoked by a lynching in Wilmington, Delaware, in which a black man accused of rape and murder was taken from prison and burned alive, but Roosevelt had been disturbed by lynching for quite a while. Roosevelt criticized lynchings publicly in other settings as well, at some risk to his political capital: see his sixth annual State of the Union address (1906), for instance. For details on the Durbin letter and its publication, see Edmund Morris, *Theodore Rex* 261–262 and 661n.

2. How to interpret the Southerner's "Jim Crow" song is a puzzle. Singing in "black" dialect familiar from minstrel shows, the character mocks his own ignorance as well as celebrates his physical ability

to "maul" his rival, "Jim Crow," and impress the "white folks" who watch. John Seelye's suggestion certainly makes some sense: "the Virginian's minstrel song is a gesture of defiance to his rival" Trampas (Wister, *Virginian* 361n46). This is not the only time in the novel when the villain Trampas is associated with being a racial other. But what is especially intriguing here is the Virginian representing his most violent inner self as non-white too.

3. In 1726, Bishop George Berkeley, in his poem "On the Prospect of Planting Arts and Learning in America," translated the medieval notion of *translatio studii* as "westward the course of empire takes its way." [. . .]

4. For two good examples of the varieties of the Scottian heroine, see Rowena's and Rebecca's different roles in *Ivanhoe*; to some degree, Wister's heroine Molly Wood embodies the qualities and actions of both. For a fuller discussion of these and related topics concerning New South authors, see my "Walter Scott, Postcolonial Theory, and New South Literature." [. . .] See also Kaplan, "Manifest Domesticity," in *Anarchy of Empire* 23–50; and Tompkins, *West of Everything* 130–155.

5. For more on the concept of imperial melancholia, see chapter 8, especially note 13.

6. Herbert Spencer, interview with E. L. Youmans, the *New York Times* (Friday, 20 October 1882), 5. I thank my colleague Kendall Johnson for this reference, to appear in chapter 3 of his forthcoming book *Henry James and the Visual* (Cambridge, 2007).

7. Scholarship on the genealogy of whiteness can hardly be summarized here, but interested readers are referred to invaluable books by Thomas Gossett and Stephen Jay Gould, as well as Nell Irvin Painter's lucid recent essay, "Why Are White People Called 'Caucasian'?" Dixon uses Caucasian as a synonym for white in *The Leopard's Spots*, 63.

8. For fine recent readings of Dixon's *Leopard's Spots* and *The Clansman* that interpret his texts and films as revealing the crises in white supremacism, see Boeckmann; Slide; Romine; and Gunning. [. . .]

9. Analysis of the social functions and contradictions of lynching and other acts of violence in maintaining racial dictatorship is now immense. I especially recommend Trudier Harris's and Sandra Gunning's books for their survey and synthesis of the work of the last three decades or so on the topic of lynching. [. . .] [Surveys other recent books and articles on the subject.]

10. Of the non-blacks who were lynched in 1892, Wells-Barnett's records show many Italian or Chinese; in addition, she notes that by 1892 nearly one-half million dollars had been paid to Italy, China, and other countries by the United States government after it was sued for the lynching deaths of those countries' citizens on U.S. soil.

11. James Allen's *Without Sanctuary* gruesomely demonstrates how lynchings were spectacles defining what a white community thought to be its *modernity*, not just its righteousness. Town centers are featured, not just nameless wilderness, and in many of the postcards spectators stare proudly toward the camera while standing near the corpse. Conversely, the black bodies often had any markers of individuality and modernity (including fashionable clothes) destroyed. Victims were sometimes also decorated, to become in death a safe embodiment of the stereotype of the complacent darky whites so needed. See especially the postcard image on the half-title page, where the corpse is painted with minstrel-like makeup.

12. Regarding Du Bois's encounter with body parts in Atlanta, see Lewis's biography, volume 1, 226. Lewis notes that this event occurred when Du Bois was on his way to the *Atlanta Constitution* editorial offices to persuade Joel Chandler Harris, one of the paper's editors, to publish Du Bois's editorial condemning lynching. [. . .]

13. For Dixon's interest in cinema, especially in having his novels filmed, see Cook, *Thomas Dixon* 109–122. [. . .] [More on recent analyses of Dixon.]

14. *Kalokagathy* is a Greek term naming the belief that external appearances accurately signify hidden character traits. See Boeckmann 54; her entire anatomization of nineteenth-century "scientific" racism is relevant, including her fine analysis of Dixon (11–97). [. . .] [Further discussion of recent scholarship on crises in late nineteenth-century discourses of racial difference.]

15. [. . .] [Further analysis of aporia in the rape scene in *The Clansman*, which is rendered only its prelude and its aftermath, until Gus's reenactment.]

16. Poe, "The Literati of New York City" 72.

# Chapter 10

1. For summaries of Page's views of educational reform and the moral grounding of U.S. imperial responsibilities, see Burton Jesse Hendrick's two volumes (especially *Training of an American* 266–272 and 389–420) and John Milton Cooper's recent biography, which extensively quotes Page's influential "Forgotten Man" speech on education, from which the illiteracy statistic is drawn (140–144). For astute brief analysis of Page's views on southern literature and a reprinting of Page's seminal 1887 essay, "Literature in the South," see Simms; for Page's relationship with Chesnutt, see McElrath; and for a history of Page's work at the *Atlantic Monthly* (a topic also covered in the biographies mentioned above), see Sedgwick. [. . .] [More discussion of scholarship on Page, particularly his novel.]

2. On Page's critique of Grady's response to Page's "pessimism," see Gaston 60–63 and 198–199. [. . .] [More discussion of Page's complicated relations with those boosting the New South after the 1880s.]

3. On Page's contacts with Booker T. Washington in the context of the 1890s and after, see J. Cooper 145–149, 217–218. Nicholas Worth's firing from his professorship may be Page's way of alluding to the controversy surrounding Professor John Spencer Bassett's comparison of Booker T. Washington to Robert E. Lee, which eventually cost him his job at Trinity College in North Carolina, Page's home state. Page supported Bassett: see J. Cooper 214–216. [. . .] [More on Page's relationship with Washington.]

4. The tone of the ending in the 1906 original emphasized the rueful pessimism in the southern pastoral tradition more strongly: "We passed from the subject [of selling the Old Place] with a laugh, as we pass by many dark tragedies that lurk just behind the hedges of our Southern life. But it may be that all gardens have sad, shadowy dwellers on the other side of their walls of roses" (*Atlantic Monthly* 98, October 1906, 488).

5. Early in Du Bois's career, Page offered him encouragement in his capacity as editor for the New York *Forum*, a journal of thought and opinion. [For the citation and further discussion, see the online notes.]

6. Nicholas Worth's speech echoes many of the ideas in an actual speech Walter Hines Page gave, "The Forgotten Man." For a paraphrase of the contents of the "Forgotten Man" speech, see J. Cooper 141–144. [. . .]

7. For an excellent introduction to the contents of Grady's speech and its role in defining the mainstream New South creed, see Gaston 23–42 and 87–90.

8. [. . .] [Further discussion of nuances in Nicholas's speech, particularly its attempted separation between whites who benefit from the social hierarchies of the postwar period and their ancestors who profited from slavery.]

9. Compare MacKethan, "Plantation Fiction," and Schmidt, "Command Performances"; the latter essay focuses directly on the paradoxical role played by black story-tellers in plantation fiction ideology.

10. In Nicholas's view, purging the remaining "shadows" (419) that slavery still casts on southern culture in the twentieth century is the most important task awaiting the next generation. [. . .] [Further discussion appropriate to an endnote of Page's revisions to southern pastoral republicanism in *Nicholas Worth*.]

# Chapter 11

1. [. . .] [Commentary on Du Bois's characters Bles Alwyn and Carolyn Wynn, including revelations from the "Silver Fleece" typescript at Fisk University.]

2. For readings of Du Bois's *Silver Fleece* that emphasize both problems of its narrative form and its engagement with contemporary history, see in particular Lewis's biography, vol. 1, 443–451; Rampersad 116–132; and essays by Lemons, Lee, and Byerman. For crucial historical background on Du Bois and the debates over vocational versus liberal arts education for blacks, see Anderson, *Education of Blacks in the South*, especially chapter 7.

3. For Du Bois's famous critique of Booker T. Washington's educational philosophy and political strategies, see *Souls of Black Folk*, chapter 3.

4. The bonfires protecting black rights in Du Bois's narrative may also be a conscious rebuke to and rewriting of the famous ending of Thomas Dixon's *The Clansman*, where bonfires signify the victory of the KKK. About the only point of agreement between Du Bois and Dixon would be that black schools functioned as sites for counterrevolution.

5. [. . .] [Further discussion of scholarship on the crop-lien system, farmers' alliances, and related topics, plus other literary depictions by contemporary authors of these topics.]

6. *Darkwater* is now in print again in Sundquist's *The Du Bois Reader*, chapter 6. For readings of *Darkwater* that influenced mine, see Lewis's biography, vol. 2, 11–23; Rampersad 170–183; Sundquist, *To Wake the Nations* 540–625 and his introduction to the *W. E. B. Du Bois Reader*; Bramen's *The Uses of Variety*, "Identity Culture and Cosmopolitanism," especially 105–111; and Kaplan, *Anarchy of Empire*, chapter 6. [. . .]

7. [. . .] [On women's identity dilemmas central to many captivity narratives popular in the United States from the early and middle colonial periods through twentieth century, including Owen Wister's *The Virginian* and Margaret Mitchell's *Lost Laysen*.]

# Chapter 12

1. Philip Butcher's solid discussion of *Lovers of Louisiana* remains the best overall, despite being several decades old. Also worth consulting are analyses by Edmund Wilson (601–604) and John Cleman (178–181); Wilson disparaged the novel and perhaps never even finished it (see his comment on 602 regarding Philip's suit), but everything he said about its topics made me want to read it immediately. [. . .] [Further discussion of Cable scholarship.]

2. Letters from Charles Scribner, Cable's publisher, confirm that the firm tried to serialize *Lovers of Louisiana* in popular magazines, like *Collier's Weekly*, the *Century*, and those owned by Charles Hearst,

but was turned down. A letter from Maxwell Perkins to Cable on 9 April 1917, notes that "the editors of the magazines to which we have submitted it speak with admiration of its qualities but seem to find it less 'timely' than the sort of fiction they are especially in search of." See also letters dated 29 December 1916 and 13 February 1917. Scribner's apparently received the manuscripts for both *Lovers* and *The Flower of the Chapdelaines* on 9 November 1916. Tulane University, Howard-Tilton Memorial Library, Special Collections, Cable Papers, box 62.

3. [. . .] [Commentary on Philip's request that his listeners forget he is white.]

4. [Note on how later speeches by Mr. Murray contain important additions added in revision in Cable's handwriting to the typescript. Tulane University, Howard-Tilton Memorial Library, Special Collections, Cable Papers, box 103.]

5. [. . .] [On sources for Cable's hero Philip Castleton and related matters.]

6. [. . .] [Analysis of some biographical connections between Philip and his creator.]

7. [. . .] [Further discussion of Cable's text and Du Bois's "African Roots of the War."]

8. [. . .] [Further discussion of Ovide Landry from the perspective of Cable's oeuvre.]

9. The parallels between Lynch's and Philip's points may not indicate direct borrowing or influence, but rather that Cable drew upon a precariously shared national discourse defending Reconstruction that was still circulating—not just among blacks—in 1913 and 1914. [. . .]

10. Philip Castleton's and Mr. Murray's praise of Bermuda in *Lovers in Louisiana* as an example of a working multiracial democracy seems rather overblown, though Bermuda's government was certainly a more just and multiracial a system than Jim Crow. [. . .] [Further critique of Cable's handling of the colonial history of Bermuda.]

# Selected Bibliography

This bibliography lists key works cited in the printed edition of *Sitting in Darkness*. For the book's full bibliography paired with its full endnotes, see www.swarthmore.edu/Humanities/pschmid1/scholarship.html.

Adams, Henry. *The Education of Henry Adams; an Autobiography.* Boston, New York: Houghton Mifflin, 1918.

Alderman, Edwin Anderson, Joel Chandler Harris, and Charles William Kent, eds. *Library of Southern Literature. Compiled Under the Direct Supervision of Southern Men of Letters.* Seventeen volumes plus a one-volume supplement. New Orleans and Atlanta: Martin and Hoyt, 1907–1923.

Alderman, Edwin Anderson. Introduction. *Library of Southern Literature. Compiled Under the Direct Supervision of Southern Men of Letters.* Ed. Edwin Anderson Alderman, Joel Chandler Harris, and Charles William Kent. New Orleans and Atlanta: Martin and Hoyt, 1907–1923. Vol. 1: xix–xxii.

———. "Sectionalism and Nationality." *Southern Prose and Poetry for Schools.* Ed. Edwin Mims and Bruce Payne. New York: Scribners, 1910. 388–400.

Alidio, Kimberly A. "'When I Get Home, I Want to Forget': Memory and Amnesia in the Occupied Philippines, 1901–1904." *Social Text* 59 (Summer 1999): 105–122.

Allen, James, ed. *Without Sanctuary: Lynching Photographs in America.* New York: Twin Palms, 2000.

Allen, Theodore W. *The Invention of the White Race.* New York: Verso, 1994.

Alvord, John W. *Inspector's Report of Schools and Finances.* U.S. Bureau of Refugees, Freemen, and Abandoned Lands. Washington, D.C.: U.S. Government Printing Office, 1866.

*Amerasia Journal* 24 (Winter 1998). Special Issue: Essays into American Empire in the Philippines.

*The American Experience: Reconstruction.* PBS documentary and Web site. 2004. http://www.pbs.org/wgbh/amex/reconstruction/.

American Tract Society. *Freedmen's Third Reader.* 1866. Rpt. New York: AMS P, 1980.

Ammons, Elizabeth. *Conflicting Stories: American Women Writers at the Turn into the Twentieth Century.* New York: Oxford UP, 1992.

Anderson, James D. *The Education of Blacks in the South, 1860–1935.* Chapel Hill: U of North Carolina P, 1988.

Anonymous. "On Negro Schools." *Harper's New Monthly Magazine* 49 (September 1874): 457–468. Illustrations by Porte Crayon.

Anonymous. [William Howard Taft, Charles Denby, John R. MacArthur, Daniel R. Williams, et al.] *Report of the Philippine Commission to the President.* Vol. 1. Washington, D.C.: Government Printing Office, 1900.

Armstrong, Samuel C. "Lessons from the Hawaiian Islands." *Journal of Christian Philosophy* 3 (1884): 200–229.

Ayers, Edward L. "Portraying Power." *Jumpin' Jim Crow: Southern Politics from Civil War to Civil Rights*. Ed. Jane Dailey, Glenda Elizabeth Gilmore, and Bryant Simon. Princeton: Princeton UP, 2000. 301–303.

———. *The Promise of the New South: Life after Reconstruction*. New York: Oxford UP, 1992.

Baker, Houston A., Jr. *Blues, Ideology, and Afro-American Literature: A Vernacular Theory*. Chicago: U of Chicago P, 1984.

———. *Turning South Again: Re-thinking Modernism, Re-reading Booker T.* Durham: Duke UP, 2001.

Baskerville, William Malone. *Southern Writers: Biographical and Critical Studies*. Two volumes. Nashville and Dallas: Publishing House of the M.E. Church South, 1903.

Beale, Howard K. *Theodore Roosevelt and the Rise of America to World Power*. Baltimore: Johns Hopkins UP, 1956.

Bean, Annemarie, James V. Hatch, and Brooks McNamara, eds. *Inside the Minstrel Mask: Readings in Nineteenth-Century Blackface Minstrelsy*. Hanover, N.H.: UP of New England [for] Weslyan UP, 1996.

Bederman, Gail. *Manliness and Civilization: A Cultural History of Gender and Race in the United States, 1880–1917*. Chicago: U of Chicago P, 1995.

Bentley, George R. *A History of the Freedmen's Bureau*. 1955. Rpt. New York: Octagon, 1974.

Blight, David W. *Race and Reunion: The Civil War in American Memory*. Cambridge: Harvard UP, 2001.

Blumenbach, Johann Friedrich. *The Anthropological Treatises of Johann Friedrich Blumenbach . . .* Trans. Thomas Bendyshe. London: Published for the Anthropological Society, by Longman et al., 1865.

Boas, Franz. *Changes in Bodily Form of Descendents of Immigrants*. New York: Columbia UP, 1912.

Boeckmann, Cathy. *A Question of Character: Scientific Racism and the Genres of American Fiction, 1892–1912*. Tuscaloosa: U of Alabama P, 2000.

Bone, Robert. *Down Home: Origins of the Afro-American Short Story*. 1975. Rpt. New York: Columbia UP, 1988.

Bramen, Carrie Tirado. *The Uses of Variety: Modern Americanism and the Quest for National Distinctiveness*. Cambridge: Harvard UP, 2000.

Brevard, Caroline Mays. *Literature of the South*. New York: Broadway P, 1908.

Brodhead, Richard H. Introduction. *The Journals of Charles W. Chesnutt*. Ed. Richard H. Brodhead. Durham: Duke UP, 1993. 1–28.

Brooks, Cleanth. "Southern Literature: The Past, History, and the Timeless." *Southern Literature in Transition: Heritage and Promise*. Ed. Philip Castille and William Osborne. Memphis: Memphis State UP, 1983. 3–16.

Brown, Richard D. *The Strength of a People: The Idea of an Informed Citizenry in America, 1650–1870*. Chapel Hill: U of North Carolina P, 1996.

Brown, Sterling. *The Negro in American Fiction*. 1937. Rpt. Port Washington, N.Y.: Kennikat P, 1968.

Brown, William Wells. *Clotel or, The President's Daughter*. 1853. Rpt. *Three Classic African American Novels*. Ed. William L. Andrews. New York: Mentor/Penguin, 1990. 71–283.

Bruce, Dickson D., Jr. *Black American Writing from the Nadir: The Evolution of a Literary Tradition, 1877–1915*. Baton Rouge: Louisiana State UP, 1989.

———. "George Marion McClellan." *Dictionary of Literary Biography*. Vol. 50: *Afro-American Writers before the Harlem Renaissance*. Ed. Trudier Harris and Thadious M. Davis. Detroit: Gale, 1986. 206–212.

Bruce, Philip Alexander. *The Plantation Negro as Freeman; Observations on his character, conditions, and prospects in Virginia*. New York: G. P. Putnam's Sons, 1889.

Bureau of Insular Affairs. *What Has Been Done in the Philippines: A Record of Practical Accomplishments under the Civil Government . . .* Washington, D.C.: Government Printing Office, 1904. American Memory Project. http://memory.loc.gov. Digital ID: (h) lcrbmrp t2420.

Burgess, John W. *The Reconciliation of Government with Liberty.* New York: Charles Scribner's Sons, 1915.

———. *Reconstruction and the Constitution, 1866–1876.* New York: Charles Scribner's Sons, 1902.

Butchart, Ronald E. *Northern Schools, Southern Blacks, and Reconstruction: Freemen's Education, 1862–1875.* Westport, Conn.: Greenwood P, 1980.

Butcher, Philip. *George Washington Cable.* New York: Twayne, 1962.

Byerman, Keith E. "Race and Romance: *The Quest of the Silver Fleece* as Utopian Narrative." *American Literary Realism* 24.3 (Spring 1992): 58–71.

———. *Seizing the Word: History, Art, and Self in the World of W. E. B. Du Bois.* Athens: U of Georgia P, 1994.

Cable, George Washington. *The Flower of the Chapdelaines.* New York: Scribners, 1918.

———. "The Freedman's Case in Equity." *Century Magazine.* January 1885. See http://etext.lib.virginia.edu/railton/huckfinn/hfequity.html.

———. *Gideon's Band: A Tale of the Mississippi.* New York: Scribners, 1914.

———. *The Grandissimes: A Story of Creole Life.* New York: Scribners, 1880.

———. *John March, Southerner.* New York: Scribners, 1894.

———. *Lovers of Louisiana (To-Day).* New York: Scribners, 1918.

———. *Madame Delphine.* New York: Scribners, 1881.

———. *The Negro Question.* New York: Scribners, 1890.

———. *Old Creole Days.* New York: Scribners, 1879.

———. *The Silent South.* New York: Scribners, 1885. Expanded edition, 1889.

Cabral, Amilcar. *Unity and Struggle: Speeches and Writings.* Trans. Michael Wolfers. New York: Monthly Review P, 1979.

Campomanes, Oscar. "1898 and the Nature of the New Empire." *Radical History Review* 73 (Winter 1999): 130–146.

———. "The New Empire's Forgetful and Forgotten Citzens: Unrepresentability and Unassimilability in Filipino-American Postcolonialities." *Hitting Critical Mass* 2.2 (Spring 1995): 145–200.

Canieso-Doronila, Maria Luisa. *Limits of Educational Change: National Identity Formation in a Philippine Public Elementary School.* Quezon City: U of the Philippines P, 1989.

Carby, Hazel V. Introduction. Frances E. W. Harper. *Iola Leroy; or Shadows Uplifted.* Boston: Beacon P, 1987. IX–XXVI.

———. *Race Men.* Cambridge: Harvard UP, 1998.

———. *Reconstructing Womanhood: The Emergence of the Afro-American Woman Novelist.* New York: Oxford UP, 1987.

Castronovo, Russ. *Necro Citizenship: Death, Eroticism, and the Public Sphere in the Nineteenth-Century United States.* Durham: Duke UP, 2001.

Cecelski, David S., and Timothy B. Tyson, eds. *Democracy Betrayed: The Wilmington Race Riot of 1898 and Its Legacy.* Chapel Hill: U of North Carolina P, 1998.

Cerny, Clayton Allen. "Reconstructing Freedom: Romance and Race in American Culture, 1877–1915." PhD diss. Northwestern University, 1996.

Cervantes, Miguel de. *Don Quixote.* Trans. Edith Grossman. New York: Ecco, 2003.

Chatterjee, Partha. *The Nation and Its Fragments: Colonial and Postcolonial Histories.* Princeton: Princeton UP, 1993.

Cheah, Pheng. *Spectral Nationality: Passages of Freedom from Kant to Postcolonial Literatures of Liberation.* New York: Columbia UP, 2003.

Chesnutt, Charles W. *The Colonel's Dream.* New York: Doubleday Page, 1905.

———. *The Conjure Woman and Other Conjure Tales.* Ed. Richard H. Brodhead. Durham, N.C.: Duke UP, 1993.

————. "The Future American: A Complete Race Amalgamation Likely to Occur." *Boston Evening Transcript.* September 1, 1900. 13. Rpt. *Charles W. Chesnutt: Essays and Speeches.* Ed. Joseph R. McElrath, Jr., Robert C. Leitz III, and Jesse S. Crisler. Stanford: Stanford UP, 1999. 121–135.

————. "The Future American: A Stream of Dark Blood in the Veins of Southern Whites." *Boston Evening Transcript.* August 25, 1900. 15. Rpt. *Charles W. Chesnutt: Essays and Speeches.* Ed. Joseph R. McElrath, Jr., Robert C. Leitz III, and Jesse S. Crisler. Stanford: Stanford UP, 1999. 121–135.

————. "The Future American: What Race Is Likely to Become in the Process of Time." *Boston Evening Transcript.* August 18, 1900. 20. Rpt. *Charles W. Chesnutt: Essays and Speeches.* Ed. Joseph R. McElrath, Jr., Robert C. Leitz III, and Jesse S. Crisler. Stanford: Stanford UP, 1999. 121–135. Rpt. *Charles W. Chesnutt: Selected Writings.* Ed SallyAnn H. Ferguson. New York: Houghton Mifflin, 2001. 47–52.

————. *The House behind the Cedars.* Boston: Houghton Mifflin, 1900.

————. *The Journals of Charles W. Chesnutt.* Ed. Richard H. Brodhead. Durham: Duke UP, 1993.

————. *The Marrow of Tradition.* Boston: Houghton Mifflin, 1901.

————. *Selected Writings.* Ed. SallyAnn H. Ferguson. New York: Houghton Mifflin, 2001.

————. *"To Be an Author": Letters of Charles W. Chesnutt, 1889–1905.* Ed. Joseph R. McElrath Jr. and Robert C. Leitz III. Princeton: Princeton UP, 1997.

————. *The Wife of His Youth and Other Stories of the Color Line.* 1899. Ridgewood, N.J.: Gregg P, 1967.

Child, Lydia Maria. *The Freedmen's Book.* Boston: Ticknor & Fields, 1865.

————. *A Lydia Maria Child Reader.* Ed. Carolyn Karcher. Durham: Duke UP, 1997.

————. *The Romance of the Republic.* 1867. Ed. Dana D. Nelson. Lexington: U of Kentucky P, 1997.

Christian, Barbara. *Black Women Novelists: The Development of a Tradition, 1892–1976.* Westport, Conn.: Greenwood P, 1980.

Cimbala, Paul A., and Randall M. Miller, eds. *The Freedmen's Bureau and Reconstruction: Reconsiderations.* New York: Fordham UP, 1999.

Cleman, John. *George Washington Cable Revisited.* New York: Twayne, 1996.

Clemens, Samuel Longhorne. See Twain, Mark.

Clevenger, Martha R. "The Igorots in the St. Louis Fair, 1904." Speech, 2004. See www.oovrag.com/essays/essay2004a-1.shtml.

Cohen, Nancy. *The Reconstruction of American Liberalism, 1865–1914.* Chapel Hill: U of North Carolina P, 2002.

Cook, Raymond Allen. *Fire from the Flint: The Amazing Careers of Thomas Dixon.* Winston-Salem, N.C.: John F. Blair, 1968.

————. *Thomas Dixon.* New York: Twayne, 1974.

Cooper, Anna Julia. *A Voice from the South.* 1892. Rpt. Ed. Mary Helen Washington. New York: Oxford UP, 1988.

Cooper, John Milton, Jr. *Walter Hines Page: The Southerner as American, 1855–1918.* Chapel Hill: U of North Carolina P, 1977.

Crummell, Alexander. *Destiny and Race: Selected Writings, 1840–1898.* Ed. Wilson Jeremiah Moses. Amherst: U of Massachusetts P, 1992.

Davis, Richard Harding. *Soldiers of Fortune.* New York: C. Scribner's Sons, 1897.

Delany, Martin R. *Blake; or, the Huts of America, a Novel.* Boston: Beacon P, 1970.

De Leon, Edwin. "The New South." *Harper's New Monthly Magazine* 48 (January 1874): 270–280. 48 (February 1874): 406–422. 49 (September 1874): 555–568.

Delmendo, Sharon. *The Star-Entangled Banner: One Hundred Years of America in the Philippines.* New Brunswick, N.J.: Rutgers UP, 2004.

Denby, Charles R. See Anonymous, *Report of the Philippine Commission to the President.*

———. "What Shall We Do with the Philippines?" *Forum* 27 (March 1899).

DeVoto, Bernard. *Mark Twain's America.* Boston: Little, Brown, 1932.

Dimock, Wai-chee. *Through Other Continents: American Literature across Deep Time.* Princeton: Princeton UP, 2006.

Diner, Steven J. *A Very Different Age: Americans in the Progressive Era.* New York: Hill and Wang, 1998.

Dixon. Thomas. *The Clansman; An Historical Romance of the Ku Klux Klan.* New York: Doubleday Page, 1905.

———. *The Leopard's Spots; A Romance of the White Man's Burden, 1865–1900.* New York: Doubleday Page, 1902.

———. *The Traitor.* 1907. *The Reconstruction Trilogy.* Ed. Samuel Dickson. Noontide P, 1994.

Dizon, Alma Jill. "Beyond the Melodramatic Vision: National Identity and the Novels of José Rizal." PhD diss. Yale University, 1996.

———. "False Vision in Two Plays by Aurelio Tolentino." *Philippine Studies* 43.4 (1995): 666–680.

Documenting the American South [database]. See http://docsouth.unc.edu.

Dorsey, Allison. *To Build Our Lives Together: Community Formation in Black Atlanta, 1875–1906.* Athens: U of Georgia P, 2004.

Douglass, Frederick. *The Life and Times of Frederick Douglass, Written by Himself.* Hartford, Conn.: Park P, 1882.

———. *Narrative of the Life of Frederick Douglass, An American Slave, Written by Himself.* 1845. *The Civitas Anthology of African American Slave Narratives.* Ed. William L. Andrews and Henry Louis Gates Jr. Washington, D.C.: Civitas/Counterpoint P, 1999. 105–194.

Du Bois, W. E. B. "The African Roots of the War." *Atlantic Monthly* 115 (May 1915): 707–714.

———. *Black Reconstruction in America.* New York: Harcourt, Brace, 1935. Rpt. Millwood, N.Y.: Kraus-Thomson, 1976.

———. *The Negro Common School.* Atlanta: Atlanta Univ. Pub. No. 6, 1901.

———. *The Oxford W. E. B. Du Bois Reader.* Ed. Eric J. Sundquist. New York: Oxford UP, 1996. This includes *Darkwater.*

———. *The Quest of the Silver Fleece.* 1911. Rpt. New York: Arno, 1969.

———. "Reconstruction and Its Benefits." *American Historical Review* 15 (July 1910): 781–799.

———. *The Souls of Black Folk.* New York: A. C. McClurg, 1903.

Dunbar, Paul Laurence. *The Strength of Gideon and Other Stories.* New York: Dodd Mead, 1900.

Dunning, William Archibald. *Essays on the Civil War and Reconstruction and Related Topics.* New York, Macmillan, 1898.

Ellison, Ralph. *The Collected Essays of Ralph Ellison.* Ed. John F. Callahan. New York: Random House/ Modern Library, 1995.

Emery, Lynne Fauley. *Black Dance from 1619 to Today.* 2nd, rev. Ed. Pennington, N.J.: Princeton Book P, 1988.

Eng, David L., and Shinhee Han. "A Dialogue on Racial Melancholia." *Loss: The Politics of Mourning.* Ed. David L. Eng and David Kazanian. Berkeley: U of California P, 2003. 343–371.

Engs, Robert Francis. *Educating the Disfranchised and Disinherited: Samuel Chapman Armstrong and Hampton Institute, 1839–1893.* Knoxville: U of Tennessee P, 1999.

Epps, Garrett. *Democracy Reborn: The Fourteenth Amendment and the Fight for Equal Rights in Post–Civil War America.* New York: Henry Holt, 2006.

Fanon, Frantz. *A Dying Colonialism.* Trans. Haakon Chevalier. New York: Grove P, 1965.

———. *Wretched of the Earth.* Trans. Constance Farrington. New York: Grove P, 1963.

Fernandez, Doreen G. "Introduction: In the Context of Political History and Dramatic Tradition." *The Filipino Drama.* Ed. Arthur Stanley Riggs. Manila: Ministry of Human Settlements, Intramuros Administration, 1981.

Ferrer, Ada. "1898: Rethinking Race, Nation, and Empire." *Radical History Review* 73 (Winter 1999): 22–46.

Fishkin, Shelley Fisher. "Crossroads of Cultures: The Transnational Turn in American Studies." *American Quarterly* 57.1 (March 2005): 17–57.

Fleischmann, Anne. "'Neither Fish, Flesh, Nor Fowl': Race and Region in the Writings of Charles W. Chesnutt." *Postcolonial Theory and the United States: Race, Ethnicity, and Literature.* Ed. Amritjit Singh and Peter Schmidt. Jackson: UP of Mississippi, 2000. 244–257.

Foner, Eric. *Reconstruction: America's Unfinished Revolution, 1863–1877.* New York: Harper and Row, 1988.

———. *Free Soil, Free Labor, Free Men: The Ideology of the Republican Party Before the Civil War.* New York: Oxford UP, 1970.

Foreman, P. Gabrielle. "'Reading Aright': White Slavery, Black Referents, and the Strategy of Histotextuality in *Iola Leroy.*" *Yale Journal of Criticism* 10.2 (Fall 1997): 327–354.

Foster, Frances Smith. Introduction. Frances E. W. Harper. *Iola Leroy, or Shadows Uplifted.* 1893. Rpt. Ed. Frances Smith Foster. New York: Oxford UP, 1988. xvii–xxxix.

———. *Written By Herself: Literary Production by African American Women, 1746–1892.* Bloomington: Indiana UP, 1993.

Franklin, John Hope. *Reconstruction: After the Civil War.* Chicago: Chicago UP, 1961.

Fredrickson, George M. *The Black Image in the White Mind: The Debate on Afro-American Character and Destiny, 1817–1914.* Middletown, Conn.: Wesleyan UP, 1971.

Freire, Paolo. *Education for Critical Consciousness.* New York: Seabury, 1973.

———. *Pedagogy of the Oppressed.* 1970. Trans. Myra Bergman Ramos. New York: Continuum, 1984.

Gaines, Kevin. "Black Americans' Racial Uplift Ideology as 'Civilizing Mission': Pauline E. Hopkins on Race and Imperialism." *Cultures of United States Imperialism.* Ed. Amy Kaplan and Donald E. Pease. Durham: Duke UP, 1993. 433–455.

Gambone, Michael D. *Documents of American Diplomacy: From the American Revolution to the Present.* Westport, Conn.: Greenwood P, 2002.

Gaston, Paul M. *The New South Creed: A Study in Southern Mythmaking.* New York: Knopf, 1970.

Gatewood, Willard B., Jr. *Black Americans and the White Man's Burden.* Urbana: U of Illinois P, 1975.

Genovese, Eugene. *Roll, Jordan, Roll: The World the Slaves Made.* New York: Pantheon, 1974.

George-Graves, Nadine. *The Royalty of Negro Vaudeville: The Whitman Sisters and the Negotiation of Race, Gender, and Class in American Theater, 1900–1940.* New York: St. Martin's P, 2000.

Giddings, Franklin Henry. *Democracy and Empire, with Studies of Their Psychological, Economic, and Moral Foundations.* New York: Macmillan, 1901.

Giddings, Paula. *When and Where I Enter: The Impact of Black Women on Race and Sex in America.* New York: William Morrow, 1984.

Gilmore, Michael T. *Surface and Depth: The Quest for Legibility in American Culture.* New York: Oxford UP, 2003.

Go, Julian, and Anne L. Foster, eds. *The American Colonial State in the Philippines: Global Perspectives.* Durham: Duke UP, 2003.

Godkin, E. L. "The White Side of the Southern Question." *Nation* 31 (19 August 1880).

Goethe, Johann Wolfgang von. *Goethe's Wilhelm Meister's Travels.* Trans. Thomas Carlyle. Introduction by James Hardin. Rpt., Columbia, S.C.: Camden House, 1991.

———. *Wilhelm Meister's Apprenticeship.* Trans. Thomas Carlyle. 1824. Rpt. New York: Collier, 1962.

Gossett, Thomas F. *Race: The History of an Idea in America.* 1963. Rpt. New York: Oxford UP, 1997.

Gould, Louis L. *America in the Progressive Era, 1890–1914.* New York: Pearson Education P, 2001.

Gould, Stephen Jay. *The Mismeasure of Man.* New York: Norton, 1981.

Grady, Henry W. "In Plain Black and White: A Reply to Mr. Cable." *Century* (April 1885). See http://etext.lib.virginia.edu/railton/huckfinn/cablans.html.

———. *The New South and Other Addresses, by Henry W. Grady.* Ed. Edna Lee Turpin. New York: Maynard, Merrill, 1904.

Grammer, John M. *Pastoral and Politics in the Old South.* Baton Rouge: Louisiana State UP, 1996.

Grantham, Dewey. *Southern Progressivism: The Reconciliation of Progress and Tradition.* Knoxville: U of Tennessee P, 1983.

Griest, Ellwood. *John and Mary; or, The Fugitive Slaves, a Tale of South-Eastern Pennsylvania.* Lancaster, Pa.: Inquirer, 1873. See http://docsouth.unc.edu/neh/griest/griest.html.

Griggs, Sutton E. *The Hindered Hand: or, The Reign of the Repressionist.* Nashville: Orion, 1905. Rpt. Miami: Mnemosyne P, 1969.

———. *Imperium in Imperio.* Cincinnati: Editor, 1899. Rpt. New York: Random House/Modern Library, 2003.

———. *Life's Demands, or According to Law.* Memphis: National Public Welfare League, 1916.

———. *Overshadowed.* Nashville: Orion, 1901. Rpt. New York: AMS P, 1973.

———. *The Story of My Struggles.* Memphis: National Public Welfare League, 1914.

Gross, Theodore. *Albion W. Tourgée.* New York: Twayne, 1963.

Gunning, Sandra. *Race, Rape, and Lynching: The Red Record of American Literature, 1890–1912.* New York: Oxford UP, 1996.

Gustafson, Sandra M. "Histories of Democracy and Empire." *American Quarterly* 59.1 (March 2007): 107–133.

Hahn, Steven. *A Nation under Our Feet: Black Political Struggles in the Rural South from Slavery to the Great Migration.* Cambridge: Harvard UP, 2003.

Handley, George. "On Reading South in the New World: Whitman, Martí, Glissant, and the Hegelian Dialectic." *Mississippi Quarterly* 56.4 (Fall 2003): 521–544.

———. *Postslavery Literatures in the Americas: Family Portraits in Black and White.* Charlottesville: UP of Virginia, 2000.

Hardwig, Bill. "Who Owns the Whip? Chesnutt, Tourgée, and Reconstruction Justice." *African American Review* 36.1 (Spring 2002): 5–20.

Harper, Frances E. W. *A Brighter Coming Day: A Frances Ellen Watkins Harper Reader.* Ed. Frances Smith Foster. New York: Feminist P, 1990.

———. *Iola Leroy, or Shadows Uplifted.* 1893. Rpt. Ed. Frances Smith Foster. New York: Oxford UP, 1988.

Harris, Joel Chandler. *Balaam and His Master and Other Sketches and Stories.* London: Osgood, McIlvaine, 1891.

———. *The Chronicles of Aunt Minervy Ann.* New York: Charles Scribner's Sons, 1899.

———. *The Complete Tales of Uncle Remus.* Ed. Richard Chase. Boston: Houghton Mifflin, 1955.

———. *Free Joe and Other Georgian Sketches.* 1887. Rpt. Ridgewood, N.J.: Gregg P, 1967.

———. *Gabriel Tolliver: A Story of Reconstruction.* 1902. Rpt. Ridgewood, N.J.: Gregg P, 1967.

———. *Joel Chandler Harris: Editor and Essayist. Miscellaneous Literary, Political, and Social Writings.* Ed. Julia Collier Harris. Chapel Hill: U of North Carolina P, 1931.

———. *Mingo and Other Sketches in Black and White.* 1884. Rpt. Edinburough: David Douglass, 1899.

———. *On the Plantation. A Story of a Georgia Boy's Adventures During the War.* 1892. Rpt. Athens: U of Georgia P, 1980.

Harris, Trudier. *Exorcising Blackness: Historical and Literary Lynching and Burning Rituals.* Bloomington: Indiana UP, 1984.

Hartman, Saidiya V. *Scenes of Subjection: Terror, Slavery, and Self-Making in Nineteenth-Century America.* New York: Oxford UP, 1997.

Healy, David. *U.S. Expansionism: The Imperialist Urge in the 1890s.* Madison: U of Wisconsin P, 1970.

Hebard, Andrew. "Romantic Sovereignty: Popular Romances and the American Imperial State in the Philippines." *American Quarterly* 57.3 (September 2005): 805–830.

Heffernan, Michael. "Inaugurating the American Century: 'New World' Perspectives on the 'Old' in the Early Twentieth Century." *The American Century: Consensus and Coercion in the Projection of American Power*. Ed. David Slater and Peter J. Taylor. Malden, Mass.: Blackwell, 1999. 117–135.

Helg, Aline. *Our Rightful Share: The Afro-Cuban Struggle for Equality, 1886–1912*. Chapel Hill: U of North Carolina P, 1995.

Hendrick, Burton J., ed. *The Life and Letters of Walter H. Page*. Vol. 1. New York: Doubleday, Page, 1924.

———. *The Training of an American: The Earlier Life and Letters of Walter H. Page, 1955–1913*. New York: Houghton Mifflin, 1928.

Henneman, John Bell. "English Studies in the South." *The South in the Building of the Nation*. Ed. Southern Historical Society. Richmond: Southern Historical Publication Society, 1909. Vol. 7: *The Literary and Intellectual Life*. 115–134.

———. "The National Element in Southern Literature." *The Library of Southern Literature, Library of Southern Literature. Compiled Under the Direct Supervision of Southern Men of Letters*. Ed. Edwin Anderson Alderman, Joel Chandler Harris, and Charles William Kent. New Orleans and Atlanta: Martin and Hoyt, 1907–1923. Vol. 14: 6273–6293.

Hentz, Caroline Lee. *Eoline; or Magnolia Vale*. Philadelphia: A. Hart, 1852.

Hobson, Fred. Introduction. *South to the Future: An American Region in the Twenty-First Century*. Ed. Fred Hobson. Athens: U of Georgia P, 2002. 1–12.

———. "The New South, 1880–1940." *Literature of the American South: A Norton Anthology*. Gen. Ed. William L. Andrews. New York: Norton, 1998.

———. "The Rise of the Critical Temper." *The History of Southern Literature*. Ed. Louis D. Rubin Jr. et al. Baton Rouge: Louisiana State UP, 1985. 252–257.

Hoganson, Kristin L. *Fighting for American Manhood: How Gender Politics Provoked the Spanish-American and Philippine-American Wars*. New Haven: Yale UP, 1998.

Holley, Marietta. *Samantha at the St. Louis Exposition, by Josiah Allen's Wife*. 1904. Excerpted and edited by Jim Zwick at www.BoondocksNet.com/expos/wfe_samantha_pv.html.

Holliday, Carl. *A History of Southern Literature*. New York: Neale P, 1906.

Holman, C. Hugh. *The Immoderate Past: The Southern Writer and History*. Athens: University of Georgia P, 1976.

———. "No More Monoliths, Please: Continuities in the Multi-Souths." *Southern Literature in Transition: Heritage and Promise*. Ed. Philip Castille and William Osborne. Memphis: Memphis State UP, 1983. xiii–xxiv.

———, ed. *The Roots of Southern Writing: Essays on the Literature of the American South*. Athens: U of Georgia P, 1972.

Hopkins, Pauline E. *Contending Forces: A Romance Illustrative of Negro Life North and South*. 1900. Rpt. Ed. Richard Yarborough. New York: Oxford UP, 1988.

———. *The Magazine Novels of Pauline Hopkins*. Ed. Hazel V. Carby. New York: Oxford UP, 1988.

Horsman, Reginald. *Race and Manifest Destiny: The Origins of American Racial Anglo-Saxonism*. Cambridge: Harvard UP, 1981.

Hubbell, Jay B. *The South in American Literature, 1607–1900*. Durham: Duke UP, 1954.

Ingraham, Ellen W. [The pseudonym Grace Lintner is listed as author on title page.] *Bond and Free: A Tale of the South*. Indianapolis: Carlon & Hollenbeck, 1882. Indianapolis: C. B. Ingraham, 1882. See http://docsouth.unc.edu/neh/lintner/menu.html.

Irwin, Robert McKee. "*Ramona* and Postnationalist American Studies: On 'Our America' and the Mexican Borderlands." *American Quarterly* 55.4 (December 2003): 539–568.

Jacobs, Harriet. *Incidents in the Life of a Slave Girl: Written by Herself*. Ed. Jean Fagan Yellin. Cambridge: Harvard UP, 1987.

Jefferson, Thomas. *Notes on the State of Virginia*. *The Portable Thomas Jefferson*. Ed. Merrill D. Peterson. New York: Viking, 1975. 23–232.

Johnson, James Weldon. *Writings*. New York: Library of America, 2004.

Johnston, Mary. *Hagar*. 1913. Rpt. Ed. Marjorie Spruill Wheeler. Charlottesville: UP of Virginia, 1994.

Jones, Jacqueline. *Labor of Love, Labor of Sorrow: Black Women, Work, and the Family from Slavery to the Present*. New York: Basic, 1985.

Jung, Moon-ho. *Coolies and Cane: Race, Labor, and Sugar in the Age of Emancipation*. Baltimore: Johns Hopkins UP, 2006.

Kaplan, Amy. *The Anarchy of Empire and the Making of U.S. Culture*. Cambridge: Harvard UP, 2002.

———. "'Left Alone with America': The Absence of Empire in the Study of American Culture." *Cultures of United States Imperialism*. Ed. Amy Kaplan and Donald Pease. Durham: Duke UP, 1993. 3–21.

———. "Romancing the Empire: The Embodiment of American Masculinity in the Popular Historical Novel of the 1890s." 1990. Rpt. *Postcolonial Theory and the U.S.: Race, Ethnicity, and Literature*. Ed. Amritjit Singh and Peter Schmidt. Jackson: UP of Mississippi, 2000. 220–243.

Kaplan, Amy, and Donald E. Pease, eds. *Cultures of United States Imperialism*. Durham: Duke UP, 1993.

Karcher, Carolyn. "Lydia Maria Child's *Romance of the Republic:* An Abolitionist Vision of America's Racial Destiny." *Slavery and the Literary Imagination*. Ed Deborah McDowell and Arnold Rampersad. Baltimore: Johns Hopkins UP, 1989. 81–103.

———. "Rape, Murder, and Revenge in 'Slavery's Pleasant Homes': Lydia Maria Child's Antislavery Fiction and the Limits of Genre." *The Culture of Sentiment: Race, Gender and Sentimentality in Nineteenth Century America*. Ed. Shirley Samuels. New York: Oxford UP, 1992. 58–72.

Kelley, Robin D. G. *Freedom Dreams: The Black Radical Imagination*. Boston: Beacon P, 2002.

Kent, Charles W. Preface. *Library of Southern Literature. Compiled Under the Direct Supervision of Southern Men of Letters*. Ed. Edwin Anderson Alderman, Joel Chandler Harris, and Charles William Kent. New Orleans and Atlanta: Martin and Hoyt, 1907–1923. Vol. 1: xv–xviii.

King, Edward. *The Great South*. Hartford, Conn.: American P, 1875. Rpt. See http://docsouth.unc.edu/nc/king/.

King, Grace. *Balcony Stories*. 1892. Rpt. Ridgewood, N.J.: Gregg P, 1968.

Kipling, Rudyard. *Poems, 1886–1929*. London: Macmillan, 1929.

Kolodny, Annette. *The Land before Her: Fantasy and Experience of the American Frontiers, 1630–1860*. Chapel Hill: U of North Carolina P, 1984.

———. "Turning the Lens on 'The Panther Captivity': A Feminist Exercise in Practical Criticism." *Critical Inquiry* 8.2 (Winter 1981): 329–345.

Kramer, Paul. "Making Concessions: Race and Empire Revisited at the Philippine Exposition, St. Louis, 1901–1905." *Radical History Review* 73 (Winter 1999): 74–114.

Kreyling, Michael. *Inventing Southern Literature*. Jackson: UP of Mississippi, 1998.

Ladd, Barbara. *Nationalism and the Color Line in George W. Cable, Mark Twain, and William Faulkner*. Baton Rouge: Louisiana State UP, 1996.

Lansing, Robert. *Papers Relating to the Foreign Relations of the United States: The Lansing Papers, 1914–1920*. Vol. 2. Washington, D.C.: United States Printing Office, 1940.

Lawton, William Cranston. *Introduction to the Study of American Literature*. New York: Globe School Book Company, 1902.

Lee, Maurice. "Du Bois the Novelist: White Influence, Black Spirit, and *The Quest of the Silver Fleece*." *African American Review* 33.3 (Fall 1999): 389–400.

Lemann, Nicholas. *Redemption: The Last Battle of the Civil War.* New York: Farrar, Straus and Giroux, 2006. Lemons, Gary L. "Womanism in the Name of the 'Father': W. E. B. DuBois and the Problematics of Race, Patriarchy, and Art." *Phylon* (2001) 49.3–4: 185–202.

Lemons, Gary L. "Womanism in the Name of the 'Father': W. E. B. Du Bois and the Problematics of Race, Patriarchy, and Art." *Phylon* (2001) 49.3–4: 185–202.

Levine, Lawrence. *Black Culture and Black Consciousness: Afro-American Folk Thought from Slavery to Freedom.* New York: Oxford UP, 1977.

Lewis, David Levering. *W. E. B. Du Bois: Biography of a Race.* Vol. 1: *1868–1919.* New York: Henry Holt, 1993.

———. *W. E. B. Du Bois: The Fight for Equality and the American Century.* Vol. 2: *1919–1963.* New York: Henry Holt, 2000.

Link, William A. *The Paradox of Southern Progressivism, 1880–1930.* Chapel Hill: U of North Carolina P, 1992.

Lintner, Grace [pseudonym]. See Ingraham, Ellen.

Logan, Rayford. *The Betrayal of the Negro from Rutherford B. Hayes to Woodrow Wilson.* New York: Collier, 1965.

Lott, Eric. "Blackface and Blackness: The Minstrel Show in American Culture." *Inside the Minstrel Mask: Readings in Nineteenth-Century Blackface Minstrelsy.* Ed. Annemarie Bean, James V. Hatch, and Brooks McNamara. Hanover, N.H.: UP of New England [for] Wesleyan University Press, 1996. 3–34.

———. *Love and Theft: Blackface Minstrelsy and the American Working Class.* New York: Oxford UP, 1993.Love, Eric T. *Race over Empire: Racism and U.S. Imperialism, 1865–1900.* Chapel Hill: U of North Carolina P, 2004.

Love, Eric T. *Race over Empire: Racism and U.S. Imperialism, 1865–1900.* Chapel Hill: U of North Carolina P, 2004.

Lowe, John. *Bridging Southern Cultures: An Interdisciplinary Approach.* Baton Rouge: LSU P, 2005.

Ludlow, Helen W. *Some Interesting Things at Hampton Institute.* [1903.] Daniel Murray Pamphlet Collection, Library of Congress. See http://memory.loc.gov. Digital ID (h)lcrbmrp t1903.

Lynch, John Roy. *The Facts of Reconstruction.* 1913. Rpt. New York: Arno, 1968.

MacKethan, Lucinda H. "Plantation Fiction, 1865–1900." *The History of Southern Literature.* Ed. Louis D. Rubin Jr. Baton Rouge: Louisiana State UP, 1985. 209–218.

Magdol, Edward. "A Note of Authenticity: Eliab Hill and Nimbus Ware in *Bricks without Straw.*" *American Quarterly* 22 (1970): 907–911.

Malone, Jacqui. *Steppin' on the Blues: The Visible Rhythms of African American Dance.* Urbana: U of Illinois P, 1996.Marschall, Richard E. "A History of *Puck, Judge,* and *Life.*" *The World Encyclopedia of Cartoons.* Ed. Maurice Horn. Chelsea House P, New York, 1980.

Martí, José. *Selected Writings.* Ed. and trans. Esther Allen. New York: Penguin, 2002.

McClellan, George Marion. "The Negro as a Writer." 1902. Rpt. *Dictionary of Literary Biography.* Vol. 50: *Afro-American Writers before the Harlem Renaissance.* Ed. Trudier Harris and Thadious M. Davis. Detroit: Gale, 1986. 308–313.

———. *Old Greenbottom Inn and Other Stories.* Louisville, 1906. Rpt. New York: AMS P, 1975.

———. *The Path of Dreams.* Nashville: A.M.E. Sunday School Union, 1916.

McElrath, Joseph R., Jr. "Collaborative Authorship: The Charles W. Chesnutt–Walter Hines Page Relationship." *The Professions of Authorship: Essays in Honor of Matthew J. Bruccoli.* Ed. Richard Layman and Joel Myerson. Columbia: U of South Carolina P, 1996. 150–168.

McHenry, Elizabeth. *Forgotten Readers: Recovering the Lost History of African American Literary Societies.* Durham: Duke UP, 2002.

McKee, Kathryn, and Annette Trefzer, eds. "Global Contexts, Local Literatures: The New Southern Studies." *American Literature* 78.4 (December 2006). Special Issue.

Michaels, Walter Benn. "Anti-imperial Americanism." *Cultures of United States Imperialism.* Ed. Amy Kaplan and Donald Pease. Durham: Duke UP, 1993. 365–391.

———. *Our America: Nativism, Modernism, Pluralism.* Durham: Duke UP, 1995.

———. "Race into Culture: A Critical Genealogy of Cultural Identity." *Critical Inquiry* 18.4 (Summer 1992): 655–685.

———. "The Souls of White Folk." *Literature and the Body: Essays on Populations and Persons.* Ed. Elaine Scarry. Baltimore: Johns Hopkins UP, 1988. 185–209.

Miller, Randall M. "Introduction. The Freedmen's Bureau and Reconstruction: An Overview." *The Freedmen's Bureau and Reconstruction: Reconsiderations.* Ed. Paul A. Cimbala and Randall M. Miller. New York: Fordham UP, 1999.

Mills, Bruce. *Cultural Reformations: Lydia Maria Child and the Work of Cultural Reform.* Athens: U of Georgia P, 1994.

Mims, Edwin. Introduction. *The South in the Building of the New Nation.* Vol. 8: *Fiction.* Richmond: Southern Historical Publication Society, 1909. xi–lxv.

Mims, Edwin, and Bruce Payne, eds. *Southern Prose and Poetry for Schools.* New York: Scribners, 1910.

Mitchell, Margaret. *Gone with the Wind.* New York: Scribner, 1936.

———. *Lost Laysen.* [1916.] Ed. Debra Freer. New York: Scribner, 1996.

Mitchell, Timothy. "Orientalism and the Exhibitionary Order." *The Visual Culture Reader.* Ed. Nicholas Mirzoeff. New York: Routledge P, 2002. 495–505.

Mixon, Wayne. *Southern Writers and the New South Movement, 1865–1913.* Chapel Hill: U of North Carolina P, 1980.

Morgan, Louis Henry. *Ancient Society.* New York: World, 1877.

Morris, Edmund. *Theodore Rex.* New York: Random, 2001.

Morris, Robert C. *Reading, 'Riting, and Reconstruction: The Education of Freedmen in the South, 1861–1870.* Chicago: U of Chicago P, 1981.

Morrison, Toni. Introduction. *Adventures of Huckleberry Finn.* Ed. Shelley Fisher Fishkin. New York: Oxford UP, 1996. xxxi–xli.

Moses, Wilson Jeremiah. *The Golden Age of Black Nationalism, 1850–1925.* New York: Oxford UP, 1978.

Mott, Luther. "The Magazine Revolution and Popular Ideas in the Nineties." *Proceedings of the American Antiquarian Society* 64 (April 1954): 195–214.

Navarro, José-Manuel. *Creating Tropical Yankees: Social Science Textbooks and U.S. Ideological Control in Puerto Rico, 1898–1908.* New York: Routledge, 2002.

Nelson, Dana D., ed. Introduction. *The Romance of the Republic.* By Lydia Maria Child. Lexington: U of Kentucky P, 1997. v–xxii.

———. *National Manhood: Capitalist Citizenship and the Imagined Fraternity of White Men.* Durham: Duke UP, 1998.

Newman, Cardinal John Henry. *On the Scope and Nature of University Education.* New York: E. P. Dutton, 1915.

Noonan, Mark James. "'Dey's Mightily in de Grass': Reconstructing the 'New' North in the Plantation Myth Fiction of *Scribner's-Century.*" Unpublished manuscript essay, 2004.

Nordhoff, Charles. *The Cotton States in the Spring and Summer of 1875.* New York: D. Appleton, 1976.

Ocampo, Ambeth R. "Bones of Contention." *Amerasia Journal* (Winter 1998): 45–74.

Olsen, Otto. *Carpetbagger's Crusade: The Life of Albion Winegar Tourgée.* Baltimore: Johns Hopkins UP, 1965.

Page, Thomas Nelson. *In Ole Virginia; or, Marse Chan and Other Stories.* 1887. Rpt. Ridgewood: Gregg P, 1968.

————. *Red Rock: A Chronicle of Reconstruction*. 1898. Rpt. Ridgewood: Gregg P, 1967.

Page, Walter Hines. "Literature in the South." 1887. Rpt. in L. Moody Simms Jr. "Walter Hines Page on Southern Literature." *Resources for American Literary Study* 6.2 (Autumn 1976): 199–208.

————. *The Rebuilding of Old Commonwealths: Being Essays towards the Training of the Forgotten Man in the Southern States*. New York: Doubleday, Page, 1902.

————. *The Southerner, A Novel. Being the Autobiography of "Nicholas Worth."* New York: Doubleday, Page, 1909.

Painter, Nell Irvin. "The Shoah and Southern History." *Jumpin' Jim Crow: Southern Politics from Civil War to Civil Rights*. Ed. Jane Dailey, Glenda Elizabeth Gilmore, and Bryant Simon. Princeton: Princeton UP, 2000. 308–310.

————. *Standing at Armageddon: The United States, 1877–1919*. New York: Norton, 1987.

————. "Why Are White People Called 'Caucasian'?" Paper given at a Yale University conference "Collective Degradation: Slavery and the Construction of Race." 2003. See www.yale.edu/glc/events/race/Painter.pdf. Accessed January 1, 2007.

Pamplin, Claire. "'Race' and Identity in Pauline Hopkins's *Hagar's Daughter*." *Redefining the Political Novel: American Women Writers, 1797–1901*. Ed. Sharon M. Harris. Knoxville: U of Tennessee P, 1995. 169–183.

Parrington, Vernon Louis. *Main Currents in American Thought*. Vol. 3: *The Beginnings of Critical Realism in America, 1860–1920*. New York: Harcourt, Brace, 1930.

Pattee, Fred Lewis. *American Literature since 1870*. New York: Century Company, 1915.

Pease, Donald E. "New Perspectives on U.S. Culture and Imperialism." *Cultures of United States Imperialism*. Ed. Amy Kaplan and Donald E. Pease. Durham: Duke UP, 1993. 22–37.

Pease, Donald E., and Robyn Wiegman, eds. *The Futures of American Studies*. Durham: Duke UP, 2002.

Pease, William Henry, and Jane H. Pease. *Black Utopia: Negro Communal Experiments in America*. Madison: Wisconsin State Historical Society, 1963.

Pérez, Louis A. *Cuba between Empires, 1878–1902*. Pittsburgh: U of Pittsburgh P, 1986.

————. *Cuba under the Platt Amendment, 1902–1934*. Pittsburgh: U of Pittsburgh P, 1986.

Perry, Bliss. *The American Spirit in Literature: A Chronicle of the Great Interpreters*. Vol. 34: *Chronicles of America*. Ed. Allen Johnson. New Haven: Yale UP, 1921.

Peterson, Carla L. *"Doers of the Word": African-American Women Speakers and Writers in the North, 1830–1880*. New York: Oxford UP, 1995.

Petteys, Chris, ed. *Dictionary of Women Artists: An International Dictionary of Women Artists Born before 1900*. Boston: G. K. Hall, 1985.

Phillips, Wendell. *Speeches, Lectures, and Letters*. Boston: Lee and Shepard, 1872.

Pike, James S. *The Prostrate State: South Carolina under Negro Government*. New York: D. Appleton, 1874.

Poe, Edgar Allan. "The Literati of New York City—No. IV." *Godey's Lady's Book*. August 1846. 72–78. See http://www.vcu.edu/engweb/transcendentalism/authors/fuller/poeonfuller.html.

Porter, Kenneth Wiggins. *The Black Seminoles: History of a Freedom Loving People*. Rev. and ed. Alcione M. Amos and Thomas P. Senter. Gainesville: UP of Florida, 1996.

Prather, H. Leon, Sr. *We Have Taken a City: Wilmington Racial Massacre and Coup of 1898*. Rutherford, N.J.: Fairleigh Dickinson UP, 1984.

Prucha, Francis Paul, ed. *Documents of United States Indian Policy*. 3rd Ed. Lincoln: U of Nebraska P, 2000.

Rafael, Vicente L. "Nationalism, Imagery, and the Filipino Intelligentsia." *Discrepant Histories: Translocal Essays on Filipino Cultures*. Ed. Vicente L. Rafael. Temple UP, 1995. 133–158.

————. "White Love: Surveillance and National Resistance in the U.S. Colonization of the Philippines." *Cultures of United States Imperialism*. Ed. Amy Kaplan and Donald E. Pease. Durham: Duke UP, 1993. 185–218.

———. *White Love and Other Events in Filipino History.* Durham: Duke UP, 2000.

Rampersad, Arnold. *The Art and Imagination of W. E. B. Du Bois.* Cambridge: Harvard UP, 1976.

Richardson, Charles F. *A Primer of American Literature.* Boston: Houghton, Osgood, 1878.

Richings, G. F. *Evidences of Progress among Colored People.* Tenth Edition. Philadelphia: George S. Ferguson P, 1903. http://docsouth.unc.edu/church/richings/richings.html.

Riggs, Arthur Stanley, ed. *The Filipino Drama.* 1905. Rpt. Manila: Ministry of Human Settlements, Intramuros Administration, 1981.

Ring, Natalie J. "Inventing the Tropical South: Race, Region, and the Colonial Model." *Mississippi Quarterly* 56.4 (Fall 2003): 619–632.

———. "The Problem South: Region, Race, and 'Southern Readjustment,' 1880–1930." PhD diss. Univ. of California, San Diego, 2003.

Romine, Scott. *The Narrative Forms of Southern Community.* Baton Rouge: Louisiana State UP, 1999.

———. "'Things Falling Apart': the Postcolonial Condition of *Red Rock* and *The Leopard's Spots.*" *Look Away! The U.S. South in New World Studies.* Ed. Jon Smith and Deborah Cohn. Durham: Duke UP, 2004. 175–200.

Roosevelt, Theodore. *The Strenuous Life: Essays and Addresses.* New York: Century P, 1901.

Root, Elihu. "Principles of Colonial Policy. Extract from the Report of the Secretary of War for 1899." Rpt. *The Military and Colonial Policies of the United States: Addresses and Reports by Elihu Root.* Ed. Robert Bacon and James Brown Scott. New York: AMS P, 1970.

Rosaldo, Renato. *Culture and Truth: The Remaking of Social Analysis.* Boston: Beacon P, 1989.

Rowe, John Carlos. *Literary Culture and U.S. Imperialism: From the Revolution to World War II.* New York: Oxford UP, 2000.

———, ed. *Post-Nationalist American Studies.* Berkeley: U of California P, 2000.

Rubin, Louis D., Jr., ed. *The Literary South.* Baton Rouge: Louisiana State UP, 1979.

Rubin, Louis D., Jr., General Editor, et al. *The History of Southern Literature.* Baton Rouge: Louisiana State UP, 1985.

Rydell, Robert W. *All the World's a Fair: Visions of Empire at American International Expositions, 1876–1916.* Chicago: U of Chicago P, 1984.

———. "Rediscovering the 1893 Chicago World's Columbian Exposition." *Revisiting the White City: American Art at the 1893 World's Fair.* Washington, D.C.: National Museum of American Art and American Portrait Gallery P, 1993. 18–61.

Samuels, Shirley. *Facing America: Iconography and the Civil War.* New York: Oxford UP, 2004.

San Juan, Epifanio, Jr. *After Postcolonialism: Remapping Philippines–United States Confrontations.* Lanham, Md.: Rowman and Littlefield, 2000.

Schechter, Patricia A. *Ida B. Wells-Barnett and American Reform, 1880–1930.* Chapel Hill: U of North Carolina P, 2001.

Schmidt, Peter. "Command Performances: Black Storytellers in Ruth McEnery Stuart's 'Blink' and Charles W. Chesnutt's 'The Dumb Witness.'" *Southern Literary Journal* 35.1 (Fall 2002): 70–96.

———. "Walter Scott, Postcolonial Theory, and New South Literature." *Mississippi Quarterly* 56.4 (Fall 2003): 543–554.

Schuyler, George. *Black No More.* 1931. Rpt. New York: Random House/Modern Library, 1999.

Sears, Lorenzo. *American Literature in the Colonial and National Periods.* Boston: Little, Brown, 1902.

Sedgwick, Ellery. "Walter Hines Page at the *Atlantic Monthly.*" *Harvard Library Bulletin* 35.4 (Fall 1987): 427–449.

See, Sarah Sarita. "*An Open Wound*: Colonial Melancholia and Contemporary Filipino/American Texts." *Vestiges of War: The Philippine-American War and the Aftermath of an Imperial Dream.* Ed. Angel Velasco Shaw and Luis H. Francia. New York: New York UP, 2002. 376–400.

———. "Southern Postcoloniality and the Improbablility of Filipino American Postcoloniality: Faulkner's *Absalom, Absalom!* and Hagedorn's *Dogeaters.*" *Mississippi Quarterly* 57.1 (Winter 2003/04): 41–54.

Seelye, John. "Introduction." *The Virginian.* By Owen Wister. New York: Penguin, 1988. vii–xxvii.Shaw, Angel Velasco, and Luis H. Francia, eds. *Vestiges of War: The Philippine-American War and the Aftermath of an Imperial Dream, 1898–1999.* New York: New York UP, 1999.

Silber, Nina. *The Romance of Reunion: Northerners and the South, 1865–1900.* Chapel Hill: U of North Carolina P, 1993.

Simms, L. Moody, Jr. "Walter Hines Page on Southern Literature." *Resources for American Literary Study* 6.2 (Autumn 1976): 199–208.

Singh, Amritjit, and Peter Schmidt. "On the Borders between U.S. Studies and Postcolonial Theory." *Postcolonial Theory and the United States: Race, Ethnicity, and Literature.* Ed. Amritjit Singh and Peter Schmidt. Jackson: UP of Mississippi, 2000. 3–69.

———, eds. *Postcolonial Theory and the United States: Race, Ethnicity, and Literature.* Jackson: UP of Mississippi, 2000.

Slide, Anthony. *American Racist: The Life and Films of Thomas Dixon.* Lexington: U of Kentucky P, 2004.

Slotkin, Joel. "Igorots and Indians: Racial Hierarches and Conceptions of the Savage in Carlos Bulosan's Fictions of the Philippines." *American Literature* 72.4 (2000): 843–866.

Slotkin, Richard. *Regeneration through Violence: The Mythology of the American Frontier, 1600–1860.* Middletown, Conn.: Wesleyan UP, 1973.

———. *The Fatal Environment: The Myth of the Frontier in the Age of Industrialization, 1800–1890.* New York: Atheneum, 1985.

———. *Gunfighter Nation: The Myth of the Frontier in the Twentieth Century.* New York: HarperPerrenial, 1993.

Smith, Jon, and Deborah Cohn, eds. *Look Away! The U.S. South in New World Studies.* Durham: Duke UP, 2004.

Southern, David W. *The Progressive Era and Race: Reaction and Reform, 1900–1917.* Wheeling, Ill.: Harlan Davidson, 2005.

Southern Historical Publication Society. *The South in the Building of the Nation: A History of the Southern States Designed to Record the South's Past in the Making of the American Nation; To Portray the Character and Genius, to Chronicle the Achievements and Progress and to Illustrate the Life and Traditions of the Southern People.* Twelve volumes. Richmond: Southern Historical Publication Society, 1909.

Stampp, Kenneth M. "The Tragic Legend of Reconstruction." *Reconstruction: An Anthology of Revisionist Writings.* Ed. Kenneth M. Stampp and Leon F. Litwack. Baton Rouge: Louisiana State UP, 1969. 3–21.

Stampp, Kenneth M., and Leon F. Litwack, eds. *Reconstruction: An Anthology of Revisionist Writings.* Baton Rouge: Louisiana State UP, 1969.

Still, William. *The Underground Railroad.* 1872. Rpt. New York: Ayer, 1992.

Stowe, Harriet Beecher. *Uncle Tom's Cabin.* 1852. Rpt. Ed. Charles Johnson. New York: Oxford UP, 2002.

Sundquist, Eric J. "Introduction: W. E. B. Du Bois and the Autobiography of Race." *The Oxford W. E. B. Du Bois Reader.* Ed. Eric J. Sundquist. New York: Oxford UP, 1996. 3–36.

———. *To Wake the Nations: Race in the Making of American Literature.* Cambridge: Harvard UP, 1993.

Taft, William Howard. See Anonymous, *Report of the Philippine Commission.*

Thomas, Brook. "The Legal Argument of Charles W. Chesnutt's Novels." *REAL: The Yearbook of Research in English and American Literature* 18 (2002): 311–334.

———. "*Plessy v. Ferguson* and the Literary Imagination." *Cardozo Studies in Law and Literature* 9.1 (Spring/Summer 1997): 54–65.

Tolentino, Aurelio. *Yesterday, Today, and Tomorrow.* In *Filipino Drama.* Ed. Arthur Stanley Riggs. 1905. Rpt. Manila: Ministry of Human Settlements, Intramuros Administration, 1981. 607–651.

Toll, Robert C. *Blacking Up: The Minstrel Show in Nineteenth-Century America.* New York: Oxford UP, 1974.

———. *On with the Show: The First Century of Show Business in America.* New York: Oxford UP, 1976.

Tompkins, Jane. *West of Everything: The Inner Life of Westerns.* New York: Oxford UP, 1992.

Tourgée, Albion. '*89. Edited from the Original Manuscript by Edgar Henry.* [pseudonym.] New York: Cassell, 1888.

———. *An Appeal to Caesar.* New York: Fords, Howard, and Hulbert, 1884.

———. *Bricks without Straw: A Novel.* 1880. Rpt. Ridgewood, N.J.: Gregg P, 1967.

———. *A Fool's Errand. 1879.* Rpt. New York: Fords, Howard, and Hulbert, 1880.

———. *The Invisible Empire.* 1880. Rpt: New York: Gregg P, 1968.

———. *The Man Who Outlived Himself.* New York: Fords, Howard, and Hulbert, 1898.

———. *Pactolus Prime.* New York: Casell and Co., 1890.

———. *A Royal Gentleman and Zouri's Christmas.* New York: Fords, Howard, and Hulbert, 1881.

———. "The South as a Field for Fiction." *Forum* 6 (December 1888): 404–413.

Trachtenberg, Alan. *The Incorporation of America: Culture and Society in the Gilded Age.* New York: Hill and Wang, 1982.

Trelease, Allen W. *White Terror: The Ku Klux Klan Conspiracy and Southern Reconstruction.* New York: Harper and Row, 1971.

Trent, William Peterfield. Introduction. *The South in the Building of the Nation.* Vol. 7: *The Literary and Intellectual Life.* Richmond: Southern History Publication Society, 1909. xv–xxxi.

———. "The Tragedy of Reconstruction." *Library of Southern Literature. Compiled Under the Direct Supervision of Southern Men of Letters.* Ed. Edwin Anderson Alderman, Joel Chandler Harris, and Charles William Kent. New Orleans and Atlanta: Martin and Hoyt, 1907–1923. Vol. 12: 5470–5477.

Turner, Arlin. *George W. Cable: A Biography.* Durham: Duke UP, 1956.

Twain, Mark. *Adventures of Huckleberry Finn.* Ed. Walter Blair and Victor Fischer. Vol. 8: *The Works of Mark Twain.* Berkeley: U of California P, 1988.

———. *Pudd'nhead Wilson and Those Extraordinary Twins.* 1894. Rpt. Ed. Sidney E. Berger. New York: Norton, 1980.

———. "To the Person Sitting in Darkness." *Vestiges of War: The Philippine-American War and the Aftermath of an Imperial Dream.* Ed. Angel Velasco Shaw and Luis H. Francia. New York: New York UP, 2002. 57–68.

United States Supreme Court. *Cherokee Nation v. State of Georgia* 30 U.S. 1 (1831).

———. Slaughterhouse cases 83 U.S. 36 (1873).

———. *U.S. v. Cruikshank* 92 U.S. 542 (1875).

———. *U.S. v. Reese* 92 U.S. 214 (1876).

———. "Civil Rights" cases 109 U.S. 3 (1883).

———. *Plessy v. Ferguson* 163 U.S. 537 (1896).

———. *Williams v. Mississippi* 170 U.S. 213 (1898).

———. Insular Cases. *Downes v. Bidwell* 182 U.S. 244 (1901).

———. Insular Cases. *Hawaii v. Mankichi* 190 U.S. 197 (1903).

Valelly, Richard M. *The Two Reconstructions: The Struggle for Black Enfranchisement.* Chicago: U of Chicago P, 2004.

Van Alstyne, R. W. *The Rising American Empire.* New York: Oxford UP, 1960.

Vergara, Benito M., Jr. *Displaying Filipinos: Photography and Colonialism in Early Twentieth-Century Philippines.* Manila: U of Philippines P, 1996.

Vienne, Véronique. "A More Perfect Union. Marrying a political agenda to a 'museum experience,' the National Constitution Center struggles for balance." *Metropolis* 23.3 (November 2003): 96–99, 131, 133, 135.

von Humbolt, Wilhelm. "Theory of Bildung." *Teaching as a Reflective Practice: The German Didaktik Tradition*. Ed. Ian Westbury, Stefan Hopmann, and Kurt Riquarts. Mahwah, N.J.: L. Erlbaum Associates, 2000. 57–62.

Warren, Kenneth W. *Black and White Strangers: Race and American Literary Realism*. Chicago: U of Chicago P, 1993.

Washington, Booker T. *Up from Slavery: An Autobiography*. New York: Doubleday, 1901.

———. "Atlanta Exposition Address." 1895. Rpt. *Plessy v. Ferguson: A Brief History*. Ed. Brook Thomas. Boston: Bedford Books, 1997. 11–124.

Waterbury, Jared Bell. *Southern Planters and the Freedmen*. New York: American Tract Society, 1865.

Wells-Barnett, Ida B. "Lynch Law in America." *Arena* 23.1 (January 1900): 15–24. Rpt. *Words of Fire: An Anthology of African-American Feminist Thought*. Ed. Beverly Guy-Sheftall. New York: Norton, 1995. 70–78.

———. *On Lynchings*. Ed Patricia Hill Collins. Amherst, N.Y.: Humanity Books P, 2002.

———. *Southern Horrors: A Red Record*. Rpt. New York: Arno, 1969.

Wiegman, Robyn. *American Anatomies: Theorizing Race and Gender*. Durham: Duke UP, 1995.

Williams, Daniel R. *The Odyssey of the Philippine Commission*. Chicago: A. G. McClurg, 1913.

Williams, William Appleman. *Contours of American History*. Cleveland: World P, 1961.

Williamson, Joel. *After Slavery: The Negro in South Carolina during Reconstruction, 1861–1877*. Chapel Hill: U of North Carolina P, 1965.

———. *The Crucible of Race: Black-White Relations in the American South since Emancipation*. New York: Oxford UP, 1984.

Wilson, Charles Reagan. *Baptized in Blood: The Religion of the Lost Cause*. Athens: U of Georgia P, 1980.

Wilson, Edmund. *Patriotic Gore; Studies in the Literature of the American Civil War*. New York: Oxford UP, 1962.

Wilson, Woodrow. *Constitutional Government in the United States*. New York: Columbia UP, 1908.

———. *The Public Papers of Woodrow Wilson: Authorized Edition*. Vol. 1: *College and State, Educational, Literary and Political Papers (1875–1913)*. Ed. Ray Stannard Baker and William E. Dodd. New York: Harper, 1925.

Winter, Marian Hannah. "Juba and American Minstrelsy." *Inside the Minstrel Mask: Readings in Nineteenth-Century Blackface Minstrelsy*. Ed. Annemarie Bean, James V. Hatch, and Brooks McNamara. Hanover, N.H.: UP of New England [for] Wesleyan UP, 1996. 223–244.

Wister, Owen. *The Virginian*. 1902. Rpt. Ed. John Seelye. New York: Penguin, 1988.

Woodson, Carter G. *The Mis-education of the Negro*. Washington, D.C.: Associated Publishers, 1933.

Woodward, C. Vann. *The Burden of Southern History*. New York: Vintage, 1961.

———. *Origins of the New South, 1877–1913*. Baton Rouge: Louisiana State UP, 1951.

———. *The Strange Career of Jim Crow*. 3rd rev. ed. New York: Oxford UP, 1974.

Woolson, Constance Fenimore. "King David." *Scribner's Monthly*, April 1878. See http://www.unl.edu/legacy/19cwww/books/elibe/woolson/kingd.htm.

———. "Rodman the Keeper." *Atlantic Monthly*, March 1877. See http://www.unl.edu/legacy/19cwww/books/elibe/woolson/rodman.htm.

———. *Rodman the Keeper: Southern Sketches*. New York: D. Appleton, 1880.

Worth, Nicholas. See Page, Walter Hines.

Yaeger, Patricia. *Dirt and Desire: Reconstructing Southern Women's Writing, 1930–1990*. Chicago: U of Chicago P, 2000.

Young, Robert J. C. *Colonial Desire: Hybridity in Theory, Culture, and Race.* New York: Routledge, 1995.

Zinn, Howard. *A People's History of the United States: 1942 to the Present.* Rev. ed. New York: Harper, 2005.

Zwick, Jim. "Mark Twain and Imperialism." *A Historical Guide to Mark Twain.* Ed. Shelley Fisher Fishkin. New York: Oxford UP, 2002. 227–256.

———. "Mark Twain's Anti-imperialist Writings in the 'American Century.'" *Vestiges of War: The Philippine-American War and the Aftermath of an Imperial Dream.* Ed. Angel Velasco Shaw and Luis H. Francia. New York: New York UP, 2002. 38–56.

———, ed. *Mark Twain's Weapons of Satire: Anti-imperialist Writings on the Philippine-American War.* Syracuse: Syracuse UP, 1992.

# Index

# Index

# Index

# Index

# Index